THE BIG BANDS GO TO WAR

The Big Bands Go To War

Chris Way

Introduction by Robert Farnon

MAINSTREAM
PUBLISHING

EDINBURGH AND LONDON

To
Robert J. Farnon
Jimmy Miller
John Miller
the late Cecil Madden
and
my dear father

First published in Great Britain 1991 by
MAINSTREAM PUBLISHING COMPANY (EDINBURGH) LTD
7 Albany Street
Edinburgh EH1 3UG

British Library Cataloguing in Publication Data

Way, Chris
  The Big Bands Go To War
  1. Military bands, history
  I. Title
  355.34

ISBN 1 85158 475 7

Typeset in 10/12 Garamond by BEECEE Typesetting Services
Printed in Great Britain by Mackays of Chatham Plc

Contents

Acknowledgments

As usual with this kind of undertaking, thanks are due to many individuals and organisations for help and advice. First and foremost, I must express my sincere appreciation to five gentlemen in particular, without any one of whom this book would not have materialised. In order, they are my good friends: ex-president Ronald Reagan, without whose help in opening many doors this book could never have been finished and who has assisted me ever since; the late Cecil Madden who offered as much information and a number of photographs held in his collection for use in this project; Robert Farnon, former leader of the Canadian Army Orchestra, better known as the Canadian Band of the AEF, who has not only given generously of his time and his recollections, but also wrote the introduction to this book; the late John Herbert Miller, better known as Herb, younger brother of Glenn Miller, whose help and guidance on rare details of his elder brother, and his own wartime service has been invaluable; and Jimmy Miller, former leader of the Royal Air Force Dance Orchestra, The Squadronaires, who at a minute's notice would drop everything, pick up his telephone and pass on rare stories and details about their wartime broadcasts and concerts. A further note of thanks to Jimmy for writing the book's preface.

To all the bandleaders and musicians who sent letters and cassettes I express my sincere thanks: Ray McKinley, Artie Shaw, the late Sam Donahue, Pat Dodd, George Chisholm, Ronnie Aldrich, Artie Malvin, John Best, John Miller (Herb Miller's son), Rubin Zeke Zarchy, George Voutsas, the late Jerry Gray, the late Johnny Desmond, Gordon Tex Beneke, the late Paul Fenoulhet, Billy Amstall, Michael Peanuts Hucko, the late Donald W. Haynes. Also, very great thanks to the many famous singers and BBC announcers who helped with this project: Anne Shelton, Gloria Brent, Paula Green, Bruce Trent, the late Bing Crosby, the late David Niven, Jean Metcalfe, Alan Dell, Richard Clegg, Sheila Tracy, the late Ronald Waldman, Teddy Gower, Max Muller, and the late Henry Whiston (CBC Canada).

In addition, many other individuals have helped in various ways: in particular Mike Morris, who sent on everything he could on many rare bands; Richard C. March (Secretary of the Glenn Miller Society), David Ades (Secretary of the Robert Farnon Society), Phillip Arnould, Geoffrey Butcher, Edward F. Polic, Tony Middleton, Larry Semmel, Harry Long, Roland Taylor

(Chairman of the Glenn Miller Society), Joannie Miller-Soper (Glenn Miller's daughter), Stephen D. Miller (Glenn Miller's son), Irene Woolfe (Glenn Miller's sister), Victor Way, Frank Driggs, William Manley, Charles Ward, John Charman, Douglas Le-Vicki, Paul Holroyd, Stan Bruce, Burt Beckham, Phillip Farlow, Geoffrey Gardner, Eric Hamilton, Glenn Mittler, William Trueden, Royal D. Frey (ex-curator of the United States Air Force Museum at Dayton, Ohio), George Way and Gerry Didymus.

Thanks are also due to those in various organisations who have willingly placed their resources at my disposal: Mrs J. Kavanagh, head of the BBC Written Archives Centre, and her staff; Miss Bobby Mitchell from the BBC Stills Library; Mr Edward Inman, director of the Imperial War Museum at Duxford Airfield, near Cambridge; the United States Archives at the US airforce base at Maxwell Field, Alabama, and the National Archives in Washington DC.

Because Glenn Miller's AAFTC/AEF Orchestra is now well documented in three books which have been published over the last five years, we have not included a day-to-day activities listing, like the other selections in this book. Please refer to either *Next to a Letter from Home* by Geoffrey Butcher, *In the Miller Mood* or *I Sustain the Wings* by Edward F. Polic.

Acknowledgments are also due to the following for use of photographs: BBC Hulton Picture Library, Bedfordshire Times, Tex Beneke, Donald W. Haynes, Cecil Madden, Jack Marshall, Louis Lawrence, Ivor Richmond, the Glenn Miller Estate, Frank Ippolito, US Army, Artie Shaw, US Air Force and Yale University.

Thanks are due to the following for permission to use copyright material: the Glenn Miller Society, the Miller Estate, the Robert Farnon Society, the US Air Force, Edward F. Polic, Geoffrey Butcher and *Melody Maker*.

My thanks to you all.

Author's Note

During the period 1939 to 1945, the world was at war. During that period more than any other in history the radio played an important role for the Allied nations at war. Along with this came perhaps some of this century's most famous names — Frank Sinatra, Bing Crosby, Anne Shelton, Vera Lynn, Glenn Miller, and many more. Just before the war had started in the late 1930s, the swing era had been born, bringing with it such famous name bands as Artie Shaw, Benny Goodman, Ambrose, Jack Payne, Tommy Dorsey, Glenn Miller and many others. From within the ranks of these orchestras came the young and very talented musicians who would be drafted into the Allied Armed Forces. It all started on a quiet Sunday morning in September 1939. The first of the famous services bands to be formed was the Royal Air Force Dance Orchestra, better known as the Squadronaires. For the next six years this uniformed band would entertain millions both on the radio and in person. The Squadronaires were formed in March 1940. By the autumn of 1940, another RAF band was formed, the Number One Balloon Centre Band, better known as the Skyrockets. Other British bands would follow — the RAOC Blue Rockets, the Royal Navy Dance Band and the Royal Marines Dance Band. Together, they contained the cream of British musicians.

With Britain at war and countries of the Empire also fighting the Nazis, it was not long before the Canadians were also forming bands and service orchestras. Over in Canada a young composer and conductor named Robert Farnon had joined the Canadian Army as a Captain. His Canadian Army Orchestra would soon travel to Britain, spreading his musical ideas both on radio and in person. The United States of America were brought into the war on Sunday, 7 December 1941 and with the Yanks came their own musicians. Many were drafted into the armed forces long before the Japanese attack on Pearl Harbour. America had been more or less on a war footing since January 1941 and the draft had affected quite a few bands, with the whole situation worsening as the year progressed. America was now on an all-out war footing. Whole bands fell apart and, to make matters worse, the United States had petrol on ration. The first leader to enlist was Artie Shaw in April 1942. Glenn Miller followed in the September of that year.

By 1943, Artie Shaw was on a tour of the Pacific and Glenn Miller was a Captain in the Army Air Forces, with another orchestra.

9

A year later Captain Glenn Miller and his Army Air Forces Orchestra were in Britain, broadcasting over the AEF (Allied Expeditionary Forces) programme and performing at bases all over the country.

Many other bands were formed and took part in similar operations all over the war-torn world. Glenn's is perhaps the most famous. As Glenn's band was known in England as 'The American Band of the AEF', what then was the British and how was that formed and run? Also what about the Canadian AEF Orchestra, whose radio work included nearly seven shows a week over the AEF programme?

Perhaps the memories for those that lived through those wartime days are now enhanced, flooding back with stories of Bing Crosby in London; Glenn Miller in Bedford; George Melachrino leading his British AEF and Army Radio Orchestra; lesser-known musicians like pianist Ronald Selby and Jack Russin; stories of Anne Shelton singing with Glenn Miller and Fred Astaire dancing at 'Rainbow Corner'.

Over the years my interest and enthusiasm for this music has, if anything, increased and I remain convinced that the AEF programme was the greatest radio network of all time.

For me, it all started with Glenn Miller and a 78rpm recording owned by my late mother and her stories of that wartime radio network. I then became curious to know how it all came about — the mysterious circumstances of Glenn Miller's death; my meeting with the late great Cecil Madden; my friendship with Glenn's brother Herb and his son John.

All this leads on to the writing of this book. Not only was there Glenn Miller, but many other famous wartime bands like our own RAF Squadronaires. Their leader was Jimmy Miller, who has provided me with some really great insights into a long forgotten story. Bob Farnon has also given so much help as well as the preface for this book. Pat Dodd, the famous pianist from the Skyrockets Band, although ill at the time, sat down and shared his ideas and stories . . .

The work is a gathering of material from many sources. It is based primarily on contemporary official documents, including British and American radio archives (particularly those of the BBC) and the US military records, together with published accounts of the bands' activities and reminiscences of people associated with the various groups listed. Other details come from the records held by the late BBC producer Cecil Madden. Many of the details were sent on for an earlier book, written and produced by me called *In the Miller Mood*, a bio-discography of the Glenn Miller Service Orchestra.

In order to make this book useful as a work of reference as well as a straight-forward story of each of the famous service bands, it has been divided into two parts: Part One gives a chronological narrative of each band — how it was formed and what it did — plus personal reminiscences of many musicians and band-leaders; Part Two gives a complete listing of the many radio broadcasts of these service bands, plus known details of recording sessions. Not all bands are listed as some never broadcast at all and only performed at troop recruiting and war bond rallies. Others only toured battle zones and never broadcast on a regular series, while other smaller bands were formed for station dances.

Foreword

Being leader of the Herb Miller Orchestra, founded here in England in 1981 by my late father Herb Miller, I am very proud to introduce this new book by my good friend Chris Way.

If you wish to acquaint yourself with the many fine service orchestras of World War Two, I cannot think of a finer piece of work than this book. It is told by perhaps the finest author in his field. Herb and myself often called Chris the greatest living expert on my late uncle, Glenn Miller. However, this book goes one step further and recalls all the other great service bands of that period.

This is without a doubt the missing chapter on some of the greatest Allied Services bands of World War Two. As my late Uncle Glenn once said, 'It brings a ''hunk o' home'' to millions upon millions of Yanks, Tommies and Johnny Cannacks'. This brings everything into focus and it tells just what happened 'When the Big Bands Went to War'.

John Miller,
February 1991

Preface

It is now just over fifty years since I became leader of the now legendary Royal
Air Force Dance Orchestra, better known as the Squadronaires. We played and
performed many times during our time in the forces, for our brother
servicemen, both here in the British Isles and on the continent of Europe, in
the later stages of World War Two. We were just one of several famous service
bands formed from the musicians being drafted into the forces. Among our
ranks were some of the finest British musicians of all time. Sadly only six of our
number now remain. But it is with great joy that we will now never be
forgotten for what we did during the period of World War Two, for you will be
able to read our story and many of the other service bands' stories in this book
by Chris Way.

What memories are evoked of the AEF orchestras, led by Major Glenn
Miller, RSM George Melachrino, and Bob Farnon. Many old friends are
included — Sam Donahue, Paul Fenoulhet, and many others. I remember with
pride the time when I sang with Captain Glenn Miller's American Band of the
AEF, on a summer evening, at Bedford in late July 1944. Other memories
come flooding back — when my wife Mary and I were in the Paris Cinema
when Bing Crosby appeared with RSM George Melachrino and his British
Band of the AEF, in late August 1944. Oh, sweet memories, but some not so
sweet — like 'Doodle-bugs', the Blitz of 1940 and rationing.

Also included in the book are good friends who are still with us today, like
George Chisholm, Harry Lewis (Dame Vera Lynn's husband), Ronnie
Aldrich, Tommy McQuater and Monty Levy, who are the remaining
members of the wartime Squadronaires, conducted by yours truly.

Perhaps this book could have been written many years ago, but it has taken
many years to piece everything together. My first meeting with Chris Way was
at the special Wycombe Abbey concert given by the Herb Miller Concert
Orchestra, on Sunday, 24 July 1988. During the interval in the VIP area we
talked at some length about Glenn Miller and the many other service bands of
World War Two. Since then we have often talked over the telephone and Chris
told me about his idea for this book. It became apparent to me that here at last
was the author for such a book, the full story of all the great service orchestras

15

and dance bands, who were in the Allied Forces during World War Two. *The Big Bands go to War* should make remarkable and fascinating reading for fans, veterans and connoisseurs all over the world.

Jimmy Miller
London, January 1991

Introduction

Throughout the years, since the end of World War Two, I have enjoyed countless conversations with musicians and members of the general public regarding the wonderful music provided by the Allied Services bands and orchestras, all of which provided morale-boosting entertainment of the highest standard for the fighting forces and citizens in the front line at home and abroad during hostilities.

A comprehensive story on the subject is long overdue and I am privileged and delighted to introduce this book by Chris Way which is gem-filled with reminiscences, photographs and fascinating information concerning the rich musical days of the many service groups.

The Canadian Band of the AEF for which I was responsible was housed at the BBC Studios in Maida Vale, London, a hive of musical activity from dawn to dusk, and frequently into the wee hours of the morning. Five of the six studios were allotted to us in order to accommodate the full orchestra and various smaller units: the jazz octet, string orchestra, mixed choir and so on. In addition to the weekly broadcasts from various venues in London, we often went on the road visiting hospitals, army camps and theatres (just to keep us out of mischief).

The varied work brought us in contact with a host of leading entertainers of stage, screen and radio, and our musical association with those great people was an education in professionalism. How nice it was for me, personally, to work with some of them again upon return to civvy street.

Several members of the AEF Groups remained in Britain after the war, and went on to achieve fame and fortune. Robert Beatty, Lois Marshall, Paul Carpenter, Lionel Murton and Edmund Hockridge to name a few.

This book holds a wealth of treasured memories for me, and may its pages provide much pleasure to readers who are familiar or otherwise with the days of the AEF Bands.

Robert Farnon
March 1991

The Army Air Forces Training Command Orchestra

The AAFTC Orchestra which replaced Captain Glenn Miller and his AAFTC Orchestra on the NBC *I Sustain the Wings* series, was conducted by both Master Sergeants Harry Bluestone and Felix Slatkin. The Commanding Officer of this 60-piece orchestra was Captain Robert Jennings. Like Captain Miller's orchestra before, the replacement orchestra also included a group of actors for the Army Air Force Dramatic playlets. The group was led by another Hollywood film star, Lieutenant William Holden. Miller's group had included Sergeant William Broderick Crawford, another famous Hollywood film star.

British-born violinist Harry Bluestone graduated from the Institute of Musical Art (later renamed Juilliard), and freelanced on numerous radio programmes in the 1930s with the Dorsey Brothers, Benny Goodman and Artie Shaw. In 1935 Harry Bluestone was on the first recordings that Glenn Miller ever made under his own name. Later that year Harry went to Hollywood with the Lennie Hayton Orchestra (which also included Manny Klein and Artie Bernstein), then featured on the *Lucky Strike* radio series. Bluestone served as concert-master on a number of film studio orchestras and recorded with many dance bands and studio orchestras.

In 1942, Harry Bluestone enlisted in the Army Air Forces and assisted Captain Eddie Dunstedter in developing the first RPU (Radio Production Unit) orchestra at Santa Ana Air Force Base, Santa Ana, California. AAFTC Headquarters in Fort Worth, Texas (Headquarters of the Eighth Air Force), requested that a similar unit be assembled in Fort Worth and in July 1943 the AAFTC Orchestra was organised there by Captain Robert Jennings and Sergeant Harry Bluestone. The orchestra conducted by Harry Bluestone grew rapidly from a small dance band to a 60-piece orchestra. Jazz pianist John 'Knocky' Parker, before an automobile accident and medical discharge from the Army Air Force, was featured as a soloist with the orchestra.

Other famous musicians within this large orchestra were Ray Cathcart (trumpet) and pianists Stan Freeman and Elmer Bernstein. Among the arrangers were Bobby Van Eps and Elmer Bernstein. Elmer's name would later become famous for film compositions.

When Captain Glenn Miller's AAFTC Orchestra went overseas in mid June 1944, the AAFTC Orchestra replaced it on the *I Sustain the Wings* series and later on the 'Fifth War Loan Bonds' tour, taking over from the Paul Whiteman Orchestra, which had taken over from Captain Glenn Miller on 12 June. The tour by the AAFTC Orchestra, led by Sergeant Harry Bluestone had included over 50 celebrities and sold more than $100,000,000 of war bonds. Then on 10 July 1944 the orchestra moved into Byers Hall, Yale University. Its first public appearance at Yale was on Tuesday, 1 August 1944. The NBC *I Sustain the Wings* broadcasts were continued on Saturdays at 6 p.m. EWT for the East Coast and at 11.30 p.m. EWT for the West Coast, from New York City. However, the programme now emanated from NBC's Radio City Studios, rather than the Vanderbilt Theatre. In addition, the orchestra was broken down into sub-units and broadcast five days a week. A breakdown of the orchestra's or sub-units' schedule was two *I Sustain the Wings* broadcasts on a Saturday; Sunday on the Blue Network, *Symphonic Flight*; Tuesday on the CBS local network *Wings for Tomorrow*; Thursday evenings *The Army Air Forces* show; and on CBS on Friday afternoons, *First in the Air*. Recordings or dress rehearsals from *I Sustain the Wings* broadcasts were also used and issued as V-discs.

In the spring of 1945, Harry Bluestone and Felix Slatkin switched assignments. Bluestone replaced Slatkin as leader of the Santa Ana Army Air Force Orchestra and Slatkin took over the AAFTC Orchestra at Yale University. For a brief period, Jack Matthias (on loan from the Army Service Forces) was with the orchestra's arranging staff in New York City. Harry Bluestone was discharged from the Army Air Forces in August 1945 and became concert-master at Eagle-Lion films for two years.

By late August 1945, with the war over, Felix Slatkin's AAFTC Orchestra was joined in New York City by Major Glenn Miller's Overseas AAF Orchestra. On 29 September 1945, with many members replaced by members of the Slatkin AAF Orchestra, Glenn Miller's Overseas Orchestra resumed its weekly *I Sustain the Wings* programmes over NBC. Up until that programme, the show had been broadcast by Felix Slatkin and his AAFTC Orchestra, but now with the ever-popular Major Glenn Miller AAF Overseas Orchestra, back home after its 13-month stay in Europe, the show was back with the orchestra that had started it all in 1943. Both orchestras began to fall apart as the soldier-musicians were slowly being demobbed back into civilian life. To keep the broadcasts up and to maintain their radio schedules, the musicians were replaced and swopped between the two outfits.

After eight weeks, with the end finally in sight, the Army Air Forces took both outfits off the air. By 1946 both no longer existed. All the musicians were back in civilian life and these two great orchestras were no more. Felix Slatkin returned to Hollywood and went back into the movies. Over the next twenty years he would become involved in some of the all-time great films. Arranger Elmer Bernstein would also become one of the all-time greats with film themes.

Tex Beneke and his US Navy Band 1943 – 1945

Gordon 'Tex' Beneke was the featured tenor saxophone player with the Glenn Miller Orchestra from 1938 until 1942, when Glenn Miller entered the United States Army with the rank of Captain. When Glenn Miller broke up his orchestra to enlist in September 1942, Tex Beneke and the Modernaires singing group toured the USA. The tour lasted until early 1943, when Tex was drafted into the United States Navy. Captain Glenn Miller wrote to Tex asking him to join his newly formed Army Air Forces Orchestra, but it was too late. Tex was already with the Navy. Tex informed Glenn, and Glenn wrote back saying, 'Of course you know the airforce is going to win the war.'

For the next two years Tex, who was a Chief Petty Officer, became a land-locked sailor at Norman, Oklahoma. It was at this base that Tex formed a very good US Navy band that included Jack Sperling on drums. The band toured that area of the USA, performing at USO dances and at war bond rallies. They never went overseas, but the band did make an extraordinary effort at the recruiting and war bond rallies. They also did some local broadcasts for the state of Oklahoma.

On 4 June 1945, CPO Tex Beneke took part in a special Glenn Miller Day broadcast and show from New York City, as a tribute to his missing boss, who had died overseas in Europe. Glenn's female singer Marion Hutton, from Miller's broken-up civilian band, also took part, along with many friends and bandleaders.

After the war, in early 1946 Tex Beneke and Don Haynes reformed the Glenn Miller Orchestra. Tex directed the enlarged orchestra (with strings) until 1950. Over the last few years he has been involved with many Glenn Miller tribute bands and is still touring around the United States, bringing memories to many thousands.

The British Band of the AEF

The British Band of the AEF, led and directed by Regimental Sergeant Major George Melachrino, was formed during mid-July 1944, from the Army Radio Orchestra. The British Army Radio Orchestra, had been put together during 1941 by BBC radio. Members of the orchestra came from every regiment in the British Army. The concert master was Eric Robinson, from the Royal Army Ordnance Corps; other members came from various other units, including the Royal Military Police. Before the war many of the orchestra players had been either in classical or swing bands. They included Alec Firman, Guardsman George Evans, Private Ronnie Selby, Lance Corporal Freddie Phillips, Private Bob Roberts, Bert Thompson, Sergeant Laurie 'Nobbie' Clarke, Jimmy Goss, George Peake, Jack Coles, Private Jack Jones, Lance Corporal Bill Bentley, Sidney 'Jock' Sutcliffe, Terence McDonagh, James Bradshaw, Private Lew Stephenson and many more. Arrangements for the orchestra were put together by George Melachrino, Bert Thompson, Jack Coles and George Evans. Evans, who had been well known before going into the Guards, was a former singer, arranger and musician with Geraldo's Orchestra.

The British Band of the AEF first broadcast live from the stage of the Queensbury All Services club, in Soho, London, on Wednesday, 26 July 1944, at 8.30 p.m. (double British summer-time). It was during the height of the V-1 'Doodle-bug' raids on London and like Glenn Miller's and Bob Farnon's AEF Bands, the British outfit had some very narrow escapes. Also in common with the American Band led by Miller, the British Band often performed with British and visiting American guest stars. The first guest stars on 26 July 1944, were Carroll Gibbons and on the distaff side Miss Evelyn Dall. The compère for the first nine weeks was Captain Franklyn Englemann, after which A/C2 Ronald Waldman of the Royal Air Force took over. The first title after the theme was the popular *Commando Patrol*, followed by a vocal by RSM George Melachrino. Then in came the first guest, Carroll Gibbons, playing piano. Evelyn Dall's song on the first broadcast was *Let us face it, we're in love*. Like Glenn Miller's American Band of the AEF, the British also performed medleys in their programmes. But, unlike the Americans, the British AEF Band would play a medley from a film like *Dixie* or *Best Foot Forward*, or any popular film or show of the period.

Like their American and Canadian counterparts, the British Band of the AEF could be broken down into sub-units. On Saturdays at 1.15 p.m., there was the Army Radio Orchestra and during September pianist Ronnie Selby was heard every Monday morning as the 'Boogieman' of the air-waves in *Piano Parade*. As well as *Piano Parade*, Selby was also heard performing with a trio made up of Freddie Phillips (guitar) and Bob Roberts (drums). The Army Radio Orchestra broadcasts on Saturdays always had guest stars. Among the female British singers to appear were Gloria Brent, Dorothy Carless, Anne Lenner, Bette Roberts, Beryl Davis, Rita Williams, Carole Carr and Paula Green. Jean Metcalfe compèred many shows, as did Corporal Douglas Marshall. The theme song for the Army Radio series was *Without a Song*, and the British Band of the AEF's theme song, composed by RSM George Melachrino, was entitled the *SHAEF Signature Tune*.

Like the American and Canadian Bands, the British also performed at many camp concerts, but in smaller formats like a small trio — they did sterling work. The large concert orchestra never actually did concerts for troops other than the weekly Wednesday Queensbury Club concerts and broadcasts.

On Wednesday, 2 August 1944, the second show went out and included guests Adelaide Hall and Teddy Brown. The following week Beryl Davis and Vic Oliver were the special guests. Beryl's song was *It's Love, Love, Love*. The programme on 16 August 1944 introduced another first, a George Evans arrangement of the AEFP call sign *Oranges and Lemons*. Later, the American Band of the AEF led by Major Glenn Miller would also produce an arrangement of the old children's song, *Oranges and Lemons*.

On Wednesday, 23 August 1944, a member of the Skyrockets Band was brought in as a guest star — Corporal Denny Dennis of the Royal Air Force. Denny sang the ever popular *Long Ago and Far Away*. Evelyn Laye also took part in that broadcast. A week later the British Band played host to their biggest star yet — The 'Old Groaner' himself, Bing Crosby. The day was Wednesday, 30 August 1944, and his first song was *I'll Be Seeing You*. Captain Franklin Englemann introduced the show, which included two other songs by Crosby — *Swinging on a Star* and Bert Thompson's arrangement of the Rogers and Hart title *With a Song in My Heart*. It was a wonder the broadcast ever took place at all because the orchestra's leader, RSM George Melachrino, had lost both his wife and young son when a V-1 'Doodle-bug' made a direct hit on their house in London. George, who was away at the time, was heart-broken and no one in the orchestra knew how he had the nerve to continue, but continue he did. Thanks to ORBS the entire broadcast still exists and is an example of the orchestra at its finest. Included is the Selby piano backed up by the strings in a really beautiful arrangement of *Sweet and Lovely*. It was a fine orchestra indeed and with Crosby it showed itself off to the full.

A week later the orchestra was on the air again and this time the British guests were Dorothy Carless and George Shearing. George played *Dancing in the Dark* and Dorothy's song was *Begin the Beguine*. A week later on 13 September, Joyce Grenfell appeared with the orchestra. This was Captain Franklin Englemann's last broadcast with the orchestra. He was sent over to the continent for the duration of the war, in a series called *AEFP on the Spot*. A/C2 Ronnie Waldman took over the announcing duties the following week, when the orchestra played for yet another big American/German film star — Marlene Dietrich. That show was broadcast on 27 September 1944. Cecil Madden remembers that first meeting very well: 'The most marvellous person. I was told I'd have great difficulty with Marlene Dietrich. In actual fact she was most co-operative. Came into the office, said ''What can I do to help? I'm very keen to work.'' She did all her funny songs — *The Boys in the Back Room* and all the rest of it, with the Melachrino Orchestra.'

The other song Marlene Dietrich sang was *Falling in Love Again*. Jessie Matthews also appeared on that show.

The compère on most of the British Band of the AEF broadcasts at that time was Ronald Waldman. Ronnie would later become the show's producer as well, whereas the early shows were produced by Cecil Madden. All the Army Radio Orchestra shows and *Piano Parade* were produced by Douglas Marshall. As well as announcing the British Band of the AEF shows, Ronnie Waldman also jointly announced the early morning *Rise 'n' Shine* programmes. Ronnie once recalled his part in the AEF programme:

> The morning show that Dick Dudley and I were doing at the time was on the air from 6 a.m. to 8 a.m., Monday through to Saturday. It was designed of course to please the troops, that's what it was for; it was on the Allied Expeditionary Forces Programme, and it was directed entirely at serving members of the American, British and Canadian Forces, both on this side of the Channel and on the other side of the Channel, when they moved.
>
> At the start of the *Rise 'n' Shine* shows we were asked to include information, in fact ordered, to include it into the programme by Supreme Headquarters. We were on the staff of Supreme Headquarters, we had been brought into and put onto the staff for this purpose. It was not propaganda, more or less information, not important, good stuff, so the boys way out in the forward areas would not be fooled by other propaganda they might be hearing. This resulted in something interesting within four or five days of us being on the air. There was an American voice, Dick, and an English voice, Ronnie, talking to each other and on a wavelength very close to ours, and it was very quickly traced to the Germans. They were trying to fool our boys to tune into the wrong wavelength and the troops thought they were listening to us, and the Germans would drop in propaganda. We had only one answer to this and one morning we told our troops what was going on, and we added that it could also happen in the other direction and we might have a lot of Nazis tuning in to us and if we have we said get the hell out of it and listen to your own show, and soon after that Dick Dudley and I were informed from another source that we had been threatened personally by the Gestapo, and we were now on their blacklist. We both used that quite a few times in the show and both found it very funny. Anyway, the idea of the show itself was purely entertainment, and they asked us to script every show which

Producer and Announcer Ronnie Waldman with Marlene Dietrich and RSM George Melachrino, during the British Band of the AEF broadcast on 27 September 1944 (Photo: Cecil Madden)

was two hours long, and send it up to SHAEF for vetting. In the end we just ad-libbed. We were able to put into the show the latest commercial discs and also special recordings by the Miller Orchestra, the Farnon Orchestra and the Melachrino Orchestra, and the V-Discs that were coming out from the United States at that time, with special performances for American Forces and being sent to places all over the world. It was a fantastic range of material. It was of course one of the most productive periods of popular music of its type that ever happened and this huge range of singers, orchestras, arrangers and composers was a pretty heady experience. There was nothing that we could not get to put on that show. There were no copyright regulations at that time, you just got it and the audience at the time must have got more out of that programme in terms of popular music, than any other programme, before or since.

Like Cecil Madden, Ronnie Waldman was one of the major producers for the AEFP and was involved in many of the network's most popular shows. On 4 October, the British Band of the AEF's guest was Vera Lynn. This was Vera's first broadcast with the British Band of the AEF; her song that evening was *I'll be Seeing You*. Later, in 1955, Vera, along with George Melachrino and most of the members of the British AEF Orchestra, would recreate the event for BBC television. The main reason it had taken so long to unite the forces' sweetheart with the British Band of the AEF on that October 1944 AEFP radio broadcast was that Vera had been overseas visiting the forgotten army in Burma.

The very next day RSM George Melachrino was the special guest on the

American Band of the AEF's broadcast. Major Glenn Miller introduced George to a packed Queensbury All Services Club, and even threw in a joke or two. George's song with Glenn was *Goodnight Good Neighbour*, from the 1943 film, *How Sweet You Are*. It was quite some night — half-way through the broadcast a V-1 'Doodle-bug' flew over the packed Services Club.

A week later on Wednesday, 11 October 1944, the orchestra played hosts to Kathleen and Webster Booth. The two sung *Why Don't You Do Right*. Then on Wednesday, 8 November 1944, the guest was Anne Shelton who sang *Time Waits for No One*. Also on the show were the famous concert pianists Rawicz and Landauer, who performed the *Hungarian Rhapsody*.

Like the other two AEF house bands the British Band was very busy during November and early December. As well as three regular broadcasts a week and their inserts into other shows, they still had their army duties to perform, and these included shows at army and air force camps in and around London.

By Christmas 1944, they, like the Canadian Band, had worked with some of the top names from both sides of the Atlantic. Visiting American guest stars were always welcomed by Cecil Madden and, whenever he got the chance, he scheduled them into AEFP shows, as well as his now famous American Eagle in Britain broadcasts. As Cecil remembered, there were various offices in the old Langham Hotel, which had become BBC offices. Cecil now picks up the story: 'There were three offices next to mine — Major Miller's, Captain Bob Farnon's, and RSM George Melachrino's. Miller hardly used his one, but Bob and George did.

'I would often select visiting American, Canadian or British guests for the three AEFP house bands. They were the finest in the world. So from a musician's point of view we could field a really big army.'

By Christmas day, 1944, the three AEFP 'house orchestras', as Cecil called them, were scheduled to perform in an extra-special broadcast containing all three, entitled *The AEF Christmas Show*. By that time Major Glenn Miller's American Band of the AEF were no longer in the United Kingdom, and were now based in Paris, but unfortunately Glenn had been posted missing on the Christmas Eve. The British and Canadian Bands of the AEF were packed onto the stage of the Queensbury All Services Club. The Canadian Band, under Captain Bob Farnon, performed their show first. After 30 minutes, the British Band came on with their 30-minute show, which included British guest star Beryl Davis. Pianist Ronnie Selby was also featured with *Prelude to Boogie*. Another guest on the show was Teddy Brown. Pianist Brown played *Some of These Days*. Beryl Davis sang *In the Spirit of the Moment* and *Just a-Whittling, and a-Whistling*. The show also featured arranger Guardsman George Evans singing *Dance with a Dolly*. Then the American Band performed their 30-minute show from the Olympia Theatre in Paris. After this there was a further 30-minute combined round-up from all three orchestras. This ended with the combined bands and audiences playing and singing *Auld Lang Syne*. The last hour of the show was broadcast by the BBC Home Service and then short-waved to the United States and Canada. It was perhaps the greatest broadcast of the war, and is still talked about to this day. It was a great shame that no copies of the two-hour programme were kept. The only part still around is the final seven minutes of the combined round-up programme, but that exists in very poor condition.

The next Wednesday, 27 December 1944, the British Band of the AEF broadcast as usual at 8.30 p.m. BST. The programme was introduced by A/C2 Ronnie Waldman, and the SHAEF announcer who brought the show on the air was Lt Charmian Samson. The guest stars were Britain's Paula Green and Vic Oliver and also Corporal Jack Powers of the US Army. Jack was better known at that time for *As a Soldier and a Song* from his three-nights-a-week AEFP show.

This programme contained Paula Green singing *His Rocking-Horse Ran Away*. Jack Powers' song was *Spring Will Be a Little Late This Year*. These two titles and the first instrumental *Put On Your Old Grey Bonnet* still exist and can be found in the BBC sound archives in London. It is sadly the only remaining broadcast that exists in the BBC of this famous orchestra.

The following week, on 3 January 1945, the guests were Jessie Matthews and saxophone player Freddie Gardner, who at that time was in the Royal Navy, with the Blue Mariners dance band. Freddie played a solo with the orchestra for the Hoagy Carmichael song *Stardust*. Jessie Matthews performed a medley of *You'll Never Know, Long Ago and Far Away* and *Spring Will Be a Little Late This Year*. It is interesting to note that the British Band of the AEF finished the broadcast with the Glenn Miller hit of 1939, *Little Brown Jug*.

The very next Wednesday, Vera Lynn was again featured along with Nat Temple. Vera's songs this time were *Little Star* and *When You Wish Upon a Star*. Nat Temple was featured in *Canzonetta*.

On Wednesday, 24 January 1945, Anne Shelton was again featured with *No One Else Will Do*. The other guest star that evening from the RAF Squadronaires was trombonist, LAC George Chisholm. George performed *My Melancholy Baby* with the British Band of the AEF. George, who had just returned from Paris with the Squadronaires, was and still is one of Scotland's greatest trombone players.

Another first for the AEFP was the broadcast of 31 January 1945. The British Band had its first French guest star, Yvonne Arnaud, playing piano with the title *La Fileuse*. Beryl Davis was also on hand singing *What a Difference a Day Made*.

Over the next few weeks, with the Allied Armies beginning to advance again, the end was in sight. By March 1945, the Allied Armies were over the River Rhine and heading straight into Nazi Germany. On 28 March Tommy Handley and Kay Cavendish from the ITMA series were featured as guest stars with the British AEF Band.

The British Band of the AEF's broadcasting schedule was increased to four

RSM George Melachrino conducts the British Band of the AEF at the 1944 Jazz Jamboree, 15 October 1944 (Photo: Ivor R. Richman)

broadcasts a week over the AEFP on Sunday, 22 April 1945. It was on this day that the entire 50-piece orchestra, directed by RSM George Melachrino, began a 30-minute programme, backing Richard Tauber. Called *The Richard Tauber Programme*, it was broadcast every Sunday evening at 8.30 p.m., DBST, until the AEFP closed down on 28 July 1945.

The Saturday afternoon Army Radio Orchestra broadcasts had continued throughout the Autumn (Fall) of 1944 and into the Spring of 1945. Every show featured a host of British female singers. Gloria Brent often participated and remembers it well: 'I worked a lot with the Army Radio Orchestra during the winter of 1944-45. Their broadcasts came mostly from the Criterion Theatre in Piccadilly. It was a fine orchestra and I sang mostly popular songs of the day.' On Saturday, 5 May 1945, the Army Radio Orchestra opened the show with a Ray McKinley composition, *Hoppin' Abroad*. Ray was a member of Major Glenn Miller's American Band of the AEF, and the composition must have been loaned to the British Band during Glenn's stay in England. As Cecil Madden remembers: 'There was great friendship between the members of the three AEF bands and their leaders.' The guest with the Army Radio Orchestra that Saturday afternoon was Helen Clare who sang *April in Paris* and *All the Things You Are*, plus an extra title, *All or Nothing At All*.

The very next Tuesday, 8 May, was 'VE Day', and the Wednesday, 9 May, British Band of the AEF broadcast was a very special show, dubbed *The Special Victory Edition*. The compère was A/C2 Ronnie Waldman, and the show included as many of the famous guests as could be packed into a

30-minute show. This show was recorded by the BBC on Saturday, 5 May 1945, and used dubbings from 16 different broadcasts. Included were guests Marlene Dietrich, Carl Barriteau, Anne Shelton, Vic Oliver, Beryl Davis, Yvonne Arnaud, Tommy Handley, Jack Train, Frank Weir, Vera Lynn, Rawicz and Landauer, Bebe Daniels, Squadron Leader Richard Murdoch and Bing Crosby, plus an instrumental at the beginning and end. It was a made-up show, but it showed off the guests, and Bing Crosby had the final song, with Rogers and Hart's beautiful *With a Song in My Heart*.

With the war in Europe over, the AEFP was nearing the end of its job. The programme's director, Maurice Gorham, called it the best entertainment programme ever to be broadcast by the BBC, and quite a bit of that was due to the three house orchestras. The AEFP closed down on Saturday, 28 July 1945, with a special thank you for a job well done from the AEF's Supreme Commander, General Dwight D. Eisenhower. The *Army Radio Orchestra Show* on that July afternoon featured five female British singers, Dorothy Carless, Anne Lenner, Edna Kaye, Bette Roberts and Vera Howe.

The British Band of the AEF's last broadcast over the BBC's AEF network was on the previous Wednesday, 25 July 1945, and included British guest stars Richard Murdoch and Kenneth Horne. The last song on that evening show was *Widdicombe Fair* which had vocals by Ronnie Selby, Bert Thompson, Alex Firman, Arthur Wilkinson, Eric Robinson, George Melachrino and producer-compère Ronald Waldman.

Both George Melachrino and the Ronnie Selby Trio were featured again on the AEFP in a special *Farewell AEFP* show from the stage of the Queensbury All Services Club, in Soho, London, on the evening of Saturday, 28 July. Only two other programmes were featured on the AEFP during its final day of transmission, and they were both recorded. The first showcased the American Band of the AEF and the last complete programme, presented by Ronald Waldman, highlighted the network's signature tune *Oranges and Lemons*. Also included in this fifteen-minute programme were nineteen of the opening themes of the most popular shows that the AEFP had featured during its thirteen months of operation over the airwaves. Among the themes performed were *SHAEF Signature Tune* which RSM George Melachrino composed, as the main theme music for the orchestra back in July 1944. Both the American and British AEF orchestras were heard performing their strikingly different versions of the old children's song, *Oranges and Lemons*. This short programme was followed by the news, a prayer and then Margaret Hubble closed the network down.

However, taking over from the AEFP was a new network. The BBC *Light Programme* opened the very next day. Although the name British Band of the AEF had disappeared along with the AEFP, the orchestra was still operating under its pre D-Day title, the Army Radio Orchestra.

With RSM George Melachrino conducting the orchestra, like Bob Farnon's Canadian Band they were often heard on this new radio network. Like the

AEFP, the BBC's *Light Programme* featured several of the former radio network's programmes. Although the BBC kept several of the large orchestra shows on the air, some of the smaller shows were dropped. Gone were Richard Tauber's show and the *Piano Parade* series. Later in the autumn of 1945, RSM George Melachrino and the Army Radio Orchestra performed at several occasions in London. One in October was the 1945 Jazz Jamboree. On another occasion they performed at the closing of the Stage-Door Canteen in Piccadilly. On that occasion they performed with the very young Petula Clark, who sang *Some of These Days*, allegedly in an imitation of Sophie Tucker!

During the early part of 1946 the members of the orchestra were demobbed and returned to civilian life. Many of the musicians stayed on with George and helped form his new orchestra. One of their first recordings was their signature tune called *First Rhapsody*. We are not sure but, as this was a George Melachrino composition, it may well have been the service orchestra's theme music, under another title. George and his orchestra recorded many fine light orchestral titles, like their version of *Moonlight Serenade*.

In 1955 George and his orchestra were reunited with Vera Lynn on a special television programme. During this show George conducted the orchestra players in their 1944 uniforms. Of course, Vera Lynn sang *I'll Be Seeing You* and they performed the *SHAEF Signature Tune*. Sadly George died in 1967, but his orchestra is still with us and is often heard in David Jacobs' Radio Two programme.

THE BRITISH BAND OF THE AEF

Wednesday, 26 July 1944 BRITISH BAND OF THE SUPREME
20.30 DBST — AEFP ALLIED COMMAND

Guest Stars: Evelyn Dall, Carroll Gibbons

Compère: Capt. Franklin Englemann

SHAEF Signature Tune -arr- George Melachrino (Theme)/Commando Patrol/Constantly -VR- GMelo/Concerto for two (featuring Carroll Gibbons, Piano)/Based on Air (featuring Carroll Gibbons, Piano)/Blues Medley: Blues in the Night; Stardust; Two Sleepy People/Skylark/Let Us Face It We're In Love -VR- Evelyn Dall/ Frenesi/Pennsylvania Polka/SHAEF Theme and Close.

Saturday, 29 July 1944 ARMY RADIO ORCHESTRA
13.15-13.45 DBST — AEFP

Compère: Cpl. Douglas Marshall

Without a Song (Theme)/Holiday for Strings/Medley: In Times Like These -VR- GMelo; I'll Get By -VR- GMelo; All My Life -VR- GMelo/Lovely Lady/ Sweet as a Song -VR- GMelo/Without a Song (Theme) and Close.

From now on the theme tunes from broadcasts are not listed as they remained the same on each broadcast.

Wednesday, 2 August 1944 — AEFP   BRITISH BAND OF THE AEF
Guest Stars: Adelaide Hall, Teddy Brown
Compère: Capt. Franklin Englemann
Cherokee/Lazy Day/Some of These Days (featuring Teddy Brown, Piano)/
Moonlight Becomes You — GMelo/Donkey Serenade/Intermezzo (featuring
Adelaide Hall)/On Ilkla Moor Baht'at.

Wednesday, 9 August 1944 — AEFP   BRITISH BAND OF THE AEF
Guest Stars: Beryl Davis, Vic Oliver
Compère: Capt. Franklin Englemann
Limehouse Blues/Canzonetta/It's Love, Love, Love -VR- Beryl Davis/Poor
Little Rich Girl/Marche Hongroise (featuring Vic Oliver)/Long Ago and Far
Away -VR- GMelo/Dixie Medley: If You Please; Sunday, Monday or Always;
Dixie; Swing Low Sweet Chariot.

Wednesday, 16 August 1944 — AEFP   BRITISH BAND OF THE AEF
Guest Stars: Patricia Burke, Stephane Grappelli, Peter Akister, George Elliott
Compère: Capt. Franklin Englemann
I Got Rhythm/Now I Know -VR- GMelo/Blue Room (featuring Grappelli,
Akister and Elliott)/Piccolini/Time On My Hands -VR- Pat Burke/Fascinating
Rhythm/Oranges and Lemons -arr- George Evans.

Saturday, 19 August 1944 — AEFP   ARMY RADIO ORCHESTRA
Compère: Jean Metcalfe
Don't Sweetheart Me/Blue Room/Yankee Doodle Dandy Medley: Mary;
Yankee Doodle Dandy; Over There/Long Ago and Far Away -VR- GMelo/
California Here I Come.

Wednesday, 23 August 1944   BRITISH BAND OF THE AEF
Guest Stars: Evelyn Laye, Cpl. Denny Dennis RAF
Compère: Capt. Franklin Englemann
Great Day/Frenesi/Long Ago and Far Away -VR- Denny Dennis/Big Boogie/
All The Things You Are/Selections from Bitter Sweet-Ziguener -VR- Evelyn
Laye; Sweet Little Café -VR- EL; The Call of Life -VR- EL; I'll See You Again
-VR- EL/Lilliburlero.

Saturday, 26 August 1944   ARMY RADIO ORCHESTRA
Guest Star: Anne Lenner
Compère: Cpl. Douglas Marshall
Bin Bam Boom/I'll Get By -VR- Anne Lenner/Fascinating Rhythm/Pedro the
Fisherman -VR- GMelo/Scrub, Brothers Scrub/Time On My Hands -VR-
Anne Lenner/Blue Skies/ Begin the Beguine -VR- GMelo/Hallelujah!

Wednesday, 30 August 1944 — AEFP   BRITISH BAND OF THE AEF
20.30-21.00 DBST
Guest Star: Bing Crosby
Compère: Capt. Franklin Englemann
BBC Disc No. SLO 60882
(Also recorded by ORBS)

(0.45) Opening Theme (SHAEF Signature tune) (George Melachrino) (2.38) Sing, Sing, Sing (Prima) -arr- Guardsman George Evans (0.47) Introductory Music for Bing Crosby (3.25) I'll Be Seeing You -VR- Bing Crosby (Fain-Kahal) (3.56) Caravan (Duke Ellington) -arr- Jack Coles (6.05) Donegal Cradle Song (Hughes) (3.08) Swinging on a Star -VR- Bing Crosby (Johnny Burke-Jimmy van Heusen) (from the 1944, Paramount film, 'Going My Way') (3.04) Sweet and Lovely (Arnheim-Lemare-Tobias) (from the 1944, MGM film, 'Two Girls and A Sailor') (featuring Ronnie Selby, Piano and the String Section) (3.55) With a Song in my Heart -VR- Bing Crosby (Rogers and Hart) -arr- Burt Thompson (from the 1944, Universal film, 'This is the Life') (0.53) Closing Theme (SHAEF Signature tune) (George Melachrino).

Saturday, 2 September 1944 — AEFP   ARMY RADIO ORCHESTRA
Guest Star: Dorothy Carless
Compère: Cpl. Douglas Marshall
Thank Your Lucky Stars/That Old Black Magic -VR- Dorothy Carless/The Peanut Vendor/Time Alone Will Tell -VR- GMelo/Lovely Lady/His Rocking-Horse Ran Away -VR- Dorothy Carless/Sophisticated Lady/The Gentleman Obviously Doesn't Believe -VR- GMelo/Holiday for Strings.

Wednesday, 6 September 1944   BRITISH BAND OF THE AEF
20.30 AEFP
Guest Stars: Dorothy Carless, George Shearing
Compère: Capt. Franklin Englemann
My Shining Hour/Dancing in the Dark (featuring George Shearing, Piano)/Indian Summer/Ca C'est Paris/Begin the Beguine -VR- Dorothy Carless/Limehouse Blues/Big Ben -arr- GMelo.

Thursday, 7 September 1944   BRITISH BAND OF THE AEF
10.01 AEFP
Recorded repeat of yesterday's broadcast in the AEFP.

Saturday, 9 September 1944   ARMY RADIO ORCHESTRA
12.15 AEFP
Guest Star: Dorothy Carless
Compère: Cpl. Douglas Marshall
Hit the Road to Dreamland/I Got It Bad and It Ain't Good -VR- Dorothy Carless/Havana's Calling Me/Stormy Weather -VR- Dorothy Carless/Tea for Two (featuring Ronnie Selby, Piano)/Darling Je Vous Aime Beaucoup -VR- Dorothy Carless/Poor Little Rich Girl/This Was the Place -VR- Dorothy Carless/Dixie Selection: Sunday, Monday or Always; If You Please; Dixie.

Wednesday, 13 September 1944   BRITISH BAND OF THE AEF
20.30 AEFP, BBC Disc No. TLO 61600
Guest Star: Joyce Grenfell
Compère: Capt. Franklin Englemann
Alexander's Ragtime Band/Now I Know -VR- GMelo/Bach Goes To Town/Turn Back the Clock -VR- Joyce Grenfell/Thank You Mr Bach/Fascinating Rhythm (featuring Ronnie Selby, Piano)/Bolero.

Thursday, 14 September 1944   BRITISH BAND OF THE AEF
10.01 AEFP
Recorded repeat of yesterday's broadcast in the AEFP.

Saturday, 16 September 1944   ARMY RADIO ORCHESTRA
12.15 AEFP
Guest Star: Beryl Davis
Compère: Cpl. Douglas Marshall
California Here I Come/This is a Lovely Way to Spend an Evening -VR- Beryl Davis/Midnight in Mayfair (featuring Ronnie Selby, Piano)/Now I Know -VR- GMelo/The Donkey Serenade/Take It Easy -VR- Beryl Davis/Canzonetta/ Zing Went the Strings of My Heart -VR- Beryl Davis/Sweet as a Song -VR- GMelo.

Monday, 18 September 1944   PIANO PARADE
11.45
(Featuring 'Boogie Woogie' Solo Piano titles by Signalman Ronnie Selby.) Chopsticks (Theme)/Fascinating Rhythm/Tea for Two/Body and Soul/No Name Boogie/untitled composition by Ronnie Selby/Chopsticks (Theme).

Wednesday, 20 September 1944   BRITISH BAND OF THE AEF
20.30 AEFP
Guest Stars: Pat Kirkwood, Richard Murdoch
Compère: Capt. Franklin Englemann
Exactly Like You/Star Eyes -VR- GMelo/Mairzy Doats (featuring Richard Murdoch)/Fantasy for Flute and Orchestra (featuring Richard Murdoch) (including: Anvil Chorus; Destiny; Donkey Serenade; Skaters' Waltz; Little Sir Echo; Chloe; The British Grenadiers; Sailor's Hornpipe; Stars and Stripes)/Piccolo/Memories of You/I've Got the World on a String -VR- Pat Kirkwood/The Girl I Left Behind Me.

Saturday, 23 September 1944   ARMY RADIO ORCHESTRA
12.15 AEFP
Guest Star: Rita Williams
Compère: Cpl. Douglas Marshall
Struttin' With Some Barbecue/A Garden in the Rain -VR- Rita Williams/ Chico's Love Song/Nightingale -VR- GMelo/Barrelhouse Boogie (featuring Ronnie Selby, Piano)/The Very Thought of You -VR- Rita Williams/Medley: Sigh No More My Ladies -VR- GMelo; Blow Blow Thou Winter Wind -VR- GMelo/Suddenly It's Spring -VR- Rita Williams/Kansas City Moods.

Monday, 25 September 1944   PIANO PARADE
11.45 AEFP
In Pinetops Footsteps/I'll Get By/Rosetta/Oh! Lady Be Good/Star Eyes/Barrelhouse Boogie.

Wednesday, 27 September 1944   BRITISH BAND OF THE AEF
20.30 AEFP
Guest Stars: Marlene Dietrich, Jessie Matthews, E. O. Pogson

Compère: A/C2 Ronald Waldman RAF

Blue Skies/My Bonnie Lies Over the Ocean (featuring E. O. Pogson and Clarinet Quartet)/Dancing on the Ceiling (introduction for Jessie Matthews)/ Medley: My Heart Stood Still -VR- Jessie Matthews; J'Attendrai -VR- Jessie Matthews; May I Have the Next Romance with You -VR- Jessie Matthews/ Brazil/Falling in Love Again -VR- Marlene Dietrich/The Boys in the Back Room -VR- Marlene Dietrich/Alouette.

Thursday, 28 September 1944   BRITISH BAND OF THE AEF
10.01 AEFP

Recorded repeat of yesterday's broadcast in the AEFP, BBC Disc No. SLO 62354.

Saturday, 30 September 1944   ARMY RADIO ORCHESTRA
13.30 AEFP

Guest Star: Carole Carr

Compère: Cpl. Douglas Marshall

Dawn Patrol/In the Spirit of the Moment -VR- Carole Carr/Cubana/Little Old Lady -VR- GMelo/Honky Tonk Train (featuring Ronnie Selby, Piano)/ Thanks Mr Censor -VR- Carole Carr/Jitterbug -VR- GMelo/The Music Stopped -VR- Carole Carr/San Fernando Valley.

Monday, 2 October 1944   PIANO PARADE
11.45

Honky Tonk Train Blues/Smoke Gets in Your Eyes/It Had to be You/Night and Day/Sophisticated Lady/At the Woodchopper's Ball.

Wednesday, 4 October 1944   BRITISH BAND OF THE AEF
20.30 AEFP (BBC Disc No. SLO 62949)

Guest Stars: Vera Lynn, Art Thompson

Compère: A/C2 Ronald Waldman RAF

Hallelujah!/The First Few Days -VR- GMelo/Persuasion (featuring Art Thompson)/Love Walked In/Great Day/Wishing (introduction for Vera Lynn)/ I'll Be Seeing You -VR- Vera Lynn (including the last few bars of I'll See You Again)/When Johnny Comes Marching Home.

Saturday, 7 October 1944   ARMY RADIO ORCHESTRA
13.30 AEFP

Guest Star: Anne Lenner

Compère: Cpl. Douglas Marshall

Jumping Jimminy/They Didn't Believe Me -VR- Anne Lenner/ Americonga/ Indian Summer -VR- GMelo/Woodchopper's Ball (featuring Ronnie Selby, Piano)/I'll Be Seeing You -VR- Anne Lenner/Milkman Keep Those Bottles Quiet -VR- GMelo/Dancing in the Dark -VR- Anne Lenner/Johnson Special/ Make Way for Tomorrow -VR- GMelo.

Monday, 9 October 1944   PIANO PARADE
11.45 AEFP

Tessa's Torch Song/Danny Boy/Eye Opener/Humoresque/I'll Never Smile Again/St Louis Blues.

Wednesday, 11 October 1944   BRITISH BAND OF THE AEF
20.30 AEFP
Guest Stars: 'Kathleen' and Webster Booth
Compère: A/C2 Ronald Waldman RAF
I Know That You Know/Going My Way -VR- GMelo/Why Don't You Do Right -VR- 'Kathleen'/Sweet and Lovely/Introductory music for Webster Booth -Comp- GMelo/On Away, Awake Beloved -VR- Webster Booth/ Yankee Doodle.

Saturday, 14 October 1944   ARMY RADIO ORCHESTRA
13.30 AEFP
Guest Star: Paula Green
Compère: Cpl. Douglas Marshall
Route Twenty-three/In the Blue of Evening -VR- Paula Green/Cubanoca/I Dream of Jeannie with the Light Brown Hair -VR- GMelo/In Pinetops Footsteps (featuring Ronnie Selby, Piano)/His Rocking Horse Ran Away -VR- Paula Green/It was a Lover and His Lass -VR- GMelo/Hallelujah!/All Or Nothing At All -VR- Paula Green /Tunisian Trail.

Sunday, 15 October 1944   JAZZ JAMBOREE
The British Band of the AEF were featured in the annual Jazz Jamboree, at the Stoll Theatre, in Kingsway, London, during the afternoon. No details remain on what titles were performed at this charity concert.

Monday, 16 October 1944   PIANO PARADE
11.45
Lady in Red/White Christmas/Blue Skies/Cherry Ripe/Jingle Bells/Twelve Bar Blues.

Wednesday, 18 October 1944   BRITISH BAND OF THE AEF
20.30 AEFP
Guest Stars: Anne Lenner, Jackie Hunter
Compère: A/C2 Ronald Waldman RAF
My Blue Heaven/Dance of the Spanish Onion -VR- Anne Lenner/Stardust -VR- Anne Lenner/Waltz in Spring-time/My Prayer/'Play-on' — The Life of the Party (featuring Jackie Hunter)/Matilda Told Such Terrible Lies (featuring Jackie Hunter)/Oranges and Lemons -arr- GE (with introduction played on the Novachord by Ronnie Waldman).

Saturday, 21 October 1944   ARMY RADIO ORCHESTRA
13.30 AEFP
Guest Star: Dorothy Carless
Compère: Cpl. Douglas Marshall
Riffs/More Than You Know -VR- Dorothy Carless/Lady in Red -VR- GMelo/The Song of the Hurricane/Scrub Me Mama, With a Boogie Beat (featuring Ronnie Selby, Piano)/Body and Soul -VR- Dorothy Carless/San Fernando Valley -VR- GMelo/Long Ago and Far Away -VR- Dorothy Carless/ Here It Is, Monday -VR- GMelo/Ode to Spring.

35

Monday, 23 October 1944   PIANO PARADE
11.45 AEFP
Lady be Good/Melody in 'F'/Rum-boogie/Elegy in Blue/Fascinating Rhythm.
Wednesday, 25 October 1944   BRITISH BAND OF THE AEF
20.30 AEFP
Guest Stars: Bebe Daniels, Max Von Stokkum
Compère: A/C2 Ronald Waldman RAF
Oh! Lady Be Good/Spring Will Be a Little Late This Year -VR- GMelo/Back Beat Boogie (featuring Max Von Stokkum, Piano)/Body and Soul/Winter Sunshine -VR- GMelo/Rio Rita (introduction to Bebe Daniels) /I Can't Love You Anymore -VR- Bebe Daniels/Deep in the Heart of Texas -VR- Bebe Daniels/The Bells of Normandy -VR- Bebe Daniels/I've Got Sixpence/Medley: Pennies from Heaven; We're in the Money; Ten Cents a Dance; Pocketful of Pennies.
Saturday, 28 October 1944   ARMY RADIO ORCHESTRA
13.30 AEFP
Guest Star: Gloria Brent
Compère: Cpl. Douglas Marshall
Stop That Dancin' Up There/Time On My Hands -VR- Gloria Brent/ Havana's Calling Me/Spring Will Be a Little Late This Year -VR- GMelo/ Holiday for Strings (featuring Ronnie Selby, Piano)/A Lovely Way to Spend an Evening -VR- Gloria Brent/Boston Bounce/Let Me Love You Tonight -VR- GMelo/The Very Thought of You -VR- Gloria Brent/Tzigane Swing.
Monday, 30 October 1944   PIANO PARADE
11.45 AEFP
Scrub Me Mama, With a Boogie Beat/My Prayer/Bublink/No Name Boogie/ The Man I Love/Holiday for Strings.
Wednesday, 1 November 1944   BRITISH BAND OF THE AEF
20.30 AEFP
Guest Stars: Elizabeth Welch, Carroll Gibbons
Compère: A/C2 Ronald Waldman RAF
Three Little Words/The Song Is You -VR- GMelo/Concerto for Carroll (featuring Carroll Gibbons, Piano)/I'm Getting Sentimental Over You/Tico Tico/Amor Amor -VR- Elizabeth Welch/Pop Goes the Weasel.
Saturday, 4 November 1944   ARMY RADIO ORCHESTRA
13.30 AEFP
Guest Star: Unknown
Compère: Cpl. Douglas Marshall
Further details remain unknown.
Monday, 6 November 1944   PIANO PARADE
11.45 AEFP
On The Sunny Side of the Street/Daybreak/She's Funny That Way/Waltz by Chopin, Opus 64, Number 1 Valse in 'D' Flat/All the Things You Are/Boogie Chromatic.

Wednesday, 8 November 1944   BRITISH BAND OF THE AEF
20.30 AEFP
Guest Stars: Anne Shelton, Rawicz and Landauer
Compère: A/C2 Ronald Waldman RAF
Keep Your Sunny Side Up/There's A Small Hotel -VR- GMelo/Introductory music for Rawicz and Landauer by GMelo/Hungarian Rhapsody (featuring the two pianos of Rawicz and Landauer)/I'll Walk Alone/Peanut Vendor/'Anne Shelton's' Theme — With a Smile and a Song/Time Waits for No One -VR- Anne Shelton/When Johnny Comes Marching Home.

Saturday, 11 November 1944   ARMY RADIO ORCHESTRA
13.30 AEFP
Guest Star: Edna Kaye
Compère: Cpl. Douglas Marshall
Come On In/As Time Goes By -VR- Edna Kaye/Conga Boom/My Prayer -VR- GMelo/Boogie Woogie Bugle Boy (featuring Ronnie Selby, Piano)/Spring Will Be a Little Late This Year -VR- Edna Kaye/War Dance of the Wooden Indians/You Belong to My Heart -VR- GMelo/Stardust -VR- Edna Kaye.

Monday, 13 November 1944   PIANO PARADE
11.45 AEFP
Undecided/My Ideal/Boogie Woogie Bugle Boy/What's New/Dear Old Southland or Deep River/Stormy Weather.

Wednesday, 15 November 1944   BRITISH BAND OF THE AEF
20.30 AEFP
Guest Stars: Adelaide Hall, Victor Feldman
Compère: A/C2 Ronald Waldman RAF
Singing in the Rain/A Fellow on a Furlough -VR- GMelo/I Got Rhythm (featuring Victor Feldman, Drums)/Canzonetta/Jeep Ride/Introductory Music for Adelaide Hall by Burt Thompson/Baby Mine -VR- Adelaide Hall/Cherry Ripe Around the Orchestra -arr- Van Phillips.

Saturday, 18 November 1944   ARMY RADIO ORCHESTRA
13.30 AEFP
Guest Star: Anne Lenner
Compère: Cpl. Douglas Marshall
Ten Days With Baby/Close To You -VR- Anne Lenner/Cubana/Whispers in the Dark -VR- GMelo/Begin the Beguine (featuring Ronnie Selby, Piano)/I'll Walk Alone -VR- Anne Lenner/Reverse the Charges/Goodnight Good Neighbour -VR-GMelo/My Shining Hour -VR- Anne Lenner.

Monday, 20 November 1944   PIANO PARADE
11.45 AEFP
Begin the Beguine/The Way You Look Tonight/Unfinished Boogie/She's My Lovely/ When Day is Done/Shoo Shoo Baby.

Wednesday, 22 November 1944   BRITISH BAND OF THE AEF
20.30 AEFP
Guest Stars: Tessie O'Shea, Monia Liter
Compère: A/C2 Ronald Waldman RAF

All God's Children Got Rhythm/I'll Be Around -VR- GMelo/Theme in 'A' (introductory music for Monia Liter)/Rhapsody on a Theme by Irving Berlin (Blue Skies) (featuring Monia Liter)/Chattanooga Choo Choo/Mean to Me/ International Rhythm -arr- Burt Thompson (including four bars of Soldiers of the King; St Louis Blues; Peanut Vendor; La Paloma; Ferdinand the Bull; The Campbells are Coming; All Through the Night; Sospanfach; Killarney; (featuring Tessie O'Shea)/Yes We Have No Bananas -arr- George Evans.

Saturday, 25 November 1944　　　　ARMY RADIO ORCHESTRA
13.30 AEFP

Guest Star: Dorothy Carless
Compère: Cpl. Douglas Marshall

Jumpin' Jimminy/More Than You Know -VR- Dorothy Carless/Americonga/ In the Still of the Night -VR- GMelo/Unfinished Boogie (featuring Ronnie Selby, Piano)/How Blue the Night -VR- Dorothy Carless/Chattanooga Choo Choo/You Belong to My Heart -VR- GMelo/Stormy Weather -VR- Dorothy Carless.

Monday, 27 November 1944　　　　PIANO PARADE
11.45

The Lady is a Tramp/Easy to Love/My Heart Belongs to Daddy/ Rosalie/I've Got You Under My Skin/I Get a Kick Out of You/F.D.R. Jones.

Wednesday, 29 November 1944　　　　BRITISH BAND OF THE AEF
20.30 AEFP

Guest Stars: Anne Zieglar, Carl Barriteau
Compère: A/C2 Ronald Waldman RAF

Zing Went the Strings of My Heart/Don't Tell a Soul -VR- GMelo/'Play-on' — 'Blues in the Night'/A Sultan Goes to Harlem (featuring Carl Barriteau)/It Could Happen to You/The Big Boogie (featuring Ronnie Selby, Piano)/Play-on Theme in 'A'/One Fine Day -VR- Anne Zieglar/Sailor's Hornpipe.

Saturday, 2 December 1944　　　　ARMY RADIO ORCHESTRA
13.30 AEFP

Guest Star: Gloria Brent
Compère: Cpl. Douglas Marshall

College Rhythm/They Didn't Believe Me -VR- Gloria Brent/Spic and Spanish/ Boogie in the Groove -VR- GMelo/There's a Lull in My Life (featuring Ronnie Selby, Piano)/Ten Days with Baby/Come Out Wherever You Are -VR- GMelo/Star Eyes -VR- Gloria Brent/Hallelujah!

Monday, 4 December 1944　　　　PIANO PARADE
11.45 AEFP

(Pre-recorded 30 November, 1944 — Disc No. SLO 65455)

Honky Tonk Train Blues/Blues in the Night/No Name Boogie -comp- Ronnie Selby/St Louis Blues/Tess's Torch Song/Barrel Boogie.

Wednesday, 6 December 1944　　　　BRITISH BAND OF THE AEF
20.30 AEFP

Guest Stars: Barbara Mullen, Frank Weir, Terrence Macdona

Compère: A/C2 Ronald Waldman RAF
Button Up Your Overcoat/A Kiss in the Night -VR- GMelo/What's New/
Concerto for Clarinet (featuring Frank Weir, Clarinet)/Lazy Day -VR-Terrence
Macdona/San Fernando Valley/Medley (featuring Barbara Mullen): Danny
Boy; I Know My Love; Eileen Oge; Let Him Go/Big Ben.

Saturday, 9 December 1944   ARMY RADIO ORCHESTRA
13.30 AEFP
Guest Star: Carole Carr
Compère: Cpl. Douglas Marshall
Riffs/May I Have the Next Romance With You -VR- Carole Carr/Chico's Love
Song/Fellow on a Furlough -VR- GMelo/Tea for Two (featuring Ronnie Selby,
Piano)/How Blue the Night -VR- Carole Carr/Rainbow Corner -VR- GMelo &
Chorus/A Kiss in the Night -VR- GMelo/Goodnight Wherever You Are -VR-
Carole Carr.

Monday, 11 December 1944   PIANO PARADE
11.45 AEFP
(Pre-recorded 30 November 1944 — BBC Disc No. SLO 65456)
If I Had You/I Cried For You/Sweet Georgia Brown/I Cover the
Waterfront/Crazy Rhythm/Out of Nowhere/I Ain't Got Nobody.

Wednesday, 13 December 1944   BRITISH BAND OF THE AEF
20.30 AEFP
Guest Stars: Evelyn Dall, Stephane Grappelli, Peter Akister, George Elliott
Compère: A/C2 Ronald Waldman RAF
Heat Wave/I Didn't Know What Time It Was -VR- GMelo/Medley (featuring
Grappelli, Akister, Elliott and Orchestra): I'll Walk Alone; It Could Happen to
You; San Fernando Valley; Donegal Cradle Song/Lover/Something for the
Boys (introductory music for Evelyn Dall)/All Reet, All Root, All Right -VR-
Evelyn Dall/The Minstrel Boy.

Saturday, 16 December 1944   ARMY RADIO ORCHESTRA
13.30 AEFP
Guest Stars: Beryl Davis
Compère: Lt. Douglas Marshall
(Pre-recorded 5 December 1944 — BBC Disc No. SLO 66580)
The Trolley Song/I'll Walk Alone -VR- Beryl Davis/Dance of the Spanish
Onion/I'll Be Around -VR- GMelo/Honeysuckle Rose (featuring Ronnie
Selby, Piano)/Spring Will Be a Little Late This Year -VR- Beryl Davis/Stop
That Dancing Up There/A Kiss in the Night -VR- GMelo/Just a-Whittling
and a-Whistling -VR- Beryl Davis.

Monday, 18 December 1944   PIANO PARADE
11.45 AEFP
(Pre-recorded Friday, 15 December 1944 — BBC Disc No. SLO 66580)
Young and Healthy/It Could Happen to You/Midnight in Mayfair/Danny
Boy/Come Out Wherever You Are/Liszt Boogie.

Wednesday, 20 December 1944   BRITISH BAND OF THE AEF
20.30 AEFP, Home Service
Guest Stars: Jack Buchanan, Sgt. Norman Sorsenson, US Army
Compère: A/C2 Ronald Waldman RAF
(Pre-recorded Thursday, 7 December 1944 — BBC Disc No. SLO 64897)
Sing, Sing, Sing/Theme in 'A' (introductory music for Norman Sorsenson)/Elegy in Blue (composition by and featuring Norman Sorsenson, Piano)/Dance with a Dolly -VR- GE (featuring George Evans, Tenor Saxophone solo)/It Could Happen to You/Come Out Wherever You Are/There Isn't Any Limit To My Love For You -VR- Jack Buchanan/When Johnny Comes Marching Home.

Saturday, 23 December 1944   ARMY RADIO ORCHESTRA
13.30 AEFP
Guest Star: Anne Lenner
Compère: Lt. Douglas Marshall
(Pre-recorded Saturday, 9 December 1944 — BBC Disc No. SLO 64898)
Everybody Dance/Time Waits For No One -VR- Anne Lenner/Cubanoca/Don't Tell a Soul -VR- GMelo/Unfinished Boogie (featuring Ronnie Selby, Piano)/Amor Amor -VR- Anne Lenner/Come Out Wherever You Are/Going My Way -VR- GMelo/Stardust -VR- Anne Lenner/Make Way For Tomorrow.

Monday, 25 December 1944   PIANO PARADE
11.45 AEFP
(Pre-recorded Thursday, 14 December 1944 — BBC Disc No. SLO 66581)
A Pretty Girl is Like a Melody/Humoresque/I'll Walk Alone/Unfinished Boogie/Love Walked In/San Fernando Valley.

Later on Christmas Day, at 6.05 p.m. on the AEFP the three bands of the AEF took part in a special *AEF Christmas Show*. The idea was that the British and Canadian Bands of the AEF would broadcast from the Queensbury All Services Club, in London. The American Band of the AEF, which was directed by Major Glenn Miller, would be recorded earlier that same day from Paris. As it turned out Major Glenn Miller had disappeared on Friday, 15 December 1944, and the American Band was directed by Sergeant Jerry Gray. The first twenty-five minutes of this special show featured the Canadian Band of the AEF (The Canadian Army Orchestra), under the direction of Captain Robert Farnon. The next thirty minutes featured the Army Radio Orchestra (a unit of the British Band of the AEF) under the direction of RSM George Melachrino. Following this, just after the news headlines at 7.01 p.m. was the thirty-minute show by the American Band of the AEF directed by Sgt. Jerry Gray from the Olympia Theatre in Paris. The final part of the two-hour show was the grand round-up, which featured all three bands, plus all the guest stars that had taken part.

Monday, 25 December 1944   BRITISH BAND OF THE AEF
18.30-19.00 AEFP
Guest Stars: Beryl Davis, Teddy Brown

Compère: A/C2 Ronald Waldman RAF
Theme/Without A Song/Everybody Dance/Just a-Whittling and a-Whistling
-VR- Beryl Davis/Prelude to Boogie (featuring Signalman Ronnie Selby,
Piano)/ In the Spirit of the Moment -VR- Beryl Davis/Dance With A Dolly
-VR- GE/Some of These Days (featuring Teddy Brown, Piano)/I'll Walk Alone
-VR- Beryl Davis/Boston Bounce/Theme and Close.

COMBINED ROUND-UP

19.30-20.00, AEFP, Home Service
(also short-waved to the USA and Canada)
Compères: A/C2 Ronald Waldman RAF, Gerry Wilmot and W/O Paul
Dudley
Canadian Band Medley: Tipperary; Keep the Home Fires Burning; Pack Up
Your Troubles/Cyril Fletcher -acc- Canadian Band - Odd Odes; Nellie Quaint;
The Blasted Heath/British Band − Lazy Day/Jackie Hunter -acc-British Band
− The Life of the Party/American Band − Oranges and Lemons -VR- JD,CC
-arr- Jerry Gray/Combined Bands and Audiences, Auld Lang Syne and Close.

Wednesday, 27 December 1944　　　**BRITISH BAND OF THE AEF**
20.30 AEFP, BBC Disc No. SLO 66345
Guest Stars: Paula Green, Vic Oliver, Cpl. Jack Powers US Army
Compère: A/C2 Ronald Waldman RAF
(Opening Theme (SHAEF Theme Song) (George Melachrino)/Put On Your
Old Grey Bonnet (Unknown) -arr- George Evans/Spring Will Be A Little Late
This Year -VR- Jack Powers (Loesser) (from the 1944 Warner Bros film
'Christmas Holiday')/His Rocking-Horse Ran Away -VR- Paula Green (Van
Heusen) -arr- Jack Coles/Memories Of You/Theme in 'A'/The Tales of
Hoffman (Vic Oliver)/Hungarian Air (Vic Oliver)/Trees (Vic Oliver)/'Patter'
by Vic Oliver/Yankee Doodle/Theme and Close.

Note: The introduction theme music and the first three titles are held by the
BBC recordings archive in London.

Saturday, 30 December 1944　　　**ARMY RADIO ORCHESTRA**
13.30 AEFP
Guest Star: Edna Kaye
Compère: Lt. Douglas Marshall
My Guy's Come Back/Zing Went the Strings of My Heart -VR- Edna Kaye/
Mi Manuclita/Oh! Lady Be Good/Blue Room/Begin the Beguine (featuring
Ronnie Selby, Piano)/Spring Will Be a Little Late This Year -VR-Edna
Kaye/Reverse the Charges/I'll Walk Alone -VR- Edna Kaye/The Trolley Song.

Monday, 1 January 1945　　　**PIANO PARADE**
11.45 AEFP
(Pre-recorded Thursday, 28 December 1944 — BBC Disc No. SLO 66553a)
On the Sunny Side of the Street/This Can't Be Love/Butterflies in the Rain/
More Than You Know/Prelude to Boogie/Cheek to Cheek.

Wednesday, 3 January 1945   BRITISH BAND OF THE AEF
20.30 AEFP
Guest Stars: Jessie Matthews, Freddie Gardner RN
Compère: A/C2 Ronald Waldman RAF
It Had To Be You/Some Other Time -VR- GMelo (Siboney/Stardust (featuring Freddie Gardner, Saxophone)/Come Out Wherever You Are/Medley: You'll Never Know; Long Ago and Far Away; Spring Will Be A Little Late This Year (all featuring Jessie Matthews, Vocal)/Little Brown Jug -arr- GMelo.

Saturday, 6 January 1945   ARMY RADIO ORCHESTRA
13.30 AEFP
Guest Star: Gloria Brent
Compère: Lt. Douglas Marshall
Atlantic Jive/What a Difference a Day Made -VR- Gloria Brent/The Conga Boom/Stay As Sweet As You Are -VR- GMelo/Prelude to Boogie (featuring Ronnie Selby, Piano)/I Said 'No' -VR- Gloria Brent/Boy Meets Horn/Tico Tico -VR- GMelo/A Journey to a Star -VR- Gloria Brent.

Monday, 8 January 1945   PIANO PARADE
11.45 AEFP
(Pre-recorded Thursday, 28 December 1944 — BBC Disc No. SLO 66554)
Ida, Sweet as Apple Cider/Lover Come Back To Me/In an Eighteenth Century Drawing Room/Out of Space/Scrub Me Mama, With a Boogie Beat/Memories of You/Loch Lomond.

Wednesday, 10 January 1945   BRITISH BAND OF THE AEF
20.30 AEFP
Guest Stars: Vera Lynn, Nat Temple
Compère: A/C2 Ronald Waldman RAF
In the Shade of the Old Apple Tree/Do You Belive in Dreams? -VR- GMelo/The Trolley Song/Canzonetta (featuring Nat Temple)/Jeep Ride/Little Star -VR- Vera Lynn/When You Wish Upon A Star -VR- Vera Lynn/Rolling Home.

Saturday, 13 January 1945   ARMY RADIO ORCHESTRA
13.30 AEFP
Guest Star: Dorothy Carless
Compère: Lt. Douglas Marshall
Sales Talk/Lover's Lullaby -VR- Dorothy Carless/Mi Cancion/Some Other Time -VR- GMelo/After the Rain (featuring Ronnie Selby, Piano)/Skylark -VR- Dorothy Carless/Bim Bam Boom/Dance with a Dolly -VR- GE (Solo Saxophone GE)/The Very Thought of You -VR- Dorothy Carless.

Monday, 15 January 1945   PIANO PARADE
11.45 AEFP
(Pre-recorded Thursday, 15 December 1944 — BBC Disc No. SLO 66580)
Recorded repeat of the Piano Parade show first broadcast by AEFP, on Monday, 18 December 1944.

Wednesday, 17 January 1945　　　　　　BRITISH BAND OF THE AEF
20.30 AEFP
Guest Stars: Anne Zieglar and Webster Booth
Compère: A/C2 Ronald Waldman RAF
Marie/I'll Remember April -VR- GMelo/You're the Cream in My Coffee -VR-
Len Stevens/Deep Purple/Tico Tico/Theme in 'A'/Liebestraum -VR- Anne
Zieglar and Webster Booth/John Twentieth Century Peel.

Saturday, 20 January 1945　　　　　　ARMY RADIO ORCHESTRA
13.30 AEFP
Guest Star: Carole Carr
Compère: Lt. Douglas Marshall
Thanks Mr. Censor -VR- Carole Carr/Americonga/Do You Believe in
Dreams? -VR- GMelo/Flag Waver/Heavenly Music -VR- Carole Carr/Sigh No
More My Lady -VR- GMelo/Blow, Blow Thou Winter Wind -VR- GMelo/
How Blue The Night -VR- Carole Carr.

Monday, 22 January 1945　　　　　　　　PIANO PARADE
11.45 AEFP
(Pre-recorded Thursday, 11 January 1945 — BBC Disc No. SLO 67530)
Sing A Song Of Sixpence/Easy to Love/The Continental/The Music Stopped/
Boogie in the Groove/The Man I Love/China Boy.

Wednesday, 24 January 1945　　　　　　BRITISH BAND OF THE AEF
20.30 AEFP
Guest Stars: Anne Shelton, LAC George Chisholm RAF
Compère: A/C2 Ronald Waldman RAF
The Sheik of Araby/Some Other Time -VR- GMelo/My Melancholy Baby
(featuring George Chisholm, Trombone)/Ye Banks and Braes/ Fascinating
Rhythm (featuring Ronnie Selby, Piano)/No One Else Will Do -VR- Anne
Shelton/Tramp, Tramp, Tramp the Boys are Marching.

Saturday, 27 January 1945　　　　　　ARMY RADIO ORCHESTRA
13.30 AEFP
Guest Star: Paula Green
Compère: Lt. Douglas Marshall
Hallelujah/There's No Two Ways About Love -VR- Paula Green/Brazil/I'll
Remember April -VR- GMelo/All or Nothing at All -VR- Paula Green/Three
Little Words (featuring Ronnie Selby, Piano)/Don't Get Around Much
Anymore -VR- Paula Green/Lovely Lady/Come Out Wherever You Are -VR-
Goodnight My Love -VR- Paula Green.

Monday, 29 January 1945　　　　　　　　PIANO PARADE
11.45 AEFP
(Pre-recorded Tuesday, 23 January 1945 — BBC Disc No. SLO 68127)
Bah Bah Black Sheep/Can I Forget You/The Trolley Song/Cocktails For Two/
St Louis Blues/Isn't It A Lovely Day/Come Out Wherever You Are/Easy To
Remember.

Wednesday, 31 January 1945   BRITISH BAND OF THE AEF
20.30 AEFP
Guest Stars: Yvonne Arnaud, Beryl Davis
Compère: A/C2 Ronald Waldman RAF
I'm Forever Blowing Bubbles/Don't You Know I Care -VR- GMelo/Winter Sunshine/'Play on' — You Made Me Love You/What A Difference a Day Made -VR- Beryl Davis/The Trolley Song/Theme in 'A'/La Fileuse (featuring Yvonne Arnaud, Piano)/The Quartermaster's Song -arr- AW.

Saturday, 3 February 1945   ARMY RADIO ORCHESTRA
13.30 AEFP
Guest Star: 'Kathleen'
Compère: Lt. Douglas Marshall
American Patrol/A Kiss in the Night -VR- GMelo/It Had To Be You -VR-'Kathleen'/Frenesi/Barrel House Boogie (featuring Ronnie Selby, Piano)/Indian Love Call -VR- 'Kathleen'/Moonlight Becomes You -VR- GMelo/Poor Little Rich Girl/I Can't Get Started -VR- 'Kathleen'.

Monday, 5 February 1945   PIANO PARADE
11.45 AEFP
(Pre-recorded Tuesday, 23 January 1945 — BBC Disc No. SLO 69128)
You're the Cream in My Coffee/Perfidia/Playing on the Seventh/Love is the Sweetest Thing/Fascinating Rhythm/Some Other Time/Great Day.

Wednesday, 7 February 1945   BRITISH BAND OF THE AEF
20.30 AEFP
Guest Stars: Gwen Catley, Frank Weir
Compère: A/C2 Ronald Waldman RAF
It Had To Be You/I'll Be Thinking Of You Easter Sunday -VR- GMelo/What's New (featuring Frank Weir)/Clarinet à la King (featuring Frank Weir, Clarinet)/These Foolish Things/I'm Young and Healthy -VR- GE/Theme in 'A'/Voices of Spring (featuring Gwen Catley)/A Life on the Ocean Wave.

Saturday, 10 February 1945   ARMY RADIO ORCHESTRA
13.30 AEFP
Guest Star: Edna Kaye
Compère: Lt. Douglas Marshall
Mop Mop/I'm in the Mood for Love -VR- Edna Kaye/Donkey Serenade/Don't You Know I Care -VR- Edna Kaye/Rosetta (featuring Ronnie Selby, Piano)/Paris in the Spring -VR- Edna Kaye/Cossack Patrol/I Didn't Know What Time It Was -VR- GMelo/The Trolley Song -VR- Edna Kaye.

Monday, 12 February 1945   PIANO PARADE
11.45 AEFP
(Pre-recorded Tuesday, 6 February 1945 — BBC Disc No. SLO 68732)
At the Woodchopper's Ball/Trees/Honeysuckle Rose/I'll Walk Alone/Barrel House Boogie/Stormy Weather.

Wednesday, 14 February 1945   BRITISH BAND OF THE AEF
20.30 AEFP
Guest Stars: Leni Lynn, Kenny Baker
Compère: A/C2 Ronald Waldman RAF
I Want to be Happy/Who Said Dreams Don't Come True -VR- GMelo/I Can't Give You Anything But Love (featuring Kenny Baker, Trumpet)/It Could Happen To You/The Peanut Vendor/Theme in 'A'/Carnival of Venice (featuring Leni Lynn, Piano)/The Girl I Left Behind Me.

Saturday, 17 February 1945   ARMY RADIO ORCHESTRA
13.30 AEFP
Guest Star: Gloria Brent
Compère: Lt. Douglas Marshall
Ten Days With Baby/It Could Happen To You -VR- Gloria Brent/Tico Tico Tico/My Prayer -VR- GMelo/Mission Hall Jump (featuring Ronnie Selby, Solo Piano)/I'm Making Believe/Fan It/Too Much Illusion -VR- Gloria Brent/ Holiday for Strings/All My Tomorrows -VR- Gloria Brent.

Monday, 19 February 1945   PIANO PARADE
11.45 AEFP
(Pre-recorded Tuesday, 6 February 1945 — BBC Disc No. SLO 68733)
In The Mood/Danny Boy/Sometimes I'm Happy/It Could Happen To You/ Unfinished Boogie/I'll Be Seeing You.

Wednesday, 21 February 1945   BRITISH BAND OF THE AEF
20.30 AEFP
Guest Stars: Patricia Leonard, Rawicz and Landauer
Compère: A/C2 Ronald Waldman RAF
So Dumb, But So Beautiful/I'll Remember April -VR- GMelo/Dance of the Spanish Onion/I'll See You In My Dreams (featuring Pat Leonard)/Poinciana (featuring Pat Leonard)/Sweet Sue/Rhapsody in Blue (featuring the two pianos of Rawicz and Landauer)/Where Oh Where Has My Little Dog Gone -arr- GMelo.

Saturday, 24 February 1945   ARMY RADIO ORCHESTRA
13.30 AEFP
Guest Star: Anne Lenner
Compère: Lt. Douglas Marshall
Jumpin' Jimminy/What a Difference a Day Made -VR- Anne Lenner/ The Morning After/Who Said Dreams Don't Come True -VR- GMelo/ Angry (featuring The Trio — Ronnie Selby, Piano; Freddie Phillips, Guitar; Bob Roberts, Bass)/Together -VR- Anne Lenner/Come On In/Pedro the Fisherman -VR- GMelo/No One Else Will Do -VR- Anne Lenner.

Monday, 26 February 1945   PIANO PARADE
11.45 AEFP
(Pre-recorded Tuesday, 20 February 1945 — BBC Disc No. SLO 69014)
AEFP Announcer: Tpr. De B. Holly, Canadian Army

45

Ida, Sweet as Apple Cider/I Dream of Jeannie with the Light Brown Hair/ 'A' Flat to 'C'/Always/Indian Summer/Willie's Return/Zing Went the Strings of My Heart.

Wednesday, 28 February 1945   BRITISH BAND OF THE AEF
20.30 AEFP

Guest Stars: Dorothy Carless, Monia Liter
Compère: Roy Williams

All God's Children Got Rhythm/I'll Break My Heart Again -VR- GMelo/Theme in 'E' -arr- GMelo/Starlight Souvenir (featuring Monia Liter)/ Flash in the Pan (featuring Monia Liter)/Estrellita/Night and Day -arr- GE/ With a Song in My Heart/All My Life -VR- Dorothy Carless/Oh! How I Hate to Get Up in the Morning.

Saturday, 3 March 1945   ARMY RADIO ORCHESTRA
13.30 AEFP

Guest Star: Dorothy Carless
Compère: Lt. Douglas Marshall

Jive Bomber/Transatlantic Lullaby -VR- Dorothy Carless/Anna Conga/Easter Sunday -VR- GMelo/Exactly Like You (Trio — Ronnie Selby, Piano; Freddie Phillips, Guitar; Bob Roberts, Bass)/The Touch of Your Lips -VR- Dorothy Carless/Ode to Spring/Did You Ever See a Dream Walking -VR- GMelo/The Trolley Song -VR- Dorothy Carless.

Monday, 5 March 1945   PIANO PARADE
11.45 AEFP

(Pre-recorded Tuesday, 20 February 1945 — BBC Disc No. SLO 69015)
SHAEF Announcer: Tpr. De B. Holly, Canadian Army

I've Found a New Baby/I'll Walk Beside You/Stomping at the Savoy/ Together/When You Wish Upon a Star/Scrub Me Mama, with a Boogie Beat/Blue Skies.

Wednesday, 7 March 1945   BRITISH BAND OF THE AEF
20.30 AEFP

Guest Stars: Elinore Farrell, Harry Hayes
Compère: A/C2 Ronald Waldman RAF

Liza/More and More -VR- GMelo/Honeysuckle Rose (Trio — Ronnie Selby, Piano; Freddie Phillips, Guitar; Bob Roberts, Bass)/'Play-on' Music -arr- GE/My Love (featuring Harry Hayes)/Body and Soul/La Cucaracha/Three Little Words (featuring Elinore Farrell)/Harlem Sandman (featuring Elinore Farrell)/The Minstrel Boy to the War Has Gone.

Saturday, 10 March 1945   ARMY RADIO ORCHESTRA
13.30 AEFP

Guest Star: Helen Raymond
Compère: Lt. Douglas Marshall

Florida Special/A Little on the Lonely Side -VR- Helen Raymond/Misirlou/ I'd Break My Heart Again -VR- GMelo/My Melancholy Baby (Trio — Ronnie Selby, Piano; Freddie Phillips, Guitar; Bob Roberts, Bass)/Time On My Hands

-VR- Helen Raymond/American Patrol/The Donkey Serenade -VR- GMelo/
Too Much Illusion -VR- Helen Raymond.

Monday, 12 March 1945   PIANO PARADE
11.45 AEFP
(Pre-recorded Saturday, 10 March 1945 — BBC Disc No. SLO 71017)
Tea For Two/People Will Say We're In Love/Ode to Chopin -comp- Ronnie
Selby/J'attendrai/Daphne/I'll Never be the Same Again/St Louis Blues.

Wednesday, 14 March 1945   BRITISH BAND OF THE AEF
20.30 AEFP
Guest Stars: Tessa Deane, Carl Barriteau
Compère: A/C2 Ronald Waldman RAF
I've Got a Feeling I'm Falling/You're So Sweet to Remember -VR- GMelo/
'Play-on' Theme in 'E' -arr- GMelo/Transatlantic Hop (featuring Carl
Barriteau)/Can I Forget You — including 'In the Gloaming' and 'You're the
Cream in My Coffee'/Waltz of the Gypsies (featuring Tessa Deane)/Dream
Lover (featuring Tessa Deane)/Show Me the Way to Go Home.

Saturday, 17 March 1945   ARMY RADIO ORCHESTRA
13.30 AEFP
Guest Star: Bette Roberts
Compère: Lt. Douglas Marshall
Tunisian Trail/How Blue the Night -VR- Bette Roberts/Havana's Calling Me/
More and More -VR- GMelo/Deed I Do (Trio — Ronnie Selby, Piano; Freddie
Phillips, Guitar; Bob Roberts, Bass)/There's a Lull in My Life -VR- Bette
Roberts/Riffs/Nightingale -VR- GMelo/Always Yours -VR- Bette Roberts.

Monday, 19 March 1945   PIANO PARADE
11.45 AEFP
(Pre-recorded Saturday, 17 March 1945 — BBC Disc No. SLO 71019)
Girl Friend/I'm in the Mood for Love/Deed I Do/Vous Qui Passez Sans Me
Voir (including 32 bars of 'Darling Je Vous Aime Beaucoup)/The Blues/
Sleepy Lagoon.

Wednesday, 21 March 1945   BRITISH BAND OF THE AEF
20.30 AEFP
Guest Stars: Judy Shirley, Sam Browne, Nat Gonella
Compère: A/C2 Ronald Waldman RAF
Three Little Words/Accentuate the Positive -VR- GMelo/Georgia (featuring
Nat Gonella, Trumpet)/Together (featuring Nat Gonella, Trumpet)/Poor
Butterfly/I Won't Dance/'Play-on' — 'Night and Day'/Wouldn't It Be Nice
-VR- Judy Shirley and Sam Browne/Love Here Is My Heart -VR- Judy Shirley
and Sam Browne/Night and Day -VR- Judy Shirley and Sam Browne/Overture
to a Housing Problem -comp- GMelo.

Saturday, 24 March 1945　　　　　　　　ARMY RADIO ORCHESTRA
13.30 AEFP
Guest Star: Anne Lenner
Compère: Lt. Douglas Marshall
Everybody Dance/A Little on the Lonely Side -VR- Anne Lenner/Cubana/I'll Remember April -VR- GMelo/Crazy Rhythm (Trio — Ronnie Selby, Piano; Freddie Phillips, Guitar; Bob Roberts, Bass)/Always Yours -VR- Anne Lenner/ My Guy's Come Back/Waiting in the Rain -VR- GMelo/A Garden in the Rain -VR- Anne Lenner.

Monday, 26 March 1945　　　　　　　　　　　PIANO PARADE
11.45 AEFP
Recorded repeat of the Piano Parade programme featuring Signalman Ronald Selby, first broadcast on 26 February 1945 — BBC Disc No. SLO 69014.

Wednesday, 28 March 1945　　　　BRITISH BAND OF THE AEF
20.30 AEFP
Guest Stars: From ITMA — Tommy Handley, Jack Train and Kay Cavendish
Compère: A/C2 Ronald Waldman RAF
(Pre-recorded Friday, 23 March 1945 — BBC Disc No. SLO 70947)
Keep Your Sunny Side Up/The Song is You -VR- GMelo/'Play-on' — Theme in 'E' -arr- GMelo/Struttin' Like a Peacock (featuring Kay Cavendish)/Mean to Me/Piccolo Pete/'Play-on' — ITMA Theme/The Trumpeter (featuring Tommy Handley and Jack Train)/Harlequin (featuring Tommy Handley and Jack Train)/When Johnny Comes Marching Home.

Saturday, 31 March 1945　　　　　　　ARMY RADIO ORCHESTRA
13.30 AEFP
(Pre-recorded earlier the same day — BBC Disc No. SLO 70475)
Guest Star: Edna Kaye
Compère: Lt. Douglas Marshall
All God's Children Got Rhythm/Too Much Illusion -VR- Edna Kaye/ Americonga/Easter Sunday -VR- GMelo/Coquette (Trio — Ronnie Selby, Piano; Freddie Phillips, Guitar; Bob Roberts, Bass)/Always Yours -VR- Edna Kaye/Sales Talk/Some Other Time -VR- GMelo/Hit the Road to Dreamland/ Two Sleepy People -VR- Edna Kaye and GMelo/Goodnight My Love -VR- Edna Kaye and GMelo.

Monday, 2 April 1945　　　　　　　　　　　PIANO PARADE
11.45 AEFP
Recorded repeat of a programme broadcast by the AEFP, on Monday, 19 February 1945 — BBC Disc No. SLO 68733.

Wednesday, 4 April 1945　　　　BRITISH BAND OF THE AEF
20.30 AEFP
Guest Stars: Dennis Noble, E. O. Pogson
Compère: A/C2 Ronald Waldman RAF
The Sheik of Araby/Waiting for Rain -VR- GMelo/Play-on Theme in 'E'/On

Hearing the First Oboe in Swing (featuring E. O. Pogson)/I'm Getting Sentimental Over You/Mr Bach Goes to Town/Play-on Theme in 'A'/Largo Al Factotum (featuring Dennis Noble)/Ballet to a Tandem.

Saturday, 7 April 1945   ARMY RADIO ORCHESTRA
14.01 AEFP
Guest Star: Lynne Shaw
Compère: Lt. Douglas Marshall
Mop Mop/Together -VR- Lynne Shaw/Come With Me Honey/April in Paris -VR- GMelo/Mary (Trio — Ronnie Selby, Piano; Freddie Phillips, Guitar; Bob Roberts, Bass)/As Time Goes By -VR- Lynne Shaw/Nine O'Clock Bounce/Accentuate the Positive -VR- GMelo/Let's Take the Long Way Home -VR- Lynne Shaw.

Monday, 9 April 1945   PIANO PARADE
11.45 AEFP
(Pre-recorded Saturday, 7 April 1945 — BBC Disc No. SLO 72138)
Honky-Tonk Train/April in Paris/Begin the Beguine/Solitude/A Pretty Girl is Like a Melody/Liza.

Wednesday, 11 April 1945   BRITISH BAND OF THE AEF
20.30 AEFP
Guest Stars: Beryl Davis, Ronald Chesney
Compère: A/C2 Ronald Waldman RAF
Great Day/More and More -VR- GMelo/'Play-on' — Theme in 'E'/Fascinating Rhythm (featuring Ronald Chesney)/They Don't Believe Me/Begin the Beguine/'Play-on' — 'You Made Me Love You'/All of a Sudden My Heart Sings -VR- Beryl Davis/Little Brown Jug -arr- GMelo.

Saturday, 14 April 1945   ARMY RADIO ORCHESTRA
14.01 AEFP
Guest Star: Helen Raymond
Compère: Lt. Douglas Marshall
The Dance of the Spanish Onion/They Didn't Believe Me -VR- Helen Raymond/Let Me Love You Tonight/More and More -VR- GMelo/To a Wild Rose (featuring George Evans, Saxophone; Ronnie Selby, Piano; Freddie Phillips, Guitar; Bob Roberts, Bass)/All of a Sudden My Heart Sings -VR- Helen Raymond/Poor Little Rich Girl/Why Do You Pass Me By -VR- GMelo/ The Very Thought of You -VR- Helen Raymond.

Monday, 16 April 1945   PIANO PARADE
11.45 AEFP
(Pre-recorded Saturday, 14 April 1945 — BBC Disc No. SLO 72619)
Cossack Patrol/I'll Remember April/Night and Day/Chelsea/Holiday for Strings/Deep Purple.

Wednesday, 18 April 1945   BRITISH BAND OF THE AEF
20.30 AEFP
Guest Stars: Edna Kaye, Victor Feldman
Compère: A/C2 Ronald Waldman RAF
Angry/Why Do You Pass Me By? -VR- GMelo/'Play-on' — 'I Got Rhythm'/
African War Dance (featuring Victor Feldman, drums)/Indian Summer/The
Birth of the Blues/Let's Take the Long Way Home -VR- Edna Kaye/Over the
Waves.

Saturday, 21 April 1945   ARMY RADIO ORCHESTRA
14.01 AEFP
Guest Star: Bette Roberts
Compère: Lt. Douglas Marshall
Perdido/Paris in the Spring -VR- Bette Roberts/Come With Me My Honey/
You're So Sweet to Remember -VR- GMelo/You'll Never Know (Trio —
Ronnie Selby, Piano; Freddie Phillips, Guitar; Bob Roberts, Bass)/Let's Take
the Long Way Home -VR- Bette Roberts/Jumpin' Jimminy/Waiting in the
Rain -VR- GMelo/Zing Went the Strings of My Heart -VR- Bette Roberts.

Sunday, 22 April 1945   THE RICHARD TAUBER SHOW
20.30 AEFP
(Pre-recorded Tuesday, 17 April, 1945 — BBC Disc No. SLO 72659)
Guest Star: Ida Haendell
Featuring: A/C2 Ronald Waldman RAF, Richard Tauber, Percy Kahn and
the British Band of the AEF
Opening Theme (You Are My Heart's Delight)/SHAEF Signature Tune/My
Heart and I -VR- RT/Overture to a Housing Problem/By the Sea -VR- RT
(accomp. by Percy Kahn, Piano)/Serenade -VR- RT (accomp. by Percy Kahn,
Piano)/La Campanella -VR- Ida Haendell/Whisperings in the Vienna Woods
-VR- RT/Closing Theme (You Are My Heart's Delight).

Monday, 23 April 1945   PIANO PARADE
11.45 AEFP
Compèred and Produced by: Lt. Douglas Marshall
Dancing in the Dark/Trees/My Guy's Come Back/Accentuate the Positive/
Without a Song/Making Whoopee.

Wednesday, 25 April 1945   BRITISH BAND OF THE AEF
20.30 AEFP
Guest Stars: Adelaide Hall, Lt. Harry Jacobson
Compèred and Produced by: A/C2 Ronald Waldman RAF
Little White Lies/I'll Remember April -VR- GMelo/'Play-on' — My Love For
You/A Dream Awakes (featuring Harry Jacobson) (from 'Daydreams')/Sweet
and Lovely/Night and Day/I'm Gonna Love that Guy -VR- Adelaide Hall/
Who's Your Lady Friend.

Saturday, 28 April 1945   ARMY RADIO ORCHESTRA
14.01 AEFP
Guest Star: Vera Howe
Compèred and Produced by: Lt. Douglas Marshall
Jive Bombers/I'll Remember April -VR- Vera Howe/Carioca/I Didn't Know What Time it Was -VR- GMelo/Pennies from Heaven (featuring Ronnie Selby, Piano; Freddie Phillips, Guitar; Bob Roberts, Bass)/More and More -VR- Vera Howe/Cossack Patrol/Begin the Beguine -VR- GMelo/Some Other Time -VR- Vera Howe.

Sunday, 29 April 1945   THE RICHARD TAUBER PROGRAMME
20.30 AEFP
Guest Star: Carroll Gibbons
Compèred and Produced by: A/C2 Ronald Waldman RAF
(Pre-recorded Tuesday, 24 April 1945 — BBC Disc No. SLO 72112)
SHAEF Signature Tune/Fear Nothing -VR- RT/Winter Sunshine/I Know of Two Bright Eyes -VR- RT (accomp. by Percy Kahn)/Drink to Me Only with Thine Eyes -VR- RT (featuring accompanist Percy Kahn)/Moment Musical ('Rosamunde')/Concerto for Carroll (featuring Carroll Gibbons, Piano)/Break of Day -VR- RT.

Monday, 30 April 1945   PIANO PARADE
11.45 AEFP
Compèred and Produced by: Lt. Douglas Marshall
(Pre-recorded Saturday, 28 April 1945 — BBC Disc No. SLO 73302)
Young and Healthy/I'll Walk Alone/Boogie Chromatic/Lover/Marie/Soho/ Pennies from Heaven.

Wednesday, 2 May 1945   BRITISH BAND OF THE AEF
20.30 AEFP
Guest Stars: Frances Day, Sqd Leader Richard Murdoch RAF
Compèred and Produced by: A/C2 Ronald Waldman RAF
Jealous/Music Brought Us Together -VR- GMelo/'Play-on' — Theme in 'E' Mairzy Doats (featuring Richard Murdoch)/Fantasy for Flute and Orchestra (featuring Richard Murdoch) (including Colonel Bogey; Anvil Chorus; Destiny: Donkey Serenade; Skaters Waltz; Little Sir Echo; Prelude Act 3 ('Lohengrin'); Chloe; The British Grenadiers)/It Could Happen To You/Piccolo Pete (featuring Geoffrey Gilbert)/It's Delightful, It's Delicious, It's D'Lovely (Play-on)/I Dream of You -VR- Frances Day/There's a Tavern in the Town.

Saturday, 5 May 1945   ARMY RADIO ORCHESTRA
14.01 AEFP
Guest Star: Helen Clare
Compère: Lt. Douglas Marshall
Hoppin' Abroad/April in Paris -VR- Helen Clare/Brazil/I Dream of You -VR- GMelo/After You've Gone (Trio — Ronnie Selby, Piano; Freddie Phillips,

Guitar; Bob Roberts, Bass)/All the Things You Are -VR- Helen Clare/Take a Deep Breath/Music Brought Us Together -VR- GMelo/All or Nothing At All -VR- Helen Clare.

Sunday, 6 May 1945   THE RICHARD TAUBER PROGRAMME
20.30 AEFP
(Pre-recorded Tuesday, 1 May 1945 — BBC Disc No. SLO 72644)
Guest Star: Yvonne Arnaud
Compèred and Produced by: A/C2 Ronald Waldman RAF
Always Keep Smiling -VR- RT/Where Oh Where Has My Little Dog Gone/ Intermezzo -VR- RT/So Deep is the Night ('Tristesse') -VR- RT/4th Impromptu in 'A' Flat (featuring Yvonne Arnaud, Piano)/Minuet/Love Comes at Blossom Time.

Monday, 7 May 1945   PIANO PARADE
11.45 AEFP
(Pre-recorded Saturday, 5 May 1945 — BBC Disc No. SLO 73496)
Blue Skies/Ah, Sweet Mystery of Life/Midnight in Mayfair/Medley: Chez Moi; Vois Qui Passez Sans Me Voir; J'Attendrai/Prelude to Boogie.

Wednesday, 9 May 1945   BRITISH BAND OF THE AEF
20.30 AEFP   (SPECIAL VICTORY EDITION)
Compèred and Produced by: A/C2 Ronald Waldman RAF
(Pre-recorded Saturday, 5 May 1945 — the following recordings were dubbed onto BBC Disc No. SLO 72558)
SHAEF THEME -arr- GMelo (SLO 73059)/Piccolo Pete (SLO 73059) Sweet and Lovely (SLO 63133)/The Boys in the Backroom -VR- Marlene Dietrich (SLO 62354-1)/A Sultan Goes to Harlem (featuring Carl Barriteau) (SLO 64845-45)/Time Waits for No One -VR- Anne Shelton (SLO 63961-35)/ Hungarian Air (featuring Vic Oliver) (SLO 66345-2)/What a Difference a Day Made -VR- Beryl Davis (SLO 68512-40)/La Fileuse (featuring Yvonne Arnaud, Piano) (SLO 68512-30)/The Trumpeter (featuring Tommy Handley and Jack Train) (SLO 70947-1)/Concerto for Clarinet (featuring Frank Weir) (SLO 65157-40)/I'll Be Seeing You -VR- Vera Lynn (SLO 62949-50)/George Gershwin Medley (featuring Rawicz and Landauer) (SLO 69988-40)/I Can't Love You Anymore -VR- Bebe Daniels (SLO 63662-40)/Mairzy Doats (featuring Richard Murdoch) (SLO 61783)/Fantasy for Flute and Orchestra (featuring Richard Murdoch) (SLO 61783)/With a Song in My Heart -VR- Bing Crosby (SLO 60882)/When Johnny Comes Marching Home (SLO 62949)/SHAEF Theme (SLO 62949).

Saturday, 12 May 1945   ARMY RADIO ORCHESTRA
14.01 AEFP
Guest Star: Bette Roberts
Compèred and Produced by: Lt. Douglas Marshall
Recorded repeat of the Army Radio Orchestra show, first broadcast on Saturday, 21 April 1945, over the AEFP — BBC Disc No. SLO 72365.

Sunday, 13 May 1945　　　　THE RICHARD TAUBER PRORAMME
20.30 AEFP
(Pre-recorded Tuesday, 8 May 1945 — BBC Disc No. SLO 72366)
Guest Star: Carole Lynne
Compèred and Produced by: A/C2 Ronald Waldman RAF
Maiden My Maiden -VR- RT/The Minstrel Boy/Last Spring -VR- RT/I Love
Thee -VR- RT/Victory March/Why Do I Love to Wake From My Dreams
-VR- Carole Lynne/Deep in My Heart -VR- Carole Lynne and RT.

Monday, 14 May 1945　　　　　　　　　　　　PIANO PARADE
11.45 AEFP
(Pre-recorded Saturday, 12 May 1945 — BBC Disc No. SLO 74159)
Over There/Tipperary/Cossack Patrol/More and More/Untitled (Boogie
Woogie title by Ronnie Selby)/Body and Soul/Daisybell.

Wednesday, 16 May 1945　　　　BRITISH BAND OF THE AEF
20.30 AEFP
Guest Stars: Cherry Lind, Rawicz and Landauer
Compèred and Produced by: A/C2 Ronald Waldman RAF
I'll Get By/I Promise You -VR- GMelo/Jeep Ride/My Love for You -VR-
Cherry Lind/Sweet Sue/'Play-on' — Theme in 'A'/Features (featuring Rawicz
and Landauer)/There's a Tavern in the Town.

Saturday, 19 May 1945　　　　ARMY RADIO ORCHESTRA
14.01 AEFP
Guest Star: Rita Williams
Compère: Lt. Douglas Marshall
Tugboat on a Frogpond/All of a Sudden My Heart Sings -VR- Rita Williams/
Annaconga/I Promise You -VR- GMelo/What Is This Thing Called Love?
(Trio — featuring Ronnie Selby, Piano; Freddie Phillips, Guitar; Bob Roberts,
Bass)/Let's Take the Long Way Home -VR- Rita Williams/Riffs/You Belong
To My Heart -VR- GMelo/Body and Soul -VR- Rita Williams.

Sunday, 20 May 1945　　　THE RICHARD TAUBER PROGRAMME
20.30 AEFP
(Pre-recorded Tuesday, 15 May 1945 — BBC Disc No. SLO 73456)
Guest Star: Moura Lympany
Compère: A/C2 Ronald Waldman RAF
Pagliacci Prologue -VR- RT/Prince Igor Dance/Chanson -VR- RT (featuring
Percy Kahn, Piano)/Elégie -VR- RT (accomp. by Percy Kahn, Piano)/
Concerto No. 2 in 'G' Minor 3rd Movement -VR- Moura Lympany/On With
the Motley -VR- RT.

Monday, 21 May 1945　　　　　　　　　　　　PIANO PARADE
11.45 AEFP
Hallelujah/Sweet Lorraine/Lullaby of Broadway/Sweet and Lovely/Rosetta/
Basin Street Blues/Honeysuckle Rose.

Wednesday, 23 May 1945   BRITISH BAND OF THE AEF
20.30 AEFP
Guest Stars: Joyce Grenfell, Leslie Gilbert
Compèred and Produced by: A/C2 Ronald Waldman RAF
Out of Space/Contrasts (featuring Leslie Gilbert)/Overture in Chaos/Mean to
Me/Prelude to Boogie (featuring Ronnie Selby, Piano)/'Play-on'/ Someday
-VR- Joyce Grenfell/Where Oh Where Has My Little Dog Gone.

Saturday, 26 May 1945   ARMY RADIO ORCHESTRA
14.01 AEFP
Guest Star: Anne Lenner
Compèred and Produced by: Lt. Douglas Marshall
Dr Livingstone I Presume/All the Things You Are -VR- Anne Lenner/
Rumba Tambah/Don't Tell a Soul -VR- GMelo/Coquette (Trio — Ronnie
Selby, Piano; Freddie Phillips, Guitar; Bob Roberts, Bass)/Darling Je Vous
Aime Beaucoup -VR- Anne Lenner/A Short Snorter/Going Home -VR-
GMelo/ I'm Gonna Love That Guy -VR- Anne Lenner.

Sunday, 27 May 1945   THE RICHARD TAUBER PROGRAMME
20.30 AEFP
(Pre-recorded Tuesday, 22 May 1945 — BBC Disc No. SLO 74672)
Guest Star: Irene Ambrus
Compèred and Produced by: A/C2 Ronald Waldman RAF
Girls Were Made to Love and Kiss -VR- RT/Moths and Butterflies/The
Question -VR- RT (accomp. by Percy Kahn, Piano)/The Post -VR- RT
(accomp. by Percy Kahn, Piano)/Knuckle on the Notes/The Laughing Song
-VR- Irene Ambrus/Let Me Awaken Your Heart -VR- RT.

Monday, 28 May 1945   PIANO PARADE
11.45 AEFP
(Pre-recorded Saturday, 26 May 1945 — BBC Disc No. SLO 75077)
Compèred and Produced by: Lt. Douglas Marshall
Coquette/A Pretty Girl is Like a Melody/Minor Confusion/I'm Gonna Love
That Guy/Liszt Boogie/These Foolish Things/Daphne.

Wednesday, 30 May 1945   BRITISH BAND OF THE AEF
20.30 AEFP
Guest Stars: Tessie O'Shea, Ted Heath
Compèred and Produced by: A/C2 Ronald Waldman RAF
Lullaby of Broadway/All the Things You Are -VR- GMelo/'Play-on' —
Lovely Weekend/Yearning (featuring Ted Heath, Trombone)/Moonlight
Seranade/ Don't Fence Me In/'Play-on' — 'Two-Ton Tessie'/Twelve Notes
in Music (featuring Tessie O'Shea)/The Quartermasters Song.

Saturday, 2 June 1945   ARMY RADIO ORCHESTRA
14.01 AEFP
Guest Star: Edna Kaye
Compère: Lt. Douglas Marshall
Dawn Patrol/I Promise You -VR- Edna Kaye/Spic and Spanish/I May Be

Wrong (Trio – Ronnie Selby, Piano; Freddie Phillips, Guitar; Bob Roberts, Bass)/What a Difference a Day Made -VR- Edna Kaye/Who's Sorry Now (Jam session by Orchestra)/Reverse the Charges/Let's Take the Long Way Home -VR- Edna Kaye/Blue Skies.

Sunday, 3 June 1945   THE RICHARD TAUBER PROGRAMME
20.30 AEFP
(Pre-recorded Tuesday, 29 May 1945 — BBC Disc No. SLO 74579)
Guest Star: Elisabeth Aveling
Compère: A/C2 Ronald Waldman RAF
There is Music in My Heart -VR- RT/Where Oh Where Has My Little Dog Gone/I'll Walk Beside You -VR- RT/My Heart is in Vienna Still -VR- RT/ Intermezzo Symphonique (British Band of the AEF, conducted by Richard Tauber)/Mimi's Farewell to the Home She Left -VR- Elisabeth Aveling/If You Are in Love -VR- Elisabeth Aveling and Richard Tauber.

Monday, 4 June 1945   PIANO PARADE
11.45 AEFP
(Pre-recorded Saturday, 2 June 1945 — BBC Disc No. SLO 75716)
Three Little Words/I Promise You/I May Be Wrong/Liebestraum/Lady Be Good.

Wednesday, 6 June 1945   BRITISH BAND OF THE AEF
20.30 AEFP
Guest Stars: Beryl Davis, Barbara Mullen, Jack Jackson
Compère: A/C2 Ronald Waldman RAF
I Never Knew/You Made Me Love You -VR- Beryl Davis/All of a Sudden My Heart Sings -VR- Beryl Davis/'Play-on' – Dancing in the Dark/Begin the Beguine -VR- Jack Jackson/Memories of You/Night and Day/'Play-on' – Danny Boy/Eileen Oge -VR- Barbara Mullen/Medley (8 bars of each): Mademoiselle from Armentieres; Take Me Back to Dear Old Blighty/ Suddenly It's Spring.

Saturday, 9 June 1945   ARMY RADIO ORCHESTRA
13.30 AEFP
Guest Star: Edna Thompson
Compère: Lt. Douglas Marshall
I've Found a New Baby/Together -VR- Edna Thompson/Brazil/Tea for Two (Trio – Ronnie Selby, Piano; Freddie Phillips, Guitar; Bob Roberts, Bass)/I'm Gonna Love That Guy -VR- Edna Thompson/Cossack Patrol/Young and Healthy/Always/Paris in the Spring -VR- Edna Thompson/Pardon Me, Pretty Baby.

Sunday, 10 June 1945   THE RICHARD TAUBER PROGRAMME
20.30 AEFP
(Pre-recorded Tuesday, 5 June 1945 — BBC Disc No. SLO 75024)
Guest Star: Billy Mayerl

Compère: A/C2 Ronald Waldman RAF
Love is My Reason -VR- RT/We'll Gather Lilacs -VR- RT/Ballet Music from 'Faust'/Fifinella -VR- RT (accomp. by Percy Kahn, Piano)/The Forgotten Forest -VR- Billy Mayerl/Waltz of My Heart -VR- RT.

Monday, 11 June 1945   PIANO PARADE
11.45 AEFP
(Pre-recorded Saturday, 9 June 1945 — BBC Disc No. SLO 76219)
Pardon Me Pretty Baby/Drink To Me Only/Irish Washerwoman/More Than You Know/Ode to Chopin/Some Other Time/Fascinating Rhythm.

Wednesday, 13 June 1945   BRITISH BAND OF THE AEF
20.30 AEFP
Guest Stars: Cpl. Jack Powers, US Army, Elinore Farrell, Frank Weir
Compèred and produced by: A/C2 Ronald Waldman RAF
One, Two, Three, Four Jump/I Dream of You -VR- Jack Powers/'Play-on' — 'What's New'/Henderson Stomp (featuring Frank Weir)/These Foolish Things/The Carioca/'Play-on' — 'Three Little Words'/I'm Beginning to See the Light -VR- Elinore Farrell/If I Had You -VR- Elinore Farrell/A Ballet to a Tandem/A Bicycle Made for Two.

Saturday, 16 June 1945   ARMY RADIO ORCHESTRA
14.01 AEFP
Guest Star: Helen Raymond
Compèred and produced by: Lt. Douglas Marshall
Happy Feet/All of a Sudden My Heart Sings -VR- Helen Raymond/Tico Tico/Soft Lights and Sweet Music (Trio — Ronnie Selby, Piano; Freddie Phillips, Guitar; Bob Roberts, Bass)/Always Young -VR- Helen Raymond/I Never Knew (Jam session by Orchestra)/Octave Jump/Body and Soul -VR- Helen Raymond/I'll See You in My Dreams.

Sunday, 17 June 1945   THE RICHARD TAUBER PROGRAMME
20.30 AEFP
Guest Stars: Rawicz and Landauer (Piano duet)
Compèred and produced by: A/C2 Ronald Waldman RAF
Vienna City of My Dreams -VR- RT/Perpetuum Mobile/My Most Romantic Memory -VR- RT/Don't Ask Me Why -VR- RT/Caprice Viennois (featuring piano duet by Rawicz and Landauer)/Medley (featuring Rawicz and Landauer): Vienna Blood; Vienna City of My Dreams; Tales from the Vienna Woods; Waltz from Fledermaus; Waltzing in the Clouds/Blue Danube -VR- RT.

Monday, 18 June 1945   PIANO PARADE
11.45 AEFP
(Pre-recorded Saturday, 16 June 1945 — BBC Disc No. SLO 76439)
Somebody Loves Me/Out of Nowhere/Isle of Capri/A Little on the Lonely Side/Unfinished Boogie (-comp.- Ronnie Selby)/I Dream of Jeannie with the Light Brown Hair/St Louis Blues.

Wednesday, 20 June 1945 BRITISH BAND OF THE AEF
20.30 AEFP
Guest Stars: Evelyn Dove, Arthur Young
Compère: A/C2 Ronald Waldman RAF
Marie/Love Walked In -VR- GMelo/Theme in 'E' − 'Play-on'/Motor Torpedo Boat Patrol (featuring Arthur Young)/Soft Lights and Sweet Music/Begin the Beguine/Body and Soul -VR- Evelyn Dove/Overture to Jaunty.

Saturday, 23 June 1945 ARMY RADIO ORCHESTRA
14.01 AEFP
Guest Star: Vivien Paget
Compère: S/Sgt. Wilf Davidson
Produced by: A/C2 Ronald Waldman RAF
Hoppin' Abroad/I'll Be Around -VR- GMelo/Rumba Tambah/I'll Get By -VR- Vivien Paget/Rosetta (Trio − Ronnie Selby, Piano; Freddie Phillips, Guitar; Rob Roberts, Bass)/You Belong to My Heart -VR- GMelo/One, Two, Three, Four Jump/I Got it Bad and That Ain't Good -VR- Vivien Paget/Blue Skies.

Sunday, 24 June 1945 THE RICHARD TAUBER PROGRAMME
20.30 AEFP
(Pre-recorded Tuesday, 19 June 1945 — BBC Disc No. SLO 75420)
Guest Star: Olga Gwynne
Compère: A/C2 Ronald Waldman RAF
My Heart and I -VR- RT/Memories of a Ballet (incorporating: Faust Ballet Music; Casse Noissette Suite; La Boutique Fantastique; Ballet Egyptien; Ballet Coppelia; Ballet Sylvia; Swan Lake; Dance of the Hours; La Source/The Last Rose -VR- RT (accomp. by Percy Kahn)/For This I Pray -VR- RT (accomp. by Percy Kahn)/A Song in the Night -VR- Olga Gwynne/Love Comes at Blossom Time -VR- RT.

Monday, 25 June 1945 PIANO PARADE
11.45 AEFP
(Pre-recorded Saturday, 23 June 1945 — BBC Disc No. SLO 76472)
Bugle Call Rag/The Song is You/Minor Confusion/She's My Lovely/No Name Boogie/I'll Get By.

Wednesday, 27 June 1945 BRITISH BAND OF THE AEF
20.30 AEFP
Guest Stars: Paula Green, George Elliott
Compère: A/C2 Ronald Waldman RAF
You're Driving Me Crazy/I've Got You Under My Skin -VR- GMelo/Theme in 'E' − 'Play-on' for George Elliott/Prelude to Jazz (featuring George Elliott)/ I'm Getting Sentimental Over You/The Lady in Red/Where or When − 'Play-on' for Paula Green/How Deep is the Ocean -VR- Paula Green/ Concerto for a Copper.

Saturday, 30 June 1945   ARMY RADIO ORCHESTRA
14.01 AEFP
Guest Star: Bette Roberts
Compère: S/Sgt. Wilf Davidson
All God's Children Got Rhythm/My Shining Hour -VR- GMelo/Mi Manuelita/ In the Blue of Evening -VR- Bette Roberts/I'm in the Market for You (Trio – Ronnie Selby, Piano; Freddie Phillips, Guitar; Bob Roberts, Bass)/Don't Tell a Soul -VR- GMelo/Mop Mop/Just a-Whittling and a-Whistling -VR- Bette Roberts/The Sheik of Araby.

Sunday, 1 July 1945   THE RICHARD TAUBER PROGRAMME
20.30 AEFP
Recorded repeat of the programme first broadcast in the AEFP, on Sunday, 6 May 1945 (Recorded Tuesday, 1 May 1945 — BBC Disc No. SLO 72644).

Monday, 2 July 1945   PIANO PARADE
11.45 AEFP
My Guy's Come Back/The Talk of the Town/The Woodchopper's Ball/ Without a Song/Stompin' at the Savoy/Isn't it Romantic/Stormy Weather.

Wednesday, 4 July 1945   BRITISH BAND OF THE AEF
20.30 AEFP
Guest Stars: Dorothy Carless, Stanley Black
Compère: A/C2 Ronald Waldman RAF
Two O'Clock Jump/The Song is You -VR- GMelo/Beautiful Love (featuring Stanley Black)/The Touch of Your Lips/Night and Day/All My Life -VR- Dorothy Carless/Four Movements to a Piece.

Saturday, 7 July 1945   ARMY RADIO ORCHESTRA
14.01 AEFP
Guest Star: Vera Howe
Compère: Lt. Douglas Marshall
Liza/Love Walked In -VR- GMelo/Let Me Love You Tonight/I Promise You -VR- Vera Howe/As Long as I Live (Trio – Ronnie Selby, Piano; Freddie Phillips, Guitar; Bob Roberts, Bass)/Why Do You Pass Me By -VR- GMelo/ Lullaby of Broadway/A Kiss in the Night -VR- Vera Howe/Two O'Clock Jump.

Sunday, 8 July 1945   THE RICHARD TAUBER PROGRAMME
20.30 AEFP
Recorded repeat of programme first broadcast by the AEFP, on Sunday, 29 April 1945 (Pre-recorded Tuesday, 24 April 1945 — BBC Disc No. SLO 72112 — O.P. 981).

Monday, 9 July 1945   PIANO PARADE
11.45 AEFP
(Pre-recorded Saturday, 7 July 1945 — BBC Disc No. SLO 77349)
Announcer: Cpl. Rudy Hartman, Canadian Army
Eye Opener/Londonderry Air/Barrel House Boogie/Star Eyes/Don't Fence Me In/Sophisticated Lady/On the Sunny Side of the Street.

Wednesday, 11 July 1945 BRITISH BAND OF THE AEF
20.30 AEFP
Guest Stars: Anne Lenner, Victor Feldman
Compèred and produced by: A/C2 Ronald Waldman RAF
Tea for Two/After a While -VR- GMelo/I Got Rhythm (featuring Victor Feldman, Drums)/Poor Butterfly/What Is This Thing Called Love/On My Way Out -VR- Anne Lenner/Oranges and Lemons -arr- George Evans.

Saturday, 14 July 1945 ARMY RADIO ORCHESTRA
14.01 AEFP
Guest Star: Edna Kaye
Compèred and produced by: Lt. Douglas Marshall
Singing' in the Rain/I've Got You Under My Skin -VR- GMelo/I'm Beginning to See the Light/You Moved Right In -VR- Edna Kaye/September in the Rain (Trio – Ronnie Selby, Piano; Freddie Phillips, Guitar; Bob Roberts, Bass)/After a While -VR- GMelo/Louise/All I Do is Dream of You -VR- Edna Kaye/Jealous.

Sunday, 15 July 1945 THE RICHARD TAUBER PROGRAMME
20.30 AEFP
Recorded repeat of programme first broadcast by the AEFP, on Sunday, 20 May 1945. (Pre-recorded Tuesday, 15 May 1945 — O.P. 984 — BBC Disc No. SLO 73456)

Monday, 16 July 1945 PIANO PARADE
11.45 AEFP
Announcer: Cpl. Rudy Hartman, Canadian Army
Saturday Night/Daybreak/I Didn't Know About You/Night and Day/Cow Cow Boogie/You, Fascinating You/Tea for Two.

Wednesday, 18 July 1945 BRITISH BAND OF THE AEF
20.30 AEFP
Guest Stars: Beryl Davis, Benny Lee, Duncan Whyte
Compère: A/C2 Ronald Waldman RAF
Between the Devil and the Deep Blue Sea/Deep Summer Music -VR- GMelo/ In a Sentimental Mood (featuring Duncan Whyte)/Dance of the Spanish Onion/Stormy Weather/'Play-on' – 'You Made Me Love You'/Our Love Affair -VR- Beryl Davis and Benny Lee/Who's Your Lady Friend.

Saturday, 21 July 1945 ARMY RADIO ORCHESTRA
14.01 AEFP
Guest Star: Anne Lenner
Compère: Lt. Douglas Marshall
You're Driving Me Crazy/The Tenement Symphony -VR- GMelo/Cubana/ You Made Me Love You (Trio – Ronnie Selby, Piano; Freddie Phillips, Guitar; Bob Roberts, Bass)/A Little on the Lonely Side -VR- Anne Lenner/ Indian Summer -VR- GMelo/Swing Rhapsody/All of a Sudden My Heart Sings -VR- Anne Lenner/I Never Knew.

Sunday, 22 July 1945   THE RICHARD TAUBER PROGRAMME
20.30 AEFP
(Pre-recorded Tuesday, 17 July 1945 — O.P. 993 — BBC Disc No. SLO 76963)
Guest Stars: John and Valerie Trimble
Song of Songs -VR- RT/Waltzing Thro' the Operettas -arr- GMelo/Falling Asleep -VR- RT/Passing By -VR- RT/Liebeslied -VR- John and Valerie Trimble/Tambourin Chinois -VR- John and Valerie Trimble/My Heart is in Vienna Still -VR- RT.

Monday, 23 July 1945   PIANO PARADE
11.45 AEFP
Announcer: Cpl. Rudy Hartman, Canadian Army
In Pinetops Footsteps/Stardust/Boogie in the Groove/The Man I Love/St Louis Blues/Body and Soul/Honky Tonk Train Blues.

Wednesday, 25 July 1945   BRITISH BAND OF THE AEF
20.30 AEFP
Guest Stars: Richard Murdoch and Kenneth Horne
Compère: A/C2 Ronald Waldman RAF
Two O'Clock Jump/The More I See You -VR- GMelo/Fascinating Rhythm (featuring Ronnie Selby, Piano)/Sweet and Lovely/Medley (featuring Richard Murdoch and Kenneth Horne): Mairzy Doats; Mama Yo Quiera; Softly Awakes My Heart; Barber of Seville; Much Binding in the Marsh/Night and Day/Widdicombe Fair (includes 4 bars of the SHAEF theme and Oranges and Lemons) -VR- Jack Coles, Ronnie Selby, Bert Thompson, Alec Firman, Arthur Wilkinson, Eric Robinson, Ronald and George Waldman.
This was the last British Band of the AEF broadcasts, although the Ronnie Selby Trio and George Melachrino were guests on the *Farewell AEFP* programme with the Bob Farnon Canadian Band of the AEF on Saturday, 28 July 1945 (see Canadian Band of the AEF listing).

Saturday, 28 July 1945   ARMY RADIO ORCHESTRA
14.01 AEFP
Guest Stars: Dorothy Carless, Anne Lenner, Edna Kaye, Bette Roberts and Vera Howe
Compèred and produced by: Lt. Douglas Marshall
Oh! Lady Be Good/The More I See You -VR- GMelo/Havana's Calling Me/ I've Had My Moments (Trio — Ronnie Selby, Piano; Freddie Phillips, Guitar; Bob Roberts, Bass)/Some Other Time -VR- Vera Howe/One Two Button My Shoe -VR- Edna Kaye/Long Ago and Far Away -VR- Anne Lenner/St. Louis Blues -VR- Bette Roberts/As Time Goes By -VR- Dorothy Carless/After You've Gone (Jam session by the Orchestra)/All God's Chillun Got Rhythm.
This was the final Army Radio Orchestra Programme. The AEFP finished broadcasting at 12 midnight Central European summer-time. The new light programme of the BBC took over on Sunday, 29 July 1945.

Lt. Larry Clinton and his AAF Band

During the period 1938–39, one of America's top band-leaders was Larry Clinton. He was well known throughout the United States with his famous theme, *The Dipsy Doodle*. By 1942, with America at war, Clinton, who had always been fascinated by flying, had developed into such a good pilot that the United States Army Air Force was delighted to accept him and gave him a Lieutenant's commission. He became a flight instructor, serving first in the United States. Later, during 1943, Clinton was moved to the China Theatre of Operations.

Then, in 1944, Larry Clinton was promoted to the rank of Captain and placed in charge of entertainment for the Allied Forces in Calcutta, India. It was during this period of August/September 1944 that Clinton formed a small dance band. Among his top aides in India was Sergeant Tony Martin. The former Corporal Tony Martin had been with Captain Glenn Miller's AAFTC Orchestra at Yale University, in 1943. Martin, better known as a Hollywood film star and singer, had been well featured with Glenn Miller's AAFTC Orchestra on their early *I Sustain The Wings* broadcasts, during the summer of 1943. During September 1943, Tony Martin, who's real name is Alfred Norris, had requested through various channels a desire to become an officer. Tony went with Glenn Miller's blessing. He had hoped to become a 2nd Lieutenant and even passed his exams at officers' training school. However, due to sheer vindictiveness by senior top brass, he failed and was returned back to duty as a Sergeant. With Glenn Miller and his large Army Air Force Orchestra about to go overseas, a request was put to headquarters for Sergeant Martin to return to his former boss. This was turned down and Tony was sent to the West Coast. However, Martin was sent overseas to India and ended up working for Captain Larry Clinton and his Army Air Force Orchestra.

Captain Larry Clinton and Sergeant Tony Martin did sterling work in India entertaining allied troops. The only known example of their work in that theatre of war was for a *Yank Bandstand* show during 1945. Both were separated from the army air forces in early 1946. Tony returned to Hollywood and the movies and later married Cyd Charisse. Larry Clinton reformed his band and recorded several albums for Herb Hendler on the Cosmo label.

Lt. Bob Crosby and his Fleet Marine Force Orchestra
1944 – 1945

George 'Bob' Crosby, younger brother of Bing Crosby, had been the leader of a large Dixieland orchestra and a small group, better known as the 'Bob Cats', since 1935. The Dixieland band was one of America's top bands through the late 1930s and their fame had spread overseas by short-wave, their records, films and world radio transcriptions. The style of the Crosby band proved such a success that Britain's first service band, the RAF Squadronaires, had copied it to a great extent.

Crosby and his band were still going strong in 1941. By the autumn (Fall) of 1942, as an increasing number of the musicians were drafted into military service, Bob disbanded the orchestra. During the spring of 1943, Van Alexander (Al Feldman) organised a band for Crosby, which he fronted. This new orchestra, led by Crosby, began the *Old Gold Cigarette Show* on 18 July 1943.

Bob Crosby disbanded this new orchestra in June 1944, and joined the US Marine corps. After training for three months, Bob formed a 30-piece orchestra for the marine corps. They were sent overseas and toured throughout the Pacific Theatre of War. They also recorded several Armed Forces Radio Service *Yank Bandstand* shows from Hawaii, during early 1945.

During the summer of 1945, while Bob and some of the members of his service orchestra were on furlough in New York City, they recorded several V-Discs with singer Martha Tilton. The group on the recordings were Lieutenant Bob Crosby and his V-Disc 'Bob Cats'.

During the autumn of 1945, with World War Two over and Bob's band returning to civilian life, Bob was assigned to the Armed Forces Radio Service in Los Angeles to become the permanent master of ceremonies on their *Swingtime* series. He was released from the marine corps in November 1945. By the spring of 1946 he was leading another orchestra, which appeared every Wednesday night on the *Ford* shows over CBS.

Sam Donahue and the US Navy Band 1944 – 1945

The Naval Reserve Band 501 that Artie Shaw had led throughout 1943, in the South Pacific Theatre of War, and better known as The Rangers, returned home to the USA on 11 November 1943. After a six-week furlough most of the band reported back for duty in early January 1944, at their former base at Treasure Island, near San Francisco. Upon arrival at the base they found that their leader Artie Shaw had been demobbed due to a nervous breakdown. They had also lost their drummer Davey Tough and trumpet player Max Kaminsky. However, the remaining members were then transferred to the US Navy school of music in Washington DC. Former trumpet player with the band, John Best, recalls their stay in Washington DC: 'We chipped in the train fare for Sam Donahue and Dick Jones to go down to the Bureau of Navy personnel in Washington, and they talked to a Captain there, and asked for permission to allow the band to stay together, and I think we had four replacements.' The band, now stationed at the Navy school of music at Anacostia, Maryland, began to reform. The four replacements were trumpeter Don Jacoby, pianist Rocky Coluccio, drummer Buzz Sithens and singer Bill Bassford. The revamped band largely dropped the Artie Shaw library. Instead it developed a new fresh style and became one of the outstanding big jazz bands of the era. The sound and style was a compound of 'Basie' light swing and the rich 'Lunceford' inspired voicings, plus leader Donahue's own originality. John Best remembers: 'We had three very fine writers in the band and Sam gave them the scope — more so than Artie Shaw.'

The ensembles would open low and subtle and then suddenly sweep into crescendos of biting brass and swirling saxes. The inclusion of Bill Bassford added a romantic note to the popular songs of the day.

In April 1944, the reformed band under Sam Donahue, was shipped overseas to England. John Best recalls: 'Originally we were supposed to be going to Appledore, North Devon. There was a lot of Navy cargo going in there, but we never did get there.'

After a particularly rough crossing of the Atlantic, in an LST (a Landing Ship Tank), the band disembarked at Plymouth, South Devon. They were then taken by Navy buses and trucks to their new base in Exeter. The late Sam Donahue recalled shortly before his death: 'We were in England for about a year, from April 1944 until March 1945. We were there during the heavy

Musician-First-Class Sam Donahue and the US Navy Dance Band during a troop concert — somewhere in England 1944

''Buzz-Bomb'' raids and the later V-2 attacks. Our first job over there was to entertain at camps and Navy bases, who were preparing for the invasion of Europe.'

From their new base in Exeter, Sam and his band, which was now retitled 'The Band of the US Navy Liberation Forces' performed at countless American Navy and Army bases throughout southern England. Many of the Yanks they performed for were preparing for the invasion of Europe. Their fame quickly spread throughout the 'hipper' servicemen. This 17-piece band could really compete with the best Britain could offer at the time. *Melody Maker* picked up their tour and in their 10 June 1944 edition, they had this to say:

ARTIE SHAW'S BAND IS IN BRITAIN

Artie Shaw's US Navy Band is in Britain! It is touring the country, entertaining American troops, but unfortunately Shaw himself is not with the bunch as he was recently discharged from the Navy through ill-health.

The band, in his absence, is led by sax-player Sam Donahue, and is the same outfit which has toured 68,000 miles during the last 12 months, including a hazardous trip through the Pacific Theatre of War, Australia, etc.

We are indebted to AC/1 G. Fackrell for some notes about a programme which this band gave last week at an Air Force station in Britain, and informs us that the personnel of the band is as follows:

Saxes: Mack Pierce, Ralph La Polla, Joe Aglora, Bill Nichols, Charlie Wade.
Trumpets: Conrad Gozzo, John Best, Frank Beach, Don Jacoby.
Trombones: Tasso Harris, Tak Takvorian, Dick Lefane, Gene Leetch.
Piano: Rocky Coluccio.
Drums: Bob Sithins.
Guitar: Al Horesh.
Bass: Barney Spieler.

Sam Donahue explained that at some camps they are to visit they may have difficulty in getting a piano, so for that reason they have an able accordionist whose name is Harold Wax.

The vocalists are Rocky Coluccio and Joe Aglora, and in a very stimulating musical programme, including commercials and swing numbers, some smashing solos were taken by Conrad Gozzo and Don Jacoby (trumpets). Rocky Coluccio (piano) and Sam Donahue (leader) on sax.

Versatile Sam also joined the trumpet section for one number, and the hit of the show was *Blues in C Sharp Minor*. A particularly interesting item in the programme was a swing arrangement entitled *Convoy* written by the boys during their crossing of the Atlantic, to England.

The next step was for the Navy to perform on the newly-opened *Allied Expeditionary Forces Programme* (AEFP) of the BBC. Cecil Madden picks up the story of how that came about:

Sam Donahue happened entirely through the Beverly Sisters — three girls who originally came from Northampton — and they knew Carmen Mastren who was guitarist with the Glenn Miller AEF Band. He had said to them, 'Did you know that Artie Shaw was on an atoll in the Pacific and hating it?' They said to him: 'You should tell Mr Madden he knows everyone — he could do something about that.' So Mastren spoke to me and I spoke to Richard Aldridge who was American representative for the Navy and he said, 'Why did you want them here?' I replied we could certainly do with them here — they'd be marvellous. And literally within five days they were in London. I met Sam Donahue and we had many happy times. The Band were transferred from Exeter to Golden Square, in Soho, London. Imagine Americans living in Soho! The poor Glenn Miller AEF Band were out in the sticks at Bedford.

Cecil arranged for Sam and his boys to record their first broadcast for the AEFP on Saturday, 26 August 1944. The show went out at 8.30 p.m. double British summer-time on Tuesday, 29 August 1944. The British guest star was Gloria Brent. Gloria still holds fond memories of Sam and his boys: 'They were a really great band and I sang two numbers with them. It was the first of many.' The British compère for the show was Captain Franklin Englemann. The show opened with two instrumentals, *Cocktails for Two* and *Long Ago and Far Away*. Next came Gloria Brent with *The Kerry Dance*. Then the band with *Holiday for Strings*. The band's own vocalist Bill Bassford was next with *I'll Be Seeing You* and then another instrumental *Somebody Loves Me*; guest star

Gloria Brent followed with *What Do You Think Those Ruby Lips Were Made For* and then the last title, another instrumental, *One O'Clock Jump*. As with all American bands and singers who met Cecil Madden, within the week they were on his *American Eagle in Britain* show. Cecil now picks up the story of those shows:

> It ran for five years. And I really never missed a week until I was ill at the end. However it was a very interesting time — it was done in Dunkers Den, which was sort of like a hole in the ground under Shaftesbury Avenue and all sorts of interesting people came including General Eisenhower himself who was determined to see it and on that particular occasion when Eisenhower came we had Captain Knight and the Golden Eagle — he would throw it out and the eagle would sail around the room as if nothing had happened at all. He did this when Eisenhower was present — I saw the General looking very apprehensive as to what was going to happen and whether the eagle was going to land on his shoulder. However, the eagle passed him and went to his master. The eagle actually went to America — the ship was torpedoed — and Captain Knight went back and rescued him from the sinking ship. The eagle was sitting in a pocket of air. The programme itself was terrific bait for the men in the Navy band and Glenn Miller's AEF band, because it was a sure-fire way that the men would have their voices recorded in London so that their wives and families would know where they were and they would be able to say something. Even the other GIs in the audience would take part. There was always quite a queue. *The American Eagle* programme was the greatest bait I ever had with Miller's and Donahue's bands.

The Navy band performed *Deep Night* on their first *American Eagle* broadcast. The recording was made on 7 September, and the show was broadcast on Saturday, 9 September, over the BBC American Red service. The recordings were made in Dunkers Den, which was part of the American Red Cross Club, at Rainbow Corner, in Piccadilly, London. Two weeks later on Thursday, 21 September 1944, the Navy band was back again for another *American Eagle in Britain* broadcast.

Later that same day they were guests on the American Band of the AEF broadcast. It was another coup for Cecil Madden who had arranged for both bands to appear at the Queensbury All Services Club, in London. It must have been some show — the British music paper, *Melody Maker*, wrote an entire page on the marvellous show and broadcast. It said, Glenn Miller's AEF Band and the Artie Shaw Navy Band on the same bill:

> The splendid co-operation of the US authorities enabled the Queensbury All Service Club to feature not only the greatest dance-band coup ever staged in London, but one of the most exciting aggregations of celebrated musicians ever lined up anywhere at once and the same time.
>
> And these words, my boys, are absolutely no exaggeration. It definitely was one of the greatest exaggerations ever — nothing less than the full GLENN MILLER ork, plus The ARTIE SHAW Naval Band — led by Sam Donahue — both together, on the vast Queensbury Club stage.

Certainly a big chapter of London's dance-band history was made that night, whilst the AEF programme could claim a really stupendous broadcast.

Passing thought: The funny part of all this is that whilst the efforts of the greatest bookers, theatrical and radio impresarios, etc., have never succeeded in getting together such a dazzling dance-band attraction as this (possibly even in the States), this war's insistent — and very proper — demand for only the very best in Services entertainment made it possible, nor for any smartly dressed audience of the élite who alone would be able to pay for such star-spangled attractions in normal times, but for the ordinary boys and girls of the Services, Privates Smith, Jones, Brown and Robinson, here in London.

First thing on the programme, the whole thing is explained and the various groups of musicians introduced by Major Glenn Miller, who makes everyone feel at home, and even essays an occasional wisecrack, without relaxing one iota of that stern, militaristic manner which so many of us have come to know so well.

The Major introduced the sections and various corner-men of his own combination, reminding us that Hank Freeman, leader of the saxes, used to be a shining light with Artie Shaw, that guitarist Carmen Mastren was with Tommy Dorsey before drafting; that Mel Powell was a gifted composer as well as a great pianist; Ray McKinley was a famous leader back home, etc.

Coming to the Naval outfit Glenn Miller paid a warm tribute to 'his old friend' Sam Donahue, praising the Naval band's extensive travels in the far Pacific, etc., in their heavy year-and-a-half's itinerary of Services entertainment half-way round the world, 'which' said Glenn Miller generously, 'completely puts our own record to shame'.

And in this fine band, we were reminded, was one of the old Miller corner-men, trumpet ace John Best.

The Major raises his baton, and there is great expectancy in the air as this battle of the bands — and the giants — gets into its stride.

Yes and in a sense it was a battle of the bands — but you couldn't say that either contestant won it; the combatants were so differently equipped. The Miller outfit's 'heavy artillery' — i.e., the massive string section, French horn etc. — made it an entirely different set-up from the Navy band, with its more or less conventional dance band instrumentation.

If Glenn Miller intended to place the issue beyond all doubt at the outset by 'slaying' us with that exquisite arrangement of *Stardust*, he certainly succeeded, so far as this critic is concerned, anyway. I defy anyone, even perhaps those not musically gifted at all, not to be completely bowled over by that incredibly beautiful bit of wizardly scoring from the band's 'Staff' arranger, Sergeant Jerry Gray, and its interpretation in the hands of this remarkable bunch of players.

Yes and Miller went on slaying us, too, one number after another, throughout this memorable broadcast. When he had exhausted all the degrees of style, versatility, exquisite tone, colour and sheer staggering technique, in which his boys specialise, he went on a different tack and brought Johnny Desmond to the microphone — and Johnny slayed us all too.

The Naval band, who played as if they might have been a trifle nervous in their first number, *Convoy*, soon warmed up and were getting in some great work also, the whole of their efforts dominated by their wonderful brass team and by the superb tenor-sax tooting of Sam Donahue himself.

> For the final number both outfits combined together in a rendering of *One O'Clock Jump*, and that glorious swell of sound made by the combined brass teams is something I will always remember.
>
> Afterwards, Mr John Harding brought the Marquis of Queensbury to the microphone, and in a short speech the Marquis warmly thanked Glenn Miller and Sam Donahue and their bands for a wonderful evening's entertainment.

The above write-up is from the *Melody Maker*'s editor Ray Sonin, who was at the AEF broadcast on 21 September 1944.

The 21 September 1944 broadcast by Sam Donahue and his boys was not their first visit to the Queensbury Club. They had performed at a concert there on Saturday, 9 September. This had also been to a packed house.

Cecil Madden was also at the Queensbury Club on the night of 21 September. 'I remember that broadcast very well. It was one of the musical sights and sounds of World War Two. And that last title of *One O'Clock Jump* was very exciting indeed'.

Bernie Priven, who was trumpet player with Glenn Miller's AEF orchestra, that evening recalls: 'The Navy Band really cut us up that evening, and Glenn knew it. He wanted a re-match, but it never came off'.

Of course more AEFP broadcasts followed for Sam and his boys. They also continued with their camp shows. Sam Donahue said, 'After our "Battle of the Big Bands" with Glenn Miller we did do a few more with Britain's Squadronaires and the Canadian AEF unit led by Captain Robert Farnon'. The first of these shows was on 21 October 1944, in a series called *AEFP Special*. Once again the broadcast was from the Queensbury All Services Club, in London.

Sam Donahue recalled just before his death in 1974: 'We were billeted in Golden Square, in Soho. It was a terrible time. We often dodged V-Bombs. That part of London was known as "Buzz-Bomb" Alley. It got even worse after September when the V-2 Rockets came over'.

On 15 December 1944, the very day Glenn Miller took off into Big Band history, Sam and the Navy Band recorded a half-hour radio programme for the AEFP. Fifteen minutes of that programme still exists in the BBC archives in London. Compère for the show was the BBC's Margaret Hubble. The titles are *St Louis Blues*, *Spring Will Be a Little Late This Year*, sung by Bill Basford, and *Dinah*. The show was recorded at the Criterion Theatre, in Piccadilly. It was broadcast the very next day, Saturday, 16 December 1944, in the AEFP.

Over Christmas 1944, Sam Donahue and his Navy band performed at quite a few camp dances, at Air and Navy bases throughout southern England.

With the announcement on Christmas Eve that Major Glenn Miller was missing in flight and with only six weeks' programmes in reserve, the AEFP was in quite a spot. How would they fill in the heavy broadcasting schedule? The situation became worse, when SHAEF informed the BBC that Glenn's orchestra would be staying in Paris for the duration of the war. New programmes had to be thought up. One of the American bands would have to

*MFC Sam Donahue with Major Glenn Miller, at the Queensbury All Services Club,
21 September 1944*

do a weekly series. In came Sam Donahue and the Navy Band of the Liberation
Forces. The series which went out at 10.06 p.m., every Thursday, was called
Navy Date. The British female singers involved were Gloria Brent, Julie Dawn
and Beryl Davis. The series lasted right through the spring of 1945. Many of
the half-hour shows were recorded in advance and even when Sam and his boys
left for home in April 1945, there were enough programmes in advance for the
series to continue. *Melody Maker* picked up the news of Donahue's Navy band
as early as 17 February 1945. In their edition dated that day they had this to
say:

Fans and enthusiasts in the British Isles will learn with considerable regret that the famous Naval Dance Orchestra of the US Liberation Forces, led — since the recall of Artie Shaw on health grounds — by tenor-sax celebrity Sam Donahue, is shortly scheduled to return to the United States.

Having been on a lengthy tour of the Pacific war zones before it ever came to this country, the band is obviously due for a visit home, since it is well over two years since the boys saw their own country.

Every thinking member of the profession over here realises the deep impression which this superb combination of US dance-band stars has made on the musicians of this country.

In spite of the comparative rarity of its broadcasts and public appearances, the work of this band, coupled with that of the more-often-heard Glenn Miller outfit, has provided a tremendous stimulus to all serious-minded dance musicians over here, and has given us at first hand a dazzling glimpse of the perfection of execution, style and technique of these top-line American outfits.

In spite of it not being heard to anything like the extent which the Glenn Miller band was when it was in this country, enthusiasts are unanimous in declaring that, considered purely as a swing combo, the Sam Donahue bunch is the more exciting of the two.

The week before last the Naval band was in London for five days and just a few London musicians and fans had an opportunity of hearing it. The outfit played at two big Forces functions, at Grosvenor House and the Dorchester Hotel respectively (when a handful of enterprising musicians gate-crashed in order to hear it) and also carried out a broadcast to the States.

On another occasion the outfit made a recording for future broadcast on the AEF wavelength at the Queensbury All Services Club, where hundreds of Forces fans gave the boys a terrific reception.

Most interesting of all the band's activities so far as the ordinary fan-in-the-street is concerned, however was the special recording of some special swing discs for future use on the AEF Programme.

The band also made some special private records at the Star Sound studios, and individual members including Donahue, relaxed in terrific style by 'sitting' in on several evenings at the Nut House Niterie.

Many of these recordings made at the BBC for AEF programme use will intrigue fans very much, since they were executed by several slightly different combinations which, besides Sam Donahue himself on tenor, featured the cream of the Naval bands' stylists, plus some of the most famous swingsters which this country can boast.

Sam Donahue and his Navy Band also did a few more *American Eagle in Britain* programmes with Cecil Madden during this period of February to March 1945. British musician Billy Amstall told me recently he often used to gate-crash into the American Red Cross Club at Rainbow Corner to see these top American bands:

My good friend, Maurice Burmann, also from the Ambrose band, and I, often used to slip into the various venues and American Red Cross clubs, in and around London, during that period. On this occasion we dropped into a club in

70

Bayswater Road, and we hoped to see one of the top American Service bands, like Sam Donahue and his boys. However, were we in for a shock. The band on the stand entertaining us were a parachute outfit. A lot of the American musicians were Jewish, like Maurice and myself. I turned to Maurice and said, 'All the members of this band look Jewish to me, maybe we should say ''Shalom'' when they've finished playing'. Maurice turned to me and said: 'I don't think so Billy, they're all Italians'. Did I feel a fool.

Billy also remembers the great friendship that grew up between the British and American musicians during that period: 'I am still great friends with many of them, and when ''Peanuts'' Hucko and his wife, Louise Tobin, come over to London, they always drop by and say hello.'

During April 1945, the US Navy Band of the Liberation Forces, led by musician-first-class Sam Donahue, returned home to the United States of America, and they had one year's stay in the European Theatre of Operations. The war in Europe was nearly over and had just a few weeks to run. The band returned home, but their singer Bill Bassford stayed on in the ETO and was heard quite a few times during late April in the *Top Ten* series with the RAF Dance Orchestra, the Squadronaires.

Meanwhile Sam and the Navy Band were given a four-week, well-earned furlough, upon their arrival back home in the USA. Then, on 11 June 1945, Sergeant George T. Simon recruited Sam Donahue and his Navy Band for two special V-Disc recording sessions, at the CBS Playhouse number 4, in New York City. The first session took place that very day. The second was on the following day on 12 June 1945. Among the titles recorded was *LST Party*, *Deep Night*, *My Melancholy Baby* and many others. George T. Simon later said, 'The V-Discs recorded by Sam on those two sessions have some of the greatest 'Big Band' sounds that ever got on record'. These V-Discs have since been re-issued on long-playing records and are still available.

Shortly after the V-Disc recording sessions in New York City took place, Sam Donahue and his Navy Band headed west across America, to Hollywood, California. Upon arrival in Hollywood, they were assigned to the Armed Forces Radio Service. Among the first shows recorded for AFRS were several *Yank Bandstand* and *Jubilee* shows. On the *Yank Bandstand* transcriptions, Sam Donahue was interviewed talking about their trip to England. Sam recalled how the title *LST Party* came about: 'This title was a tribute to the LSTs that transported us to England.' Sam and his band had performed this title on perhaps their most famous broadcast ever with the Glenn Miller AEF Orchestra, on Thursday, 21 September 1944. On the *Jubilee* shows the band was introduced by Ernie 'Bubbles' Whitman, the 'jive-talking' master of ceremonies.

The Navy band spent the whole of the month of September recording AFRS transcriptions. During early August the Sam Donahue Navy Band had also played a couple of times in the Hollywood canteen for allied servicemen and women. They also performed at many naval bases and stations throughout California and the west coast. After this they played on regular and short-wave broadcasts. Then after a short sojourn to the Navy's school of music in Washington DC, 70 per cent of the musicians from the band were discharged from the Navy and sent back into civilian life. After all, the world was by this time at peace. The war with Japan ended during August 1945.

The need for bands like the Sam Donahue US Navy Band, and the other service bands finished when the war ended. The newly-formed Navy band under Sam Donahue returned to the west coast during early December 1945. The band, now containing nearly all regular Navy musicians, continued on. Sam Donahue and the remaining 30 per cent from the original overseas unit were discharged from the service soon after. Sam Donahue left the Navy on 22 December 1945.

In the spring of 1946, Sam Donahue organised a new civilian orchestra, which included several members from his Navy band. Once again the band was a major success. In later years Sam Donahue led the famous Tommy Dorsey Orchestra, after Tommy's death in 1956. Sam Donahue died in Reno, Nevada, on 22 March 1974. Several of the Navy band's musicians are still alive and well.

SAM DONAHUE AND THE US NAVY DANCE BAND OF THE LIBERATION FORCES AUGUST 1944 – MARCH 1945

Tuesday, 29 August 1944   US NAVY DANCE ORCHESTRA
20.30-21.00
(Pre-recorded at the Queensbury All Services Club, Soho, London, on Saturday, 26 August 1944 — BBC Disc No. SLO 61185)
Over AEFP
Guest Star: Gloria Brent
Compère: Capt. Franklin Englemann
Opening Theme (Convoy)/Cocktails for Two/Long Ago and Far Away/The Kerry Dance -VR- Gloria Brent/Holiday for Strings/I'll Be Seeing You -VR- Bill Bassford/Somebody Loves Me/What Do You Think Those Ruby Lips Were Made For -VR- Gloria Brent/One O'Clock Jump and Close.

Thursday, 7 September 1944   AMERICAN EAGLE IN BRITAIN
(Pre-recording made at the American Red Cross Club, 'Dunker's Den', Piccadilly, London)
Broadcast by the BBC American Service, on Saturday, 9 September 1944
Compère and producer: Cecil Madden
Featuring: Sam Donahue and his US Navy Dance Band, Major Ken Tredwell.
Opening Introduction/Over There -VR- Bill Bassford and Audience/Major Ken Tredwell interviews with the audience/Convoy (US Navy Band)/The

Roving Microphone, introducing members of the Band: Rocky Collucio, Sam Donahue, Charlie Wade, Bill Nichol, Max Pierce, Ralph La Polla, Joe Anglora, Al Horish, Barney Spieler, Buzz Sithens, John Best, Conrad Gozzo, Frank Beach, Don Jacoby, Tasso Harris, Dick Le Fave, Gene Leetch, Tak Takvorian, Bill Bassford, Dick Jones, and Dave Rose/Spotlighting WSYB Vermont/Bebe Daniels from France/Ken Harvey with Cecil Madden/One O'Clock Jump (featuring Ken Harvey, Guitar)/Rainbow Corner (The Century Bombers Band) -VR- Trio/Major Ken Tredwell Interview/Closing Theme (US Navy Band).

Saturday, 9 September 1944　　　　　　HANDS ACROSS THE SEA
Broadcast recorded at the Queensbury All Services Club, Soho, London (BBC Disc No. TLO 61626). Broadcast by AEFP on Wednesday, 13 September 1944
12.15 - 13.00 DBST
Featuring: The US Navy Dance Band of the Liberation Forces, directed by MFC Sam Donahue, the RAF Dance Orchestra, directed by Sgt. Jimmy Miller, with Beryl Davis
Compère: A/C2 Ronald Waldman RAF and Sgt. Dick Dudley
Opening Themes (There's Something in the Air — RAF Squadronaires) — (Convoy — US Navy Dance Band)/When Buddy Smiles (RAF Squadronaires)/ Wrap Your Troubles in Dreams -VR- Beryl Davis (RAF Squadronaires)/How Am I To Know (US Navy Dance Band)/Amor Amor -VR- Bill Bassford (US Navy Band)/Walk Jenny Walk (RAF Squadronaires)/Milkman Keep Those Bottles Quiet -VR- Beryl Davis (RAF Squadronaires)/Goodnight Wherever You Are (US Navy Band)/It's Love, Love, Love -VR- Rocky Coluccio (US Navy Band)/Blues in 'C' Sharp Minor (RAF Squadronaires)/Hobo's Prayer (RAF Squadronaires)/My Melancholy Baby (US Navy Dance Band)/I Got Rhythm (US Navy Band)/Closing Theme (There's Something in the Air — RAF Squadronaires); (Convoy — US Navy Band).

Thursday, 21 September 1944　　　　AMERICAN EAGLE IN BRITAIN
(Recording made at the American Red Cross Club, 'Dunker's Den', Piccadilly, London) for future broadcast over short-wave by the BBC American Service, on Saturday, 23 September 1944
Compère and producer: Cecil Madden
Featuring: Sam Donahue and the US Navy Dance Band of the Liberation Forces with Bill Bassford and Major Ken Tredwell
Further details remain unknown.

Thursday, 21 September 1944　　　　AMERICAN BAND OF THE AEF
20.30 - 21.00
Broadcast live from the Queensbury All Services Club, Soho, London
Over AEFP
Guest Stars: Music I/C, the Sam Donahue US Navy Dance Band of the Liberation Forces
Compère: Major Glenn Miller

Announcer: Cpl. Paul Dubov
Intro: Theme (Moonlight Serenade)/Flying Home/I'll Be Seeing You -VR-
Johnny Desmond/Somebody Loves Me (US Navy Band)/Medley: I Dream of
Jeannie; I Couldn't Sleep a Wink Last Night -VR- Johnny Desmond and The
Crew Chiefs; Begin the Beguine; Blue Rain/LST Party (US Navy Band)/One
O'Clock Jump (combined Miller and US Navy Bands)/Closing Theme
(Moonlight Serenade).

Monday, 16 October 1944 TOP TEN
21.05-21.35
Broadcast live from Studios No. 1 Aeolian Hall, London
Over AEP
Featuring: The RAF Dance Orchestra. Directed by Sgt. Jimmy Miller, the
Singing Strings and the Brass Hats, with Beryl Davis
Special Guest Stars: Sam Donahue and the US Navy Dance Band
Compère: Cpl. Douglas Marshall
Intro: Theme (A Pretty Girl is Like a Melody)/Unknown Title (US Navy
Band)/Spring Will Be a Little Late This Year -VR- Beryl Davis (The Singing
Strings)/Yearning (RAF Squadronaires)/My Prayer -VR- Bill Bassford (US
Navy Band)/Chinatown My Chinatown (The Brass Hats)/I'm Gonna Sit Right
Down and Write Myself a Letter -VR- Beryl Davis (RAF Squadronaires)/When
It's Sleepy Time Down South (Combined Bands)/Vous Qui Passez Sans Me
Voir -VR- Beryl Davis (The Singing Strings)/Unknown Title (US Navy Band)/
All Alone -arr- George Evans (Combined RAF Squadronaires and US Navy
Dance Bands)/Closing Theme (A Pretty Girl is Like a Melody).

Saturday, 21 October 1944 AEF SPECIAL
Recorded from the Queensbury All Services Club, Soho, London, for broadcast
on Sunday, 22 October 1944 — BBC Disc No. SLO 62783)
17.15-18.00 DBST
Featuring: The Canada Show Dance Band (A Unit of the Canadian Band of
the AEF), directed by Capt. Robert Farnon, the RAF Dance Orchestra,
directed by Sgt. Jimmy Miller, the US Navy Dance Band, directed by MFC
Sam Donahue
Compère: Lt. Charmian Samson, CWAC
Introduction/Isle of Capri (Canada Dance Band)/I Heard You Cried Last Night
-VR- Beryl Davis (RAF Squadronaires)/What Can I Say Dear After I Say I'm
Sorry (US Navy Dance Band)/Basin Street Blues/Somebody Loves Me/The
First Few Days -VR- Paul Carpenter (Canada Dance Band)/Stompin' at the
Savoy (US Navy Dance Band)/Do Nothin' Till You Hear From Me -VR- Beryl
Davis (RAF Squadronaires)/Is You Is or Is You Ain't My Baby? -VR- Don
Jacoby (US Navy Dance Band)/Swinging on a Star -VR- Paul Carpenter
(Canada Dance Band)/The Touch of Your Lips (RAF Squadronaires)/'C' Jam
Blues (US Navy Dance Band) and Close.

Saturday, 16 December 1944   THE US NAVY BAND
18.30
(Pre-recorded at The Paris Cinema, Lower Regent Street, London, on Friday, 15 December 1944 between 13.30 - 14.00 — BBC Disc No. SLO unknown)
Over AEFP
Compère: Margaret Hubble
Producer: Sgt. Harry Lyle, US Army
Intro: Theme/St Louis Blues/Spring Will Be a Little Late This Year -VR- Bill Bassford/Dinah/East of the Sun/Is You Is or Is You Ain't My Baby? -VR-Don Jacoby/Five O'Clock Drag/Time Waits for No One -VR- Bill Bassford/Bugle Call Rag/Closing Theme.
Note: Part of this broadcast is held in the BBC archives in London.

Tuesday, 6 February 1945   SAM DONAHUE'S US NAVY BAND
(Pre-recorded at the Queensbury All Services Club, Soho, London, on Friday, 2 February 1945 — BBC Disc No. SLO 68375)
Over AEFP
Guest Star: Gloria Brent
Compere: Seaman 1st Class Charles MacMahon
Intro: Theme/Moten Swing/I'll Walk Alone -VR- Gloria Brent/Deep Night/ I'll Remember April -VR- Bill Bassford/I Can't Give You Anything But Love -VR- Rocky Coluccio/I Surrender Dear/When They Ask About You -VR- Gloria Brent/St Louis Blues/Closing Theme.

Thursday, 22 March 1945   NAVY DATE
22.06
Broadcast live from the Maida Vale Studios, London
Over AEFP
Featuring: Sam Donahue and the US Navy Dance Band
Guest Star: Julie Dawn
Compère: Yeoman Lou Brown, US Navy
Producer: Norman Sickel, US Navy
Opening Theme/I Found a New Baby/Mean To Me/Little on the Lonely Side -VR- Julie Dawn/Cossack Patrol/Some Other Time -VR- Bill Bassford/On the Alamo/Sweet and Lovely -VR- Julie Dawn/Gangway/Theme and Close.

Thursday, 29 March 1945   NAVY DATE
22.06
Broadcast live from the Maida Vale Studios, London
Over AEFP
Featuring: Sam Donahue and the US Navy Dance Band with Bill Bassford
Guest Star: Beryl Davis
Compère: Yeoman Lou Brown, US Navy
Details remain unknown.

Friday, 6 April 1945   NAVY DATE
20.01-20.29
(Pre-recorded at The BBC Studios, Maida Vale, London, mid-March 1945 —
BBC Disc No. SLO 68375)
Over AEFP
Featuring: Sam Donahue and the US Navy Dance Band with Bill Bassford
Guest Star: Gloria Brent
Compère: Yeoman Lou Brown, US Navy
Details remain unknown.

Friday, 13 April 1945   NAVY DATE
20.01
(Pre-recorded at The BBC Studios, Maida Vale, London, mid-March 1945 —
BBC Disc No. SLO unknown)
Over AEFP
Details remain unknown.

Friday, 20 April 1945   NAVY DATE
20.01
(Pre-recorded at The BBC Studios, Maida Vale, London, mid-March 1945 —
BBC Disc No. SLO unknown)
Over AEFP
Featuring: Sam Donahue and the US Navy Dance Band with Bill Bassford
Details remain unknown.

Note: The *Navy Date* programmes were taken over by Hank Frabotti and his
US Navy Dance Band during late April 1945. The Donahue US Navy Dance
Band were transported home during April 1945 and recorded many V-Discs
in New York City, plus several *Yank Bandstand* programmes for AFRS.

Eighth Air Force Dance Bands

Between 1942 and 1945, many 8th Air Force bases throughout the United Kingdom had their own small dance bands. These were put together mainly to provide entertainment at camp dances and events such as mission parties. Over the two-year period from 1942 until the build-up for D-Day in June 1944, all the bases could do to provide entertainment was to form their own base bands. With the arrival of Glenn Miller's American Band of the AEF and Sam Donahue's US Navy band, the whole situation had changed. Their tour of the bases from July to October 1944 put less pressure on these small bands.

Before this and the opening of the American Forces Network in July 1943, however, such small bands would back visiting US stars and singers. Many bands were formed, among the most famous being The Flying Eagles from the 4th Fighter Group at Debden, 'The Jive Pilots' of the 305th Bomb Group stationed at Underwood, 'The Bomb Beats' of the 401st Bomb Group stationed at Deenthorpe, and 'The Flying Yanks'.

Another famous dance band was 'The Gremlins' from the 2nd Air Depot, led by PFC Lyman Wood, with six brass, five reeds and four rhythm. Among their musicians were Sergeant Russell Newcomb, Corporal John Evans (both trombones), PFC Lyman Wood (saxophone, clarinet and leader) and PFC John Kane (tenor saxophone). On piano was Private Joseph Ivey and vocals were by Sergeant Raymond (Ray) Arias. The 1st Strategic Air Depot Band was called 'The Yanks' and were led by T/Sgt Jack Manwell. The 3rd Air Depot band were called 'The Continentals' and were led by Sergeant Peter Kara, with PFC Nick Giammerese as vocalist. The 4th Strategic Air Depot band were led by Private Dick Motter and were called 'The High Flyers'; their vocalist was Private Hershel Ayres. 'The Gremlins' became very famous and were even included in a few live broadcasts over the AEFP during February and March 1945. All four of the Air Depot bands appeared at a special Carnival of Music at the Grenada Cinema in Bedford, on Sunday, 26 November 1944. The Master of Ceremonies was Lt. Colonel Ben Lyon and Major Glenn Miller was also on hand.

Some bands did not even have a name and just used their fighter or bomb group numbers. These included the 56th fighter group dance band based at Boxted near Colchester, Essex, the 355th fighter group dance band based for a time at Steeple Morden, Cambridgeshire, and the 466th bomb group dance band based at Attlebridge, near Norwich, Norfolk. Many of these small bands came into their own right backing famous USO and ENSA stars, like Bing Crosby, Marlene Dietrich, Frances Langford and Bob Hope. Bing Crosby and Marlene Dietrich came over in August and September 1944; Frances Langford and Bob Hope came on a USO tour around Britain in 1943. Bing Crosby visited many airfields during his tour of the ETO from August to September 1944. Perhaps his most famous was at Duxford Airfield, Cambridgeshire. These small bands also backed British singers touring bases. Gloria Brent and Anne Shelton often performed at American bases after the D-Day landings, as did Dorothy Carless and Vera Lynn.

Many of these small bands disappeared at the end of the war, never to be seen or heard again.

Captain Robert Farnon and the Canadian Band of the AEF July 1944 – December 1945

On Monday, 4 September 1944 at 8.30 p.m. double British summer-time, the AEF programme brought to the air the first of a series of broadcasts, called *The Canada Show*. It introduced the new Canadian Band of the AEF, commanded and directed by Captain Robert Farnon. This unit replaced the original Canadian boadcasting unit, which had been on the air since 24 July under the direction of Warrant Officer Reg Newman. This first Canadian Band of the AEF had been broadcasting for six weeks over the Allied Expeditionary Forces Programme, and had included several very well-known British guest stars. On the first show broadcast, Paula Green, from the ITMA Series, had been featured.

This new unit of the Canadian Army Overseas had been brought to Britain for the primary purpose of broadcasting entertainment programmes for

Captain Bob Farnon conducts the new Canadian Band of the AEF in the BBC Studios during a rehearsal, Thursday, 24 August 1944 (Photo © BBC)

Captain Robert J. Farnon in 1944 (Photo © BBC)

everyone serving in the AEF in Europe. The unit consisted of more than fifty soldier-musicians and entertainers, known collectively as the Canadian Band of the AEF. Its chief assignment each week was *The Canada Show* on Monday evenings and, like Major Glenn Miller's American Band of the AEF, it included subsidiary musical units, which took part in their own as well as other AEF programmes.

In the basic sections were an orchestra of thirty, a mixed chorus of fourteen voices, a group of actor-announcers, and two soloists — a CWAC and a private soldier. The eight female members of the unit were members of the Canadian Women's Army Corps, so that the band was representative of many corps and formations in the Canadian Army, as well as every province in Canada.

This broadcasting unit was formed in Canada for use in recruiting programmes, radio work in connection with Victory Loans, and so on. As with Major Glenn Miller's orchestra, SHAEF had requested their transfer to Europe for radio programmes and concerts for the Allied Invasion forces. Accordingly, the unit was reinforced and sent over the Atlantic in record time.

The fifty soldier-musicians and entertainers arrived in Britain on Wednesday, 26 July 1944.

Bob Farnon himself picks up the story: 'We were stationed first at Aldershot for a short period, before moving into London. Our base was at the BBC studios in Maida Vale, and the personnel were housed in various digs around West London.'

Like everyone in London during that time, the members of the band faced bombing and V-1 raids.

Every member of the unit − women, as well as men − was a soldier, so routine and discipline had to be maintained throughout. Bob Farnon remembers: 'Discipline was rigid, with daily inspection outside the studios in Delaware Road, in the early morning, followed by a route march around the W2 district. Close shaves with doodle-bugs were a regular experience. While on the march on one occasion our doom was almost sealed when a bomb exploded less than 200 yards in front of the parade as we approached Lord's Cricket ground. On another occasion we were too close for comfort when a V-2 rocket dropped on Speaker's Corner at Marble Arch.'

Captain Robert Farnon, one of the Dominion's outstanding young conductor-composers and arrangers, was in charge, both militarily and musically. He will be remembered by thousands of Canadians as Bob Farnon of the CBC's famous *Happy Gang* programmes, and more recently he has become known throughout North America as a serious composer of unusual promise. In the realm of popular music, Bob was and still is a brilliant arranger and composer. The striking orchestral and choral effects which were a feature of *The Canada Show* exemplified his unique arranging talents, and the programmes signature tune, *March Along, Joe Soldier*, is one of his compositions.

The band's second-in-command, and the man in charge of the actor-announcers and writers was Lieutenant Douglas Montgomery, whose name is very familiar to film buffs. He was one of many Canadians to find fame on the American stage and screen. He will be remembered for his roles in such films as *Waterloo Bridge*, *Paid* and the British-made *Everything is Thunder*. Montgomery acquired much broadcasting experience in the United States and had already done quite a few broadcasts with Beatrice Lillie in the AEF Programmes *Night Cap* series on Thursday evenings.

The two featured singers with *The Canada Show* were Private Joanne Dallas, CWAC, and Private Paul Carpenter.

Joanne Dallas, from Winnipeg, and Paul Carpenter, from Montreal, would really make names for themselves over the next year's broadasting. Both would feature in two of the unit's sub-units, on Thursday evenings with the *Canada Swing Show*, featuring the eight-piece Dixie-style unit, and on Saturday mornings with the *Canada Dance Band Show*, with the full dance band.

Bob Farnon had this to say about Paul Carpenter: 'Among the solo vocalists in the band was one, Paul Carpenter, who led the life of Reilly and regarded his Army duties as an interruption to his activities on a grand scale in the company of film and theatre stars about town. He usually arrived for morning parade in a taxi and wore a Colombo-style raincoat which concealed ''slept-in'' uniform and tarnished buttons. All of us loved the guy.'

After the first *Canada Show* on 4 September which introduced the entire orchestra and chorus members to the radio audience, but had no guest stars, their next show was a sub-unit show on Thursday, 7 September, when the eight-piece Dixieland Band led by Bob were featured. Then on Monday, 11 September 1944, *The Canada Show* was again on the air and the first guest star, Beatrice Lillie, was featured. Many others would follow on Monday evenings. As well as working on their radio series, the Canadian Band of the AEF also performed at camp shows all over the south-east of England. Bob Farnon again picks up the story: 'In addition to five to six weekly broadcasts at the studios and venues around town, we played many ''one-niters'' at hospitals, army camps, etc. up and down the country. Sub-units were formed for small entertainment shows in and out of London. It was great fun for me to take a small jazz combo gigging at army camps, where I led the group from the piano. One evening at Sandhurst I was approached at the bandstand by a 1st Lieutenant, ordering me (a Captain) to play a certain song. Disliking the man, drawing myself to full height and showing three pips, he quickly disappeared without trace.'

The following Saturday (9 September), another sub-unit were on the air with the full *Canada Dance Band Show*, singers Joanne Dallas and Paul Carpenter. This unit performed many of the all-time greats from Glenn Miller's book to Benny Goodman. It was a great band and could really swing.

Also on Thursday evenings at 10.30 p.m., double British summer time, the Canada Dance Band, led by Bob Farnon, did another show called *Night Cap*. The series included Beatrice Lillie. The next *Canada Show* to include a guest star was on Monday, 25 September 1944. The guest was harmonica player Ronald Chesney. The first half of this broadcast is to be found in the BBC archives. It also includes Paul Carpenter singing *Poinciana*. Chesney performed *My Prayer*. That same week, on Wednesday, 27 September, another member of the orchestra was featured in his own programme. The programme was *Piano Parade* and featured pianist Dick Misener from Vancouver. Each week, the *Piano Parade* series was broadcast daily at 11.45 a.m., DBST, from Monday through to Saturday. Monday featured Ronnie Selby, pianist from the British Band of the AEF, Wednesday was Dick from the Canadian Band of the AEF and Saturday was PFC Jack Russin from the American Band of the AEF, while in between were other civilian and service pianists. Each programme involved uninterrupted piano music in various styles, from Boogie-Woogie to the classics.

Dick Misener was featured with the entire chorus in another Canadian AEF show called the *Canada Sing Show* on Friday evenings. This was very much like our contemporary *Sing Something Simple* series featured by the BBC on Radio 2. The *Canada Sing Show* series' first broadcast was on Friday, 22 September 1944. The chorus was led by Private Cliff McAree.

As well as working on the regular series, the entire Canada Show were often featured in the Series *AEF Special* from the stage of the Queensbury All Services Club in Soho, London.

Hence, on Sunday, 22 October, from the Queensbury All Services Club, a truly historic *AEF Special* was broadcast that featured not only the Canadian Band of the AEF, conducted by Captain Bob Farnon, but also the US Navy Band directed by Sam Donahue, together with the RAF Dance Orchestra, The Squadronaires, conducted by Sgt. Jimmy Miller. The compère was Pilot Officer Robin Ordell from the RAAF. It was another Cecil Madden coup. Cecil had already teamed the great Glenn Miller AEF Orchestra and the Sam Donahue US Navy Band at the club, and had presented Spike Jones, Dinah Shore and Bing Crosby on various programmes from that venue.

As well as the regular series and the *AEF Specials* which Bob and his orchestra were involved with, they also performed on the AEFP Series *Johnny Canuck's Revue* on Friday evenings from 10.01 p.m. until 10.30 p.m. Also included in each show was singer Sergeant Ted Hockridge. The title theme, written and composed by Bob Farnon, was *Canadian Caravan*. After the war, Bob recorded this title and it became very well known. Most of the programmes by the sub-units were either recorded in, or broadcast, from the BBC studios in Maida Vale. Only the *Canada Shows* and AEFP Specials came from the Queensbury All Services Club. Bob has related a very light-hearted story about one of the rehearsals: 'We were rehearsing for a broadcast and the orchestra broke for a half-hour break before the broadcast. We arranged with the studio attendant to set the clocks forward fifteen minutes. What happened was we called the orchestra in and they thought, ''Oh, five minutes to go''. Then eventually the red light came on and they thought we were on the air. And the ones that were in on this little gag — the drummer and one of the trumpet players — started swearing and saying outrageous things. One said, ''I don't want to sing that f------ thing.'' This was all unknown to the producer — everyone knew about it, including the engineer, the studio attendant, but not the producer. Of course, he was tearing his hair out and he lost ten years of his life, going out on the air with this crowd causing pandemonium.'

During late 1944, the Canadian Band of the AEF made two feature films — *I Live in Grosvenor Square* and *Piccadilly Incident*. Bob recalls: 'I sort of remember that Glenn Miller's American Band of the AEF was supposed to be in that film *Piccadilly Incident* with us, but it turned out too expensive.'

By Christmas 1944, the Canadian Band of the AEF had played host to many guests both in and out of the services. Bob again remembers: 'In regard to guest stars appearing with the band, I reckon that we worked with most of the artistes around and about. Gracie Fields, Vera Lynn, Anne Shelton, Beatrice Lillie, Cyril Fletcher, Ronald Chesney, Kenneth Horne, Richard Murdoch,

```
──────────── PROGRAMME ────────────

             A.E.F.  SPECIAL
           " THE  CANADA  SHOW "
     THE NEW CANADIAN BAND OF THE A.E.F.
     Conducted by Captain ROBERT FARNON (Canada's foremost Composer)
```

Trumpets ... ... GEORGE ANDERSON	The "Canada Show" Chorus MARGARET HUBBARD, C.W.A.C
FRED DAVIS	HELEN FARRELL, C.W.A.C.
HARRY FREEDMAN	PHYLLIS GILLIARD, C.W.A.C.
RON NEAR	EVELYN SCAMAN, C.W.A.C.
Trombones ... ... FLOYD ROBERTS	ILA CLENDINNING, C.W.A.C.
GARY HUGHES	GEORGE HARRISON
BOB BLAND	GERRY TRAVERS
Saxophones ... ... JACK WACHTER	JACK MCÜEACHIE
NORM BARBER	ALBERT LOVE
GEORGE NAYLOR	WALLY GOERTZ
KEN HELM	MAC PACE
WALDO FARNHAM	GABE LALONDE
Violins ... ... STAN KOLT	Writing Staff ... ... JOY PORTEOUS, C.W.A.C.
JOE BARATT	SHERRY WELLS, C.W.A.C.
LOU HERSCHENHOREN	BILL VALENTINE
BOB LITTNER	WILF DAVIDSON
GEORGE YACHNICKI	DICK MISENER
REUBEN SAGINUR	DE B. HOLLY
ROY ROME	Lieut. DOUGLASS MONTGOMERY
JACK SANDHAM	Arrangers ... ... TONY BRADEN
Violas ... ... LEN DUNELYK	BOB FARNON
GIL MARGISON	Administrative Staff ... S.Q.M.S. QUARTERLEY
Cellos ... ... TADEUSZ KADZIULAWA	J. DUFF
CHARLES DOJACK	M. GIBSON
Piano ... ... CLIFF MCAREE	Announcer: Lieut. CHARMIAN SANSOM, C.W.A.C.
Celeste ... ... JOANNE DALLAS, C.W.A.C.	Guest Stars:–
Guitar ... ... GEORGE ARTHUR	TOMMY HANDLEY– ITMA in Person
Bass ... ... HOWIE BARNES	SUZETTE TARRI– the Popular Commedienne
Drums ... ... CUTH KNOWLTON	RONALD CHESNEY– the Hamonica Star
Soloists ... ... JOANNE DALLAS, C.W.A.C.	MC: GERRY WILMOT (Producer of "Johnny Canuck's
PAUL CARPENTER	Revue", etc.)
	Producer: Lieut. CAM RITCHIE

```
        In charge of A.E.F. Production: CECIL MADDEN

    Producer for the Queensberry All-Services Club: JOHN HARDING
```

Anna Neagle, Gert and Daisy, The Crazy Gang, Irene Manning, Beryl Davis are some names that come to mind.'

On Christmas Day 1944, Bob and the Canadian Band of the AEF were involved in the *AEF Christmas Show*. This involved the British and Canadian AEF bands on the stage of the Queensbury All Services Club in London, and Major Glenn Miller's American Band of the AEF in Paris. The day before Christmas Eve, the BBC had announced that Major Glenn Miller was missing over the English Channel. The broadcast went ahead, first with the Christmas *Canada Show*, directed by Bob Farnon at 6.05 p.m., then at 6.30 p.m. the British Band of the AEF took over. Then, at 7.01 p.m., it was the turn of the American Band of the AEF from Paris. Bob again picks up the story: 'We just did not know what was happening in Paris. We knew Glenn wasn't there, but the band was. We waited and waited. We performed our half-hour show, then Melachrino performed his. Still nothing from Paris, they came on and the American Band was directed by Jerry Gray.' After the American band's half-hour show, there was a combined round-up from both London and Paris. This last hour was broadcast via short-wave to the USA and Canada.

Bob has said of that Christmas Day broadcast: 'It turned out a very sad evening for all of us, with Glenn missing.'

Another series which the Canadian Band of the AEF broadcast over the AEF Programme was the *Canada Guest Show* on Tuesday afternoon at 5.15 p.m. Unlike on most of the other sub-unit programmes, the orchestra was conducted by Gunner Bruce Campbell. Many British, American and Canadian guest stars filled each programme. With six regular programmes a week, plus visits to the Queensbury Club for AEFP Specials and also camp shows, the orchestra and its singers were very busy indeed. Even so Bob worked very hard composing and arranging for each show on top of conducting the full *Canada Show* on Monday evenings and several other shows during each week over the AEFP.

Bob Farnon has recalled many happy memories from this period: 'The signature tune of the Canadian Band of the AEF was a thing appropriately called "Canadian Caravan". It was done in rather broad, slow treatment, but, after the war, I rewrote it and made it rather an exciting piece. I used to conduct with my left hand (I am left-handed), and it wasn't until I took over the Army Orchestra that I was allowed to practise on those poor suffering musicians, and there was a transition in learning to conduct with my right hand. Those were wonderful times — a great collection of musicians. We had a ball: there was great fraternity among the three bands. It improved our players a lot, I know.'

The three bands were the American Band of the AEF, directed by Major Glenn Miller, the British Band of the AEF, directed by RSM George Melachrino, and the Canadian, directed by Bob Farnon. The Canadian band, unlike its American and British counterparts, contained three brothers. There was conductor and leader Bob Farnon, and his two brothers: Brian, who played alto saxophone, and Denny, who played trumpet.

Another highlight each Monday evening was the *Symphonettes*. These compositions were short and amusing burlesque of classic symphony, usually in the traditional three movements, and were usually based on fairy-tales or nursery rhymes. Bob Farnon wrote each one and they were similar to the famous *Peter and the Wolf* recording which was featured in the 1950s children's radio show with Uncle Mac.

Bob also wrote other great titles while with the Canadian AEF unit, as well as theme music for each of the six programmes.

Like the American Band of the AEF, the Canadian Band had its own home-town singer for the vocals of *Is You Is or Is You Ain't My Baby?* and many more. This was drummer Lance Corporal Cuth Knowlton. The polished vocals were left to Paul Carpenter and Gerry Travers. On the *Canada Guest Show*s, vocals were left to Captain Cam Ritchie, who also introduced quite a few of these shows.

On 1 January 1945, the first *Canada Show* of 1945 was broadcast. However, the show was pre-recorded on 18 December 1944, and no guest

Capt. Bob Farnon, seated, with the Canadian Band's two featured singers, Privates Joanne Dallas and Paul Carpenter, 1944-45 (Photo: © BBC)

stars were featured. The following Monday (8 January 1945), the show was broadcast live from the Queensbury All Services Club, with guest star, pianist Kay Cavendish. She played *Kay Tico Tico, Come Out Wherever You Are* and *Spring Will be a Little Late This Year*. All through the winter of 1945, the Canadian band did its full share of AEFP broadcasts. By early spring, with the river Rhine crossed and the advance into Germany well under way, the AEFP kept up with its commitments, continuing with all its popular radio entertainment.

Bob and his Canadian Band of the AEF played host to many American,

The entire chorus from The Canada Show *are featured in their own ten-minute Friday evening show, the* Canada Sing Show, *which also highlighted L/Cpl. Dick Misener, BBC Studios, London 1944-45 (Photo:* © *BBC)*

British and Canadian stars while in London, with most of the broadcasts being compèred by one of the following members of the orchestra: Paul Carpenter, Dick Misener, Wilf Davidson and Gerry Wilmot. When the band performed on AEF Specials from the Queensbury All Services Club, other guest announcers were brought in from the AEFP. Among those who worked with Bob Farnon and his orchestra were Jean Metcalfe, Margaret Hubble, Lt. Charmian Sansom, CWAC, as well as many others.

During April 1945, pianist Dick Misener was replaced by Corporal Denny Vaughan on the *Piano Parade* shows. Misener, who was also one of the arrangers for the orchestra, was far too busy in this latter capacity and was reassigned by Bob. As well as writing for the band, Bob also did some under-the-counter arrangements for some of the famous civilian bands in Britain. Bob explains: 'Towards the end of the war, during the last few months or so, a friend of mine, Bruce Campbell, who was also in our unit, and had been in Britain before the war, helped me to get to know people like Ted Heath and Geraldo — the orchestras of the day. Unbeknown to the army commanding officers, I used to do the odd arrangement for these bands — under-the-counter, as it were! When I received my discharge in Britain, I took up writing for these bands on a regular basis. As a matter of fact, I signed up with Geraldo for a year's exclusive contract, just writing for his orchestra.'

Another *Canada Show* still extant is the full programme from Monday, 30 April 1945. The guests were the Master Singers.

Up until 'VE-Day' the Canadian Band of the AEF used *March Along, Joe Soldier* as their theme tune for the regular Monday *Canada Shows*. This was included in the programme of 30 April. Following the theme, the orchestra and chorus continued with *That's An Order From the Army* and then, as usual, the Canada Dance Band went on to *Liza*, and the dance band could really swing. There is no doubt that Bob's orchestra was a great band. After 'VE-Day' on 8 May 1945, the *Canada Show*'s theme changed to another Bob Farnon composition, *Canadian Caravan*.

The Allied Expeditionary Forces Programme had only about ten more weeks to be broadcast, under an agreement between the BBC and SHAEF. However, it was still a busy time for Bob and his boys — after all, they were all still in the army and the war out in the Pacific was still being fought. All their six weekly broadcasts would continue up until the end of the AEFP on Saturday, 28 July 1945. Even on that last Saturday, Bob and his band would be working and broadcasting to the Allied Forces all over Europe. On that very last Saturday, Bob Farnon and his Canadian Band of the AEF were featured along with the RAF Squadronaires Dance Band in a very special programme broadcast from the Queensbury All Services Club. This programme was called *Farewell AEFP!*, and also featured many American, British and Canadian guest stars, including: Lt. Charmian Sansom, Lt. Douglas Marshall, RSM George Melachrino, Staff Sergeant Wilf Davidson, Sgts. Dick Dudley, Keith Jameson, George Monaghan, Corporal Jack Powers, Private Joanne Dallas, Private Paul Carpenter, A/C2 Ronald Waldman RAF, Gerry Wilmot, Margaret Hubble, Jill Balcon, Betty McLoughlin, Dorothy Carless, Beryl Davis, and Pat Frost. The show lasted from 21.05 to 22.00 DBST, and was a Cecil Madden production. Needless to say, the whole recording was one of the broadcasts kept by the BBC and is still to be found in the BBC sound archives in London.

Although the AEFP was closed down, the very next day (29 July 1945), a brand new network was opened by the BBC. This was the new BBC light programme and, because the Canadian Band of the AEF was the youngest of the three AEFP house bands, it was still broadcasting in a series called *Canadian Caravan* every Monday evening at 8.30 until 9.00 p.m. on the said programme. The series would run from 30 July until 24 September 1945.

As in *The Canada Show*, some guests were featured in the nine-week series. Some of the early broadcasts were performed from the Queensbury All Services Club. Slowly, as London went back to its peacetime normality, Bob and the Canadian Band of the AEF transferred the venue to the famous pre-war *Monseigneur* night spot. Just as it did on the late *Canada Show* broadcasts over the AEFP, the band used Bob Farnon's composition of *Canadian Caravan* as its theme tune for the series.

Captain Bob Farnon and his Canadian Band of the AEF's last radio broadcast as a unit was on the BBC light programme on Saturday, 15 December 1945, from 7.45 to 8.15 p.m. This special programme, produced by Stephen Williams and Cecil Madden, was a BBC tribute to the American Forces Network. The network was closed down that evening and moved to Germany. It had opened in Britain two-and-a-half years before. Taking part in that special programme (called *Farewell AFN*) were Captain Bob Farnon's Canadian Band, Jackie Hunter, Dorothy Carless, Ronald Waldman, Dick Dudley, PFC Byron Kane, Brigadier General Claude M. Thiel and BBC announcer Margaret Hubble. It was the last show of many for the old Canadian Band of the AEF, now simply known (since August 1945) as Captain Bob Farnon's Canadian Band. Over the next few months, into early 1946, most of the Canadian Army Orchestra would be demobbed and sent home to Canada. However, Bob Farnon and Paul Carpenter, together with a few others, stayed on in Britain. Paul found his way into the newly formed Ted Heath Band and Bob Farnon joined Geraldo. Paul is now, sadly, no longer with us. He gave some tremendous performances during the late 1940s and 1950s and he is still widely remembered by everyone. He died on 12 June 1966.

Bob Farnon went on to even greater things, first with Geraldo and later with film and television themes. Bob has worked with most of the all-time greats and his compositions *Westminster Waltz* and the *Theme from Colditz* will always be remembered. Bob is alive and very well and now lives in the Channel Islands. He still directs orchestras and writes compositions.

CAPTAIN ROBERT FARNON AND THE CANADIAN BAND OF THE AEF SEPTEMBER 1944 – DECEMBER 1945

Monday, 4 September 1944   CANADA SHOW
20.30-21.00
Broadcast live from the Queensbury All Services Club, Soho, London
Over AEFP
Featuring: The Canadian Band of the AEF, conducted by Capt. Robert Farnon, with Pvts. Paul Carpenter and Joanne Dallas, and the Canada Show Chorus
Compère: Gerry Wilmot
Opening Theme (March Along, Joe Soldier -VR- The Unit Choir)/Stomping at the Savoy/The Music Stopped -VR- Paul Carpenter/Old Man River/Embraceable You -VR- Joanne Dallas/San Fernando Valley -VR- Paul Carpenter and The Unit Choir/'Joe Medley' (featuring vocals by The Unit Choir): Why Am I Always Joe; Joe, Joe, What D'Ya Know, Joe?; Joe Worker; Unessential Joe; Schooldays; Joe-see-fus Jones; Parrididdle Joe; Ragtime Cowboy Joe; Old Black Joe; Joseph Joseph; I Came Here to Talk for Joe/Closing Theme (March Along, Joe Soldier -comp- Robert Farnon).

Thursday, 7 September 1944   CANADA SHOW IN
17.00-17.30   'SWING TIME'
Broadcast live from the BBC Studios, Maida Vale, London
Over AEFP
Featuring: The Canada Show's eight-piece Dixieland Band, conducted by Captain Robert Farnon
Compère: Cpl. W. T. Valentine
Opening Theme (The Blues)/Royal Garden Blues/I'll Get By -VR- Joanne Dallas/Indiana/It Had to be You -VR- Paul Carpenter/Five Foot Two/Taking a Chance on Love -VR- Joanne Dallas/Ding Dong Daddy/I'll Be Around -VR- Paul Carpenter/Who's Sorry Now?/Closing Theme (The Blues).

Thursday, 7 September 1944   NIGHT CAP
22.30-23.00
Broadcast live from the BBC Studios
Over AEFP
Featuring: Beatrice Lillie, The Canada Dance Band, conducted by Capt. Robert Farnon
Compère: Pvt. Dick Misener
Opening Theme (Cocktails for Two)/Sketch 'To Entertain the Troops' (featuring Beatrice Lillie)/How Could You?/Honeysuckle Rose/Medley (featuring Beatrice Lillie with the Canada Dance Band): Michigan; Black Eyes Susan; Lazy; Suzannah's Squeaking Shoes/Goodnight Wherever You Are -VR- Paul Carpenter and Close.

Saturday, 9 September 1944   CANADA SHOW
08.30-09.00   DANCE ORCHESTRA
Broadcast recorded from the Queensbury All Services Club, Soho, London, on Friday, 8 September 1944 — BBC Disc No. SLO 61494
Compère: Pvt. Dick Misener
Opening Theme (Canadian Capers)/Stomping at the Savoy/Day In Day Out -VR- Joanne Dallas/Caroline/Body and Soul/The Night We Called it a Day -VR- Paul Carpenter/One O'Clock Jump/Say a Prayer for the Boys Over There -VR- Joanne Dallas/For Me and My Gal/Singing on a Star -VR- Paul Carpenter/Bugle Call Rag/Closing Theme (Canadian Capers).

Monday, 11 September 1944   CANADA SHOW
20.30-21.00
Broadcast live from the Queensbury All Services Club, Soho, London
Over AEFP
Guest Star: Beatrice Lillie
Compère: Gerry Wilmot, Lt. R. D. Montgomery
Opening Theme (March Along, Joe Soldier -comp- Capt. Robert Farnon and Lt. R. D. Montgomery)/T'Aint Necessarily So -VR- Chorus/Now I Know -VR- Joanne Dallas/Land of Promise -VR- Beatrice Lillie/'Sketch' — with Beatrice Lillie/ Paree -VR- Beatrice Lillie/Put on Your Old Grey Bonnet/The

Night We Called it a Day -VR- Paul Carpenter/Canadian Tapestry -VR-Choir/Canada Medley (featuring The Canada Show Chorus): Maple Leaf Forever; Kerry Dancers; Annie Laurie; Country Garden; All Through the Night; Devil's Drum; A la Claire Fontaine; Alouette; Last Round Up; Come to the Fair; Shanandoah; Dark Eyes; O Sole Mio; Oh! Canada/Closing Theme (March Along, Joe Soldier).

Thursday, 14 September 1944   CANADA SWING SHOW
17.01-17.30
Broadcast live from the BBC Studios, Maida Vale, London
Over AEFP
Compère: Cpl. W. T. Valentine
Opening Theme (The Blues)/Muskrat Ramble/What is This Thing Called Love -VR- Joanne Dallas/I'm Forever Blowing Bubbles/Paducah -VR- Paul Carpenter/Honeysuckle Rose/Basin Street Blues -VR- Joanne Dallas/Benny's Bugle/As Long As You're Not in Love -VR- Paul Carpenter/When My Sugar Walks Down the Street/Closing Theme (The Blues).

Thursday, 14 September 1944   NIGHT CAP
22.30-22.59
Broadcast live from the BBC Studios, Maida Vale, London
Over AEFP
Compère: Lt. R. D. Montgomery, Lt. Charmian Samson
Opening Theme (Cocktails for Two)/My Blue Heaven/Baby Doesn't Know -VR- Beatrice Lillie/Skit — 'After the Show'/Body and Soul/Nanette -VR-Beatrice Lillie/Skit — 'Snaps' (featuring Beatrice Lillie)/Margie and Close.

Saturday, 16 September 1944   CANADA DANCE BAND
08.30-09.00
Pre-recorded 15 September 1944 — BBC Disc No. SLO unknown
Compère: Pvt. Dick Misener
Details remain unknown.

Sunday, 17 September 1944   CANADA SHOW —
18.05-18.45   AEF SPECIAL
Broadcast recorded at the Queensbury All Services Club, Soho, London, on Saturday, 16 September 1944 — BBC Disc No. SWN 19324
Over AEFP
Compère: Charmian Samson, CWAC
Guest Stars: Tommy Handley, Ronald Chesney
Opening Theme (March Along, Joe Soldier)/Three Little Words -VR- Canada Chorus/How Blue the Night -VR- Paul Carpenter/'Skit' with Tommy Handley (includes Colonel Bogey/Jolly Brothers)/Stomping at the Savoy/Embraceable You -VR- Joanne Dallas/Deep River/My Blue Heaven/Liebestraum -VR- Chorus/Hallelujah! (featuring Ronald Chesney)/Poinciana (featuring Ronald Chesney)/Holiday for Strings (featuring Ronald Chesney)/San Fernando Valley -VR- Paul Carpenter/T'Aint Necessarily So -VR- Canada Chorus/Closing Theme (March Along, Joe Soldier).

Monday, 18 September 1944 CANADA SHOW
20.30-21.00
Broadcast live from the Queensbury All Services Club, Soho, London
Over AEFP
(Repeated the following morning, Tuesday, 19 September 1944,
10.01-10.30 a.m. — BBC Disc No. unknown)
Compère: Gerry Wilmot
Opening Theme (March Along, Joe Soldier)/My Blue Heaven/Time Alone
Will Tell -VR- Paul Carpenter/Deep River/I'll Be Seeing You -VR- Joanne
Dallas/Chopsticks/Tico Tico -VR- Paul Carpenter/Symphonette — 'The
Princess and the Ugly Frog' — Music and Dialogue by Robert Farnon, and
Close.

Wednesday, 20 September 1944 PIANO PARADE
11.45-12.00
Broadcast live from the BBC Studios, Maida Vale, London
Over AEFP
Featuring: Pvt. Dick Misener at the piano
Opening Theme (Chopsticks)/I Can't Escape From You/Deep Purple/Lazy
River/Cocktails for Two/Body and Soul/All of Me/Closing Theme
(Chopsticks).

Thursday, 21 September 1944 CANADA SWING SHOW
17.15-17.45
Broadcast live from the BBC Studios, Maida Vale, London
Over AEFP
Compère: Cpl. W. T. Valentine
Opening Theme (The Blues)/The Band Played On/Amor Amor -VR- Joanne
Dallas/I May Be Wrong/Ain't Misbehavin' -VR- Paul Carpenter/Tea for Two/
All of Me -VR- Joanne Dallas/When I Grow Too Old to Dream/Too Much in
Love -VR- Paul Carpenter/Button Up Your Overcoat/Closing Theme (The
Blues).

Thursday, 21 September 1944 NIGHT CAP
22.30
Broadcast live from the BBC Studios, Maida Vale, London
Over AEFP
Compères: Gerry Wilmot and Lt. Charmian Samson, CWAC
Opening Theme (Cocktails for Two)/Isle of Capri/Medley: My Heart Belongs
to Daddy -VR- Beatrice Lillie; I Get a Kick Out of You -VR- Beatrice
Lillie/Wind -VR- Beatrice Lillie/I Surrender Dear/You Took Advantage of Me
-VR- Beatrice Lillie/Give Me a Night at the Ballroom (featuring Beatrice Lillie)
and Close.

Friday, 22 September 1944 CANADA SWING SHOW
21.05-21.15
Broadcast live from the BBC Studios, Maida Vale, London
Over AEFP

Featuring: The Canadian Army Choir, under Pvt. Cliff McAree, with Pvt. Dick Misener at the piano
Compère: Cpl. Wilf Davidson
Opening Theme (By the River St Marie)/Oh! Dear What Can the Matter Be/ When Day is Done/My Buddy -VR- Joanne Dallas and Choir/Where or When/ Closing Theme (By the River St Marie).

Saturday, 23 September 1944   CANADA DANCE BAND
08.30-09.00
Broadcast recorded at the BBC Studios, at Maida Vale, London — Friday, 22 September 1944 — BBC Disc No. unknown
Over AEFP
Compère: Unknown
Details remain unknown.

Monday, 25 September 1944   CANADA SHOW
20.30
Broadcast live from the Queensbury All Services Club, Soho, London
Over AEFP
(Repeated by AEFP, Tuesday, 26 September 1944 — 10.01-10.30 a.m. — BBC Disc No. SWN 19269)
Compère: Gerry Wilmot
Guest Star: Ronald Chesney
Intro: Theme (March Along, Joe Soldier)/Oh! Dear What Can the Matter Be -VR- Chorus/Isle of Capri/Poinciana -VR- Paul Carpenter/My Prayer (featuring Ronald Chesney, Harmonica)/Hallelujah! (featuring Ronald Chesney)/The Girl I Left Behind Me/My Shining Hour -VR- Joanne Dallas/Darktown Strutters Ball/Cocktails for Two/Closing Theme (March Along, Joe Soldier).

Wednesday, 27 September 1944   PIANO PARADE
11.45
Broadcast live from Aeolin Hall Studios, London
Over AEFP
Opening Theme (Chopsticks)/Soliloquy/Time on My Hands/A Pretty Girl is Like a Melody/Poor Butterfly/In the Middle of a Kiss/Theme and Close (Chopsticks).

Thursday, 28 September 1944   CANADA SWING SHOW
17.45
Broadcast live from Aeolin Hall Studios, London
Over AEFP
Compère: Cpl. W. T. Valentine
Opening Theme (The Blues)/Bennys Bugle/When They Ask About You -VR- Joanne Dallas/Kerry Dances/Forget-me-nots in Your Eyes -VR- Paul Carpenter/Royal Garden Blues/My Heart Stood Still -VR- Joanne Dallas/Lady Be Good/You're My Little Pin-Up Girl -VR- Paul Carpenter/I Never Knew/ Theme and Close (The Blues).

Thursday, 28 September 1944   NIGHT CAP
22.30
Broadcast live from Aeolin Hall Studios, London
Over AEFP
Compère: Lt. Charmian Samson, CEAC
Opening Theme (Cocktails for Two)/Ja Da/A Baby's Best Friend is its Mother
-VR- Beatrice Lillie/'Skit' – Telephone Tangle (featuring Beatrice Lillie)/
Confessin'/Mad Dogs and Englishmen -VR- Beatrice Lillie/'Skit' – 'Speak As
You Read' (featuring Beatrice Lillie)/I'll Be There with You -VR- Beatrice
Lillie/Girl of My Dreams/Closing Theme (Goodnight Wherever You Are).

Friday, 29 September 1944   CANADA SWING SHOW
21.05
Broadcast live from Aeolin Hall Studios, London
Over AEFP
Compère: Cpl. Wilf Davidson
Opening Theme (By the River St Marie)/Three Little Words -VR- Chorus/
Stormy Weather -VR- Gerry Travers/Flying Down to Rio -VR- Quartet/Blue
Moon -VR- Choir/Closing Theme (By the River St Marie).

Saturday, 30 September 1944   CANADA DANCE BAND
08.25
(Pre-recorded Friday, 29 September 1944 — BBC Disc No. SLO unknown
Over AEFP
Compère: unknown
Details remain unknown.

Sunday, 1 October 1944   CANADA SHOW — AEF SPECIAL
20.30-21.00
Broadcast recorded from the Queensbury All Services Club, Soho, London, on
Saturday, 30 September 1944 — BBC Disc No. FLO 62948
Over AEFP
Guest Stars: Vera Lynn, Pat Frost, Jackie Hunter
Compère: Gerry Wilmot
Opening Theme (March Along, Joe Soldier -VR- Chorus)/Love is in the Air
Tonight/Ja Da/Knuckledust (featuring Pat Frost)/San Fernando Valley
(featuring Pat Frost)/My Prayer (featuring Pat Frost)/Sweet Sue (featuring Pat
Frost)/My Shining Hour -VR- Joanne Dallas/Put On Your Old Grey Bonnet/
'Skit' – Jackie Hunter/Someday I'll Meet You Again -VR- Paul Carpenter/
Long Ago and Far Away -VR- Vera Lynn/The Man I Love -VR- Vera Lynn/
The First Few Days -VR- Vera Lynn/Closing Theme (March Along, Joe
Soldier).

Monday, 2 October 1944   CANADA SHOW
20.30
Broadcast live from the Queensbury All Services Club, Soho, London
Over AEFP

(Repeated by AEFP, 'Morning After', Tuesday, 3 October 1944, 10.01-10.30 a.m., BBC Disc No. unknown)
Guest Star: Frances Day
Compère: Gerry Wilmot
Love is in the Air Tonight -VR- Chorus/Ja Da/Someday I'll Meet You Again -VR- Paul Carpenter/A Fine Romance -VR- Frances Day/Parody on 'A Nightingale Sang in Berkley Square' -VR- Frances Day/When I Grow Too Old to Dream/That Soldier of Mine -VR- Joanne Dallas/Blue Moon -VR- Chorus.
Note: From now on, we do not list themes which remained the same until VE Day.

Wednesday, 4 October 1944   PIANO PARADE
11.45
Broadcast live **Over AEFP**
Announcer: Pvt. Dick Misener
I Had the Craziest Dream/Lover's Lullaby/The Very Thought of You/Indian Summer/Whispers in the Dark.

Thursday, 5 October 1944   CANADA SWING SHOW
17.15
Broadcast live from the BBC Studios, London
Over AEFP
Compère: Cpl. W. T. Valentine
Pack Up Your Troubles/My Ideal -VR- Joanne Dallas/Sweet Lorraine/Pretty Kitty Blue Eyes -VR- Paul Carpenter/Way Down Yonder in New Orleans/Blue Skies -VR- Joanne Dallas/The Girl Friend/In Times Like These -VR- Paul Carpenter/It's a Long Way to Tipperarary.

Thursday, 5 October 1944   NIGHT CAP
22.30
Broadcast live from the BBC Studios, London
Over AEFP
Compère: Lt. Charmian Samson, CWAC
Promenade/Nanette -VR- Beatrice Lillie/Skit — 'How To Get There (featuring Beatrice Lillie, Gerry Wilmot, Charmian Samson, De B. Holly and Grant Tyler)/Ain't Misbehavin'/Paris -VR- Beatrice Lillie/Skit — 'Inaudibility' (featuring Beatrice Lillie, Charmian Samson and Gerry Wilmot)/Mouse Mouse -VR- Beatrice Lillie/When Johnny Comes Marching Home/Goodnight Wherever You Are.
Note: This was the last programme in this series. From the following week, the AEFP would replace 'Night Cap' with a recorded programme from Canada.

Friday, 6 October 1944   CANADA SING SHOW
21.05
Broadcast live from the BBC Studios, London
Over AEFP
Compère: Cpl. Wilf Davidson
My Little Banjo -VR- Chorus/Water Boy -VR- Pvt. Macpace/Deep River -VR- Chorus/The Battle of Jericho -VR- Chorus.

Saturday, 7 October 1944   CANADA DANCE BAND
08.25
Broadcast live from the BBC Studios, Maida Vale, London
Over AEFP
Opening Theme (Canadian Capers)/Stomping at the Savoy/Time on My Hands
-VR- Joanne Dallas/Girl of My Dreams/Emaline/Irresistible You -VR- Paul
Carpenter/Blue Room/Love Me or Leave Me -VR- Joanne Dallas/Button Up
Your Overcoat/My Melancholy Baby/Forget-me-nots in Your Eyes -VR- Paul
Carpenter/Promenade/Closing Theme (Canadian Capers).

Monday, 9 October 1944   CANADA SHOW
20.30
Broadcast live from the Queensbury All Services Club, Soho, London
Over AEFP
(Repeated by AEFP, 'Morning After', Tuesday, 10 October 1944 –
10.01 - 10.30 a.m.)
Compères: Cpl. Wilf Davidson and Gerry Wilmot
You Are My Lucky Star -VR- Chorus/Stomping at the Savoy/Il Suffit d'une
Petite Femme -VR- Paul Carpenter/Symphonette – The Three Bears –
Narrator Sgt. G. Stuart/Somebody Loves Me/Time on My Hands -VR- Joanne
Dallas/The Old Grey Bonnet/Dancing in the Dark -VR- Chorus.

Wednesday, 11 October 1944   PIANO PARADE
11.45
Broadcast live from the BBC Studios, London
Over AEFP
If I Had You/I'm Getting Sentimental Over You/It Can't be Wrong/Stardust/
It Had to be You.

Thursday, 12 October 1944   CANADA SWING SHOW
17.15
Broadcast live from the BBC Studios, London
Over AEFP
Compère: Cpl. W. T. Valentine
Who's Sorry Now/How Sweet You Are -VR- Joanne Dallas/Cherry/I'll Be
Home for Christmas -VR- Paul Carpenter/Digga Digga Do/Can't Get Out of
this Mood -VR- Joanne Dallas/Sweet Sue/Don't Believe Everything You
Dream -VR- Paul Carpenter/The Sheik of Araby.

Friday, 13 October 1944   CANADA SING SHOW
21.05
Broadcast live from the BBC Studios, London
Over AEFP
Compère: Cpl. Wilf Davidson
Love is on the Air Tonight -VR- Chorus/L'amour Toujours L'amour -VR-
Pvt. J. McGeachie/Somebody Loves Me -VR- Chorus/Falling in Love with
Love -VR- Chorus.

Saturday, 14 October 1944   CANADA DANCE BAND
08.25
(Pre-recorded Friday, 13 October 1944 — BBC Disc No. TLO 62250)
Compère: Pvt. Dick Misener
I Want to be Happy/I'll be Seeing You -VR- Joanne Dallas/Paducah -VR- Paul Carpenter/In a Little Spanish Town/I've Got the World on a String/When They Ask About You -VR- Joanne Dallas/In Times Like These -VR- Paul Carpenter/The Sheik of Araby/Basin Street Blues -VR- Joanne Dallas/Don't Blame Me/How Blue the Night -VR- Paul Carpenter/Carving Session (Original by G. Hughes).

Monday, 16 October 1944   CANADA SHOW
20.30
Broadcast live from the Queensbury All Services Club, London
Over AEFP
Guest Star: Sub-Lt. Eric Barker
Compères: Cpl. Wilf Davidson, Gerry Wilmot, Pvt. Dick Misener
Oh! How I Hate to Get Up in the Morning -VR- Chorus/In a Little Spanish Town/ J'Attendrai -VR- Paul Carpenter/'Patter' — Eric Barker/Bicycle Built for Two/The First Few Days -VR- Joanne Dallas/Three Little Words -VR- Chorus/Night and Day/San Fernando Valley -VR- Chorus.

Tuesday, 17 October 1944   VARIETY BANDBOX
13.01-13.55 Overseas Service
Recorded at the Queensbury All Services Club, Soho, London, on Sunday, 15 October 1944 — BBC Disc No. OP 823 — SLO 62797
Featuring: The Canadian Band of the AEF, directed by Capt. Robert Farnon, with the Canada Show Chorus, Vera Lynn, Janet Joyce, Irving Kaye, Phil Park, Master Thomas Criddle, Kathleen Moody, Jackie Hunter
Compère: Lilli Palmer
Opening Theme (I Love to Sing)/March Along, Joe Soldier -VR- Chorus/Oh! Dear What Can the Matter Be -VR- Chorus/'Impressions' (featuring Janet Joyce)/Whistle Your Blues Away (featuring Irving Kaye)/Medley: (featuring Irving Kaye, Violin): Jolly Brothers; Humoresque; Old Folks at Home (Swanee River)/Medley (featuring Irving Kaye, Whistling): Neila Valse; Over the Waves; Blue Danube; Voices of Spring/Captain Phil Park with Composer Cavalcade — My Kind of Music; How Beautiful You Are; Take the World Exactly as You Find it; What a Surprise for the Duce; Where the Blue Begins (featuring -VR- Master Thomas Criddle)/Indian Love Call -VR- Kathleen Moody/The Wren (featuring Kathleen Moody)/Old Man River/ 'Patter' — Miss Otis Regrets (featuring Jackie Hunter)/Echo of a Serenade (featuring Jackie Hunter)/Skyline -VR- Vera Lynn/All of My Life -VR- Vera Lynn/It Could Happen to You -VR- Vera Lynn/Dancing in the Dark -VR- Chorus/Closing Theme (Let's Have Another One -VR- Combined Artists and Audience).

Tuesday, 17 October 1944   CANADA GUEST SHOW
17.15-17.55
Broadcast live from the Paris Cinema, Lower Regent Street, London
Over AEFP
Featuring: The Canadian Band of the AEF, directed by Capt. Robert Farnon
Guest Stars: A. J. Powell, Miss Daphne Kelf, Lyle Evans, Bennett and Williams
Compères: Gerry Wilmot, Capt. F. J. Lynch
Opening Theme (Anything Goes)/Twelfth Street Rag (featuring A. J. Powell, Xylophone)/Xylophone Rag (featuring A.J. Powell, Xylophone)/This is the Army (A. J. Powell, Xylophone)/In the Mood (A. J. Powell, Xylophone)/Always -VR- Daphne Kelf/Waltz of My Heart -VR- Daphne Kelf/When the Home Bells Ring -VR- Daphne Kelf/Phonofiddle Duet − There's Nothing Like Music (featuring Bennett and Williams)/My Blue Heaven/The Girl I Left Behind Me/I'd Much Rather Sing a Song -VR- Lyle Evans/Can't You Hear Me Calling Caroline -VR- Lyle Evans/Tattooed Lady -VR- Lyle Evans/Closing Theme /Anything Goes -arr- Capt. Robert Farnon).

Wednesday, 18 October 1944   PIANO PARADE
11.45
Broadcast live from the BBC Studios, London
Over AEFP
Tea for Two/Body and Soul/Soliloquy/If I Had My Way/You Made Me Love You/Ain't Misbehavin'.

Thursday, 19 October 1944   CANADA SWING SHOW
17.15
Broadcast live from the BBC Studios, Maida Vale, London
Over AEFP
Compère: Pvt. Dick Misener
Benny's Bugle/When They Ask About You -VR- Joanne Dallas/Indiana/Paducah -VR- Paul Carpenter/Button Up Your Overcoat/My Ideal -VR- Joanne Dallas/Kerry Dance/Ain't Misbehavin' -VR- Paul Carpenter/Pack Up Your Troubles.

Friday, 20 October 1944   CANADA SING SHOW
21.05
Broadcast live from the BBC Studios, London
Over AEFP
Compère: Cpl. Wilf Davidson
We Joined the Navy -VR- Chorus/Shenandoah -VR- G. Lalande/Jolly Roger -VR- Chorus/Sing Me a Shanty -VR- G. Lalande and Chorus.

Saturday, 21 October 1944   CANADA DANCE BAND
17.15
Recorded at the BBC Studios, Maida Vale, London, on Friday, 20 October 1944 — BBC Disc TLO 63372
Compère: Pvt. Dick Misener

Farewell Blues/We Mustn't Say Goodbye -VR- Joanne Dallas/At Sundown/ Liza/One Alone -VR- Paul Carpenter/Stardust/Long Ago and Far Away -VR- Joanne Dallas/The Girl Friend/Swinging on a Star -VR- Paul Carpenter/ Confessin'/Isle of Capri.

Sunday, 22 October 1944 AEF SPECIAL
17.15 - 17.55
Pre-recorded at the Queensbury All Services Club, Soho, London, on Saturday, 21 October 1944 — BBC Disc No. SLO 62783
Featuring: The Canada Show Band, conducted by Capt. Robert Farnon, the RAF Dance Orchestra, conducted by Sgt. Jimmy Miller, the US Navy Dance Band, conducted by Sam Donahue
Compère: Lt. Charmian Samson, CWAC
Script and production by: Pat Dixon
Opening Theme (Red, White and Blue)/Isle of Capri (Canada Dance Band)/I Heard You Cried Last Night -VR- Beryl Davis (RAF Squadronaires)/What Can I Say Dear, After I Say I'm Sorry (US Navy Dance Band)/Basin Street Blues (Canada Dance Band)/Somebody Loves Me (RAF Squadronaires)/The First Few Days -VR- Joanne Dallas (Canada Dance Band)/Stompin' at the Savoy/ Do Nothin' Till You Hear From Me -VR- Beryl Davis (RAF Squadronaires)/Is You Is or Is You Ain't My Baby? -VR- Don Jacoby (US Navy Band)/ Swinging on a Star -VR- Paul Carpenter (Canada Dance Band)/The Touch of Your Lips (RAF Squadronaires)/'C' Jam Blues (US Navy Dance Band)/Closing Theme (Red, White and Blue).

Monday, 23 October 1944 CANADA SHOW
20.30
Broadcast live from the Queensbury All Services Club, Soho, London
Over AEFP
(Repeated by AEFP on 'Morning After', Tuesday, 24 October 1944 10.01 - 10.30 a.m.)
Guest Stars: Nan Kenway, Douglas Young
Pack Up Your Troubles -VR- Chorus/Lullaby of Broadway/Paducah -VR- Paul Carpenter/'Skit' (featuring Kenway and Young)/Anything Goes/Embraceable You -VR- Joanne Dallas/Liza/I've Got You Under My Skin/The Empire is Marching -VR- Chorus.

Tuesday, 24 October 1944 CANADA GUEST SHOW
17.15
Broadcast live from the BBC Studios, London
Over AEFP
Guest Stars: Wren Audrey Pullen, Carroll Gibbons, Stephane Grappelli
Compère: Capt. F. J. Lynch
I Want to be Happy/Roses of Picardy -VR- Audrey Pullin/Homing -VR- Audrey Pullin/Bicycle Built for Two/On the Air (featuring Carroll Gibbons, Piano)/In 'D' Major (featuring Carroll Gibbons, Piano)/More than You Know (featuring Carroll Gibbons, Piano)/Dearly Beloved (featuring Carroll Gibbons,

Piano)/In a Little Spanish Town/Great Day -VR- Cam Ritchie/Time Alone
Will Tell (featuring Stephane Grappelli, Violin)/Lady be Good (featuring
Stephane Grappelli, Violin)/Vous Qui Passez Sans Me Voir (featuring
Stephane Grappelli, Violin)/The Girl Friend (featuring Stephane Grappelli,
Violin)/Old Grey Bonnet.

Wednesday, 25 October 1944 PIANO PARADE
11.45
Broadcast live from the BBC Studios, London
Over AEFP
Please/Jealous/Cocktails for Two/I Surrender Dear/Paper Doll/Smoke Gets in
Your Eyes.

Thursday, 26 October 1944 CANADA SWING SHOW
17.15
Broadcast live from the BBC Studios, London
Over AEFP
Compère: Pvt. Dick Misener
Exactly Like You/Georgia -VR- Joanne Dallas/Somebody Loves Me/My
Melancholy Baby -VR- Paul Carpenter/I Can't Give You Anything But Love/
For the First Time -VR- Joanne Dallas/I May be Wrong/San Fernando Valley
-VR- Paul Carpenter/Five Foot Two.

Friday, 27 October 1944 CANADA SING SHOW
21.05
Broadcast live from the BBC Studios, London
Over AEFP
Of Thee I Sing -VR- Chorus/A Pretty Girl is Like a Melody -VR-
Chorus/Drums in My Heart -VR- Chorus/Goodnight Soldier -VR-Chorus.

Saturday, 28 October 1944 CANADA DANCE BAND
08.25
(Pre-recorded Friday, 27 October 1944 — BBC Disc No. TLO 63419)
Over AEFP
Compère: Pvt. Dick Misener
Lullaby of Broadway/Humpty Dumpty Heart -VR- Joanne Dallas/Sweet
Georgia Brown/As Long as You're Not in Love with Anyone Else -VR- Paul
Carpenter/Body and Soul/Dolores -VR- Paul Carpenter/Tipperary/It Could
Happen to You -VR- Joanne Dallas/The Night we Called it a Day/One
O'Clock Jump.

Monday, 30 October 1944 CANADA SHOW
20.30
Broadcast live from the Queensbury All Services Club, Soho, London
Over AEFP
Compères: Cpl. Wilf Davidson, Gerry Wilmot, Pvt. Dick Misener
We Saw the Sea -VR- Chorus/When Johnny Comes Marching Home/One
Alone -VR- Paul Carpenter/Symphonette – 'The Valiant Little Tailor'

(Narrator for Symphonette — Sgt. G. Stuart)/Small Fry -VR- Joanne Dallas/ Sweet Sue/You and the Night and the Music/Till Men Again are Free -VR- Chorus.

Tuesday, 31 October 1944   CANADA GUEST SHOW
17.15
Broadcast live from the BBC Studios, London
Over AEFP
Featuring: Canadian Army Radio Orchestra, conducted by Gnr. Bruce Campbell
Guest Stars: Anne Lenner, Ronald Chesney, Lt. Marian Signunt, Lt. Kolac Zkowski
Compère: Capt. F. J. Lynch
Ja Da/Don't Sweetheart Me -VR- Anne Lenner/I'll Walk Alone -VR- Anne Lenner/I'll be Seeing You -VR- Anne Lenner/When Johnny Comes Marching Home/All or Nothing at All (featuring Ronald Chesney, Harmonica)/Flight of the Bumble Bee (featuring Ronald Chesney, Harmonica)/You and the Night and the Music/Tomorrow -VR- Marian Signunt (accomp. by Kolac Zkowski)/Maciek -VR- Marian Signunt (accomp. by Kolac Zkowski)/ Polish Mountaineers Song -VR- Marian Signunt (accomp. by Kolac Zkowski)/Loch Lomond -VR- Marian Signunt (accomp. by Kolac Zkowski)/Chopsticks/Old Man River.

Wednesday, 1 November 1944   PIANO PARADE
11.45
Broadcast live from the BBC Studios, London
Over AEFP
It Had To Be You/Without a Word of Warning/Beside a Babbling Brook/You Belong to My Heart/Smoke Gets in Your Eyes/Peg of My Heart.

Thursday, 2 November 1944   CANADA SWING SHOW
17.15
Broadcast live from the BBC Studios, London
Over AEFP
Compère: Pvt. Dick Misener
Digga Digga Do/Small Fry -VR- Joanne Dallas/I Found a New Baby/Parlez-Moi d'Amour -VR- Paul Carpenter/Tea for Two/Blue Skies -VR- Joanne Dallas/ Way Down Yonder in New Orleans/Somebody Else is Taking My Place -VR-Paul Carpenter/Lady be Good.

Friday, 3 November 1944   CANADA SING SHOW
21.05
Broadcast live from the BBC Studios, London
Over AEFP
Compère: Cpl. Wilf Davidson
Oh! How I Hate to Get Up in the Morning -VR- Chorus/Sometime -VR-Chorus/Can't You Hear Me Calling Caroline -VR- W. Goertz/Dancing in the Dark -VR- Chorus.

Saturday, 4 November 1944   CANADA DANCE BAND
08.25
(Pre-recorded at the BBC Studios, London, on Friday, 3 November 1944 —
BBC Disc No. TLO 64170)
Compère: Pvt. Dick Misener
Caribbean Clipper/Day In Day Out -VR- Joanne Dallas/Promenade/I
Surrender Dear/Too Much in Love -VR- Paul Carpenter/Margie/That Soldier
of Mine -VR- Joanne Dallas/Exactly Like You/I'm Making Believe -VR- Paul
Carpenter/The Sheik of Araby/Don't Blame Me/Out of Nowhere.

Monday, 6 November 1944   CANADA SHOW
20.30
Broadcast live from the Queensbury All Services Club, London
Over AEFP
Guest Star: Gwen Catley
Compères: Gerry Wilmot, Pvt. Dick Misener, De B. Holly
Tico Tico -VR- Chorus/My Blue Heaven/People Like You and Me -VR-
Joanne Dallas/Lo, Hear the Gentle Lark -VR- Gwen Catley/Good News/Milk-
man Keep Those Bottles Quiet -VR- Paul Carpenter/Medley: There's a Long
Trail Awinding; Keep the Home Fires Burning/I Give Thanks For You -VR-
Gwen Catley/A Brown Bird Singing -VR- Gwen Catley/Love is on the Air
Tonight -VR- Chorus.

Tuesday, 7 November 1944   CANADA GUEST SHOW
17.15
Broadcast live from the BBC Studios, London
Over AEFP
Guest Stars: Unknown
Compère: Unknown
Details remain unknown.

Wednesday, 8 November 1944   PIANO PARADE
11.45
Broadcast live from the BBC Studios, London
Over AEFP
Details remain unknown.

Thursday, 9 November 1944   CANADA SWING SHOW
17.15
Broadcast live from the BBC Studios, London
Over AEFP
Compère: Cpl. Wilf Davidson
Indiana/I'll Get By -VR- Joanne Dallas/I Can't Give You Anything but Love/
So You're the One -VR- Paul Carpenter/Is You Is or Is You Ain't My Baby
-VR- Cuth Knowlton/What is this Thing Called Love -VR- Joanne Dallas/
Cherry/How Blue the Night -VR- Paul Carpenter/Lady be Good.

Friday, 10 November 1944   CANADA SING SHOW
21.05
Broadcast live from the BBC Studios, London
Over AEFP
Compère: Cpl. Wilf Davidson
Till Men Again Are Free -VR- Chorus/This is Worth Fighting for -VR- G. I. Harrison/Jerusalem -VR- Chorus.

Saturday, 11 November 1944   CANADA DANCE BAND
08.25
(Pre-recorded at the BBC Studios, London, on Friday, 10 November 1944 — BBC Disc No. TLO 64244)
Compère: Pvt. Dick Misener
That's A-Plenty/Love Me or Leave Me -VR- Joanne Dallas/Ja Da/Ain't Misbehavin'/You Belong to My Heart -VR- Paul Carpenter/I'm Forever Blowing Bubbles/We Mustn't Say Goodbye -VR- Joanne Dallas/Can't You Hear Me Calling Caroline/I'll Walk Alone -VR- Paul Carpenter/Kerry Dance/Softly as in a Morning Sunrise.

Monday, 13 November 1944   CANADA SHOW
20.30
Broadcast live from the Queensbury All Services Club, Soho, London
Over AEFP
Guest Star: L/Cpl. Roger Doucet
Compères: Gerry Wilmot, Cpl. Wilf Davidson, Pvt. Dick Misener
Shoulder to Shoulder -VR- Chorus/In a Little Spanish Town/There's a New World Over the Skyline -VR- Joanne Dallas/Dans Mon Coeur -VR- Roger Doucet/I Can't Give You Anything but Love -VR- Roger Doucet/For Me and My Gal/Everything I Have is Yours -VR- Paul Carpenter/Russian Lullaby/Begin the Beguine/Roses of Picardy -VR- Roger Doucet/You are My Lucky Star -VR- Chorus.

Tuesday, 14 November 1944   CANADA GUEST SHOW
17.15
Broadcast live from the BBC Studios, London
Over AEFP
Guest Stars: Norman Dawn, Emilio, The Edmundo Ross Thumba Band
Compère: Capt. F. J. Lynch
For Me and My Gal/Invitation to the Dance (featuring Emilio, accordion)/The Man I Love (featuring Emilio, Accordion)/Always -VR- Norma Dawn/Long Ago and Far Away -VR- Norma Dawn/I Want to be Happy/Bicycle Built for Two/William Tell Overture (featuring Emilio, Accordion)/Stardust (featuring Emilio, Accordion)/The Song is You -VR- Capt. Cam Ritchie/Tico Tico (featuring Edmundo Ross and his Thumba Band)/Mario La O (featuring Edmundo Ross and his Thumba Band)/Conga Boom (featuring Edmundo Ross and his Thumba Band)/How Could You.

Wednesday, 15 November 1944   PIANO PARADE
11.45
Broadcast live from the BBC Studios, London
Over AEFP
Ain't Misbehavin'/Honolulu Eyes/So Close to Me/Where Was I/If I Didn't
Care/I Don't Want to Set the World on Fire/I Surrender Dear.

Thursday, 16 November 1944   CANADA SWING SHOW
17.15
Broadcast live from the BBC Studios, London
Over AEFP
Compère: Pvt. Dick Misener
China Boy/All of Me -VR- Joanne Dallas/Sweet Sue/Goodnight Wherever You
Are -VR- Paul Carpenter/Somebody Loves Me/Humpty Dumpty Heart -VR-
Joanne Dallas/Ding Dong Daddy/My Melancholy Baby -VR- Paul Carpenter/
What Can I Say Dear.

Friday, 17 November 1944   CANADA SING SHOW
21.05
Broadcast live from the BBC Studios, London
Over AEFP
Compère: Cpl. Wilf Davidson
One Alone -VR- Chorus/The Desert Song -VR- Chorus/Stouthearted Men
-VR- Chorus/Lover Come Back to Me -VR- Chorus.

Saturday, 18 November 1944   CANADA DANCE BAND
08.30
(Pre-recorded at the BBC Studios, London, on Friday, 17 November 1944 —
BBC Disc No. TLO unknown)
Compère: Pvt. Dick Misener
Lullaby of Broadway/It Could Happen to You -VR- Joanne Dallas/Blue
Room/Emaline/This is a Lovely Way to Spend an Evening -VR- Paul
Carpenter/Girl of My Dreams/Don't You Know I Care -VR- Joanne Dallas/
Swanee River/Irresistible You -VR- Paul Carpenter/Someone Rocking My
Dream Boat.

Monday, 20 November 1944   CANADA SHOW
20.30
Broadcast live from the Queensbury All Services Club, Soho, London
Over AEFP
Guest Stars: Sgts. Johnny Wayne and Frank Shuster
Compères: Gerry Wilmot, Cpl. Wilf Davidson, Pvt. Dick Misener
Zing Went the Strings of My Heart -VR- Chorus/Lullaby in Rhythm/Dark-
town Strutter's Ball/Sketch with Sgts. Wayne and Shuster, Gerry Wilmot,
Orchestra and Chorus (How About a Cheer for the Navy) -VR- Wayne and
Shuster/April Showers/Il Suffit D'une Petite Femme -VR- Paul Carpenter/To a
Wild Rose/Oh! How I Hate to Get Up in the Morning -VR- Chorus.

Tuesday, 21 November 1944   CANADA GUEST SHOW
17.15
Broadcast live from the BBC Studios, London
Over AEFP
Guest Stars: Unknown
Compère: Cpl. Wilf Davidson
Details remain unknown.

Wednesday, 22 November 1944   PIANO PARADE
11.45
Broadcast live from the BBC Studios, London
Over AEFP
You'll Never Know/Out of Nowhere/All the Things You Are/I Hear a
Rhapsody/Stardust/Serenade in Blue.

Thursday, 23 November 1944   CANADA SWING SHOW
17.15
Broadcast live from the BBC Studios, London
Over AEFP
Compère: Pvt. Dick Misener
Ain't She Sweet/Exactly Like You/I Never Mention Your Name -VR- Paul
Carpenter/I Never Knew/Georgia on My Mind -VR- Joanne Dallas/After
You've Gone/Forget-me-nots in Your Eyes -VR- Paul Carpenter/Pack Up
Your Troubles.

Friday, 24 November 1944   CANADA SING SHOW
21.05
Broadcast live from the BBC Studios, London
Over AEFP
Compère: Sgt. Wilf Davidson
What Do You Do in the Infantry -VR- Chorus/The World is Waiting for the
Sunrise -VR- Chorus/The Drum -VR- Chorus/The Victory Polka -VR-Chorus.

Saturday, 25 November 1944   CANADA DANCE BAND
08.30
(Pre-recorded at the BBC Studios, London, on Friday, 24 November 1944 —
BBC Disc No. TLO 64764)
Over AEFP
Compère: Pvt. Dick Misener
Lullaby in Rhythm/I'll Pray for You -VR- Joanne Dallas/Exactly Like You/
Don't Blame Me/Confessin'/You Fascinating You -VR- Paul Carpenter/At
Sundown/Humpty Dumpty Heart/Tipperary -VR- Joanne Dallas/I'm Making
Believe -VR- Paul Carpenter/I Would do Anything for You.

Sunday, 26 November 1944   AEF SPECIAL
17.15-17.50
Broadcast live from the Queensbury All Services Club, Soho, London
Over AEFP

Featuring: The Canada Show Orchestra and Chorus, conducted by Captain Robert Farnon, Pat Kirkwood, John Bucklemaster, US Army
Compère: Sgt. Keith Jameson, US Army
Producer: Sgt. Syl Binkin, US Army
Script by: Sgt. Varner Paulsen, US Army
Opening Theme (Red White and Blue)/Zing Went the Strings of My Heart -VR- Chorus/Swinging on a Star -VR- Pat Kirkwood/You and the Night and the Music/San Fernando Valley -VR- Paul Carpenter/I've Got the World on a String -VR- Pat Kirkwood/Pvt. John Buckmaster – Act – Dr Anthony and Nazi Film/Stomping at the Savoy/Medley: Long Ago and Far Away -VR-Pat Kirkwood; It Had to be You -VR- Pat Kirkwood; Time Alone will Tell -VR- Pat Kirkwood/Closing Theme (Red, White and Blue).

Monday, 27 November 1944 CANADA SHOW
20.30
Broadcast live from the Queensbury All Services Club, Soho, London
Over AEFP
Guest Star: Jack Warner
Compères: Gerry Wilmot, Sgt. Wilf Davidson, Pvt. Dick Misener
Big Broad Smile -VR- Chorus/I Would do Anything for You/Swinging on a Star -VR- Paul Carpenter/You Can't Help Laughing -VR- Jack Warner/Good Ship Ballyhoo -VR- Jack Warner/The Ranch is Gone -VR- Jack Warner/The Girl I Left Behind Me/Confessing/All My Life -VR- Joanne Dallas/The Man I Love/Dancing in the Dark -VR- Chorus.

Tuesday, 28 November 1944 CANADA GUEST SHOW
17.15
Broadcast live from the BBC Studios, London
Over AEFP
Guest Stars: Cherry Lind, Carroll Gibbons, George Armitage
Compère: Capt. F. J. Lynch
April Showers/Tales from Vienna -VR- Cherry Lind/Spring will be a Little Late this Year -VR- Cherry Lind (accomp. by Pvt. Dick Misener, Piano)/ Exactly Like You/Songs of Songs -VR- George Armitage/Those You Have Loved -VR- George Armitage/On the Air (featuring Carroll Gibbons, Piano)/Somebody Loves Me (featuring Carroll Gibbons, Piano)/Someone to Watch Over Me (featuring Carroll Gibbons, Piano)/They Can't Take that Away (featuring Carroll Gibbons, Piano)/My One and Only (featuring Carroll Gibbons, Piano)/Swanee River/Night and Day -VR- Cherry Lind/It Had to be You (featuring Carroll Gibbons, Piano)/I'll be Around (featuring Carroll Gibbons, Piano)/Donkey Serenade (featuring Carroll Gibbons, Piano)/Today is Ours -VR- George Armitage/Someone is Rocking My Dreamboat.

Wednesday, 29 November 1944 PIANO PARADE
11.45
Broadcast live from the BBC Studios, London
Over AEFP
Details remain unknown.

106

Thursday, 30 November 1944   CANADA SWING SHOW
17.15
Broadcast live from the BBC Studios, London
Over AEFP
Compère: Pvt. Dick Misener
You Can Depend on Me -VR- Cuth Knowlton/Am I Blue -VR- Joanne Dallas/
The Girl Friend/Why Don't We do this More Often -VR- Paul Carpenter/
Muskrat Ramble/Can't Get Indiana Off My Mind -VR- Joanne Dallas/There'll
be Some Changes Made/Parlez-Moi D'Amour -VR- Paul Carpenter/The Sheik
of Araby -VR- Cuth Knowlton.

Friday, 1 December 1944   CANADA SING SHOW
21.05
Broadcast live from the BBC Studios, London
Over AEFP
Compère: Sgt. Wilf Davidson
Big Broad Smile -VR- Chorus/Now I Know -VR- Chorus/San Fernando Valley
-VR- Chorus/I'll Walk Alone -VR- Chorus.

Saturday, 2 December 1944   CANADA DANCE BAND
09.30 - 10.00
(Pre-recorded at the BBC Studios, London, on Friday, 1 December 1944 —
BBC Disc No. TLO 64958)
Over AEFP
Compère: Pvt. Dick Misener
Stomping at the Savoy/Time Waits for No One -VR- Joanne Dallas/On the
Alamo/Holiday for Strings/Spring Will Be a Little Late This Year -VR- Paul
Carpenter/Caribbean Clipper/People Like You and Me -VR- Joanne Dallas/
Humoresque/Dolores -VR- Paul Carpenter/One O'Clock Jump.

Monday, 4 December 1944   CANADA SHOW
20.30
Broadcast live from the Queensbury All Services Club, Soho, London
Over AEFP
Guest Star: C.S.M. Jimmy Shields
Compères: Gerry Wilmot, Sgt. Wilf Davidson, Pvt. Dick Misener
Three Little Words -VR- Chorus/Humoresque/Now I Know -VR- Joanne
Dallas/Phil The Fluter's Ball (featuring Jimmy Shields)/Something to
Remember You By (featuring Jimmy Shields)/Old Grey Bonnet/Poinciana
-VR- Paul Carpenter/Cocktails for Two/I'll Take You Home Again Kathleen
-VR- Jimmy Shields/Somebody Loves Me -VR- Chorus.

Tuesday, 5 December 1944   CANADA GUEST SHOW
17.15
Broadcast live from the BBC Studios, London
Over AEFP
Guest Stars: Derek Roy, Triss Henderson, Roland Peachey
Compère: Capt. F. J. Lynch

Caribbean Clipper/Medley (featuring Roland Peachey, Guitar): Aloha; Rendezvous in Honolulu; Goodbye Hawaii/Begin the Beguine -VR- Triss Henderson (featuring Roland Peachey, Guitar)/Is You Is or Is You Ain't My Baby? -VR- Triss Henderson (featuring Roland Peachey, Guitar)/Cow Cow Boogie -VR- Triss Henderson/Good News/'Patter' – Derek Roy/Doctor Roy -VR- Derek Roy/On the Alamo/I'll Walk Alone -VR- Triss Henderson/ Goodbye Now -VR- Triss Henderson and Derek Roy/Hawaiian War Chant (featuring Roland Peachey, Guitar)/The Girl I Left Behind Me.

Wednesday, 6 December 1944   **PIANO PARADE**
11.45
Broadcast live from the BBC Studios, London
Over AEFP
I'm Getting Sentimental Over You/Sophisticated Lady/April in My Heart/ Kind o' Lonesome/A Little Kiss at Twilight/The Man I Love.

Thursday, 7 December 1944   **CANADA SWING SHOW**
17.15
Broadcast live from the BBC Studios, London
Over AEFP
Compère: Pvt. Dick Misener
Shine/It's the Talk of the Town -VR- Joanne Dallas/I Can't Give You Anything But Love/Come Out, Come Out Wherever You Are -VR- Paul Carpenter/I Found a New Baby/Small Fry -VR- Joanne Dallas/Digga Digga Do/Goodnight Wherever You Are -VR- Paul Carpenter/When I Take My Sugar to Tea -VR- Cuth Knowlton.

Friday, 8 December 1944   **CANADA SING SHOW**
21.05
Broadcast live from the BBC Studios, London
Over AEFP
Compère: Sgt. Wilf Davidson
Czechoslovakian Dance Song -VR- Chorus/And Russia is Her Name -VR- Chorus/Medley: Song of the Volga Boatmen -VR- Chorus; Dark Eyes -VR- Chorus (featuring Dick Misener, Piano and J. Barati, Violin); Red Army March Song -VR- Chorus; Soviet Land so Dear to Every Toiler -VR-Chorus.

Saturday, 9 December 1944   **CANADA DANCE BAND**
09.30
(Pre-recorded at the BBC Studios, London, on Friday, 8 December 1944 — BBC Disc No. TLO 65253)
Compère: Pvt. Dick Misener
In a Little Spanish Town/As Long as There's Music -VR- Joanne Dallas/ That's A-Plenty/I Surrender Dear/Where the Blue Begins -VR- Paul Carpenter/You're Driving Me Crazy/Don't You Know I Care -VR- Joanne Dallas/Can't We be Friends/Unknown Title.

Monday, 11 December 1944   CANADA SHOW
20.30
Broadcast live from the Queensbury All Services Club, Soho, London
Over AEFP
(Repeated on 'Morning After', Tuesday, 12 December 1944, 10.01-10.30
a.m. — BBC Disc No. SWN 19636)
Guest Star: Miss Margaret Eaves
Compères: Gerry Wilmot, Sgt. Wilf Davidson, Pvt. Dick Misener
S'Wonderful -VR- Chorus/Isle of Capri/You Fascinating You -VR- Joanne
Dallas/The Stars Look Down -VR- Margaret Eaves/One Day When We Were
Young -VR- Margaret Eaves/Old Man River/By the River of Roses -VR- Gerry
Travers/You and the Night and the Music/Birds Sang in the Rain -VR-
Margaret Eaves/Big Broad Smile -VR- Chorus.

Tuesday, 12 December 1944   CANADA GUEST SHOW
17.15
Broadcast live from the Paris Cinema, Lower Regent Street, London
Over AEFP
Guest Stars: Frank Weir, Anne Lenner, Michael Moore (Comedian)
Compère: Capt. F. J. Lynch
Sunny/It Could Happen to You -VR- Anne Lenner/Swinging on a Star -VR-
Anne Lenner/Clarinet à la King (featuring Frank Weir, Clarinet)/I Would Do
Anything for You/Comedy Spot (featuring Michael Moore)/When You're
Away -VR- Cam Ritchie/I Get a Kick Out of You/When They Ask About
You -VR- Anne Lenner/Clarinet Concerto (featuring Frank Weir, Clarinet)/
Humoresque.

Wednesday, 13 December 1944   PIANO PARADE
11.45
Broadcast live from the BBC Studios, London
Over AEFP
The Very Thought of You/You and the Night and the Music/All of Me/It's a
Crying Shame/I Can't Escape from You/The Hour of Parting.

Thursday, 14 December 1944   CANADA SWING SHOW
17.15
Broadcast live from the BBC Studios, London
Over AEFP
Compère: Pvt. Dick Misener
Five Foot Two/My Favourite Dream -VR- Joanne Dallas/I'm Gonna Sit Right
Down and Write Myself a Letter/Have Yourself a Merry Little Christmas -VR-
Paul Carpenter/What Can I Say Dear/When We're Alone -VR- Joanne Dallas/
Opus and a Half/Echo of a Serenade -VR- Paul Carpenter/After You've Gone.

Friday, 15 December 1944   CANADA SING SHOW
21.05
Broadcast live from the BBC Studios, London
Over AEFP
Compère: Sgt. Wilf Davidson
Details remain unknown.

Saturday, 16 December 1944   CANADA DANCE BAND
09.30
(Pre-recorded at the BBC Studios, London, on Friday, 15 December 1944 —
BBC Disc No. TLO 66004)
Compère: Pvt. Dick Misener
Song of the Volga Boatmen/A Fellow on a Furlough -VR- Joanne Dallas/On
the Sunny Side of the Street/Ain't Misbehavin'/Dance with a Dolly -VR- Paul
Carpenter/Somebody Loves Me/I'll be Seeing You -VR- Joanne Dallas/Beyond
the Blue Horizon/You Belong to My Heart -VR- Paul Carpenter/Ja Da.

Monday, 18 December 1944   CANADA SHOW
20.30
Broadcast live from the Queensbury All Services Club, Soho, London
Over AEFP
Guest Star: Leslie Hutchinson
Compères: Gerry Wilmot, Sgt. Wilf Davidson, Pvt. Dick Misener
We Saw the Sea -VR- Chorus/Song of the Volga Boatmen/As Long as There's
Music -VR- Joanne Dallas/No One Else Will Do -VR- Leslie Hutchinson/
Lovely Day -VR- Leslie Hutchinson/The Army Air Corps Song/The Ranch
has Gone -VR- Jerry Travers/To a Wild Rose/A Kiss in the Night -VR- Leslie
Hutchinson/Zing Went the Strings of My Heart -VR- Chorus.

Tuesday, 19 December 1944   CANADA GUEST SHOW
17.15
Broadcast live from the Paris Cinema, Lower Regent Street, London
Over AEFP
Guest Stars: Helen Clare, Stanley Andrews, Jack and Eddy Eden
Compère: Capt. F. J. Lynch
The Girl I Left Behind Me/Love Must be Free -VR- Helen Clare/Begin the
Beguine -VR- Helen Clare/The Sparks Fly Onwards (featuring Stanley
Andrews, Violin)/Sweet and Low (featuring Stanley Andrews, Violin)/Song of
the Volga Boatmen/Original Music -VR- Jack and Eddy (accomp. by Dick
Misener, Piano)/Chopsticks/All or Nothing at All -VR- Helen Claire/Poor
Butterfly (featuring Stanley Andrews, Violin)/Beyond the Blue Horizon.

Wednesday, 20 December 1944   PIANO PARADE
11.45
Broadcast live from the BBC Studios, London
Over AEFP
I'll Never Let a Day Pass By/Manhattan Serenade/I'll Walk Alone/I Don't
Want to Walk Without You/Take it from There.

Thursday, 21 December 1944   CANADA SWING SHOW
17.15
Broadcast live from the BBC Studios, London
Over AEFP
Compère: Pvt. Dick Misener
Button Up Your Overcoat/Way Down Yonder in New Orleans -VR- Cuth

110

Knowlton/I Never Knew/A Fellow on a Furlough -VR- Paul Carpenter/Blue Skies/I May be Wrong -VR- Cuth Knowlton/Don't Blame Me/Texas Polka -VR- Paul Carpenter/The Kerry Dance.

Friday, 22 December 1944   CANADA SING SHOW
21.05
Broadcast live from the BBC Studios, London
Over AEFP
Compère: Sgt. Wilf Davidson
Good King Wenceslas -VR- Chorus/I Saw Three Ships -VR- Chorus/Nouvelle Agréable -VR- Chorus/Hark the Herald Angels Sing -VR- Chorus.

Saturday, 23 December 1944   CANADA DANCE BAND
09.30
(Pre-recorded at the BBC Studios, London, on Friday, 22 December 1944 — BBC Disc No. TLO 66112)
Over AEFP
Compère: Pvt. Dick Misener
My Blue Heaven/The Sheik of Araby -VR- Cuth Knowlton/Emaline/All of Me/Come Out, Come Out Wherever You Are -VR- Paul Carpenter/Swanee River/You Can Depend On Me -VR- Cuth Knowlton/By the River St Marie/ Spring Will Be a Little Late This Year -VR- Paul Carpenter/Isle of Capri.

Monday, 25 December 1944   AEF CHRISTMAS SHOW
18.04-18.30   CHRISTMAS CANADA SHOW
Broadcast live from the Queensbury All Services Club, Soho, London
Over AEFP
Special Guest Star: Gwen Catley
Compère: Gerry Wilmot
Announcer: A/C2 Ronald Waldman RAF
Opening Theme (March Along, Joe Soldier -VR- Chorus)/The Time is Now -VR- Chorus/You, Fascinating You -VR- Joanne Dallas/Humoresque/Caro Nomee -VR- Gwen Catley/Jubilate -VR- Gwen Catley/Symphonette − The Valiant Little Tailor (Narrator: Gil Stewart) -comp- Robert Farnon/ Closing Theme (March Along, Joe Soldier).

Broadcast live from the Queensbury   AEF CHRISTMAS SHOW
All Services Club, Soho, London   GROUND ROUND-UP
(with pre-recorded insert from the Olympia Theatre, Paris)
Over AEFP, BBC Home Service,
BBC North American Service (relayed to NBC (USA) and CBC (Canada))
Compères: A/C2 Ronald Waldman RAF, Gerry Wilmot, W/O Paul Dudley, Lt. Don Haynes
Canadian AEF Medley: Tipperary; Keep the Home Fires Burning; Pack Up Your Troubles/Cyril Fletcher -acc- Canadian Band − 'Odd Odes': Nellie Quaint; The Blasted Heath/British AEF Band − Lazy Day/Jackie Hunter -acc- British AEF Band − 'The Life of the Party'/American AEF Band − Oranges and Lemons -VR- JD, CC -arr- Jerry Gray/Combined bands and audiences − Auld Lang Syne and Close.

Tuesday, 26 December 1944　　　　　　　CANADA GUEST SHOW
17.15
Broadcast live from the Paris Cinema, Lower Regent Street, London
Over AEFP
Guest Stars: Kay Young, Lorna Martin, King and Gibson (comedians)
Compère: Capt. F. J. Lynch
Army Air Corps Song/Dance of the Tumblers (featuring Lorna Martin, Accordion)/A Kiss in the Night (featuring Lorna Martin, Accordion)/ Medley: Smoke Gets in Your Eyes -VR- Kay Young; I'm Old Fashioned -VR- Kay Young; All the Things You Are -VR- Kay Young/By the River St Marie/ Original Material (King and Gibson)/Wagon Wheels -VR- Cam Ritchie/ The Flight of the Bumble Bee (featuring Lorna Martin, Accordion)/Day Break -VR- Kay Young/One O'Clock Jump.

Tuesday, 26 December 1944　　　　　　ALI SADSACK AND THE
20.15-21.00　　　　　　　　　　　FORTY QUARTERMASTERS
Broadcast live from the Queensbury All Services Club, Soho, London
Over AEFP

A SPECIAL PANTOMIME FOR THE AEF

Featuring:

Sgt. Dick Dudley	Pvt. Ali Sadsack, US AAC
Joan Young	The Fairy Queen
Pvt. Joanne Dallas	Cpl. Mary Morgan, CWAC
Sqd/Ldr Richard Murdoch	Sqd/Ldr Hereward Prince-Goodhart
W/Cdr Kenneth Horne	An Air Vice-Marshall
Sgt. Leo Kaye	Sgt. Ed Cassim, US AAC

With the Forty Quartermasters: Cpl. Alex Munro, Cpl. Dick Crawford, Sgt. Gil Stuart, Pvt. Ken Heady, Gerry Wilmot and The Canada Show Chorus, led by Pvt. Cliff McAree
With Geraldo and his Orchestra
Opening Fanfare/Fairy Queen Motif/The Curtain Rises/Opening Chorus -VR- Canada Show Chorus/I'll Be Seeing You -VR- Joanne Dallas/The Quack Quack Song -VR- Richard Murdoch/Potato Blues -VR- Dick Dudley/Saddlebags Spot (featuring Cpl. Saddlebags and the AEF Ranchhouse Gang)/ Quartermaster's Song -VR- Canada Show Chorus/Fairy Queen Motif/ 'Patter' – Richard Murdoch and Kenneth Horne/Because/Much Binding in the Marsh/ Fairy Queen Motif/Quartermaster's Song -VR- Canada Show Chorus/ I'll Pray For You -VR- Joanne Dallas/Fairy Queen Motif/ Quartermaster's Song/Flagwaver/I Love a Lassie/'Patter' – Alex Munro/ Fanfare/Happy Wedding Day -VR- Chorus/Finale (with A/C2 Ronald Waldman RAF and the entire cast).

Wednesday, 27 December 1944　　　　　　　PIANO PARADE
11.45
Broadcast live from the BBC Studios, London
Over AEFP

Poor Butterfly/Without a Word of Warning/Smoke Gets in Your Eyes/My Prayer/Ain't Misbehavin'/Body and Soul.

Thursday, 28 December 1944   CANADA SWING SHOW
17.15
Broadcast live from the BBC Studios, London
Over AEFP
Compère: Pvt. Dick Misener
Ain't She Sweet -VR- Cuth Knowlton/Stormy Weather -VR- Gerry Travers/ Exactly Like You/Where the Blue Begins -VR- Paul Carpenter/Somebody Loves Me/Blue Skies -VR- Gerry Travers/Lamplighters Serenade -VR- Paul Carpenter/I'll Always be in Love with You.

Friday, 29 December 1944   CANADA SING SHOW
21.05
Broadcast live from the BBC Studios, London
Over AEFP
Compère: Sgt. Wilf Davidson
All for One -VR- Chorus/S'Wonderful -VR- Chorus/Rose O'Day -VR- Chorus/Zing Went the Strings of My Heart -VR- Chorus/More Than You Know -VR- Chorus.

Saturday, 30 December 1944   CANADA DANCE BAND
09.30-10.00
(Pre-recorded at the BBC Studios, London, on Friday, 29 December 1944 — BBC Disc No. TLO 66454)
Over AEFP
Compère: Pvt. Dick Misener
'C' Jam Blues/Time Waits for No One -VR- Gerry Travers/I Would do Anything for You/Holiday for Strings/My Melancholy Baby -VR- Paul Carpenter/Bell Bottom Boogie/You Go to My Head -VR- Gerry Travers/ Lullaby in Rhythm/People Like You and Me -VR- Paul Carpenter/Stardust.

Monday, 1 January 1945   CANADA SHOW
20.30
(Pre-recorded at the Queensbury All Services Club, Soho, London, on Monday, 18 December 1944 — BBC Disc No. SOX 42759)
Compères: Gerry Wilmot, Sgt. Wilf Davidson, Pvt. Dick Misener
Love is in the Air Tonight -VR- Chorus/I Would Do Anything For You/There's a New World Over the Skyline -VR- Joanne Dallas/Symphonette – The Three Bears (Narrator – Sgt. Gil Stuart)/Ding Dong Daddy/By the River of Roses -VR- Gerry Travers/Night and Day/Big Broad Smile -VR- Chorus.

Tuesday, 2 January 1945   CANADA GUEST SHOW
17.15
Broadcast live from the BBC Studios, London
Over AEFP

Canadian Band of the AEF replaced on this broadcast by Canadian Air Forces Band.

Wednesday, 3 January 1945   PIANO PARADE
11.45
(Pre-recorded at the BBC Studios, London, on Wednesday, 27 December 1944 — BBC Disc No. SLO 67315)
Over AEFP
Tea for Two/Where Was I/Soliloquy/If I Had My Way/If I Had You/When Day is Done.

Thursday, 4 January 1945   CANADA SWING SHOW
17.15
(Pre-recorded at the BBC Studios, London, on Thursday, 30 November 1944 — BBC Disc No. SWN 19714)
Compère: Pvt. Dick Misener
Pack Up Your Troubles/My Ideal -VR- Joanne Dallas/Sweet Lorraine/Pretty Kitty Blue Eyes -VR- Paul Carpenter/Way Down Yonder in New Orleans/Blue Skies -VR- Joanne Dallas/The Girl Friend/In Times Like These -VR- Paul Carpenter/Tipperary.

Friday, 5 January 1945   CANADA SING SHOW
21.05
(Pre-recorded at the BBC Studios, London, on Friday, 1 December 1944 — BBC Disc No. SOX 42745)
Over AEFP
Hallelujah! -VR- Chorus/Nobody Knows the Trouble I've Seen -VR- Chorus/Kentucky Babe -VR- Chorus/Me and My Little Banjo -VR- Chorus.

Saturday, 6 January 1945   CANADA DANCE BAND
09.30
(Pre-recorded at the BBC Studios, London, on Friday, 1 December 1944 — BBC Disc No. TLO 65668)
Over AEFP
Compère: Pvt. Dick Misener
Lullaby of Broadway/Humpty Dumpty Heart -VR- Joanne Dallas/Body and Soul/Dolores -VR- Paul Carpenter/Tipperary/It Could Happen to You -VR- Joanne Dallas/Vilia/The Night We Called it a Day -VR- Paul Carpenter/One O'Clock Jump.

Monday, 8 January 1945   CANADA SHOW
20.30
Broadcast live from the Queensbury All Services Club, Soho, London
Over AEFP
Guest Star: Kay Cavendish
Compères: Gerry Wilmot, Sgt. Wilf Davidson, Pvt. Dick Misener
You are My Lucky Star -VR- Chorus/Piccadilly Commotion -comp- Robert Farnon/Georgia on My Mind -VR- Joanne Dallas/Kitten-on-the-keys — Theme (featuring Kay Cavendish, Piano)/Is You Is or Is You Ain't My Baby?

(featuring Kay Cavendish, Piano)/Boogie in the Groove (featuring Kay Cavendish, Piano)/Kitten-on-the-keys – Theme (featuring Kay Cavendish, Piano)/Captains of the Clouds/I Sent You a Kiss in the Night -VR- Gerry Travers/Meditation – Thais/Tico Tico (featuring Kay Cavendish, Piano)/Come Out, Come Out Wherever You Are (featuring Kay Cavendish, Piano)/Spring Will Be a Little Late This Year (featuring Kay Cavendish, Piano)/ S'Wonderful -VR- Chorus.

Tuesday, 9 January 1945   CANADA GUEST SHOW
17.15
Broadcast live from the Paris Cinema, Lower Regent Street, London
Over AEFP
Guest Stars: Wren Audrey Pullin RN, Johnny Green, Derek Roy (comedian)
Compère: Capt. F. J. Lynch
Captains of the Clouds/Some Other Time -VR- Johnny Green/Swingin' on a Star -VR- Johnny Green/'C' Jam Blues/Always -VR- Audrey Pullin/Thoughts -VR- Audrey Pullin/Original 'Patter' – Derek Roy/The Trolley Song -VR- Derek Roy/Oh! Susannah/Friend of Mine -VR- Cam Ritchie/Piccadilly Commotion -comp- Robert Farnon /You are Love -VR- Audrey Pullin/ Where or When -VR- Johnny Green/You're Driving Me Crazy.

Wednesday, 10 January 1945   PIANO PARADE
11.45
Broadcast live from the BBC Studios, London
Over AEFP
Jealous/I Surrender Dear/You Belong to My Heart/Honolulu Eyes/So Close to Me/Cocktails for Two.

Thursday, 11 January 1945   CANADA SWING SHOW
17.15
Broadcast live from the BBC Studios, London
Over AEFP
Compère: Pvt. Dick Misener
Sweet Sue/May I Love You Again -VR- Gerry Travers/There'll be Some Changes Made/I Surrender Dear -VR- Paul Carpenter/Who's Sorry Now/Am I Blue -VR- Gerry Travers/Ding Dong Daddy/Goodnight Wherever You Are -VR- Paul Carpenter/You can Depend on Me -VR- Cuth Knowlton/Back Home in Indiana.

Friday, 12 January 1945   CANADA SING SHOW
21.05
(Pre-recorded at the BBC Studios, London, on Thursday, 11 January 1945 — BBC Disc No. SLO 67945)
Over AEFP
Compère: Sgt. Wilf Davidson
Give a Cheer for the Navy -VR- Chorus/Blow the Man Down -VR- Chorus/ What Do You Do with a Drunken Sailor -VR- Chorus/Les Berceaux -VR- G. Lalande/We Saw the Sea -VR- Chorus.

Saturday, 13 January 1945   CANADA DANCE BAND
09.30
(Pre-recorded at the BBC Studios, London, on Friday, 12 January 1945 —
BBC Disc No. DLO 67484)
Over AEFP
Compère: L/Cpl. Dick Misener
Piccadilly Commotion -comp- Capt. Robert Farnon/So Little Time -VR-Joanne
Dallas/Someone's Rocking My Dreamboat/Tunisian Trail/Je Tire Ma
Reverence -VR- Paul Carpenter/Deed I Do/Time Waits for No One -VR-
Joanne Dallas/When I Grow Too Old to Dream/Dance with a Dolly -VR-Paul
Carpenter/At Sundown.

Monday, 15 January 1945   CANADA SHOW
20.30
Broadcast live from the Queensbury All Services Club, Soho, London
Over AEFP
Guest Star: Lorna Martin
Compères: Gerry Wilmot, Sgt. Wilf Davidson, L/Cpl. Dick Misener
Pack Up Your Troubles -VR- Chorus/Lullaby in Rhythm/My Prayer -VR-
Joanne Dallas/Andante and Rondo Capriccioso (featuring Lorna Martin,
Concertina)/Some Other Time -VR- Gerry Travers/Good News/To a Wild
Rose/Stardust (featuring Lorna Martin, Concertina)/Mosquito (featuring Lorna
Martin, Concertina)/The Time is Now -VR- Chorus.

Tuesday, 16 January 1945   CANADA GUEST SHOW
17.15
Broadcast live from the Paris Cinema, Lower Regent Street, London
Over AEFP
Guest Stars: Inga Anderson, Cpl. Jack Powers, US Army, Stephane Grappelli
Compère: Capt. F. J. Lynch
Jersey Bounce/See No Evil -VR- Inga Anderson/In Paree, It's Love -VR- Inga
Anderson/Ten Days with Baby (featuring Stephane Grappelli, Violin)/Where
the Blue Begins (featuring Stephane Grappelli, Violin)/Henderson Stomp
(featuring Stephane Grappelli, Violin)/Tunisian Trail/Some Other Time -VR-
Jack Powers/I'll be Around -VR- Jack Powers/April Showers/The Faith I
Have in You -VR- Cam Ritchie/It Had to be You -VR- Inga Anderson/Shine
on Harvest Moon -VR- Inga Anderson/Come Out, Come Out Wherever You
Are -VR- Inga Anderson/Vous Qui Passez Sans Me Voir (featuring Stephane
Grappelli, Violin)/The Girl Friend (featuring Stephane Grappelli, Violin)/What
a Difference a Day Made -VR- Jack Powers/Bicycle Built for Two.

Wednesday, 17 January 1945   PIANO PARADE
11.45
Broadcast live from the BBC Studios, London
Over AEFP
I'll Never Let a Day Pass By/More than You Know/No One Else will Do/
Apple Blossoms in the Rain/I'm Making Believe/Stardust/A Pretty Girl is Like
a Melody.

Thursday, 18 January 1945   CANADA SWING SHOW
17.15
Broadcast live from the BBC Studios, London
Over AEFP
Compère: L/Cpl. Dick Misener
Louise/Keep an Eye on Your Heart -VR- Joanne Dallas/The Band Played On/
Sleepy Time Gal -VR- Paul Carpenter/Alexander's Ragtime Band/When I
Take My Sugar to Tea/Can't Get Indiana Off My Mind -VR- Joanne Dallas/
Digga Digga Do/Don't Blame Me/Come Out, Come Out Wherever You Are
-VR- Paul Carpenter/I Can't Give You Anything but Love.

Friday, 19 January 1945   CANADA SING SHOW
21.05
Broadcast live from the BBC Studios, London
Over AEFP
What Do You Do in the Infantry -VR- Chorus/Night and Day -VR- Chorus/
Oh! Dear What Can the Matter Be -VR- Chorus/Irresistible You -VR- Chorus.

Saturday, 20 January 1945   CANADA DANCE BAND
09.30
(Pre-recorded at the BBC Studios, London, on Friday, 19 January 1945 —
BBC Disc No. TLO 67846)
Compère: L/Cpl. Dick Misener
Hot Chestnuts/Too Much in Love -VR- Joanne Dallas/Can't We be Friends/
Vous Qui Passez Sans Me Voir -VR- Paul Carpenter/Music Makers/A Fellow
on a Furlough -VR- Joanne Dallas/Jersey Bounce/Spring Will Be a Little Late
This Year -VR- Paul Carpenter/My Blue Heaven.

Monday, 22 January 1945   CANADA SHOW
20.30
Broadcast live from the Queensbury All Services Club, Soho, London
Over AEFP
Guest Star: Leading Bandsman Doug Allan
Compères: Gerry Wilmot, Sgt. Wilf Davidson, L/Cpl. Dick Misener
The Empire is Marching -VR- Chorus/Lullaby of Broadway/My Shining Hour
-VR- Joanne Dallas/I Cover the Waterfront (featuring Doug Allan)/Long Ago
and Far Away (featuring Doug Allan)/Liza/Apple Blossoms in the Rain -VR-
Gerry Travers/To a Wild Rose/Time Waits for No One -VR- Cavalry of the
Steppes -VR- Chorus.

Tuesday, 23 January 1945   CANADA GUEST SHOW
17.15
Broadcast live from the Paris Cinema, Lower Regent Street, London
Over AEFP
Guest Stars: Helen Raymond, Robin Richmond, Jackie Hunter
Compère: Capt. F. J. Lynch
Liza/I'll Remember April -VR- Helen Raymond/When They Ask About You

-VR- Helen Raymond/When the Red Red Robin — 'Theme' (featuring Robin Richmond, Organ)/Whistler and his Dog (featuring Robin Richmond, Organ)/Promenade (featuring Robin Richmond, Organ)/Music Makers/Theme — 'You Too Can Be the Life of the Party'/Sketch (featuring Jackie Hunter and F. J. Lynch)/Sam You Made the Pants Too Long -VR- Jackie Hunter/Bell Bottom Boogie/Shortnin' Bread -VR- Cam Ritchie/Medley (featuring Robin Richmond, Organ): Ain't She Sweet; On the Sunny Side of the Street; Avalon/When the Red Red Robin — Theme for Robin Richmond/It Had to Be You -VR- Helen Raymond/Humoresque.

Wednesay, 24 January 1945   PIANO PARADE
11.45
Broadcast live from the BBC Studios, London
Over AEFP
Sophisticated Lady/I've Had This Feeling Before/Ain't Misbehavin'/Body and Soul/Time on My Hands.

Thursday, 25 January 1945   CANADA SWING SHOW
17.15
Broadcast live from the BBC Studios, London
Over AEFP
Compère: L/Cpl. Dick Misener
Details remain unknown.

Friday, 26 January 1945   CANADA SING SHOW
21.05
(Pre-recorded at the BBC Studios, London, on Thursday, 25 January 1945 — BBC Disc No. DLO 68485)
Compère: Sgt. Wilf Davidson
Drums in My Heart -VR- Chorus/Deep River -VR- Chorus/Shortnin' Bread -VR- Pvt. Goertz/Drink to Me Only -VR- Chorus.

Saturday, 27 January 1945   CANADA DANCE BAND
09.30
(Pre-recorded at the BBC Studios, London, on Friday, 26 January, 1945 — BBC Disc No. TLO 68172)
Compère: L/Cpl. Dick Misener
Humoresque/Every Day of My Life -VR- Joanne Dallas/I Would Do Anything For You/Body and Soul/Night and Day -VR- Paul Carpenter/Always/Love Me or Leave Me -VR- Joanne Dallas/When Johnny Comes Marching Home/I'll Walk Alone -VR- Paul Carpenter/'C' Jam Blues.

Monday, 29 January 1945   CANADA SHOW
20.30
Broadcast live from the Queensbury All Services Club, Soho, London
Over AEFP
Guest Star: Lt. Dixie Dean

Compères: Gerry Wilmot, Sgt. Wilf Davidson, L/Cpl. Dick Misener
Love Is On the Air Tonight -VR- Chorus/My Blue Heaven/How Sweet You Are -VR- Joanne Dallas/Dark Eyes (featuring Dixie Dean, Piano Accordion)/Hora Staccato (featuring Dixie Dean)/I Know that You Know/I'm So In Love -VR- Gerry Travers/Deep River/Munitions Train (featuring Dixie Dean)/War Medley: Tipperary; Keep the Home Fires Burning -VR- Chorus; Pack Up Your Troubles.

Tuesday, 30 January 1945   CANADA GUEST SHOW
17.15
Broadcast live from the Paris Cinema, Lower Regent Street, London
Over AEFP
Guest Stars: Eric Winstone, Michel Morel, Maria Parelli
Compère: Capt. F. J. Lynch
I Know that You Know/Spring is in My Heart -VR- Maria Parelli/The Song Is You -VR- Maria Parelli/Stage Coach/Medley (featuring Eric Winstone, Piano): Mirage; Evening; Bottle Party/You and the Night and the Music/ Medley (featuring Michael Morel, Piano): Louise; You Brought a New Kind of Love to Me; I Was Lucky; Valentine; My Love Parade; Le Jardin du Mois de Mai; Sur le Fil/Lullaby of Broadway/Pony Express (featuring Eric Winstone, Accordion)/Oasis (featuring Eric Winstone, Accordion)/Stage Coach (theme for Eric Winstone)/Neapolitan Nights -VR- Cam Ritchie/Sunny/ Darling Je Vous Aime Beaucoup -VR- Michel Morel/Where the Blue Begins -VR- Maria Parelli/Ja Da.

Wednesday, 31 January 1945   PIANO PARADE
11.45
Broadcast live from the BBC Studios, London
Over AEFP
Please/Smoke Gets In Your Eyes/Little Thoughts/I Surrender Dear/ Poor Butterfly.

Thursday, 1 February 1945   CANADA SWING SHOW
17.15
Broadcast live from the BBC Studios, London
Over AEFP
Compère: Unknown
Details remain unknown.

Friday, 2 February 1945   CANADA SING SHOW
21.05
Broadcast live from the BBC Studios, London
Over AEFP
Compère: Sgt. Wilf Davidson
Details remain unknown.

Saturday, 3 February 1945   CANADA DANCE BAND
09.30
(Pre-recorded at the BBC Studios, London, on Friday, 2 February 1945 — BBC Disc No. TLO 68371)

Over AEFP
Compère: L/Cpl. Dick Misener
In a Little Spanish Town/I Go For You -VR- Joanne Dallas/Stars Fell on Alabama/I Surrender Dear/As Long as There's Music -VR- Paul Carpenter/Undecided/Don't You Know I Care -VR- Joanne Dallas/Bell Bottom Boogie/Come Out Wherever You Are -VR- Paul Carpenter/One O'Clock Jump.

Monday, 5 February 1945   CANADA SHOW
20.30
Broadcast live from the Queensbury All Services Club, Soho, London
Over AEFP
Guest Star: Derek Roy
Compères: Gerry Wilmot, Sgt. Wilf Davidson, L/Cpl. Dick Misener
Parody: Ta Ra Ra Boom Der A -VR- Chorus (Lyrics − Gil Stuart)/ Stompin' at the Savoy/A Brown Bird Singing -VR- Joanne Dallas/Theme: 'I Want to be Happy'/Original Patter − Derek Roy/A Dream World is Waiting -VR- Derek Roy/Great Day/I'll be Around -VR- Gerry Travers/I've Got You Under My Skin/Clap Your Hands -VR- Chorus.

Tuesday, 6 February 1945   CANADA GUEST SHOW
17.15
Broadcast live from the Paris Cinema, Lower Regent Street, London
Over AEFP
Guest Stars: Charles Ernesco, Ronald Chesney, Sgt. Bill Smith
Compère: Capt. F. J. Lynch
Always/Dance of the Hours (featuring Ronald Chesney, Harmonica)/A Kiss in the Night -VR- Bill Smith/The Ranch has Gone -VR- Bill Smith/I Would Do Anything for You/Smoke Gets in Your Eyes -VR- Charles Ernesco/Stompin' at the Savoy/There's a New World Over the Skyline -VR- Joanne Dallas/Cherokee (featuring Ronald Chesney, Harmonica)/The Song of the Shirt -VR- Cam Ritchie (Solo Piano − Dick Misener)/Swanee River/Don't Worry Mom -VR- Bill Smith/Two Guitars -VR- Charles Ernesco/Undecided.

Wednesday, 7 February 1945   PIANO PARADE
11.45
Broadcast live from the BBC Studios, London
Over AEFP
Played by: L/Cpl. Dick Misener
I Don't Want to Walk Without You/If I Could be Without You/Lazy Rhapsody/April in My Heart/A Kiss at Twilight.

Thursday, 8 February 1945   CANADA SWING SHOW
17.15
Broadcast live from the BBC Studios, London
Over AEFP
Compère: L/Cpl. Dick Misener
The Band Played On/How About You -VR- Joanne Dallas/Honeysuckle Rose/I Surrender Dear -VR- Paul Carpenter/Louise/Can't Get Indiana Off My Mind

-VR- Joanne Dallas/Royal Garden Blues/So Dumb but So Beautiful -VR- Paul Carpenter/When I Grow Too Old to Dream/My Buddy.

Friday, 9 February 1945　　　　　　　　　CANADA SING SHOW
21.05
(Pre-recorded earlier the same day at the BBC Studios, London — BBC Disc No. SLO 69081)
Over AEFP
Fun to be Fooled -VR- Chorus/My Wish (featuring Pvt. McGeachie, Piano)/ Mama Don't Allow -VR- Chorus/I'm Looking Over a Four Leaf Clover -VR- Chorus/Three Little Words -VR- Chorus.

Saturday, 10 February 1945　　　　　　　CANADA DANCE BAND
09.30
(Pre-recorded at the BBC Studios, London, on Thursday, 8 February 1945 — BBC Disc No. TLO 68470)
Compère: L/Cpl. Dick Misener
Piccadilly Commotion -comp- Robert Farnon/Don't You Notice Anything New -VR- Joanne Dallas/The Sheik of Araby/Confessin'/Le Fiacre -VR- Paul Carpenter/Oh! Look At Me Now -VR- Cuth Knowlton/And So Little Time -VR- Joanne Dallas/'Deed I Do/My Melancholy Baby -VR- Paul Carpenter/ Bugle Call Rag.

Monday, 12 February 1945　　　　　　　　CANADA SHOW
20.30
Broadcast live from the Queensbury All Services Club, Soho, London
Over AEFP
(Repeated — 'Morning After', Tuesday, 13 February 1945, 10.01 - 10.30 a.m.)
Guest Star: Lt. Marion Zigmunt
Compères: Gerry Wilmot, Sgt. Wilf Davidson, L/Cpl. Dick Misener
S'Wonderful -VR- Chorus/'C' Jam Blues/Do You Ever Dream of Tomorrow -VR- Joanne Dallas/Carpathian Bridge -VR- Marion Zigmunt/Annie Laurie -VR- Marion Zigmunt (accomp by Dick Misener — Solo Piano)/I Got Rhythm/Easter Sunday -VR- Gerry Travers/Yesterdays/When the King Went Forth to War -VR- Marion Zigmunt/The Time is Now -VR- Chorus.

Tuesday, 13 February 1945　　　　　　　CANADA GUEST SHOW
17.15
Broadcast live from the Paris Cinema, Lower Regent Street, London
Over AEFP
Guest Stars: Gloria Brent, Douglas Allen, Roland Peachey
Compère: Capt. F. J. Lynch
In a Little Spanish Town/Intro Music for Douglas Allen — 'All the Nice Girls Love a Sailor'/I'll Be Around -VR- Douglas Allen/I'm So in Love -VR- Douglas Allen/Medley (featuring Roland Peachey, Guitar): Aloha Oe; Song of the Islands; On Ami Ami Oui Oui Isle/Russian Lullaby/Medley: What do You Think Those Ruby Lips Were Made For -VR- Gloria Brent; Do it Again -VR-

Gloria Brent; No Doubt About it -VR- Gloria Brent; Let's Always be Together -VR- Gloria Brent/On the Alamo/Dark Eyes -VR- Cam Ritchie/ Wabash Blues (featuring Roland Peachey, Guitar)/Some Other Time -VR- Douglas Allen/'Deed I Do/Fond Affection -VR- Gloria Brent/I Get a Kick Out of You.

Wednesday, 14 February 1945   PIANO PARADE
11.45
Broadcast live from the BBC Studios, London
Over AEFP
My Ideal/Talk of the Town/Adorable/Was it Rain/Stardust.

Thursday, 15 February 1945   CANADA SWING SHOW
17.15
Broadcast live from the BBC Studios, London
Over AEFP
Compère: L/Cpl. Dick Misener
Digga Digga Do/Not Mine -VR- Joanne Dallas/Tea for Two/Meet the Sun Halfway -VR- Paul Carpenter/Lady Be Good/Basin Street Blues -VR- Joanne Dallas/Straighten Up and Fly Right -VR- Cuth Knowlton/Ain't Misbehavin' -VR- Paul Carpenter/Somebody Loves Me.

Friday, 16 February 1945   CANADA SING SHOW
21.05
(Pre-recorded at the BBC Studios, London, on Thursday, 15 February 1945 — BBC Disc No. SLO 69082)
Over AEFP
Oh! How I Hate to Get Up in the Morning -VR- Chorus/The World is Waiting for the Sunrise -VR- Chorus/The Three Crows -VR- Chorus/In the Gloaming -VR- Chorus.

Saturday, 17 February 1945   CANADA DANCE BAND
09.30
(Pre-recorded at the BBC Studios, London, earlier the same day — BBC Disc No. SLO 68777)
Over AEFP
Compère: L/Cpl. Dick Misener
When Johnny Comes Marching Home/Till All Our Prayers are Answered -VR- Joanne Dallas/Ja Da/It's Always You/Some Other Time -VR- Paul Carpenter/How Could You/Every Day of My Life -VR- Joanne Dallas/ Humoresque/Je Tire Ma Reverence -VR- Paul Carpenter/Unknown Title.

Monday, 19 February 1945   CANADA SHOW
20.30
Broadcast live from the Queensbury All Services Club, Soho, London
Over AEFP
Guest Star: Miss Lorna Martin
Compères: Gerry Wilmot, Sgt. Wilf Davidson, L/Cpl. Dick Misener
Califor-ni-ay -VR- Chorus/Isle of Capri/My Buddy -VR- Joanne Dallas/

Pavanne (featuring Lorna Martin, Accordion)/Perpetual Motion (featuring Lorna Martin, Accordion)/Liza/Drink To Me Only With Thine Eyes -VR-Quartet/Cocktails for Two/Dizzy Fingers (featuring Lorna Martin, Accordion)/ Poinciana -VR- Gerry Travers.

Tuesday, 20 February 1945   CANADA GUEST SHOW
17.15
Broadcast live from the Paris Cinema, Lower Regent Street, London
Over AEFP
Guest Stars: Julie Dawn, Benny Lee, Stanley Andrews, The Canadian Navy Show Quartet
Compère: Capt. F. J. Lynch
The Army Air Corps Song/Besame Mucho -VR- Julie Dawn/Accent on Strings (featuring Stanley Andrews, Violin)/Believe Me In All Those Endearing Young Charms (featuring Stanley Andrews, Violin)/Lullaby of Broadway/When They Ask About You -VR- Benny Lee/Let Yourself Go -VR-Benny Lee/Theme: Roll Along Wavy Navy -VR- Navy Show Quartet/ Medley (featuring The Navy Show Quartet): I do Like to be Beside the Seaside; Sweet Genevieve; By the Light of the Silvery Moon/My Girl's a Corker -VR-Canadian Navy Show Quartet/Yesterdays/Road to the Isles -VR- Cam Ritchie (Piano Solo by Dick Misener)/Beautiful Love -VR-Julie Dawn/Whispering Grass (featuring Stanley Andrews, Violin)/My Ideal -VR- Benny Lee/ Undecided.

Wednesday, 21 February 1945   PIANO PARADE
11.45
Broadcast live from the BBC Studios, London
Over AEFP
I Can't Escape From You/If I Had You/If I Had My Own Way/It Had to be You/Tea for Two/Soliloquy.

Thursday, 22 February 1945   CANADA SWING SHOW
17.15
Broadcast live from the BBC Studios, London
Over AEFP
Compère: L/Cpl. Dick Misener
Dr Heckle and Mr Jive/Says My Heart -VR- Joanne Dallas/I Found a New Baby/As Long as There's Music -VR- Paul Carpenter/The Girl Friend/Am I Blue -VR- Joanne Dallas/Five Foot Two/Dance with a Dolly -VR- Paul Carpenter/All the Nice Girls Love a Sailor/The Sheik of Araby.

Friday, 23 February 1945   CANADA GUEST SHOW
21.05
Broadcast live from the BBC Studios, London
Over AEFP
Of Thee I Sing Baby -VR- Chorus/Together -VR- Chorus/The Drum -VR-Chorus/Dance with a Dolly -VR- Chorus.

Saturday, 24 February 1945　　　　　　　　　CANADA DANCE BAND
09.30
(Pre-recorded at the BBC Studios, London, on Friday, 23 February 1945 —
BBC Disc No. SLO 69153)
Over AEFP
Compère: L/Cpl. Dick Misener
Song of the Volga Boatmen/I Go For You -VR- Joanne Dallas/Taking a
Chance on Love/Street of Dreams/No One Else Will Do -VR- Paul Carpenter/
Exactly Like You/Too Much in Love -VR- Joanne Dallas/Ida/Night and Day
-VR- Paul Carpenter/In a Little Spanish Town.

Monday, 26 February 1945　　　　　　　　　　　CANADA SHOW
20.30
Broadcast live from the Queensbury All Services Club, Soho, London
Over AEFP
Guest Star: Pvt. J. Groob, Violin
Compères: Gerry Wilmot, Sgt. Wilf Davidson, L/Cpl. Dick Misener
Can't Help Singing -VR- Chorus/Piccadilly Commotion -comp- Robert
Farnon/The Very Thought of You -VR- Gerry Travers/Medley (featuring J.
Groob, Violin): All the Things You Are; Where or When; I've Got You
Under My Skin/Dark Eyes (featuring J. Groob, Violin)/I Know That You
Know/Georgia On My Mind -VR- Joanne Dallas/Chopsticks/Smoke Gets In
Your Eyes (featuring J. Groob, Violin)/Blue Moon -VR- Chorus.

Tuesday, 27 February 1945　　　　　　　　　CANADA GUEST SHOW
17.15
Broadcast live from the BBC Studios, London
Over AEFP
Guest Stars: Unknown
Compère: Capt. F. J. Lynch
Details remain unknown.

Wednesday, 28 February 1945　　　　　　　　　PIANO PARADE
11.45
Broadcast live from the BBC Studios, London
Over AEFP
A Pretty Girl Is Like a Melody/Ain't Misbehavin'/She's Funny That Way/All
of Me/I'm Getting Sentimental Over You.

Thursday, 1 March 1945　　　　　　　　　　CANADA SWING SHOW
17.15
Broadcast live from the BBC Studios, London
Over AEFP
Compère: L/Cpl. Dick Misener
Song of the Wanderer/Two's a Crowd -VR- Joanne Dallas/Sweet Sue/There
Goes That Song Again -VR- Paul Carpenter/Coquette/What a Difference a
Day Made -VR- Joanne Dallas/Alexander's Ragtime Band/Where the Blue
Begins -VR- Paul Carpenter/When I Take My Sugar To Tea -VR- Cuth
Knowlton/Rosetta.

Friday, 2 March 1945   CANADA SING SHOW
21.05
(Pre-recorded at the BBC Studios, London, on Friday, 1 March 1945 — BBC
Disc No. SLO 69873)
Over AEFP
Painting the Clouds with Sunshine -VR- Chorus/Taps Till Reveille -VR-
Chorus/Swinging on a Star -VR- Chorus/Beautiful Sari Marais -VR- Chorus.

Saturday, 3 March 1945   CANADA DANCE BAND
09.30
(Pre-recorded at the BBC Studios, Maida Vale, London, on Friday, 2 March
1945 — BBC Disc No. SLO 70092)
Over AEFP
Compère: L/Cpl. Dick Misener
March of the Toys/Don't You Notice Anything New -VR- Joanne Dallas/
Cinquantaine/She's Funny That Way -VR- Paul Carpenter/Sleepy Time Gal/
I'll Be Seeing You -VR- Joanne Dallas/I Would Do Anything for You/Vous
Qui Passez Sans Me Voir -VR- Paul Carpenter/Stompin' at the Savoy.

Monday, 5 March 1945   CANADA SHOW
20.30
Broadcast live from the Queensbury All Services Club, Soho, London
Over AEFP
Guest Comedian: L/Cpl. Jack Madden
Compères: Gerry Wilmot, Sgt. Wilf Davidson, L/Cpl. Dick Misener
Oh! How I Hate to Get Up in the Morning -VR- Chorus/March of the Toys/
The Boy Next Door -VR- Joanne Dallas/Annie's Cousin Fanny -VR- Jack
Madden/Sam's Medal (featuring Jack Madden with Dick Misener, Piano)/Fine
and Dandy/There Goes That Song Again -VR- Gerry Travers/The Girl with
the Flaxen Hair/The Birthday Song -VR- Jack Madden accomp. by Dick
Misener at the piano/Sari Marais -VR- Chorus.

Tuesday, 6 March 1945   CANADA GUEST SHOW
17.15
Broadcast live from the Paris Cinema, Lower Regent Street, London
Over AEFP
Guest Stars: Triss Henderson, Les Allen, Bernard Miles
Compère: Capt. F. J. Lynch
Great Day/My Guy's Come Back -VR- Triss Henderson/I'm Gonna Love
That Guy -VR- Triss Henderson/Ida/Hello Mom -VR- Les Allen/A Kiss in the
Night -VR- Les Allen/To be a Farmers Boy -VR- Bernard Miles/'Comedy
Dialogue' (featuring Bernard Miles)/To be a Farmers Boy -VR- Bernard
Miles/The Broad Highway -VR- Cam Ritchie accompanied by piano/Cow Cow
Boogie -VR- Triss Henderson/Liza/Medley: Goodnight Wherever You Are
-VR- Les Allen; The Very Thought of You -VR- Les Allen/Always/You and
the Night and the Music/In a Little Spanish Town.

Wednesday, 7 March 1945   PIANO PARADE
11.45
Broadcast live from the BBC Studios, Maida Vale, London
Over AEFP
Featuring: Denny Vaughan, Piano
It Could Happen to You/Smoke Gets in Your Eyes/Where or When/Always.

Thursday, 8 March 1945   CANADA SWING SHOW
17.15
Broadcast live from the BBC Studios, Maida Vale, London
Over AEFP
Compère: L/Cpl. Dick Misener
When I Grow Too Old to Dream/Two's a Crowd -VR- Joanne Dallas/After
You've Gone/Roseanna -VR- Paul Carpenter/When I Take My Sugar to Tea
-VR- Cuth Knowlton/Please Don't Talk About Me When I'm Gone/Blue
Skies -VR- Joanne Dallas/There'll be Some Changes Made/So Dumb But So
Beautiful -VR- Paul Carpenter/Tipperary/Blue Lou.

Friday, 9 March 1945   CANADA SING SHOW
21.05
(Pre-recorded at the BBC Studios, Maida Vale, London, on Thursday, 8
March 1945 — BBC Disc No. SLO 69792)
Over AEFP
Compère: Capt. Cam Ritchie.
Pedro the Fisherman -VR- Chorus/Bluebird of Happiness -VR- Chorus/Where
or When -VR- Chorus.

Saturday, 10 March 1945   CANADA DANCE BAND
09.30
(Pre-recorded at the BBC Studios, Maida Vale, London, on Friday, 9 March
1945 — BBC Disc No. SLO 70519)
Over AEFP
Compère: L/Cpl. Dick Misener
Lullaby in Rhythm/As Long as There's Music -VR- Joanne Dallas/Mexican
Hat Dance/Any Old Time/There Goes That Song Again -VR- Paul Carpenter/
My Blue Heaven/Time Waits for No One -VR- Joanne Dallas/You Took
Advantage of Me/Some Other Time -VR- Paul Carpenter/One O'Clock Jump.

Monday, 12 March 1945   CANADA SHOW
20.30
Broadcast live from the Queensbury All Services Club, Soho, London
Over AEFP
Guest Star: Cherry Lind
Compères: Gerry Wilmot, Pvt. Paul Carpenter, L/Cpl. Dick Misener
The Trolley Song -VR- Chorus/You Fascinating You -VR- Joanne Dallas/
Song of the Volga Boatmen/One Fine Day -VR- Cherry Lind/Old Grey
Bonnet/Easter Sunday -VR- Gerry Travers/We Could Make Such Beautiful
Music Together/Medley: All Through the Night -VR- Cherry Lind; When

Irish Eyes Are Smiling -VR- Cherry Lind; Coming Through the Rye -VR-
Cherry Lind/Big Broad Smile -VR- Chorus.

Tuesday, 13 March 1945   CANADA GUEST SHOW
17.15
Broadcast live from the Paris Cinema, Lower Regent Street, London
Over AEFP
Guest Stars: Dorothy Carless, Don Kenito, Josephine Sera
Compère: Capt. Cam Ritchie
I Know that You Know/Brazil/Besame Mucho -VR- Don Kenito/Kiss Me
Again -VR- Don Kenito/I'm Gonna Love That Girl -VR- Don Kenito/Ja Da/
Romance -VR- Josephine Sera/Schoen Rosmarin -VR- Josephine Sera/Old
Man River/With a Song in My Heart − Theme for Dorothy Carless/All My
Life -VR- Dorothy Carless/Begin the Beguine -VR- Dorothy Carless/Fine and
Dandy/Canzonetta -VR- Josephine Sera with Piano/Stormy Weather -VR- Don
Kenito/Accentuate the Positive -VR- Dorothy Carless/March of the Toys.

Wednesday, 14 March 1945   PIANO PARADE
11.45
Broadcast live from the BBC Studios, Maida Vale, London
Over AEFP
Played by Cpl. Denny Vaughan
Ain't Misbehavin'/I'll Get By/Taking a Chance on Love/I'll Be Seeing You/
There Goes That Song Again.

Thursday, 15 March 1945   CANADA SWING SHOW
17.15
Broadcast live from the BBC Studios, Maida Vale, London
Over AEFP
Compère: L/Cpl. Dick Misener
The Kerry Dance/When They Ask About You -VR- Gerry Travers/Mary
Lou/Accentuate the Positive -VR- Paul Carpenter/Sweet Sue/Sweet Dreams,
Sweetheart -VR- Gerry Travers/All the Nice Girls Love a Sailor/Sleepy Time
Gal -VR- Paul Carpenter/Somebody Loves Me/Between the Devil and the
Deep Blue Sea.

Friday, 16 March 1945   CANADA SING SHOW
21.05
(Pre-recorded at the BBC Studios, Maida Vale, London, on Thursday, 15
March 1945 — BBC Disc No. SLO 70256)
Over AEFP
Compère: L/Cpl. Dick Misener
MacNamara's Band -VR- Chorus/You're Irish and You're Beautiful -VR-
Chorus/A Little Bit of Heaven -VR- Chorus/Too Ra Loo Ra Loo Ra -VR-
Chorus/When Irish Eyes Are Smiling -VR- Chorus.

Saturday, 17 March 1945   CANADA DANCE BAND
09.30
(Pre-recorded at the BBC Studios, Maida Vale, London, on Friday, 16 March
1945 — BBC Disc No. SLO 70546)

Over AEFP
Compère: L/Cpl. Dick Misener
Paramount March (The Eyes and Ears of the World)/Every Day of My Life
-VR- Gerry Travers/Oh Look at Me Now -VR- Cuth Knowlton/Ain't
Misbehavin'/What a Difference a Day Made -VR- Paul Carpenter/Deed I
Do/Don't You Know I Care -VR- Gerry Travers/Lullaby of Broadway/As
Long as There's Music -VR- Paul Carpenter/American Patrol.
Monday, 19 March 1945   CANADA SHOW
20.30
Broadcast live from the Queensbury All Services Club, Soho, London
Over AEFP
Guest Stars: The Vincent Raff Trio
Compères: Gerry Wilmot, S/Sgt. Wilf Davidson, L/Cpl. Dick Misener
S'Wonderful -VR- Chorus/I Would Do Anything For You/Our Waltz -VR-
Gerry Travers/Hungarian Impressions -VR- The Vincent Raff Trio/Play
Gypsy (featuring The Vincent Raff Trio)/Why?/My Buddy -VR- Joanne
Dallas/Yesterdays/Czardas (featuring The Vincent Raff Trio)/San Fernando
Valley -VR- Paul Carpenter.
Tuesday, 20 March 1945   CANADA GUEST SHOW
17.15
Broadcast live from the Paris Cinema, Lower Regent Street, London
Over AEFP
Guest Stars: Anne Lenner, Douglas Allen, The Canadian Navy Show
Accordion Trio
Compère: Capt. Cam Ritchie
Mexican Hat Dance/Stardust -VR- Anne Lenner/A Little on the Lonely Side
-VR- Anne Lenner/All the Nice Girls Love a Sailor – Theme (for The
Canadian Navy Trio)/Rushing Around (featuring The Canadian Navy
Accordion Trio)/Accordiana (featuring The Canadian Navy Accordion
Trio)/In the Still of the Night/A Kiss in the Night -VR- Douglas Allen/
Together -VR- Douglas Allen/Manhattan Serenade (featuring Dixie Dean,
accordion)/The Hills of Home -VR- Cam Ritchie/The Girl I Left Behind Me/
Time On My Hands -VR- Anne Lenner/Twelfth Street Rag (featuring The
Canadian Navy Accordion Trio)/There Goes That Song Again -VR- Douglas
Allen/Taking a Chance on Love.
Wednesday, 21 March 1945   PIANO PARADE
11.45
Broadcast live from the BBC Studios, London
Over AEFP
Played by: Cpl. Denny Vaughan
My Blue Heaven/All the Things You Are/Confessin'/More and More/I May
be Wrong.
Thursday, 22 March 1945   CANADA SWING SHOW
17.15
Broadcast live from the BBC Studios, Maida Vale, London

Over AEFP
Compère: L/Cpl. Dick Misener
Indiana/Love Me or Leave Me -VR- Joanne Dallas/Georgia On My Mind/
Let's Take the Long Way Home -VR- Paul Carpenter/Button Up Your
Overcoat/How About You -VR- Joanne Dallas/I Never Knew/Sunday,
Monday or Always -VR- Paul Carpenter/Exactly Like You/Avalon.
Friday, 23 March 1945   CANADA SING SHOW
21.05
(Pre-recorded at the BBC Studios, Maida Vale, London, on Thursday, 22
March 1945 — BBC Disc No. SAL 19785)
Over AEFP
Announcer: S/Sgt. Wilf Davidson
The Trolley Song/Easter Sunday -VR- Chorus/When Day is Done -VR-
Chorus/Tico Tico Tico -VR- Chorus.
Saturday, 24 March 1945   CANADA DANCE BAND
09.30
(Pre-recorded at the BBC Studios, Maida Vale, London, on Friday, 23 March
1945 — BBC Disc No. SLO 70733)
Over AEFP
Compère: L/Cpl. Dick Misener
King Porter Stomp/Who Said Dreams Don't Come True -VR- Joanne Dallas/
Colonel Bogey/I Surrender Dear/Accentuate the Positive -VR- Paul Carpenter/
Ida/Till All Our Prayers are Answered -VR- Joanne Dallas/Ghost of a
Chance/No One Else Will Do -VR- Paul Carpenter/March of the Toys.
Monday, 26 March 1945   CANADA SHOW
20.30
Broadcast live from the Queensbury All Services Club, Soho, London
Over AEFP
Guest Star: Peter Cavanaugh (impressionist)
Compères: Gerry Wilmot, S/Sgt. Wilf Davidson, L/Cpl. Dick Misener
Califor-ni-ay -VR- Chorus/Humoresque/The Very Thought of You -VR-Gerry
Travers/'Original Dialogue for Impressions' (featuring Peter Cavanaugh)/You
Are My Heart's Delight -VR- Peter Cavanaugh/Great Day/ The Boy Next
Door -VR- Joanne Dallas/Poinciana -VR- Paul Carpenter and Chorus/You and
the Night and the Music/Can't Help Singing -VR- Chorus.
Tuesday, 27 March 1945   CANADA GUEST SHOW
17.15
Broadcast live from the Paris Cinema, Lower Regent Street, London
Over AEFP
Guest Stars: Rita Marlowe, Mario Lorenzi (Harp), Alvar Lidell, Carl Asplund
Compère: Capt. Cam Ritchie
When Johnny Comes Marching Home/Begin the Beguine -VR- Rita
Marlowe/My Guy's Come Back -VR- Rita Marlowe/Liebestraum (featuring
Mario Lorenzi, Harp)/Why?/The Little Red Caboose Behind the Tree -VR-

Carl Asplund (accomp. by George Arthur, Guitar)/Where'er You Walk -VR-Alvar Lidell (accomp. by Dick Misener, Piano)/Linden Lea -VR- Alvar Lidell (accomp. by Dick Misener, Piano)/I Got Rhythm/ Three for Jack -VR- Cam Ritchie (with Dick Misener, Piano)/American Patrol/Medley (featuring Mario Lorenzi, Harp): Tico, Tico, Tico; Always Yours; I Love to Sing/I'm Gonna Love That Guy -VR- Rita Marlowe/ Yodelling Ranger -VR- Carl Asplund/Paramount March.

Wednesday, 28 March 1945   PIANO PARADE
11.45
Broadcast live from the BBC Studios, London
Over AEFP
Piano selections played by Cpl. Denny Vaughan
Avalon/Don't Blame Me/I Cried for You/I'm Gonna Love That Guy/Exactly Like You.

Thursday, 29 March 1945   CANADA SWING SHOW
17.15
Broadcast live from the BBC Studios, Maida Vale, London
Over AEFP
Compère: L/Cpl. Dick Misener
I'll be With You in Apple Blossom Time/If You Build a Better Mouse Trap -VR- Joanne Dallas/All the Nice Girls Love a Sailor/The Echo of a Serenade -VR- Paul Carpenter/Straighten Up and Fly Right -VR- Cuth Knowlton/May I Never Love Again -VR- Joanne Dallas/Louise/Meet the Sun Halfway -VR-Paul Carpenter/Shine/Rose Room.

Friday, 30 March 1945   CANADA SING SHOW
21.05
(Pre-recorded at the BBC Studios, London, on Thursday, 29 March 1945 — BBC Disc No. SLO 71630)
Announcer: S/Sgt. Wilf Davidson
Legend -VR- Chorus/Oh Lord Most Holy -VR- Chorus/The Mummers Carol -VR- Chorus/The Festival Carol -VR- Chorus.

Saturday, 31 March 1945   CANADA DANCE BAND
09.30
(Pre-recorded earlier the same day at the BBC Studios, Maida Vale, London — BBC Disc No. SLO 70915)
Over AEFP
Compère: L/Cpl. Dick Misener
Take Me Out to the Ball Game/Too Much in Love -VR- Joanne Dallas/Mary -VR- Paul Carpenter/Body and Soul/More and More -VR- Paul Carpenter/Ja Da/I Go For You -VR- Joanne Dallas/Sweet Lorraine/There Goes That Song Again -VR- Paul Carpenter/Piccadilly Commotion -comp- Robert Farnon.

Monday, 2 April 1945   CANADA SHOW
20.30
Broadcast live from the Queensbury All Services Club, Soho, London
Over AEFP
Guest Stars: Jack and Daphne Barker
Compères: Gerry Wilmot, S/Sgt. Wilf Davidson, L/Cpl. Dick Misener
Free For All -VR- Chorus/March of the Toys/Accentuate the Positive -VR-
Paul Carpenter/Barker Theme − 'I'll Get By'/They All Got Together -VR-
Jack and Daphne Barker/We Do Have Fun in the Garden Don't We -VR- Jack
and Daphne Barker/I'll Get By/Bicycle Built for Two/Sweet Dreams,
Sweetheart -VR- Gerry Travers/Drink to Me Only With Thine Eyes -VR-
Quartet/Hour of Parting/The Trolley Song -VR- Chorus.

Wednesday, 4 April 1945   PIANO PARADE
11.45
Broadcast live from the BBC Studios, London
Over AEFP
Played by: Cpl. Denny Vaughan
I Can't Give You Anything But Love/You're So Sweet to Remember/All of
My Life/Embraceable You/It Had to be You.

Wednesday, 4 April 1945   CANADA GUEST SHOW
17.15
Broadcast live from the Queensbury All Services Club, Soho, London — BBC
Disc No. TLO 71370
Over AEFP
Guest Stars: Edna Kaye, Ronald Chesney, Chief Petty Officer Tony Russell
and The Navy Trio
Compère: Capt. Cam Ritchie
Take Me Out to the Ball Game/A Kiss in the Night -VR- Edna Kaye/The
Trolley Song -VR- Edna Kaye/Yes My Darling Daughter -VR- The Navy
Trio/April Showers/That Old Black Magic (featuring Ronald Chesney,
Harmonica)/The Riff Song -VR- Cam Ritchie/For Me and My Gal/Take Me in
Your Arms -VR- The Navy Trio/What a Difference a Day Made -VR- Edna
Kaye/Fascinatin' Rhythm (featuring Ronald Chesney, Harmonica)/
L'Espagnola -VR- The Navy Trio/Undecided.

Thursday, 5 April 1945   CANADA SWING SHOW
17.15
Broadcast live from the BBC Studios, London
Over AEFP
Compère: L/Cpl. Dick Misener
Who's Sorry Now/More and More -VR- Paul Carpenter/Song of the
Wanderer/You Took Advantage of Me/The Very Thought of You -VR- Gerry
Travers/I Can't Give You Anything But Love/I Surrender Dear -VR- Paul
Carpenter/Ja Da.

Friday, 6 April 1945   CANADA SING SHOW
19.05
(Pre-recorded Thursday, 5 April 1945, at the BBC Studios, London — BBC
Disc No. SLO 71905)
Over AEFP
Announcer: S/Sgt. Wilf Davidson
Sing Me a Chanty -VR- Chorus/Blow the Man Down -VR- Chorus/Rhene
Baten -VR- Chorus/Shenandoah -VR- Chorus.

Saturday, 7 April 1945   CANADA DANCE BAND
09.30
(Pre-recorded at the BBC Studios, Maida Vale, London, on Friday, 6 April
1945 — BBC Disc No. SAL 20095)
Compère: L/Cpl. Dick Misener
Carioca/And So Little Time -VR- Gerry Travers/It's the Talk of the Town/
Confessin'/Together -VR- Paul Carpenter/Humoresque/It Could Happen to
You -VR- Gerry Travers/Dinah/I'll Walk Alone -VR- Paul Carpenter/Lady Be
Good.

Monday, 9 April 1945   CANADA SHOW
20.30
Broadcast live from the Queensbury All Services Club, Soho, London
Over AEFP
Guest Star: Derek Roy
Compères: Gerry Wilmot, S/Sgt. Wilf Davidson, L/Cpl. Dick Misener
Cavalry of the Steppes -VR- Chorus/In a Little Spanish Town/A Brown Bird
Singing -VR- Joanne Dallas/Original Comedy 'Patter' — Derek Roy/I'm a
Gooseberry -VR- Derek Roy/I Know That You Know/Dance with a Dolly
-VR- Paul Carpenter/If There Is Someone Lovelier Than You/War Medley:
Tipperary -VR- Gerry Travers and Chorus; Keep the Home Fires Burning
-VR- Gerry Travers and Chorus; Pack Up Your Troubles -VR-Gerry Travers
and Chorus.

Wednesday, 11 April 1945   PIANO PARADE
11.45
Broadcast live from the BBC Studios, London
Over AEFP
Played by Cpl. Denny Vaughan
Who's Sorry Now/Long Ago and Far Away/When They Ask About You/
Sweet Lorraine/My Melancholy Baby.

Wednesday, 11 April 1945   CANADA GUEST SHOW
17.15
(Pre-recorded at the Queensbury All Services Club, Soho, London, on
Tuesday, 10 April 1945 — BBC Disc No. SAL 20137)
Over AEFP
Guest Stars: Robin Richmond, Cpl. Mae Meads, The Navy Quintette
Compère: Capt. Cam Ritchie

Good News/Wanting You -VR- Mae Meads/Liza (featuring The Navy Quintette)/Long Ago and Far Away -VR- Douglas Allen (with The Navy Quintette)/King Porter Stomp/Theme for Robin Richmond – 'When the Red, Red Robin'/Vibrollini (featuring Robin Richmond, Organ)/The Little Irish Girl -VR- Cam Ritchie (accomp. by Robin Richmond, Organ)/St Louis Blues (The Navy Quintette)/Fall In Love With Me -VR- Mae Meads/My Blue Heaven/Medley (featuring Robin Richmond, Organ): When It's Sleepy Time Down South; That Grand and Glorious Feeling; A Tisket, A Tasket/ Don't Ever Change (The Navy Quintette) -VR- Douglas Allen/Golden Wedding.

Thursday, 12 April 1945   CANADA SWING SHOW
17.15
Broadcast live from the BBC Studios, Maida Vale, London
Over AEFP
Compère: L/Cpl. Dick Misener
Pack Up Your Troubles/What a Difference a Day Made -VR- Joanne Dallas/ Doctor Heckle and Mr Jive/I'm Gonna Love That Girl -VR- Paul Carpenter/ Way Down Yonder in New Orleans -VR- Cuth Knowlton/Two's a Crowd -VR- Joanne Dallas/Accentuate the Positive -VR- Paul Carpenter/Rose Boom.

Friday, 13 April 1945   CANADA SING SHOW
19.05
(Pre-recorded at the BBC Studios, Maida Vale, London, earlier at 15.05-15.15 — BBC Disc No. SLO 71906)
Over AEFP
Accouncer: S/Sgt. Wilf Davidson
For You -VR- Chorus/Constantly -VR- Chorus/Mama Don't Allow -VR- Chorus/Taps Till Reveille -VR- Chorus.

Saturday, 14 April 1945   CANADA DANCE BAND
09.30
(Pre-recorded at the BBC Studios, London, on Friday, 13 April 1945 — BBC Disc No. SLO)
Compère: L/Cpl. Dick Misener
Details remain unknown.

Monday, 16 April 1945   CANADA SHOW
20.30
Broadcast live from the Queensbury All Services Club, Soho, London
Over AEFP
Guest Star: L/Cpl. Roger Doucet
Compères: Gerry Wilmot, S/Sgt. Wilf Davidson, L/Cpl. Dick Misener
Keep 'Em Smiling -VR- Chorus/Colonel Bogie/When Irish Eyes are Smiling -VR- Joanne Dallas/Dans Mon Coeur -VR- Roger Doucet/In the Still of the Night -VR- Roger Doucet/Great Day/Fence Around Texas -VR- Paul Carpenter/Meditation/In a Monastery Garden -VR- Roger Doucet and Chorus/ Pedro the Fisherman -VR- Gerry Travers and Chorus.

Wednesday, 18 April 1945   PIANO PARADE
11.45
Broadcast live from the BBC Studios, London
Over AEFP
Played by Cpl. Denny Vaughan
S'Wonderful/On the Sunny Side of the Street/My Heart Stood Still/I'll Remember April/I'm Gonna Sit Right Down and Write Myself a Letter.

Wednesday, 18 April 1945   CANADA GUEST SHOW
17.15
(Pre-recorded at the Queensbury All Services Club, Soho, London, on Tuesday, 17 April 1945 — BBC Disc No. SLO 71744)
Over AEFP
Guest Stars: Rita Williams, Benny Lee, Allan Bristow
Compère: Capt. Cam Ritchie
Old Man River/A Little on the Lonely Side -VR- Rita Williams/Accentuate the Positive -VR- Benny Lee/Captain Stratton's Fancy -VR- Cam Ritchie (accomp. by Dick Misener, Piano)/Pearls on Velvet (featuring Allan Bristow, Piano)/Oh! Susannah/Come Out Wherever You Are -VR- Rita Williams/Emaline/ Serenade/ What a Difference a Day Made -VR- Benny Lee/Lady Be Good.

Thursday, 19 April 1945   CANADA SWING SHOW
17.30
Broadcast live from the BBC Studios, Maida Vale, London
Over AEFP
Compère: L/Cpl. Dick Misener
Ding Dong Daddy/All Of My Life -VR- Joanne Dallas/Sweet Sue/Apple Blossoms in the Rain -VR- Paul Carpenter/The Band Played On/Not Mine -VR- Joanne Dallas/Cherry/Sweet Lorraine -VR- Paul Carpenter/Between the Devil and the Deep Blue Sea.

Friday, 20 April 1945   CANADA SING SHOW
19.05
(Pre-recorded at the BBC Studios, London, on Thursday, 19 April 1945 — BBC Disc No. SLO 72671)
Over AEFP
Announcer: S/Sgt. Wilf Davidson
Medley: By the Light of the Silvery Moon -VR- Chorus; When You Wore a Tulip -VR- Chorus; Alice Blue Gown -VR- Chorus; In the Gloaming -VR- Chorus; In the Good Old Summer Time -VR- Chorus; Mary's A Grand Old Name -VR- Chorus; Bicycle Built for Two -VR- Chorus; I Want a Girl Just Like the Girl -VR- Chorus.

Saturday, 21 April 1945   CANADA DANCE BAND
09.30
(Pre-recorded at the BBC Studios, London, on Friday, 20 April 1945 — BBC Disc No. unknown)

Compère: L/Cpl. Dick Misener
Details remain unknown.
Monday, 23 April 1945   CANADA SHOW
20.30
Broadcast live from the Queensbury All Services Club, Soho, London
Over AEFP
Guest Star: Al Phillips
Compères: Gerry Wilmot, S/Sgt. Wilf Davidson, L/Cpl. Dick Misener
The Trolley Song -VR- Chorus/March Militaire/Don't Fence Me In -VR- Paul
Carpenter/Dancing in the Dark -VR- Al Phillips/That Old Black Magic -VR-
Al Phillips/I Got Rhythm/Small Fry -VR- Joanne Dallas/Parade of the Wooden
Soldiers/All the Things You Are -VR- Al Phillips/Sometime -VR- Chorus.
Wednesday, 25 April 1945   PIANO PARADE
11.45
Broadcast live from the BBC Studios, London
Over AEFP
Played by Cpl. Denny Vaughan
Ain't She Sweet/Spring Will Be a Little Late This Year/Rosetta/How Deep is
the Ocean/Come Out Wherever You Are.
Wednesday, 25 April 1945   CANADA GUEST SHOW
17.15
(Pre-recorded at the Queensbury All Services Club, Soho, London, on
Tuesday, 24 April 1945 — BBC Disc SLO 72121)
Over AEFP
Guest Stars: Sally Douglas, Len Camber, Cpl. Neil Chotem and Sgt. Ken Bray
(Piano Team)
Compère: Capt. Cam Ritchie
Fine and Dandy/My Heart Sings -VR- Sally Douglas/I'll Remember April -VR-
Len Camber/In a Little Spanish Town/Cavalry of the Steppes (featuring the
'Two Pianos' of Neil Chotem and Ken Bray)/Home on the Range -VR- Cam
Ritchie/Piccadilly Commotion -comp- Robert Farnon/William Tell Overture
(featuring the 'Two Pianos' of Neil Chotem and Ken Bray)/Cherokee/What a
Difference a Day Made -VR- Sally Douglas/I Surrender Dear/The Song Is You
-VR- Len Camber/One O'Clock Jump.
Thursday, 26 April 1945   CANADA SWING SHOW
17.30
Broadcast live from the BBC Studios, Maida Vale, London
Over AEFP
Compère: L/Cpl. Dick Misener
Details remain unknown.
Friday, 27 April 1945   CANADA SING SHOW
19.05
(Pre-recorded at the BBC Studios, London, on Thursday, 26 April 1945 —
BBC Disc No. SLO 72191)

Over AEFP

Announcer: S/Sgt. Wilf Davidson

Me and My Little Banjo -VR- Chorus/Mah Lindy Lou (featuring C. Trotman, Piano)/The Battle of Jericho -VR- Chorus/Old Man River -VR- Chorus.

Saturday, 28 April 1945   CANADA DANCE BAND
09.30

(Pre-recorded at the BBC Studios, London, on Friday, 27 April 1945 — BBC Disc No. SAL 20262)

Over AEFP

Compère: L/Cpl. Dick Misener

Isle of Capri/He's the Image of You -VR- Joanne Dallas/American Patrol/Liza/ Don't Fence Me In -VR- Paul Carpenter/Lullaby in Rhythm/Ain't Misbehavin'/Every Day of My Life -VR- Joanne Dallas/Between the Devil and the Deep Blue Sea/More and More -VR- Paul Carpenter/When I Grow Too Old To Dream.

Monday, 30 April 1945   CANADA SHOW
20.30

Broadcast live from the Queensbury All Services Club, Soho, London

Over AEFP

(Repeated by AEFP, 'Morning After', Tuesday, 1 May 1945 – 10.01-10.30 a.m. — BBC Disc No. SAL)

Guest Stars: The Master Singers

Compères: Gerry Wilmot, S/Sgt. Wilf Davidson

Announcer: L/Cpl. Dick Misener

That's An Order From The Army -VR- Chorus/My Blue Heaven/More and More -VR- Paul Carpenter/Theme – 'Rise and Shine' -VR- The Master Singers/Macushla -VR- Master Singers (accomp. by Dick Misener)/ Liza/We'll Gather Lilacs -VR- Joanne Dallas/The Hour of Parting/Pedro the Fisherman -VR- The Master Singers (accomp. by Dick Misener, Piano)/The Music Stopped -VR- Gerry Travers and Chorus.

Wednesday, 2 May 1945   PIANO PARADE
11.45

Broadcast live from the BBC Studios, London

Over AEFP

Played by Cpl. Denny Vaughan

Tea for Two/A Little on the Lonely Side/Love Me or Leave Me/The Man I Love/That Old Feeling.

Wednesday, 2 May 1945   CANADA GUEST SHOW
17.15

(Pre-recorded at the Queensbury All Services Club, Soho, London, on Tuesday, 1 May 1945 — BBC Disc No. SLO 73314)

Over AEFP

Guest Stars: Triss Henderson, George Shearing, The Army Trio (Bdr. Pete Barry, Pvt. W. Crouter and Pvt. B. Lovett)

Compère: Capt. Cam Ritchie
The Army Air Corps Song/A Little on the Lonely Side -VR- Triss Henderson/
'Radio Sketch' — The Army Trio/Between the Devil and the Deep Blue Sea/I
Didn't Know About You (featuring George Shearing, Piano)/Lindy Lou -VR-
Cam Ritchie/Lullaby in Rhythm/Accentuate the Positive -VR- Triss
Henderson/Boogie Ride (featuring George Shearing, Piano)/Confessin'/The
Waiter and the Porter and the Upstairs Maid -VR- The Army Trio/The
Doodle Bug Song -VR- The Army Trio/American Patrol.

Thursday, 3 May 1945   CANADA SWING SHOW
17.30
Broadcast live from the BBC Studios, Maida Vale, London
Over AEFP
Compère: L/Cpl. Dick Misener
Tipperary/My Buddy -VR- Joanne Dallas/I Never Knew/Too Much Illusion
-VR- Paul Carpenter/I Found a New Baby/If You Build a Better Mousetrap
-VR- Joanne Dallas/Georgia/Sleepy Time Gal -VR- Paul Carpenter/When I
Grow Too Old to Dream.

Friday, 4 May 1945   CANADA SING SHOW
19.05
(Pre-recorded at the BBC Studios, London, on Thursday, 3 May 1945 — BBC
Disc No. SLO 73047)
Over AEFP
MacNamara's Band -VR- Chorus/Drink To Me Only -VR- Chorus/Scots Wha
Hae -VR- Chorus/All Through the Night -VR- Chorus.

Saturday, 5 May 1945   CANADA DANCE BAND
09.30
(Pre-recorded at the BBC Studios, Maida Vale, London, on Friday, 4 May
1945 — BBC Disc No. SAL 20385)
Over AEFP
Compère: L/Cpl. Dick Misener
Rosetta/I Go For You -VR- Joanne Dallas/In a Little Spanish Town/Oh Look at
Me Now -VR- Cuth Knowlton/I Didn't Know About You -VR- Paul
Carpenter/Sometimes I'm Happy/Too Much in Love -VR- Joanne Dallas/You
Took Advantage of Me/Accentuate the Positive -VR- Paul Carpenter/'C' Jam
Blues.

Monday, 7 May 1945   CANADA SHOW
20.30
Broadcast live from the Queensbury All Services Club, Soho, London
Over AEFP
Guest Star: Alfredo Campoli, Violin
Compères: Gerry Wilmot, S/Sgt. Wilf Davidson, L/Cpl. Dick Misener
The Empire is Marching -VR- Chorus/March of the Toys/What a Difference a
Day Made -VR- Paul Carpenter/Ave Maria (featuring Alfredo Campoli,

Violin)/Oh! Susannah/The Boy Next Door -VR- Joanne Dallas/Chopsticks/ Witches Dance (featuring Alfredo Campoli, Violin)/My Shining Hour -VR- Gerry Travers and Chorus.

Note: This was the last Canada Show broadcast that used the Bob Farnon composition, 'March Along, Joe Soldier', as its opening and closing theme.

Wednesday, 9 May 1945   PIANO PARADE
11.45

Broadcast live from the BBC Studios, London

Over AEFP

Played by Cpl. Denny Vaughan

Tea for Two/What a Difference a Day Made/Poor Butterfly/I Married an Angel/There Goes That Song Again.

Wednesday, 9 May 1945   CANADA GUEST SHOW
17.15

(Pre-recorded at the Queensbury All Services Club, Soho, London, on Tuesday, 8 May 1945 — BBC Disc No. SLO 73276)

Over AEFP

Guest Stars: Betty Webb, Stanley Andrews, Pvt. Colyn Trotman

Compère: Capt. Cam Ritchie

For Me and My Gal/I Give Thanks For You -VR- Betty Webb/Water Boy -VR- Colyn Trotman/Isle of Capri/The Sparks Fly Upwards (featuring Stanley Andrews, Violin)/The Broad Highway -VR- Cam Ritchie/Body and Soul/April Showers/Always -VR- Betty Webb/One O'Clock Jump/Oh Didn't It Rain -VR- Colyn Trotman/Moonlight Madonna (featuring Stanley Andrews, Violin)/Humoresque/Invictus (Piano Solo by Cam Ritchie)/Cavalry of the Steppes.

Thursday, 10 May 1945   CANADA SWING SHOW
17.30

Broadcast live from the BBC Studios, Maida Vale, London

Over AEFP

Compère: L/Cpl. Dick Misener

When You Wore a Tulip/Just a Little Fond Affection -VR- Joanne Dallas/ Louise/Mexico -VR- Paul Carpenter/Between the Devil and the Deep Blue Sea/ Confessin'/How About You -VR- Joanne Dallas/Please Don't Talk About Me When I'm Gone/Apple Blossoms in the Rain -VR- Paul Carpenter/All the Nice Girls Love a Sailor.

Friday, 11 May 1945   CANADA SING SHOW
19.05

(Pre-recorded at the BBC Studios, London, on Thursday, 10 May 1945 — BBC Disc No. SLO 72981)

Over AEFP

That's an Order From the Army -VR- Chorus/Parlez-Moi d'Amour -VR- Chorus/Rolling Down to Rio -VR- Chorus/Something to Remember -VR- Chorus.

Saturday, 12 May 1945   CANADA DANCE BAND
09.30
(Pre-recorded at the BBC Studios, Maida Vale, London, on Friday, 11 May 1945 — BBC Disc No. SAL 20569)
Over AEFP
Compère: L/Cpl. Dick Misener
The Girl Friend/Small Fry -VR- Joanne Dallas/By the Light of the Silvery Moon/Carioca/Candy -VR- Paul Carpenter/Moonlight on the Ganges/He's the Image of You -VR- Joanne Dallas/I Would Do Anything For You/Night and Day -VR- Paul Carpenter/One O'Clock Jump.

Monday, 14 May 1945   CANADA SHOW
20.30
Broadcast live from the Queensbury All Services Club, Soho, London
Over AEFP
(Repeated by AEFP, 'Morning After', Tuesday, 15 May 1945, 10.01-10.30 a.m.)
Guest Star: Cyril Fletcher
Compères: Gerry Wilmot, S/Sgt. Wilf Davidson
Announcer: L/Cpl. Dick Misener
Opening Theme ('New Theme' by Robert Farnon)/Can't Help Singing -VR- Chorus/The Girl Friend/I Didn't Know About You -VR- Paul Carpenter/Theme for Cyril Fletcher — Entry of the Gladiators/Original Dialogue — Cyril Fletcher/Old Grey Bonnet/Too Much in Love -VR- Joanne Dallas/I've Got You Under My Skin/Medley: Bless 'Em All -VR- Chorus; The White Cliffs of Dover -VR- Chorus; I've Got Sixpence -VR- Chorus; We'll Meet Again -VR- Chorus; Roll Out the Barrel -VR- Chorus/Closing Theme (Original by Robert Farnon).

Wednesday, 16 May 1945   PIANO PARADE
11.45
Broadcast live from the BBC Studios, London
Over AEFP
Played by Cpl. Denny Vaughan
Don't Be That Way/I Didn't Know About You/Taking a Chance on Love/A Pretty Girl is Like a Melody/When They Ask About You.

Wednesday, 16 May 1945   CANADA GUEST SHOW
17.15
(Pre-recorded at the Queensbury All Services Club, Soho, London, on Tuesday, 15 May 1945 — BBC Disc No. SLO 73463)
Over AEFP
Guest Stars: Bette Roberts, Emilio, Cpl. Jack Kelly, Max and Harry Nesbit
Compère: Capt. Cam Ritchie
Fine and Dandy/There's a Lull in My Life -VR- Bette Roberts/Medley (featuring Emilio, Accordion): Voices of Spring; Liebes Freud; Faust; Waltzes of

139

Spring/Rosetta/Four Jolly Sailormen -VR- Cam Ritchie/Theme for the Nesbits − 'I Want to be Happy'/My Dreams Are Getting Better All the Time -VR- Nesbit Bros/At the End of the Day -VR- Nesbit Bros/Melody in 'F' -VR- Nesbit Bros/I Wanna Sleep on Feavers -VR- Nesbit Bros/Why?/The Man I Love (featuring Emilio, Accordion)/Carioca/Original Dialogue − Jack Kelly/Ain't Misbehavin'/Honeysuckle Rose -VR- Bette Roberts/The Girl Friend.

Thursday, 17 May 1945   CANADA SWING SHOW
17.30
Broadcast live from the BBC Studios, Maida Vale, London
Over AEFP
Compère: L/Cpl. Dick Misener
Button Up Your Overcoat/Anywhere -VR- Joanne Dallas/On the Sunny Side of the Street/Sentimental Journey -VR- Paul Carpenter/Pack Up Your Troubles/My Favourite Dream -VR- Joanne Dallas/I Can't Give You Anything but Love/More and More -VR- Paul Carpenter/There'll be Some Changes Made/Honeysuckle Rose.

Friday, 18 May 1945   CANADA SING SHOW
19.05
(Pre-recorded at the BBC Studios, London, on Thursday, 17 May 1945 — BBC Disc No. SLO 73477)
Over AEFP
How About a Cheer for the Navy -VR- Chorus/Pedro the Fisherman -VR- Chorus/Captain Mac -VR- Chorus/We Saw the Sea -VR- Chorus.

Saturday, 19 May 1945   CANADA DANCE BAND
09.30
(Pre-recorded at the BBC Studios, Maida Vale, London, on Friday, 18 May 1945 — BBC Disc No. SAL 20789)
Over AEFP
Compère: L/Cpl. Dick Misener
Song of the Volga Boatmen/I Never Mention Your Name -VR- Joanne Dallas/Digga Digga Do/Any Old Time/Struttin' Like a Peacock -VR- Paul Carpenter/Old Spinning Wheel/As Long as There's Music -VR- Joanne Dallas/A Little on the Lonely Side -VR- Paul Carpenter/Indiana.

Monday, 21 May 1945   CANADA SHOW
20.30
Broadcast live from the Queensbury All Services Club, Soho, London
Over AEFP
Guest Stars: Rawicz and Landauer
Compères: Gerry Wilmot, S/Sgt. Wilf Davidson, L/Cpl. Dick Misener
There's No Need to Worry Anymore -VR- Chorus/Digga Digga Do/Candy -VR- Paul Carpenter/Voices of Spring (featuring Rawicz and Landauer, pianos)/Great Day/Small Fry -VR- Paul Carpenter/To a Wild Rose/The Bee's Wedding

(featuring Rawicz and Landauer, Pianos)/Now I Know -VR- Gerry Travers and Chorus.

Wednesday, 23 May 1945   PIANO PARADE
11.45
Broadcast live from the BBC Studios, London
Over AEFP
Three Little Words/I'm Gonna Love That Guy/Exactly Like You/So Beats My Heart for You/What Can I Say Dear After I Say I'm Sorry.

Wednesday, 23 May 1945   CANADA GUEST SHOW
17.15
(Pre-recorded at the Queensbury All Services Club, Soho, London, on Tuesday, 22 May 1945 — BBC Disc No. SLO 79643)
Over AEFP
Guest Stars: Rita Williams, Smn. Alex Firman, Bosn's Mate First Class Bill Bassford — U.S.N.
Compère: Capt. Cam Ritchie
Old Man River/How Blue the Night -VR- Rita Williams/Dinah -VR- Rita Williams (accomp. by Cam Ritchie, Piano)/Theme — 'Anchors Aweigh'/ Embraceable You -VR- Bill Bassford/Indiana/I Love Life -VR- Cam Ritchie/ Portrait of a Lady (featuring Alex Firman, Violin) (original by George Melachrino)/Old Spinning Wheel/Let's Take the Long Way Home -VR- Rita Williams/Cocktails for Two/Take Me Out to the Ball Game/Some Other Time -VR- Bill Bassford/Hejre Kati (featuring Alex Firman, Violin)/Cherokee.

Thursday, 24 May 1945   EMPIRE DAY PROGRAMME
17.30
Broadcast live from the Queensbury All Services Club, Soho, London
Over AEFP
Featuring: The Canadian Army Radio Orchestra, under Captain Robert Farnon, and The Canada Show Chorus, with Pvt. Gerry Travers
Compère: L/Cpl. Dick Misener
Opening Theme (Original by Robert Farnon)/The Empire is Marching -VR- Chorus/All Through the Night -VR- Helen Farrell/The Kerry Dance/ To a Wild Rose/Bretonnes -VR- G. Lalande/Medley: Keep the Home Fires Burning; There's a Long, Long Trail Awinding/My Ain Folk -VR- Gerry Travers/ There's No Need to Worry Anymore -VR- Chorus/Oh Canada -VR- Chorus and Close.

Friday, 25 May 1945   CANADA SING SHOW
19.05
(Pre-recorded at the BBC Studios, London, on Thursday, 24 May 1945 — BBC Disc No. SLO 74464)
Over AEFP
Of Thee I Sing -VR- Chorus/Love Walked In -VR- Chorus/Clap Yo' Hands -VR- Chorus/S'Wonderful -VR- Chorus.

141

Saturday, 26 May 1945   CANADA DANCE BAND
09.30
(Pre-recorded at the BBC Studios, Maida Vale, London, on Friday, 25 May 1945 — BBC Disc No. SAL 20940)
Over AEFP
Compère: L/Cpl. Dick Misener
Please Don't Talk About Me When I'm Gone/Am I Blue/Big Cecilia's Jump Joint (original by Denny Farnon)/Sentimental Journey -VR- Paul Carpenter/ La Cinquantaine/And So Little Time -VR- Gerry Travers/I Apologise/ One Alone -VR- Paul Carpenter/My Blue Heaven.

Monday, 28 May 1945   CANADA SHOW
20.30
Broadcast live from the Queensbury All Services Club, Soho, London
Over AEFP
Guest Star: Ronald Chesney
Compères: Gerry Wilmot, S/Sgt. Wilf Davidson
Announcer: L/Cpl. Dick Misener
Free for All -VR- Chorus/Indiana/A Little on the Lonely Side -VR- Paul Carpenter/Believe Me if All Those Endearing Young Charms (featuring Ronald Chesney, Harmonica)/Hallelujah! (featuring Ronald Chesney, Harmonica)/I'm Just Wild About Harry/In the Middle of Nowhere -VR- Gerry Travers/Yesterdays/All or Nothing at All (featuring Ronald Chesney, Harmonica)/The Trolley Song -VR- Chorus.

Wednesday, 30 May 1945   PIANO PARADE
11.45
Broadcast live from the BBC Studios, London
Over AEFP
Honeysuckle Rose/More and More/Come Out, Come Out Wherever You Are/I'm in the Mood for Love/Blue Skies.

Wednesday, 30 May 1945   CANADA GUEST SHOW
17.15
(Pre-recorded at the Queensbury All Services Club, Soho, London, on Tuesday, 29 May 1945 — BBC Disc No. SLO 74580)
Over AEFP
Guest Stars: Carla Forbes, Cpl. Jack Powers, L/Cpl. Freddie Phillips
Compère: Capt. Cam Ritchie
I'm Just Wild About Harry/Waltz Medley: Invitation to the Dance -VR-Carla Forbes; Tales from the Vienna Woods -VR- Carla Forbes; Blue Danube -VR- Carla Forbes/When Your Lover Has Gone -VR- Jack Powers/Please Don't Talk About Me When I'm Gone/Come to the Fair -VR- Cam Ritchie/ Fandanguillo (featuring Freddie Phillips, Guitar)/I Apologise/I'm Gonna See My Baby on Victory Day -VR- Jack Powers/Toroba's Fandanguillo (Piano and Cellist)/Oh! Susannah/La Villanelle -VR- Carla Forbes/When It's Sleepy Time Down South (featuring Freddie Phillips, Guitar)/My Blue Heaven.

Thursday, 31 May 1945   CANADA SWING SHOW
17.30
Broadcast live from the BBC Studios, Maida Vale, London
Over AEFP
Compère: L/Cpl. Dick Misener
The Band Played On/More Than You Know -VR- Gerry Travers/Bye Bye Baby/Like Someone in Love -VR- Paul Carpenter/South Rampart Street Parade/Sweet Dreams Sweetheart -VR- Gerry Travers/Rose Room/I'm Gonna Love That Girl -VR- Paul Carpenter.

Friday, 1 June 1945   CANADA SING SHOW
19.05
(Pre-recorded at the BBC Studios, London, on Thursday, 31 May 1945 — BBC Disc No. SLO 74643)
Over AEFP
Louisiana Hay Ride -VR- Chorus/Wagon Wheels -VR- Chorus/San Fernando Valley -VR- Chorus/The West, a Nest and You -VR- Chorus.

Saturday, 2 June 1945   CANADA DANCE BAND
09.30
(Pre-recorded at the BBC Studios, Maida Vale, London, on Friday, 1 June 1945 — BBC Disc No. SAL 21040)
Over AEFP
Compère: L/Cpl. Dick Misener
March of the Toys/Always Yours -VR- Denny Vaughan/Take Me Out to the Ball Game/Sleepy Town Train/A Ghost of a Chance -VR- Paul Carpenter/ London Bridge is Falling Down/I Go For You -VR- Gerry Travers/Cocktails for Two/Candy -VR- Paul Carpenter/Humoresque.

Monday, 4 June 1945   CANADA SHOW
20.30
(Pre-recorded at the Queensbury All Services Club, Soho, London, on Friday, 9 February 1945 — BBC Disc No. SLO 68474)
Over AEFP
Compères: Gerry Wilmot, S/Sgt. Wilf Davidson
Announcer: L/Cpl. Dick Misener
Opening Theme (March Along, Joe Soldier) -VR- Chorus/Song of the Steppes -VR- Chorus/Lullaby of Broadway/I Go For You -VR- Joanne Dallas/Great Day/Shortnin' Bread -VR- Cam Ritchie/Ain't She Sweet/Drink to Me Only -VR- Chorus (Piano Solo by Denny Vaughan)/Night and Day/I'll Be Around -VR- Gerry Travers/Clap Yo' Hands -VR- Chorus/Closing Theme (March Along, Joe Soldier)

Wednesday, 6 June 1945   PIANO PARADE
11.45
(Pre-recorded at the BBC Studios, London, on Wednesday, 30 May 1945 — BBC Disc No. SWN 20404)
Over AEFP

Bye Bye Baby/The First Few Days/How About You/These are the Things I Love/I'm Gonna Sit Right Down and Write Myself a Letter.

Wednesday, 6 June 1945   **CANADA GUEST SHOW**
17.15

(Recorded repeat of the programme broadcast on Wednesday, 11 April 1945 — BBC Disc No. SAL 20137)

Over AEFP.

Thursday, 7 June 1945   **CANADA SWING SHOW**
17.30

(Pre-recorded at the BBC Studios, Maida Vale, London, on Thursday, 4 January 1945 — BBC Disc No. SWN 19714)

Over AEFP.

Friday, 8 June 1945   **CANADA SING SHOW**
19.05

(Pre-recorded at the BBC Studios, London, on Thursday, 26 April 1945 — BBC Disc No. SLO 72191)

Over AEFP

Recorded repeat of programme first broadcast by the AEFP on Friday, 27 April 1945.

Saturday, 9 June 1945   **CANADA DANCE BAND**
09.30

(Pre-recorded at the BBC Studios, London, on Friday, 9 March 1945 — BBC Disc No. SLO 70519)

Over AEFP

Recorded repeat of programme first broadcast by the AEFP on Saturday, 10 March 1945.

Monday, 11 June 1945   **CANADA SHOW**
20.30

Broadcast live from the Queensbury All Services Club, Soho, London

Over AEFP

Guest Star: Jackie Hunter

Compères: Gerry Wilmot, S/Sgt. Wilf Davidson, L/Cpl. Dick Misener

Opening Theme ('New Theme' – Original music by Robert Farnon)/We Saw the Sea -VR- Chorus/London Bridge/Sentimental Journey -VR- Paul Carpenter/Down by the Vinegar Works -VR- Jackie Hunter/Arthur Murray Taught Me Dancing in a Hurry -VR- Jackie Hunter/I Got Rhythm/The Night has Known More Tears -VR- Gerry Travers/Summertime/Poinciana -VR- Gerry Travers and Chorus/Closing Theme (Original music by Robert Farnon).

Wednesday, 13 June 1945   **PIANO PARADE**
11.45

Broadcast live from the BBC Studios, London

Over AEFP

Sweet Georgia Brown/We'll Gather Lilacs/All My Life/Dianne/Love Me or Leave Me.

Wednesday, 13 June 1945 CANADA GUEST SHOW
17.15
(Pre-recorded earlier the same day at the Paris Cinema, Lower Regent Street, London — BBC Disc No. SLO 75336)
Over AEFP
Guest Stars: Julie Dawn, Denny Dennis RAF, Cliff Gordon
Compère: Capt. Cam Ritchie
Sunny/Tess' Torch Song -VR- Julie Dawn/The Touch of Your Lips -VR- Julie Dawn/A Kiss in the Night -VR- Denny Dennis/I Would Do Anything for You/Give Me the Open Road -VR- Cam Ritchie/Original Comedy — Cliff Gordon/London Bridge/The Very Thought of You -VR- Gerry Travers/It Can't be Wrong -VR- Julie Dawn/I Got Rhythm/You're So Sweet to Remember -VR- Denny Dennis/March of the Toys.

Thursday, 14 June 1945 CANADA SWING SHOW
17.30
Broadcast live from the BBC Studios, Maida Vale, London
Over AEFP
Compère: L/Cpl. Dick Misener
Sweet Sue/Stormy Weather -VR- Gerry Travers/Jeepers Creepers/Vous Qui Passez Sans Me Voir -VR- Paul Carpenter/Digga Digga Do/You're So Sweet to Remember -VR- Gerry Travers/Tea for Two/I Promise You -VR- Paul Carpenter/Lady Be Good.

Friday, 15 June 1945 CANADA SING SHOW
19.05
(Pre-recorded at the BBC Studios, London, on Thursday, 14 June 1945 — BBC Disc No. SLO 75173)
Over AEFP
That's an Order from the Army -VR- Chorus/I Give Thanks for You -VR- Chorus/Together -VR- Chorus/I'm Looking Over a Four Leaf Clover -VR- Chorus.

Saturday, 16 June 1945 CANADA DANCE BAND
09.30
(Pre-recorded at the BBC Studios, London, on Friday, 15 June 1945 — BBC Disc No. SAL 21281)
Over AEFP
Compère: L/Cpl. Dick Misener
All By Myself/It Could Happen To You -VR- Gerry Travers/Shine On Harvest Moon/Hayfoot Strawfoot/Dance with a Dolly -VR- Paul Carpenter/Solitude/You Go to My Head -VR- Gerry Travers/In a Little Spanish Town/Struttin' Like a Peacock -VR- Paul Carpenter/I Let a Song Go Out of My Heart.

Monday, 18 June 1945   CANADA SHOW
20.30
Broadcast live from the Queensbury All Services Club, Soho, London
Over AEFP
Guest Star: Joyce Grenfell
Compères: Gerry Wilmot, S/Sgt. Wilf Davidson
Announcer: L/Cpl. Dick Misener
Pedro the Fisherman -VR- Chorus/Ja Da/What a Difference a Day Made -VR-
Paul Carpenter/Monologue − Joyce Grenfell/I'll Remember April -VR- Joyce
Grenfell/Oh! Susannah/Ma Curly Headed Baby -VR- Joanne Dallas/Parade of
the Wooden Soldiers/All My Tomorrows -VR- Joyce Grenfell/Tico, Tico -VR-
Chorus.

Wednesday, 20 June 1945   PIANO PARADE
11.45
Broadcast live from the BBC Studios, London
Over AEFP
Ain't She Sweet/Like Someone In Love/Confessin'/These Foolish Things/That
Old Feeling.

Wednesday, 20 June 1945   CANADA GUEST SHOW
17.15
(Pre-recorded at the Queensbury All Services Club, Soho, London, on Tuesday
1 May 1945 — BBC Disc No. SLO 73314)
Over AEFP
Recorded repeat of programme first broadcast by AEFP on Wednesday, 2 May
1945 — 17.15.

Thursday, 21 June 1945   CANADA SWING SHOW
17.30
Broadcast live from the BBC Studios, Maida Vale, London
Over AEFP
Compère: L/Cpl. Dick Misener
Five Foot Two/Time On My Hands -VR- Gerry Travers/Straighten Up and
Fly Right -VR- Cuth Knowlton/Mary Lou/When They Ask About You -VR-
Gerry Travers/Coquette/Too Much Illusion -VR- Paul Carpenter/I'm Forever
Blowing Bubbles.

Friday, 22 June 1945   CANADA SING SHOW
19.05
(Pre-recorded at the BBC Studios, London, on Thursday, 21 June 1945 —
BBC Disc No. SLO 75661)
Over AEFP
Announcer: L/Cpl. Dick Misener
Czechoslovakian Dance Song -VR- Chorus/Passing By -VR- Chorus/Morning
Chappell -VR- Chorus/Little Red Drum -VR- Chorus.

Saturday, 23 June 1945   CANADA DANCE BAND
09.30
(Pre-recorded at the BBC Studios, Maida Vale, London, on Friday, 22 June
1945 — BBC Disc No. SAL 21369)
Over AEFP
Compère: L/Cpl. Dick Misener
I Would Do Anything for You/I Never Mention Your Name -VR- Denny
Vaughan/Perdido/Body and Soul/When Your Lover Has Gone -VR- Paul
Carpenter/Take Me Out to the Ball Game/Don't You Know I Care -VR-
Denny Vaughan/Carioca/More and More -VR- Paul Carpenter/Indian Love
Call.

Monday, 25 June 1945   CANADA SHOW
20.30
Broadcast live from the Queensbury All Services Club, Soho, London
Over AEFP
Guest Star: Miss Harriet Cohen
Compères: Gerry Wilmot, S/Sgt. Wilf Davidson, L/Cpl. Dick Misener
Free For All -VR- Chorus/All By Myself/Why do You Pass Me By -VR- Paul
Carpenter/Cornish Rhapsody (featuring Harriet Cohen, Piano)/I'm Just Wild
About Harry/Time On My Hands -VR- Joanne Dallas/Darktown Strutters
Ball/The Hills of Home -VR- Cam Ritchie/Dancing in the Dark -VR- Chorus.

Wednesday, 27 June 1945   PIANO PARADE
11.45
Broadcast live from the BBC Studios, London
Over AEFP
Jeepers Creepers/Barrel Organ Rhapsody/Coquette/Cocktails for Two/Exactly
Like You.

Wednesday, 27 June 1945   CANADA GUEST SHOW
17.15
(Pre-recorded from the Queensbury All Services Club, Soho, London, on
Tuesday, 26 June 1945 — BBC Disc No. SLO 75477)
Over AEFP
Guest Stars: Betty Webb, Stanley Andrews, Jack Watson
Compère: Capt. Cam Ritchie
Liza/Love Here is My Heart -VR- Betty Webb/Accent on Strings (featuring
Stanley Andrews, Violin)/On the Alamo/Without a Song -VR- Cam Ritchie/
All Over the Place (Theme for Jack Watson)/Original Dialogue — Jack
Watson/Dianne (Piano Solo)/Carioca/Old Man River -VR- Chorus (accomp. by
Cliff McAree, Piano)/Little Red Drum -VR- Chorus (accomp. by Cliff McAree,
Piano)/Whispering Grass (featuring Stanley Andrews, Violin)/Beautiful
Dreamer -VR- Betty Webb/Stomping at the Savoy.

Thursday, 28 June 1945   CANADA SWING SHOW
17.30

Broadcast live from the BBC Studios, Maida Vale, London
Over AEFP
Compere: L/Cpl. Dick Misener
When You Wore a Tulip/Junior and Me -VR- Joanne Dallas/September in the Rain/I'm Beginning to See the Light -VR- Paul Carpenter/Just a Little Fond Affection -VR- Joanne Dallas/Blue Lou/I'm Gonna Sit Right Down and Write Myself a Letter/Sentimental Journey -VR- Paul Carpenter/Button Up Your Overcoat.

Friday, 29 June 1945   CANADA SING SHOW
19.05
(Pre-recorded at the BBC Studios, London, on Thursday, 28 June 1945 — BBC Disc No. SLO 76003)
Over AEFP
Announcer: L/Cpl. Dick Misener
Fiesta -VR- Chorus/That's Why Darkies Were Born -VR- Chorus/Stout Hearted Men -VR- Chorus/Irish Medley: Too-Ra-Loo-Ra-Loo-Ra -VR- Chorus; When Irish Eyes Are Smiling -VR- Chorus.

Saturday, 30 June 1945   CANADA DANCE BAND
09.30
(Pre-recorded at the BBC Studios, Maida Vale, London, on Friday, 29 June 1945 — BBC Disc No. SAL 21543)
Over AEFP
Compère: L/Cpl. Dick Misener
Isle of Capri/As Long as There's Music -VR- Denny Vaughan/Lazy River/ Lullaby of Rhythm/Robin Hood -VR- Paul Carpenter/La Cinquantaine/I Cover the Waterfront -VR- Denny Vaughan/Rosetta/Accentuate the Positive -VR- Paul Carpenter/Business in the AEF -comp.- Cpl. G. Hughes.

Monday, 2 July 1945   CANADA SHOW
20.30
Broadcast live from the Queensbury All Services Club, Soho, London
Over AEFP
Guest Star: Alfredo Campoli
Compères: Gerry Wilmot, S/Sgt. Wilf Davidson, L/Cpl. Dick Misener
Fiesta -VR- Chorus/Please Don't Talk About Me When I'm Gone/When Your Lover Has Gone -VR- Paul Carpenter/On Wings of Song (featuring Alfredo Campoli, Violin)/Isle of Capri/Junior and Me -VR- Joanne Dallas/ Chopsticks/Polonaise (featuring Alfredo Campoli, Violin)/With a Song in My Heart -VR- Gerry Travers.

Wednesday, 4 July 1945   PIANO PARADE
11.45
Broadcast live from the BBC Studios, London
Over AEFP
Three Little Words/I Didn't Know About You/Annie Laurie/How Deep is the Ocean/What Can I Say Dear, After I Say I'm Sorry.

Wednesday, 4 July 1945   CANADA GUEST SHOW
17.15
(Pre-recorded on Tuesday, 3 July 1945 — BBC Disc No. SLO 76160)
Over AEFP
Guest Stars: Beryl Davis, Johnny Green, Lorna Martin
Compère: Capt. Cam Ritchie
I'm Just Wild About Harry/You Made Me Love You (Theme for Beryl Davis)/All of a Sudden My Heart Sings -VR- Beryl Davis/Blues in the Night -VR- Johnny Green/Accentuate the Positive -VR- Johnny Green/Indian Love Call/Greensleeves (featuring Lorna Martin, Accordion)/Roadways -VR- Cam Ritchie/For Me and My Gal/Big Cecilia's Jump Joint -VR- Denny Farnon/Mosquito (featuring Lorna Martin, Accordion)/Up a Lazy River (featuring Lorna Martin, Accordion)/Robin Hood -VR- Johnny Green/What a Difference a Day Made -VR- Beryl Davis/Rosetta.

Thursday, 5 July 1945   CANADA SWING SHOW
17.30
Broadcast live from the BBC Studios, Maida Vale, London
Over AEFP
Compère: L/Cpl. Dick Misener
Blue Skies/Wouldn't it be Nice -VR- Joanne Dallas/Pack Up Your Troubles/Saturday Night -VR- Paul Carpenter/The Sheik of Araby -VR- Cuth Knowlton/If You Build a Better Mousetrap -VR- Joanne Dallas/Ding Dong Daddy/I Surrender Dear -VR- Paul Carpenter/China Boy.

Friday, 6 July 1945   CANADA SWING SHOW
19.05
(Pre-recorded at the BBC Studios, London, on Thursday, 5 July 1945 — BBC Disc No. SLO 76174)
Over AEFP
Compere: S/Sgt. Wilf Davidson
Till Men are Free Again -VR- Chorus/Home on the Range -VR- Chorus/Medley (featuring G. Lalande, Solo): C'est L'Aviron; Laboureur; Ah! Si Mon Moine Voulez Danser; The West, a Nest and You.

Saturday, 7 July 1945   CANADA DANCE BAND
09.30
(Pre-recorded at the BBC Studios, London, on Friday, 6 July, 1945 — BBC Disc No. SAL 21666)
Over AEFP
Compère: L/Cpl. Dick Misener
Humoresque/More Than You Know -VR- Joanne Dallas/Sweet Georgia Brown/Things Ain't What They Used to Be/I'm Beginning to See the Light -VR- Paul Carpenter/Dream a Little Dream of Me/Always Yours -VR- Joanne Dallas/I Still Get a Thrill/A Ghost of a Chance -VR- Paul Carpenter/Idaho.

Monday, 9 July 1945   CANADA SHOW
20.30
Broadcast live from the Queensbury All Services Club, Soho, London
Over AEFP
Guest Star: Mario Lorenzi, Harp
Compères: Gerry Wilmot, S/Sgt. Wilf Davidson
Announcer: L/Cpl. Dick Misener
The Trolley Song -VR- Chorus/Idaho/Robin Hood -VR- Paul Carpenter/Poet and Peasant (featuring Mario Lorenzi, Harp)/Cherokee/Too Much in Love -VR- Joanne Dallas/Stairway to the Stars/The Men of Harlech (featuring Mario Lorenzi, Harp)/Loch Lomond (featuring Mario Lorenzi, Harp)/Poinciana -VR- Gerry Travers and Chorus.

Wednesday, 11 July 1945   PIANO PARADE
11.45
Broadcast live from the BBC Studios, London
Over AEFP
Played by: Cpl. Denny Vaughan
Don't be That Way/Every Day of My Life/Wouldn't it be Nice/I Know Why/ Ain't Misbehavin'.

Wednesday, 11 July 1945   CANADA GUEST SHOW
17.15
(Pre-recorded at the Queensbury All Services Club, Soho, London, on Tuesday, 10 July, 1945 — BBC Disc No. SLO 76426)
Over AEFP
Guest Stars: Dorothy Carless, Benny Lee, Frank Weir
Guest Announcer: Sgt. George Monahan (US Army)
Compère: Capt. Cam Ritchie
I Got Rhythm/A Ghost of a Chance -VR- Dorothy Carless/Cry and You Cry Alone -VR- Benny Lee/Perdido/Clarinet Concerto (featuring Frank Weir, Clarinet)/The Song of the Shirt -VR- Cam Ritchie/Candy -VR- Dorothy Carless/Trumpet Concerto in 'E' Flat (featuring Cam Ritchie, Piano and G. Anderson, Trumpet)/I Ain't Got Nothing but the Blues -VR- Benny Lee/ Henderson Stomp (featuring Frank Weir, Clarinet)/Piccadilly Commotion -comp- Robert Farnon.

Thursday, 12 July 1945   CANADA SWING SHOW
17.30
Broadcast live from the BBC Studios, London
Over AEFP
Compère: L/Cpl. Dick Misener
Indiana/The Cows in the Meadow -VR- Joanne Dallas/Poor Butterfly/We'll Gather Lilacs -VR- Paul Carpenter/Ain't Misbehavin'/Says My Heart -VR- Joanne Dallas/Sweet Lorraine/I Promise You -VR- Paul Carpenter/When I Grow Too Old To Dream.

Friday, 13 July 1945   CANADA SWING SHOW
19.05
(Pre-recorded at the BBC Studios, London, on Thursday, 12 July 1945 —
BBC Disc No. SLO 76339)
Over AEFP
Compère: S/Sgt. Wilf Davidson
Scots Wha Hae -VR- Chorus/Medley: Loch Lomond -VR- Chorus; Wi' a
Hundred Pipers -VR- Chorus; Ye Banks and Braes -VR- Chorus; Border
Ballad -VR- Chorus; My Ain Folk -VR- Chorus.

Saturday, 14 July 1945   CANADA DANCE BAND
09.30
(Pre-recorded at the BBC Studios, London, on Friday, 13 July 1945 — BBC
Disc No. SAL 21825)
Over AEFP
Compère: L/Cpl. Dick Misener
Japanese Sandman/A Friend of Yours -VR- Joanne Dallas/Hayfoot Strawfoot/
Indian Summer/Saturday Night -VR- Paul Carpenter/You You Darling/I Go
For You -VR- Joanne Dallas/Am I Blue/When Your Lover has Gone -VR-
Paul Carpenter/In a Little Spanish Town.

Sunday, 15 July 1945   CANADA SWING SHOW
16.01
(Pre-recorded at the BBC Studios, Maida Vale, London, on Thursday, 12 July
1945 — BBC Disc No. SLO 77099)
Over AEFP
Compère: L/Cpl. Dick Misener
Who's Sorry Now/Every Day of My Life -VR- Joanne Dallas/Somebody Loves
Me/Like Someone in Love -VR- Paul Carpenter/Rosetta/Blue Skies -VR-
Joanne Dallas/Things Ain't What They Used to Be/Accentuate the Positive
-VR- Paul Carpenter/Exactly Like You.

Monday, 16 July 1945   CANADA SHOW
20.30
Broadcast live from the Queensbury All Services Club, Soho, London
Over AEFP
Guest Star: Ronald Chesney
Compères: Gerry Wilmot, S/Sgt. Wilf Davidson, L/Cpl. Dick Misener
That's an Order from the Army -VR- Chorus/Japanese Sandman/I'm
Beginning to See the Light -VR- Paul Carpenter/Fascinating Rhythm
(featuring Ronald Chesney, Harmonica)/Schoen Rosmarin (featuring Ronald
Chesney, Harmonica)/Old Man River/I'll Be Seeing You -VR- Joanne Dallas/
All the Things You Are/Medley: Bless 'Em All -VR- Gerry Travers and
Chorus; White Cliffs of Dover -VR- Gerry Travers and Chorus; I've Got
Sixpence -VR- Gerry Travers and Chorus; We'll Meet Again -VR- Gerry
Travers and Chorus; Roll Out the Barrel -VR- Gerry Travers and Chorus.

Tuesday, 17 July 1945   VARIETY HANDBOX
13.01-14.00
(Pre-recorded at the Queensbury All Services Club, Soho, London, on Sunday, 15 July 1945 — BBC Disc No. OP 901 — SLO 76817)
Over AEFP and BBC General Overseas Service
With Special Guests: The BBC Revue Orchestra, conducted by Alan Crookes, the Canadian Band of the AEF, conducted by Robert Farnon, Raymond Newell, Ronald Chesney, Nat Mills and Bobbie, Daria Bayan, Gerry Wilmot, Gil Stewart, Bill Smith, Pat Leonard
Compère: Rene Ray
Announcer: Harry Middleton
Producer: Stephen Williams
Editor: Cecil Madden
Opening Theme (I Love to Sing)/Fanfare (BBC Revue Orchestra)/Great Day (Canadian Band of the AEF)/Border Ballad (Raymond Newell)/Green Eyed Dragon (Raymond Newell)/Flight of the Bumble Bee (BBC Revue Orchestra)/ Believe Me if All Those Endearing Young Charms (featuring Ronald Chesney, Harmonica)/Holiday for Strings (Ronald Chesney, Harmonica)/Comedy Act (Nat Mills and Bobbie)/Winnie the Whistler (Canadian Band of the AEF)/ Theme of the first and second movements from Symphony in Db Major (Robert Farnon, Piano)/Beautiful Lady (Daria Bayan)/Ave Maria /Daria Bayan)/Night and Day (Canadian Band of the AEF)/Comedy Act (featuring Gerry Wilmot, Bill Smith and Gil Stewart)/Laura -VR- Pat Leonard (accomp. by Johnny Franz)/ A Little on the Lonely Side -VR- Pat Leonard (accomp. by Johnny Franz, Piano)/I'll See You In My Dreams -VR- Pat Leonard (Theme Tune)/ I'm Just Wild About Harry (Canadian Band of the AEF)/Liza (Canadian Band of the AEF)/Closing Theme (Let's Have Another One).

Wednesday, 18 July 1945   PIANO PARADE
11.45
(Pre-recorded at the BBC Studios, London, on Wednesday, 30 May 1945 between 12.45 and 13.00 — BBC Disc No. SWN 20404)
Over AEFP
Played by: Cpl. Denny Vaughan
Bye Bye Baby/The First Few Days/How About You/These Are the Things I Love/I'm Gonna Sit Right Down and Write Myself a Letter.

Wednesday, 18 July 1945   CANADA GUEST SHOW
17.15
(Pre-recorded at the Queensbury All Services Club, Soho, London, on Tuesday, 17 July 1945 — BBC Disc No. SLO 76958)
Over AEFP
Guest Stars: Cherry Lind, Alan Bristow, Lt. Bill O'Connor
Compère: Capt. Cam Ritchie
April Showers/Invitation to the Waltz -VR- Cherry Lind/Together -VR- Bill O'Connor/Carioca/Three for Jack -VR- Cam Ritchie (also featuring Cam

Ritchie, Solo Piano)/Drink to Me Only With Thine Eyes (featuring Alan Bristow, Piano)/Great Day/Romance/My Blue Heaven/All the Things You Are -VR- Cherry Lind/Goodnight Wherever You Are/The Very Thought of You -VR- Bill O'Connor/Old Spinning Wheel.

Friday, 20 July 1945   CANADA SING SHOW
19.05
(Pre-recorded at the BBC Studios, London, on Thursday, 19 July 1945 — BBC Disc No. SLO unknown)
Over AEFP
Details remain unknown.

Saturday, 21 July 1945   CANADA DANCE BAND
09.30
(Pre-recorded at the BBC Studios, London, on Friday, 20 July 1945 — BBC Disc No. SAL 21925)
Over AEFP
Compère: L/Cpl. Dick Misener
Perdido/Wouldn't it be Nice -VR- Joanne Dallas/Ja Da/Play Fiddle Play/ Maria Mia -VR- Paul Carpenter/Tea for Two/And So Little Time -VR- Joanne Dallas/All By Myself/Robin Hood -VR- Paul Carpenter/'C' Jam Blues.

Sunday, 22 July 1945   CANADA SWING SHOW
16.01
(Pre-recorded at the BBC Studios, Maida Vale, London, on Thursday, 19 July 1945 — BBC Disc No. SLO 77400)
Over AEFP
Compère: L/Cpl. Dick Misener
September in the Rain/Basin Street Blues -VR- Joanne Dallas/Jazz Me Blues/ When I Take My Sugar to Tea -VR- Cuth Knowlton/I Found a New Baby/ How About You -VR- Joanne Dallas/Love is the Sweetest Thing/I'm Beginning to See the Light -VR- Paul Carpenter/There'll be Some Changes Made.
Note: This was the last programme by the Canadian Army Swing Group directed by Cpl. Denny Vaughan, over the AEFP.

Monday, 23 July 1945   CANADA SHOW
20.30
Broadcast live from the Queensbury All Services Club, Soho, London
Over AEFP
Guest Stars: P/O Ted Hockridge, Sub-Lt. Eric Barker, Les Lieber
Compères: Gerry Wilmot, S/Sgt. Wilf Davidson
Announcer: L/Cpl. Dick Misener
Three Little Words -VR- Chorus/Tea for Two/Tin Whistle Rhapsody (featuring Les Lieber, Tin Whistle)/Embraceable You -VR- Joanne Dallas/ Original Dialogue — Eric Barker/Old Grey Bonnet/I Get a Kick Out of You/ Begin the Beguine -VR- P/O Ted Hockridge/In a Monastery Garden -VR- Chorus.

Wednesday, 25 July 1945   PIANO PARADE
11.45
Broadcast live from the BBC Studios, London
Over AEFP
Played by: Cpl. Denny Vaughan
Exactly Like You/Like Someone in Love/Coquette/More Than You Know/ My Blue Heaven.
Note: This was the last Piano Parade Programme by members of the Canadian Band of the AEF.

Wednesday, 25 July 1945   CANADA GUEST SHOW
17.15
(Pre-recorded at the Queensbury All Services Club, Soho, London, on Tuesday, 24 July 1945 — BBC Disc No. SLO 77551)
Over AEFP
Guest Stars: Marilyn Williams, Billy Mayerl, Pvt. Paul Carpenter (Canadian Army)
Compère: Capt. Cam Ritchie
The Girl I Left Behind Me/April's Fools (Piano Solo by Billy Mayerl)/ Saturday Night is the Loneliest Night -VR- Paul Carpenter/Play Fiddle Play/Shortnin' Bread -VR- Cam Ritchie (Piano Solo by Cam Ritchie)/Sketch (featuring Gerry Wilmot, Dick Misener, Gil Stuart, Pvt. Porteous, H. Farrell and A. Laing)/I Got Rhythm/All of a Sudden My Heart Sings -VR- Marilyn Williams/Blue Again -VR- Marilyn Williams/Ja Da/Marigold (Piano Solo by Billy Mayerl)/Candy -VR- Paul Carpenter/Business in AEF (Original by G. Hughes).
Note: This was the last Canada Guest Show programme broadcast by the AEFP.

Friday, 27 July 1945   CANADA SING SHOW
21.05
(Pre-recorded at the BBC Studios, Maida Vale, London, on Thursday, 26 July 1945 — BBC Disc No. SLO 77705)
Over AEFP
Compère: L/Cpl. Dick Misener
Louisiana Hayride -VR- Chorus/Shenandoah -VR- Chorus/Mama Don't Allow -VR- Chorus/Russia is Her Name -VR- Chorus.
Note: This was the last Canada Sing Show broadcast by the AEFP.

Saturday, 28 July 1945   CANADA DANCE BAND
09.30
(Pre-recorded at the BBC Studios, London, on Friday, 27 July 1945 — BBC Disc No. SAL 22080)
Over AEFP
Compère: L/Cpl. Dick Misener
I'm Forever Blowing Bubbles/I Should Care -VR- Joanne Dallas/Maria Elena/ Emaline/I Wish I Knew -VR- Paul Carpenter/More Than You Know -VR-

Joanne Dallas/There'll be Some Changes Made/Sentimental Journey -VR- Paul Carpenter/March of the Toys/Sweet Lorraine (Piano Solo by Denny Vaughan).
Note: This was the last Canada Dance Band programme broadcast by the AEFP.

Saturday, 28 July 1945   'FAREWELL AEFP'
21.05-22.00
Broadcast live from the Queensbury All Services Club, Soho, London
Over AEFP
(Repeated in edited form by the BBC Light Programme, Sunday, 29 July 1945, 16.00-16.30)
Featuring: The Canadian Band of the AEF, conducted by Robert Farnon, Pat Frost, Dorothy Carless, Beryl Davis, Cpl. Jack Powers, RSM George Melachrino, Richard Tauber, Cpl. Ronnie Selby and his Trio, RAF Dance Orchestra, conducted by Sgt. Jimmy Miller
Compères: Gerry Wilmot, Lt. Douglas Marshall, Jill Balcon, Margaret Hubble, A/C Ronald Waldman RAF, Lt. Charmian Samson, S/Sgt. Wilf Davidson, Sgt. Dick Dudley
Opening Theme (Fanfare) (Canadian Band of the AEF)/Marie (RAF Dance Orchestra)/Candy -VR- Paul Carpenter (Canadian AEF Band)/Don't Fence Me In -VR- Dorothy Carless (Canadian AEF Band)/On Another Track (Pat Frost with RAF Dance Orchestra)/Patter (Cam Ritchie and Red Finlay)/My Heart Sings -VR- Beryl Davis (Canadian AEF Band)/Red, White and Blue (Canadian AEF Band)/What a Difference a Day Made -VR- Jack Powers (Canadian AEF Band)/A Brown Bird Singing -VR- Joanne Dallas (Canadian AEF Band)/Patter – Ronald Waldman and Dick Dudley/Rise and Shine Blues/ SHAEF Theme (Canadian AEF Band)/The More I See You -VR- George Melachrino (Canadian AEF Band)/What is This Thing Called Love? (Ronnie Selby Trio)/Whisperings in the Vienna Woods -VR- Richard Tauber/ (accomp. by Percy Kahn)/General Eisenhower Speech/Auld Lang Syne (both bands with artists and audience) and Close.

Monday, 30 July 1945   CANADIAN CARAVAN
20.30-21.00
Broadcast live from the Queensbury All Services Club, Soho, London
Over the BBC Light Programme
Featuring: The Canadian Army Radio Orchestra, conducted by Capt. Robert Farnon, with Pvt. Joanne Dallas and Pvt. Paul Carpenter and Gerry Travers
Compères: Gerry Wilmot, Rudy Hartman
Opening Theme (Original by Robert Farnon)/I'm Just Wild About Harry/ The More I See You -VR- Gerry Travers/Maria Elena/Sketch (featuring Dick Misener, Joy Porteous, G. Harrison, G. Murray and A. Laing)/Liza/Wouldn't it be Nice -VR- Joanne Dallas/Cocktails for Two/I Wish I Knew -VR- Paul Carpenter/Oh! Susannah/Closing Theme (Original by Robert Farnon).

Monday, 6 August 1945   CANADIAN CARAVAN
20.30
Broadcast live from the Queensbury All Services Club, Soho, London

Over the BBC Light Programme
Compères: Gerry Wilmot, Rudy Hartman
When I Grow Too Old to Dream/Just a Prayer Away -VR- Gerry Travers/
There'll Be Some Changes Made/Sketch (featuring Joy Porteous, G. Murray,
Dick Misener and G. Harrison)/Great Day/I Should Care -VR- Joanne
Dallas/We Could Make Such Beautiful Music/The Gypsy -VR- Paul
Carpenter/Put on Your Old Grey Bonnet.

Monday, 13 August 1945   CANADIAN CARAVAN
20.30
Broadcast live from the Queensbury All Services Club, Soho, London
Over the BBC Light Programme
Compères: Gerry Wilmot, Rudy Hartman
Lady Be Good/Let Me Love You Tonight -VR- Gerry Travers/March of the
Toys/Sketch (featuring Gerry Wilmot, Dick Misener, A. Laing, Gil Stuart, G.
Murray and G. Harrison)/I Know That You Know/I Walked In -VR- Joanne
Dallas/I've Got You Under My Skin/ Robin Hood -VR- Paul
Carpenter/Cherokee.

Monday, 20 August 1945   CANADIAN CARAVAN
20.30
Broadcast live from the Monseigneur Club, London
Over the BBC Light Programme
Compères: Gerry Wilmot, Rudy Hartman
All the Nice Girls Love a Sailor/On My Way Out -VR- Gerry Travers/Perfidia/
Sketch (featuring Robert Farnon, Dick Misener, G. Murray, A. Laing, and G.
Harrison)/Bicycle Built For Two/You've Got Me Where You Want Me -VR-
Joanne Dallas/Take Me Out to the Ball Game/Pablo the Dreamer -VR- Paul
Carpenter/When I Grow Too Old to Dream.

Monday, 27 August 1945   CANADIAN CARAVAN
20.30
Broadcast live from the Queensbury All Services Club, Soho, London
Over the BBC Light Programme
Guest Star: Sgt. Ned Ciachini
Compères: Gerry Wilmot, Rudy Hartman
I Got Rhythm/Just a Prayer Away -VR- Gerry Travers/Way Down Yonder in
New Orleans/Sketch (featuring Dick Misener, A. Laing, G. Murray, G.
Harrison, Gil Stuart, and Davis)/I'm Beginning To See The Light -VR- Joanne
Dallas/Little Way to the Stars (featuring Ned Ciachini, Piano-Accordion)/Out
of This World -VR- Paul Carpenter/Stairway to the Stars (featuring Piano Solo
by Dick Misener).

Monday, 3 September 1945   CANADIAN CARAVAN
20.30
Broadcast live from the Queensbury All Services Club, Soho, London
Over the BBC Light Programme
Compères: Gerry Wilmot, Rudy Hartman

Hallelujah!/Coming Home -VR- Gerry Travers/Confessin'/Sketch/Button Up Your Overcoat/Sketch/Believe Me if All Those Endearing Young Charms -VR- Joanne Dallas/Sketch/There I've Said it Again -VR- Paul Carpenter/ Sketch/Begin the Beguine -arr- Capt. Bob Farnon.

Monday, 10 September 1945 CANADIAN CARAVAN
20.30
Broadcast live from the Queensbury All Services Club, Soho, London
Over the BBC Light Programme
Compères: Gerry Wilmot, Rudy Hartman
I Got Rhythm/Sketch/June Comes Around Every Year -VR- Gerry Travers/ Sketch/Take Me Out to the Ball Game/Sketch/Jeepers Creepers/I'd Rather be Me -VR- Joanne Dallas/Sketch/Digga Digga Do/Sentimental Journey -VR- Paul Carpenter/Sketch/I Want to be Happy.

Monday, 17 September 1945 CANADIAN CARAVAN
20.30
Broadcast live from either the Monseigneur Club or the Paris Cinema, London
Over the BBC Light Programme
Compères: Gerry Wilmot, Rudy Hartman
I Got Rhythm/That Old Black Magic -VR- Gerry Travers/Dinah/Sketch/South Rampart Street Parade/Sketch/A Brown Bird Singing -VR- Joanne Dallas/ Maria Mia -VR- Paul Carpenter/Sketch/I Know That You Know.

Monday, 24 September 1945 CANADIAN CARAVAN
20.30
Broadcast live from the Paris Cinema, Lower Regent Street, London
Over the BBC Light Programme
Compères: Gerry Wilmot, Rudy Hartman
I Want to be Happy/Sketch/Just a Prayer Away -VR- Gerry Travers/When I Grow Too Old to Dream/Sketch/Bicycle Built for Two/First Few Days -VR- Joanne Dallas/Sketch/Pack Up Your Troubles/What a Difference a Day Made -VR- Paul Carpenter/Sketch/Hallelujah!

Monday, 30 September 1945 CANADIAN CARAVAN
20.30
Broadcast live from the Monseigneur Club, London
Over the BBC Light Programme
Compères: Gerry Wilmot, Rudy Hartman
Details remain unknown.

Monday, 8 October 1945 CANADIAN CARAVAN
20.30
Broadcast live from the Monseigneur Club, London
Over the BBC Light Programme
Compères: Gerry Wilmot, Rudy Hartman
Details remain unknown.

Saturday, 15 December 1945   FAREWELL AFN
19.45-20.15
Broadcast live from the Paris Cinema, Lower Regent Street, London
Over the BBC Light Programme
(A BBC tribute to the AFN in the United Kingdom, on closing after two-and-a-half years)
Featuring: Capt. Robert Farnon's Canadian Army Radio Orchestra, Jackie Hunter, Dorothy Carless, A/C2 Ronald Waldman RAF, Dick Dudley, PFC Byron Kane, Brigadier General Claude M. Thiel
Compère: Sgt. Dick Dudley
Announcer: Margaret Hubble
Opening Theme (Original by Robert Farnon)/Speech by Claude M. Thiel, of the UK base of the US Army/Somebody Loves Me/ Interview between Ronald Waldman and Dick Dudley/When I Got in the Army -VR- Dick Dudley (accompanied by Ronald Waldman, Piano) Medley: Sentimental Journey; As Time Goes By; Shoo Shoo Baby; I'll be Seeing You/Men of Arnhem -VR- Byron Kane/Begin the Beguine -VR- Dorothy Carless/I Hate Guys and Dames -VR- Jackie Hunter/Auld Lang Syne -VR- Band and Audience and Close.

Jimmy Heffner and the Seabees Dance Orchestra

The Seabees Dance Orchestra, conducted and led by Jimmy Heffner, were based at Camp Parks, California. Not much is known of this swinging fifteen-piece band. They were formed about late 1943 to early 1944 and made several appearances on the Armed Forces Radio Services 'Yank Bandstand' series of radio programmes during late 1944. It was a wonderful little band, with some memorable clarinet and saxophone playing. The vocals were given by Seaman Bill Barr. The group were broken up sometime in late 1945. They were never featured on V-Discs, but did make several appearances at the Hollywood Canteen and on war bond rallies.

Captain Wayne King and his US Army Band
1942 – 1944

Wayne King was an orchestra leader during the early 1940s. He was famous for his waltz recordings for RCA from 1940 until 1942. His famous theme, *The Waltz You Saved for Me*, was often borrowed by Glenn Miller and his Orchestra during early 1942. Later, Glenn Miller's Army Air Force Orchestra also used the theme in one of their medleys.

Wayne King, like Glenn Miller, had joined the United States Army in 1942, at the rank of Captain. He was stationed in the Chicago area and directed all military show units for the US Army Sixth Service Command. He also contributed greatly to the work of the US Treasury Department at War Bond Rallies during 1943. The orchestra also appeared at recruiting rallies and Red Cross drives throughout the mid-West and Chicago areas during 1943. Wayne King was promoted to the rank of Major late in 1943. He left the Army late in 1944 and reorganised his civilian orchestra in 1945.

Manhattan Beach Coast Guard Band 1942 – 1945

The Manhattan Beach Coast Guard Band was formed in early 1942 by Chief Musician Norbert O'Conner. The 35-piece concert/marching band was stationed at the Manhattan Beach Coast Guard Training Centre, at Brooklyn, New York. The orchestra was often broken down into a very good dance band. The three groups played separately, but combined for parades. Shortly after the formation of the orchestra, O'Conner was replaced by ex-symphony orchestra conductor, Ensign Richard Korn. Musician Third Class Clare Grundman arranged for the band and served as assistant conductor. Grundman conducted the band for Coast Guard radio broadcasts over WEAF/NBC and short recruiting and propaganda films.

The dance band was formed in early 1942, by Grundman and popular song writer Jack Lawrence. Lawrence soon left for the Merchant Marines and former orchestra leader Chief Musician Jack Stabile took over the dance band. One of Glenn Miller's ex-musicians, bass player Edward 'Doc' Goldberg, joined this band around the autumn of 1942. Another well-known musician who was also in this band was drummer Sheldon 'Shelly' Manne.

The concert marching band recorded for V-Discs in late October, 1943. These V-Discs were in the series, *Music for Marching Men*. The band also appeared at war bond rallies in and around New York.

As far as is known, the unit was disbanded in 1945.

Maritime Service Training Station Band 1942 – 1945

The Maritime Service Training Station Band was formed in November 1942 by bandleader Phil Harris (from the Jack Benny radio show), with the help of Hollywood contractor Dave Klein. The musicians joined as Petty Officers Third Class and went on active duty at Avalon, Catalina Island, California, on 26 November 1942. Phil Harris was commissioned as a Lieutenant Junior Grade and was in charge of the band. His assistant was Lieutenant Junior Grade Curt Roberts.

The band made an appearance on the Jack Benny radio show in late 1942 and played at military functions on top of their bi-monthly trips to Los Angeles to play for war bond rallies and at the Hollywood Canteen.

The orchestra contained forty-one musicians and a smaller dance band. Among the famous sailor-musicians in its ranks were Wilbour 'Willie' Schwartz from the Glenn Miller Band, Mahlon Clark from the Ray McKinley Band, and Walter 'Pee Wee' Hunt from the Glen Gray Casa Loma Orchestra.

Phil Harris was released from active duty in late 1943 and returned to the Jack Benny radio show. Lieutenant Curt Roberts took over both the large orchestra and the dance band until about June 1945, when Warrant Officer Simon 'Sy' Waronker (musical contractor for the Twentieth Century Fox studios) replaced him and remained in charge until the unit was dissolved in either late 1945 or early 1946.

Glenn Miller and his Army Air Force Orchestra
1943 – 1945

Of all the big bands of the Second World War, perhaps the band or orchestra that Glenn Miller led and directed from May 1943 until late 1945 evokes more memories and nostalgia than any other. Ask anyone to produce a war film or play of World War Two and two people's music will certainly be playing in the background: Dame Vera Lynn's and Glenn Miller's. Their music represents the whole epoch.

It may well have been the way in which Glenn died and the mystery surrounding that fateful day of Friday, 15 December 1944 which continues to ensure his popularity. Glenn's nephew, John Miller, said recently on a radio interview that he believed that Glenn would not want anybody to uncover the mystery because it was good for business. Maybe John is right, because even today the records are still selling and Glenn continues to be one of the all-time greats of popular music.

Born on 1 March 1904 in a sleepy mid-West town called Clarinda, in the state of Iowa, his rise to fame really began in 1939, when the world was still at peace. For many years, he had been an arranger and trombonist for many bands. In 1935, he had put together his first studio band. It lasted for one recording session. In 1937, he had put together another. A year later, it failed. Nobody seemed interested and Glenn had problems with his wife Helen's health. A couple of months later, he tried again and put together yet another band. This one included a young saxophone player called Gordon 'Tex' Beneke and Ray Eberle. By early 1939, this new band had started to take off. Then, on 17 May 1939, they opened at Glen Island Casino, at New Rochelle, near New York City. They had hit the big time. Tex recently said, 'The band started to draw big crowds and in no time we became household names from coast to coast. Recordings flowed with hits like *Little Brown Jug*, *In the Mood* and our famous theme written by Glenn himself, *Moonlight Serenade*.'

By 27 December 1939, the band was to be heard coast to coast on CBS for Chesterfield Time. They stayed with the cigarette company until Glenn went to war in September 1942. The Chesterfield shows were aired three nights a week. Business was very brisk indeed and included recording sessions, broadcasts and personal appearances throughout the United States and Canada. During August 1941, Glenn produced a further programme, paid for out of his own pocket, which saluted service camps throughout the USA. America was already preparing for war. Nazi U-boats had already attacked US ships and Japan was having talks about its Empire out in the Pacific. The United States had begun a call-up of its young men as early as January that year. Glenn's salute was aimed at them: he invited the camps to choose their favourite top tune, the public voted and the camp that won was awarded a radio-phonograph (a radio and record player) and fifty records. During the spring, Glenn and the band went to Hollywood and made a film called *Sun Valley Serenade*; this was released during the autumn and it proved a great success too. Then, on Sunday, 7 December 1941, the Japanese suddenly attacked Pearl Harbour and America was at war. Everything was turned over to the war effort. America was on the march. The Glenn Miller Orchestra had just ten months to go and then Glenn would enter the army. During the spring, Glenn and the band made one further film in Hollywood — *Orchestra Wives*.

At the beginning of September 1942, Glenn applied for a commission in the army. He had tried to enter the Navy during June, but was turned down because of his age. He was 38 and short-sighted. The Army Specialist Corps accepted him and by 26 September 1942, the band was disbanded. It was on that night that Glenn and the band performed their highly emotional farewell show in Passaic, New Jersey. It was a tear-stained event. An emotional Glenn said, 'I turned from the band to see the whole audience bawling their eyes out.' From this dramatic farewell, Glenn would take his music a step further. The most successful commercial band of all time had passed into history. Glenn took his next step into what was to become his destiny.

On 7 October 1942, the newly created Captain Alton Glenn Miller reported for duty at the US Army Specialist Corps headquarters at Omaha, Nebraska. The week before, Glenn and his wife, Helen, had spent their time with his mother and his elder brother, Deane. Upon arrival at Omaha, Glenn was told to report to the Army Specialist Training Centre at Fort George Meade, Maryland. Glenn would stay there until he had completed his training in early December 1942. He did not attempt very much on the musical side since he had to cope with the purely military side of his training. However, he did appear a couple of times with the post band, directing military music. On 4 December he was transferred from the Army to the Army Air Forces Technical Training Command. Some astute young officer had found out Glenn's first name and had transferred him. The Army Air Force gained the bandleader to their ranks, and the Army lost him.

Glenn was next transferred to the Army Air Forces headquarters at Maxwell Field, Alabama. It was there that Glenn and Lieutenant Colonel Richard E. Daley were put in charge of all bands for the Technical Training Command of the Army Air Forces. By deploying the enormous amount of musical talent being drafted into the Army Air Forces, Glenn could put together many brand-new bands, bringing versatile music right up to date. He had, unfortunately, failed to take into account the conservatism of the chain of

Captain Glenn Miller with Corporals Ray McKinley and Hollywood film star Broderick Crawford during a CBS I Sustain the Wings *broadcast (early summer of 1943)*

command above him. Still, he did manage to salvage a couple of the projects. Most important of all was the idea of a new super-band, featuring the top musical talent from the big bands now at the training centre at Atlantic City. Among them were many old friends from Glenn's time with the Dorsey brothers and Ray Noble. Musicians like former bandleaders and drummer Ray McKinley, pianist and arranger Mel Powell (from the Benny Goodman Band), and many more. There were also quite a few from Glenn's own disbanded band, including Glenn's arranger friend Jerry Gray, and trumpeter Zeke Zarchy. Glenn swapped musicians for those he really wanted. Also included in the line-up was a string section of some twenty players. Many had come from the top symphony orchestras in New York City and Boston.

Drawing all the best musicians from the popular, jazz and symphonic worlds together at Atlantic City and picking the very best, Glenn began to put together the ultimate all-purpose band, a kind of super-big band orchestra, that no civilian bandleader could ever match. The cost of such a super-band would have staggered anyone putting together such a star line-up in peacetime. Glenn's scheme was to syphon off the musicians he thought he needed as the draft brought them into the armed forces. He would also contact certain chosen instrumentalists to ask them to let him know when their call-up was imminent; he would then pull out all the stops to get them into his mammoth new project. In one instance, he even swapped six soldier-musicians for his old bass player, Herman 'Trigger' Alpert. The new orchestra would be like none ever put together by the services. It would include its own script writer,

Hollywood film star, Broderick Crawford, and would provide dramatic playlets to extol the efforts of the Army Air Forces in the war-torn world; they would also encourage and invite young men and women to join the Army Air Forces and would give out propaganda.

By late April 1943, the newly created 418th AAFTC Band, which was now stationed at Yale University, in New Haven, Connecticut, was nearly ready to start a series of radio programmes called *I Sustain the Wings*. The first six programmes were to go out live from Yale University every Saturday afternoon over the local CBS radio station. The first show was broadcast on 29 May 1943. They were a success from the word go. The Army Air Forces were so pleased that they gave the go-ahead for the series to be broadcast coast to coast over the CBS network. The first show on 10 July was cancelled, however, due to technical problems, although it was recorded. A week later, on 17 July 1943, much to the delight of the American radio public coast to coast, the first show was aired. Once again it was a success and included the orchestra with Hollywood film star (now Corporal) Tony Martin singing and Corporal Broderick Crawford in the dramatic sketch.

Although the radio orchestra were an outstanding success, this did not necessarily loosen the attitude of the top brass to Glenn's version of *St Louis Blues March* and *Blues in the Night March*.

Glenn and the newly created marching band ran straight into trouble with them over their 'swinging' marches. Many old-style military bandmasters started to question Glenn's ideas. This resulted in Glenn and the Major of the cadets at Yale meeting face to face. The Major said, 'Tell me, Captain, we did pretty good with Sousa in the last war.' To which Glenn snapped, 'Tell me, Major, are we still flying the same planes we flew then?' The band continued with their swinging marching music, much to the delight of the cadets and the general public in and around New Haven.

After just two months of broadcasts over CBS with *I Sustain the Wings*, the show was switched to the NBC Network. Moreover, Tony Martin left during September and would be replaced on 16 October 1943 by Johnny Desmond. Johnny was perhaps Miller's best-ever vocalist. He was called the 'G.I.s Sinatra', and fitted very well into the orchestra. Also in late October, Glenn and the band were in the RCA Victor studios to wax their first V-Discs for the American Forces. They recorded several marches, including two by the full forty-piece orchestra — the ever beautiful *Stardust* and *Stormy Weather*.

During the summer of 1943, the full orchestra had taken part in several war bond rallies and concerts. More would take place in and around New Haven over the next few months.

The orchestra now became a multi-purpose unit which could function as a complete unit or be broken down into a string orchestra, led by Staff Sergeant George Ockner, a swing/dance band, a small jazz group, or even a jazz trio, led by Sergeant Mel Powell at the piano. The first broadcast by the dance band was on 20 October 1943 in a series called *Wings for Tomorrow*. The group was led by Corporal Ray McKinley. The String Orchestra made its first radio broadcast on 30 November 1943 in a programme called *Strings With Wings*. This was the forerunner of the ETO *Swing Shifts* and *Strings With Wings* programmes which became so popular over the BBC's AEF programme. The orchestra could also be broken down into small sections when they visited hospitals so that they could tour the wards and play for wounded and sick servicemen.

The *I Sustain the Wings* radio broadcast on Christmas Day, 1943, performed at Halloran General Hospital (in the auditorium), was memorable insomuch that it was the first broadcast that Glenn missed. He was taken ill with flu just before air time and went home sick.

Captain Miller was back the following week on New Year's Day of 1944 for a live *Atlantic Spotlight* broadcast aimed at the British Isles and the American troops stationed there. Later that day the orchestra performed their *I Sustain the Wings* show from New York City.

Later that month Glenn and the orchestra performed at the opening of the Fourth War Loan Drive, on a special broadcast. Also taking part was Hollywood film star Ronald Reagan, now a Lieutenant in the Army Air Forces. Today, he speaks very fondly of Glenn and the orchestra and is still a big fan. Glenn and the orchestra performed at many places all over the Eastern USA for the Fourth War Loan Drive. Glenn still wanted to do more, remembers Ray McKinley: 'We recorded V-Discs that would wind up in every corner of the war-torn world.'

On 18 February 1944, Captain Glenn Miller was transferred from the AAF headquarters at Maxwell Field to Yale University, to take over the leadership of the orchestra. Although he had conducted the orchestra up until that time, he was not listed as the commanding officer until this date. Glenn's dream of producing a group of orchestras and bands for the war effort had never really got off the ground. All he had was two bands: the large orchestra and a small dance band, which were really the overflow of musicians also stationed at Yale University. His next dream was to take the super-orchestra overseas to the fighting men 'Over There'! After all, bandleader Artie Shaw had just finished a year's service on tour in the South Pacific with his US Navy Rangers band, and Glenn wanted to do the same, if the top brass would let him. Again, officialdom stood in his way, and it is not clear to this day whether it was due to sheer vindictiveness at the top or whether the Miller Orchestra had by this time become such potent fund-raisers for war bonds, the Red Cross, and at recruiting rallies and other patriotic causes that they were genuinely felt to be more useful at home than overseas, Again, fate stepped into the picture in the shape of Colonel Edward Kirby, who was part of General Dwight D. Eisenhower's staff at SHAEF in England. Ed was in New York City on 6 May 1944 and went along to see the Glenn Miller AAFTC Orchestra performing on their live broadcast. After the show, Kirby was taken backstage and introduced to Glenn and Don Haynes. The three left the theatre and went for a

Capt. Glenn Miller directs the AAFTC Orchestra during its final I Sustain the Wings radio broadcast over NBC, at the Service Men's Centre in Chicago, Saturday, 10 June 1944

coffee in the restaurant next door. Colonel Kirby told Miller about his problems and his need for an orchestra in London to become part of the Allied team for D-Day, the great Invasion of Europe. Glenn said, 'What about my orchestra?' Kirby went on to explain the problems, but said he would see what could be done at SHAEF when he got back to London.

Suddenly, events began to move in Miller's favour. During late May, arrangements were made for the transfer of the entire unit to England. Glenn and the orchestra still carried on with their broadcasts and the Fifth War Loan Drive. The news came through while Glenn and the orchestra were on tour that the D-Day landings in Normandy had taken place on 6 June. This was the sign that they too were heading overseas. They performed their last *I Sustain the Wings* broadcast on 10 June from Chicago and the following day they left by train for Yale University. The next week would be one of lectures, rifle training and injections. Glenn considered every aspect of the trip. He even obtained relief musicians.

On 18 June Glenn and T/Sgt. Paul Dudley flew to the United Kingdom. The orchestra members left by ship on 23 June. The 62 members of the orchestra arrived in the United Kingdom on 28 June. Captain Miller met them at Gourock, in Scotland. He told them that, over the last few days, London had been under Nazi blitz from V-1's or Doodle-bugs. The unit travelled overnight by train from Glasgow and arrived at Euston station. Army trucks were waiting to take them to their new billets in Chelsea, right bang in the area known as 'Buzz-Bomb' Alley, where those dreaded Doodle-bugs came over.

Glenn could see a chance that, if he did not get them out soon, he may not have a band left to lead.

While the band settled into its new billets, Miller, Haynes and Dudley went by staff car to SHAEF at Bushey Park, near Teddington, Middlesex, to meet Colonel David Niven, the British film star and a SHAEF transport officer, who, at Miller's request, was already trying to obtain transport to move the band out of London. The band had been billeted in London to meet its broadcasting commitments, prior to the V-1 'Doodle-bug' bombardment on 13 June 1944. Miller wanted the band moved out as soon as possible.

After lunch, twice interrupted by air-raid warnings, Niven took the three men to Bedford. Also present was the BBC engineer assigned to the band, Teddy Gower. Teddy remembers the first trip to Bedford with Niven, Miller, Haynes and Dudley. 'Miller, Haynes, Dudley, Maurice Gorham and Dr Alexander and I drove up to Bedford at that time, and we saw this hall, which was a social hall belonging to the Gas Company. Anyway, it was all we could get, and it was not really large enough. Acoustic-wise, it was pretty terrible; anyway, we had to have it and there we stayed for six months — more or less everybody recording or doing live transmissions.'

During that period, Miller, Haynes, Dudley, plus many AEFP staff, had many meetings at Broadcasting House. Miller was even given an office in the Langham Hotel, which, as Cecil Madden recalls, he never used. However, he also had a suite at the Mount Royal Hotel, near Marble Arch, although, during this period, Miller, Haynes and Dudley spent most of their time in the deep BBC air-raid shelter. The V-1 flying bombs were coming over day and night. The band soon found out this was not the quiet of New Haven that they had all known so well.

Because of the hollowness of Co-Partners Hall, it had to be lined with sandbags and shelter halfs. Another thing that the band soon encountered in England was the rationing. After all, Britain had been at war nearly five years and they found bomb sites everywhere they went in London. It was certainly a world away from the United States of America, which had only certain things rationed. This was the civilian front line, with death and destruction everywhere!

Singer Artie Malvin remembers their billet in Sloane Square: 'Our first night in London, most of the band headed for the neighbourhood bomb shelters with their blankets, but several heroes, or idiots — you make the choice — by name Johnny Desmond, Steve and Gene Steck, Jack Steele and myself, put on our steel helmets and climbed to the roof of our house to watch the rockets with their flaming tails flying over the city. Fortunately for us they were concentrated on targets at some distance from our perch. When the flame coming out the rear bomb went out, the engine would cut out and, in a brief few seconds it seemed, a thunderous explosion would follow, with ensuing death and destruction.'

'Glenn's intuition was surely working overtime when he insisted we be moved out of London no later than Sunday, 2 July 1944! The American motor pool said, ''We don't work Sundays''. It is my recollection that Glenn proceeded to make a deal with the Royal Air Force to provide transportation to our new billets in Bedford, which was to be our new base. In exchange for the lorries, we would play a concert for the Royal Air Force. A very good deal that was. At noon on Sunday, we travelled the 55 miles or so to Bedford, and the very next morning, Monday, 3 July at 8.00 a.m., a V-Bomb struck behind our former billet on Sloane Court. Twenty-five military policemen seated in a truck were killed, as were several women of the American Women's Corps — their first overseas casualties. The women had been in formation ready to march to the local mess-hall for breakfast. Glenn's intuition surely saved some of our lives — tragic that we couldn't save his!'

Don Haynes was near Sloane Square on that morning of 3 July. He spent most of his time there, helping to dig out the wounded and injured casualties from the remains of the band's former billet. It was the first of many narrow escapes that the orchestra would encounter in the European Theatre of Operations. The situation would get worse, because, during September, the Nazis started bombarding the south-east of England with long-range rockets — V-2's. These gave no warning whatsoever.

The orchestra would also encounter other problems with the BBC schedule, their tour of the bases and travelling. Artie Malvin recalls: 'Mulling over the term ''adverse'', it could easily apply to those kidney-jarring rides in what seemed to be springless half-ton trucks, delivering us to some Air Force base to play a concert.'

Glenn's band, now known as the American Band of the Supreme Allied Command, broadcast their first programme over the Allied Expeditionary Forces Programme on Sunday, 9 July 1944. This special broadcast took place live from the Bedford Corn Exchange, on direct line to the AEFP and BBC Home Service. Taking part in the programme were British guest stars Dorothy Carless and Bruce Trent. Bruce remembers with pride his broadcasts with Glenn Miller: 'The first member of the orchestra I met was the young red-haired trumpet player, Bobby Nichols. I asked him what he thought of his famous boss. Bobby answered: ''We think the world of him; he is the greatest.'' It was some experience singing with this large soldier orchestra. My song on that first broadcast was *I Couldn't Sleep a Wink Last Night*. Dorothy's song was *Begin the Beguine*. Leslie Mitchell and Glenn Miller introduced us.' The following Thursday, 13 July 1944, both Dorothy and Bruce were back again as the British guest stars. Young Jean Metcalfe helped out with the introductions.

The impact of the orchestra on Britain can scarcely be imagined within the week of broadcasts which showed off the band's many-faceted units. These units included the dance band, directed by the much-loved drummer and singer, Sergeant Ray McKinley, the Uptown Hall Swing Sextet, led by pianist and composer Sergeant Mel Powell (from the Benny Goodman band) and the

Captain Glenn Miller directs the entire American Band of the AEF in the Corn Exchange in Bedford July – August 1944 (Photo: Bedford Record)

string orchestra, led by concert master Sergeant George Ockner, which played light and classical songs on the *Strings With Wings* programmes. Singer Sergeant Johnny Desmond had his own programme every Sunday lunch-time with the entire orchestra, conducted by Master Sergeant Norman Leyden. This programme, introduced by Johnny himself, was called *Johnny Desmond Sings: A Soldier and a Song*, and included the orchestra and Johnny singing many of the hit songs of the day. Among these were *I'll Get By, I'll Be Seeing You, Going My Way* and many others. There was also a solo piano programme by the orchestra's relief pianist, PFC Jack Russin. In the beginning, they were called *Keyboard Contrasts* and, much later, in September, *Piano Parade*; they were broadcast over AEFP every Saturday morning at 11.45 a.m., for fifteen minutes.

Then on Friday evening, 14 July 1944, Captain Glenn Miller and the Orchestra began their now famous tour of the bases. Their first major concert was at the heavy bomber base at Thurleigh Airfield. The late Jerry Gray remembered with pride their tour of the bases in England: 'When we saw the look of those G.I.s the very first time, that was enough for me: I knew we did a good thing by going there, because you could just see the looks on those guys' eyes and, as Glenn said, "We gave them a 'Hunk o' Home'." '

Glenn told Colonel Kirby during the concert at Thurleigh Airfield: 'Making all the money in the big-band business could never make me this rich.' If this first concert was anything to go by, the G.I.s wanted as much as they could get! On Sunday, 16 July 1944, during the afternoon, Captain Glenn Miller and the American Band of the Supreme Allied Command performed at the 8th Air Force Service Command Headquarters at Milton Ernest Hall, just outside

Captain Glenn Miller and the orchestra in the grounds of Milton Ernest Hall, near Bedford, 16 July 1944

Bedford. These were the headquarters of General Goodrich and his executive officer, Lt. Colonel Norman Baessell. This was the base where the band were fed, and this Sunday afternoon concert was at the back of the hall, under the trees. It was a very sunny, hot afternoon and British singer Dorothy Carless performed with the orchestra.

Glenn's next performance was at the Ordnance Depot at Melchbourne Park. The orchestra played on a flat-bed truck in front of the hall. It was an overcast day and very chilly, but the music was not and the G.I.s loved every minute of it.

On Thursday, 20 July 1944, the American Band of the Supreme Allied Command broadcast included two guests, both British and both famous. One was the forces' sweetheart, Vera Lynn, and the other was Sergeant Jimmy Miller, leader of the famous RAF Dance Orchestra, the Squadronaires. Jimmy now picks up the story of that broadcast: 'Dame Vera Lynn drove us both down to Bedford from London during the afternoon. I sung the first with a song from a Frank Sinatra film, *A Lovely Way to Spend an Evening*. The orchestra was really great and I shall never forget that, at the rehearsal, Glenn raised one hand and the orchestra hushed. They even stood to attention when he entered. Compared to the Squadronaires, that was the only way to lead an orchestra. The band were great, but not my vocals. Vera sang towards the end with Besame Mucho. Afterwards, Vera and I returned by car back to London. Vera drove again and, due to the blackout, we nearly drove off the road. I shall never forget that day when I met my namesake.'

Captain Glenn Miller and the American Band of the Supreme Allied Command entertaining the G.I.s at Melchbourne Park, Friday, 21 July 1944

A week later, on Thursday, 27 July 1944, Anne Shelton was the guest star, but this programme was recorded at Bedford on Sunday, 23 July. Anne remembers with pride her guest-star role with Glenn and his orchestra: 'I remember we first met in Co-Partners Hall. He said, ''You're the little gal that sings in G flat.'' I said, ''Well, I sing with Mr Ambrose and all big orchestras.'' He said, ''We're gonna get along just fine.'' ' Anne sang *I'll Get By* on the broadcast and later, she also sang *And the Angels Sing.* Glenn told her that when she sang that, it made the eagle on his cap take wing and fly. Anne remembers: 'That was when I made my biggest boob, by telling Mel Powell to stop running up and down the keyboard on his piano during my song of *Blues in the Night.* Glenn turned and said, ''I've been telling him that for years.'' The orchestra fell about laughing.' Earlier that day, some members of the band attended the Royal visit by Her Majesty The Queen (The Queen Mother) at the American Red Cross Club in Bedford. Her Royal Majesty told Don Haynes that the future queen and her sister, Princess Margaret, were great fans of the Glenn Miller Orchestra and listened to the radio every Thursday for their broadcasts. This must have pleased Glenn when he heard it from Don.

The orchestra were on the air over the AEFP nearly every day of the week, including Sunday. Most of the programmes were live at this time, although a few were recorded in advance, when Glenn and the band were touring the fighter and bomber bases. Up until now the orchestra had been seen only by the Armed Forces, although their broadcasts netted a wider audience in the United Kingdom through the BBC Home Service on Thursday evenings. This would soon change, because, during late July, Glenn and Maurice Gorham of the BBC had an argument over the full band's Thursday show. Gorham told Miller: 'The trouble was that, when the orchestra performed its low mellow passages on certain tunes, civilian listeners had complained that they had thought that the BBC had gone off the air.' Glenn retorted 'We did not come here to entertain civilians, but to entertain the fighting men of the Allied Forces.' So, on 10 August 1944, the American Band of the AEF, as it was now named, performed its last show on the BBC Home Service. From then on, the orchestra would broadcast only over the BBC AEFP and General Forces programmes.

The orchestra's tour of the bases continued and began to move outwards from the Bedford area. The band began to fly by transport aircraft to bases. Sometimes, they even used bombers such as the B-17s and B-24s. On 24 July 1944, the dance band and its leader performed at a concert at Wattisham, near Ipswich, in Suffolk.

So far, London had not seen much of the orchestra since its move to Bedford, although Glenn and Don Haynes had spent quite a bit of time in the Doodle-bug-hit city, at meetings, with Cecil Madden, and Lt. Colonel David Niven, at Teddington and at Broadcasting House. It was Cecil Madden who put forward the idea that the dance orchestra section should appear on his long-running *American Eagle in Britain* programme. So, to kill two birds with one stone, Glenn and the dance band appeared on 27 July in the American Red Cross Club's Dunkers Den, better known as 'Rainbow Corner' — in Piccadilly Circus. Later in the afternoon, Glenn and the full orchestra, including the string section, performed at the charity première of the new Bing Crosby film, *Going My Way*, at the Plaza Cinema. It was a star-studded occasion, with many famous celebrities and British bandleaders in the audience.

The charity was in aid of the Stage Door Welfare fund. The new London Stage Door Canteen was due to be opened in mid-August 1944 at 201 Piccadilly, and would be unique in providing all non-commissioned ranks of men and women of the armed forces of the Allied Nations with entertainment, dancing and light refreshments. The new canteen would open daily and on hand would be prominent stars of stage, screen and radio to serve and dance with those present.

The day after the band's charity performance in London, Glenn and the orchestra were at the B-17 base at Polebrook, some 25 miles north of Bedford. They performed for 10,000 American airmen at this concert. This was the base at which another famous American had been stationed during his stay in the United Kingdom: Captain Clark Gable.

The very next day, 29 July, would prove quite an experience in itself for Glenn, Don and the entire orchestra. In the afternoon, they performed at

General Jimmy Doolittle's special headquarters at Wycombe Abbey, in the centre of High Wycombe. These were the headquarters of the 8th Air Force and were the nerve-centre of the Allied Air Forces. In 1944, the location was top secret and was codenamed 'Pinetree'. Doolittle was famous for his B-25 bomber raid on Tokyo in early 1942. Glenn and the orchestra performed on a flat-bed open truck in front of the abbey. Today, the building is a top girls' school. Recently, the event was recreated with the Herb Miller Concert Orchestra, directed by Glenn's nephew, John Miller — and what an experience it turned out to be! Although 44 years had passed, a healthy number of people turned out for a very special event indeed, which, like its 1944 predecessor, was recorded on film.

After the 1944 concert, General Doolittle made his now famous remark: 'Next to a letter from home, your music is the greatest morale booster in the ETO.' This was the concert that featured in the Hollywood film *The Glenn Miller Story*, made in 1954, in which a flying bomb comes over during the playing of *In the Mood*. Although in reality the flying bomb incident happened on 16 August 1944 at Bently Priory, near Stanmore.

On Sunday, 30 July, Glenn and the orchestra were back in London for the recording of the weekly variety show, *Variety Bandbox*. This was another Cecil Madden production. Glenn and Cecil were very great friends and, just before his death, Cecil recalled their friendship: 'He was a truly great bandleader and a really nice chap to talk to, although he knew exactly what he wanted.' Cecil went on to tell me a story about Glenn and the orchestra: 'He wanted microphones everywhere and, after a few words — and I knew I would not convince him — we dug up these really old-type microphones. Glenn was very pleased and he turned to me and said, ''There you are, Cecil. It sounds much better.'' What we never told him was that we had only activated the original ones.' The *Variety Bandbox* show included British film star, Margaret Lockwood, and was performed at the Queensbury All Services Club, in Soho, London (now the Prince Edward Theatre in Old Compton Street). Of that club, the late Colonel Ed Kirby wrote just before his death, 'You saw what Major Miller meant when you looked down on the faces of three thousand Allied faces in the Queensbury All Services Club in London — British, Canadian, French, Polish, Dutch and American — their expressions and reactions the same. You couldn't tell their nationality by looking at their faces. You had to wait until the full lights were turned on to learn their insignia.'

The *Variety Bandbox* was packed with a forces audience that night. But there were another 1,000 service personnel waiting outside who could not get in. So Glenn told the theatre's manager, John Harding, that the orchestra would give a second performance like that every evening to allow those outside a chance to see and hear them.

On 2 August, Glenn and the orchestra performed at the AAF base at Kimbolton. Once again, Dorothy Carless was with the band. The following day, 3 August, the orchestra — now called, yet again, the American Band of

Captain Glenn Miller with Hal Monty, Cecil Madden, Margaret Lockwood, Bertha Wilmot, Peter Sinclair and John Blore at the Queensbury All Services Club, 30 July 1944

the AEF — did its weekly broadcast live from Bedford. This week's guest stars were Dinah Shore and British male singer, Sam Browne. Dinah has just arrived in England on a United Services Tour (USO was the American version of ENSA). She would be in the ETO for just over a month. Her first British broadcast was with Miller's orchestra. She sang two titles: *Long Ago and Far Away* and *I'll be Seeing You.*

As well as the live broadcast, Dinah also recorded four titles for future use with the Swing Sextet, better known as the Uptown Hall group, led by pianist Sergeant Mel Powell. These were recorded at a special session directly after the full orchestra broadcast in Co-Partners Hall in Bedford.

The late Captain Franklin Englemann recalled just before his death how Glenn and his boys often ate fish and chips. He said: 'One of the sights I will always remember was of Glenn dressed in his officer's uniform queueing outside the fish and chip shop, near Co-Partners Hall. He would often come out with them in newspaper and eat them. He loved the idea of eating them from the newspaper . . . It was often very hard to see or meet him, as often, he would be surrounded by high-ranking American officers wearing Patton-type pistols, and yet, down at the fish and chip shop, anyone could see and talk with the ''Moonlight Serenader''. There was no doubt in anybody's mind that here was a hard-boiled showman and bandleader. He was more like a school teacher than a bandleader, but he knew every move and phrase the orchestra used when they performed.'

The next day, Friday, 4 August, turned out to be another red-letter day for

176

the orchestra and Captain Glenn Miller. Don Haynes had arranged for the unit to perform at another base concert in the south of England. A SHAEF Staff Officer, Major Stearns, had arranged everything with Haynes, but for security reasons had not informed him of the location and exactly who they were going to play for. During the afternoon, Stearns sent three C-54 transport planes to Twinwoods Farm Airfield, just outside Bedford, to pick up the entire unit. It was not until they were airborne that the men discovered they were heading for General Eisenhower's advance headquarters — SHAEF (Forward), code-named 'Sharpener' — near Portsmouth. When they landed at the airstrip on Thorney Island, they were picked up and taken by trucks and staff cars through eight miles of densely-wooded countryside. The concert was under camouflage netting. About a thousand SHAEF personnel attended, including the Supreme Commander himself. Eisenhower thanked Glenn in person at the end of the concert.

On Sunday, 6 August, Captain Miller and the dance band played at two airfield concerts. The first, at Halesworth, East Suffolk, was arranged that very day at Twinwoods Farm airfield. The scheduled one was at the 56th fighter group base at Boxted airfield, near the village of Langham, some six miles north of Colchester, in Essex. This was an evening concert. However, being a fighter base, B-24s from the bomber base at Halesworth had been asked to pick up the band. One of the pilots asked Captain Miller: 'When are you going to perform at our base?' After a quick telephone call to Halesworth to the commander there, it was arranged for Glenn and the dance band to do a second performance there as well.

Next day, the dance band and Captain Miller headed west to the 192nd General Hospital at Cirencester, in Gloucestershire. They performed two concerts in the park. Glenn also split up the dance band and toured the wards of the hospital.

Two days later, on Wednesday, 9 August, Glenn and the full orchestra played for the personnel of SHAEF at Bushey Park, Teddington, Middlesex.

On Thursday, the orchestra were back in London for their AEFP Home Service broadcast. The guest star this week was Paula Green. Paula, who at that time was in the popular ITMA series, remembers the broadcast very well. 'I was absolutely thrilled to sing with the great Glenn Miller Band. It was the ultimate to have sung with the Miller Band. I sang three times and I also appeared at a base concert in a hangar and, during my song, the microphone went dead.' This was the first broadcast from the Paris Cinema, a BBC studio in Lower Regent Street still used by the BBC today, and Glenn's last broadcast for the BBC Home Service.

Earlier that same afternoon, Ray McKinley and the dance band had made their second appearance on Cecil Madden's *American Eagle in Britain* broadcast. Recorded by the BBC for later broadcast by short wave to the United States, it also included members of the G.I. audience sending messages home to their families. Ray and several members of the band also joined in to say hello to their families.

Also included in the thirty-minute show were four selections by the dance band, with the vocal group 'The Crew Chiefs' singing *G.I. Jive*. Cecil said: 'I directed and produced the *American Eagle in Britain* show for nearly five years. It ran from September 1940 until 8 September 1945. I only missed one show due to illness and, throughout the Blitz, V-bombs and all, I continued. I compèred nearly every show and we included live links with the forces in Europe from the invasion of Italy in 1943 until the end of the war in Europe. Every show was recorded from ''Dunkers Den'', beneath the pavement in the American Red Cross Club, in Piccadilly, in London. The title of the show was taken from the American RAF Eagle Squadron that came here during the Battle of Britain in 1940. The impact of the broadcasts was fantastic after the Americans entered the war. It was natural to include Glenn and his boys at the place. The American band visited us five times and made broadcasts every time. Glenn loved the idea of broadcasting back home from war-torn London.'

On Sunday, 13 August, Glenn and the dance band flew from Twinwoods Farm airfield to Northern Ireland. The dance band played two concerts there: one at the American Red Cross Club in Belfast, and the other at the USAAF base at Langfordlodge. Then they returned to the British mainland, landing at Wharton airfield, near Blackpool. They stayed overnight at this base, and the following day they played a concert for 10,000 officers and other ranks. They stayed another night and Glenn, Don and Paul Dudley went sightseeing in nearby Blackpool. The next day, 15 August, the dance band played two concerts at the largest base in the United Kingdom — Burtonwood. They played for an audience of some 17,000 service personnel at these two shows. British bandleader Joe Loss and the forces' sweetheart, Vera Lynn, were also on hand at the afternoon show.

During the late evening, Glenn and the band returned to Bedford. On 16 August, Captain Miller and Lt. Don Haynes were flying from Twinwoods Farm to Hendon airfield in North London, and, as their transport plane was coming in to land, they had a near disaster with a B-17 'Flying Fortress' taxying for take-off. The pilot only just missed the bomber. This was only one of many hair-raising experiences Glenn would encounter whilst flying and would confirm his abhorrence of that means of travel.

Glenn later described how he thought he would die to Cecil Madden: 'You know, Cecil, I will probably get mine in one of those old beat-up wrecks we have to fly in.' Ray McKinley recently told how Glenn hated flying so much and was so nervous just before take-off that he would walk up and down smoking — a complete wreck. Ray also tells of other incidents that the band were involved in, during flights around the United Kingdom. One concerns an incident over East Anglia, when the band travelled in three B-17 'Flying Fortress' aircraft. Because of the cramped space, the band used the bomb bays to transport their band stands and Ray's drum kit. Ray recalls: 'We used to use plywood to cover the bomb bay area and then load my drum kit and

''Trigger's'' double bass into the bay. Often as not, because of the limited space in the bomber, three or four of us would lay on top. During one trip, someone in the cockpit moved the bomb release lever that opens the bomb doors. We travelled quite a long way until somebody noticed. We were very lucky indeed not to have fallen out over the English countryside and ended up dead!' Another story about Glenn's problems with flying comes from the late Don Haynes' diary. Of one trip, Don writes: 'Glenn was so worried about the close-formation flying of the B-24 bombers that picked us up, that, at the destination, he was white with fright.'

During the afternoon, Captain Miller and the entire orchestra played at another special concert. This time it was at RAF Headquarters at Bentley Priory, near Stanmore. It was at this concert that, during the band's version of *In the Mood*, a V-1 'Doodle-bug' flying bomb came over. Glenn hushed the band, but they continued to play. The incident was recreated in the Miller bio-film, *The Glenn Miller Story*.

Back in late April before the orchestra came to England, Glenn had been recommended for promotion to the rank of Major. On 8 August 1944, the promotion had come through to SHAEF, but it was not passed on to Glenn until 17 August. So, on the Thursday evening broadcast, Glenn was introduced as Major Glenn Miller. The British guest star was Beryl Davies. Beryl was famous for her broadcasts on the AEFP with the RAF Squadronaires in the *Top Ten* series on Monday evenings. Her song with Glenn was *It's Love, Love, Love*.

The next day, Major Glenn Miller and the American Band of the AEF performed at Steeple Morden, a USAAF P-51 fighter base, near Royston, in Cambridgeshire. Five thousand attended this concert. Later, during the afternoon, the orchestra were picked up from Steeple Morden and flown to Attlebridge base, near Norwich, Norfolk. At 8.30 p.m., Major Miller and his orchestra gave their now famous 'Hunk o' Home' to 10,000 officers, enlisted men and their guests, at the 100th mission party at Attlebridge. After the concert, they were forced to stay overnight due to bad weather. The next morning, they had to travel by road back to their base in Bedford.

Another promotion was in the offing too. This was for T/Sgt. Paul Dudley. Dudley was the orchestra's programme director. He was promoted to the rank of warrant officer. Cecil Madden tells the story behind this: 'We had one problem with Dudley. Unlike Miller and Haynes, who were officers, Dudley was only a sergeant and could not attend programme planning meetings with Miller, Haynes, Niven and myself. I went to Colonel Kirby and he called Miller into the meeting to resolve the problem. So Paul was given an officer's rank. I myself was offered a rank, but I stayed a civilian.'

For the next few days, the weather remained bad and the band stayed in Bedford. Their next concert was at the AAF base at Podington, twenty-five miles west of Thurleigh. This was the home of the 92nd bomb group. Glenn and the orchestra, including the string section, performed on two flat-bed trucks in the open air for 3,000 airmen. Their performance lasted 90 minutes. Then they packed up and were flown to the 390th bomb group base at Framlingham for another 100 mission party. Major Miller and the orchestra stayed overnight at Framlingham, and then flew back on the morning of 24 August to Bedford.

Later that evening their weekly full band show included Geraldo's singer, Doreen Villiers. Doreen sang the Marion Hutton hit, *That's Sabotage* with Glenn. Also on this show, Glenn introduced his very last composition, *I'm Heading For California*. The words were by Artie Malvin, a member of the vocal group, 'The Crew Chiefs'. Glenn may have been dreaming of his new home there, after the war, with this song. It suggests he was homesick, like any other G.I. Other things began to show too in Glenn. He had began to lose weight, and the tailored uniforms began to hang on his tall frame, rather loose. During a meal at his billet in Bedford, Glenn showed Cecil Madden, Lt. Colonel David Niven and the BBC sound engineer attached to the band, Teddy Gower, a model of the proposed ranch he was planning to build in California. The name of the development was 'Tuxedo Junction', taken from the bandleader's great hit of the same name. Cecil said: 'Glenn told us, ''You know, somehow I don't think I will ever get to see it.'' David Niven gave me a strange look. Glenn was white when he said it.'

On Friday, 25 August, Paris was liberated by the advancing Allied armies. Major Glenn Miller and the American Band of the AEF played at two AAF bomber bases: one at Knettishall, near Thetford, but the first was at the B-17 base at Wendling during the early afternoon. One of Wendling's B-17s was christened 'Moonlight Serenader'. Glenn — named the 'Moonlight Serenader' after his theme song — insisted on travelling to Knettishall in her. After the evening concert at Knettishall, Glenn and the orchestra were forced by bad weather to spend the night at the base. They returned on the Saturday morning by road transport to Bedford.

That Sunday, in beautiful sunshine, the orchestra performed for over 1,000 RAF personnel, at RAF Twinwoods Farm Airfield. This was the airfield just outside Bedford that Glenn and the band used to travel all over the United Kingdom. This Sunday afternoon the full orchestra performed on crash trucks in the open air. RAF Twinwoods Farm was a satellite of RAF Cranfield some ten miles to the south-west.

While Glenn and the orchestra performed at Twinwoods Farm, their relief pianist, PFC Jack Russin, was travelling by staff-car to the Queensbury All Services Club, in Soho, London. Jack was scheduled to play for one of America's greatest stars, who had just arrived in England on his first visit. Bing Crosby was at last here. The British *Melody Maker* pronounced the news and the following week announced, 'Bing went the Strings of our Hearts'. As well as performing with Bing, Russin was also to play for our own Anne Shelton. Anne recalls: 'Cecil Madden phoned me, and asked me to come along to the Queensbury Club to sing with Bing Crosby. I said, ''I am sorry, but I'm

Cecil Madden, T/Sgt. Paul Dudley and S/Sgt. George Voutsas during a meeting at the Queensbury All Services Club, London, 30 July 1944 (Photo: Cecil Madden)

having tea with the king.'' I thought it was a joke. Cecil then phoned back and told me again. I said, ''Is that really you, Cecil?'' He said it was and it was no joke — Bing was really here and wanted to do a duet with me. I was really proud. I'd already appeared with Glenn Miller and now I was to do a duet with one of the greatest entertainers of all time.' Anne and Bing sang the Irving Berlin number *Easter Parade*. The Queensbury Club was packed for the *Variety Bandbox* recording.

The next day, with hardly a break, Glenn and the orchestra flew from Twinwoods Farm for a series of concerts for the Navy down in Plymouth, Devon. Once again they were weathered in for two days. They did not get back to Bedford until Wednesday dinner-time, and who should be at Twinwoods Farm airfield, but the Old Groaner himself, Bing Crosby! Bing had returned to Bedford with Russin on Tuesday. Glenn and Bing were old friends from the early thirties, when they were both in the Dorsey Brothers Band. The two greats were scheduled to do a series of broadcasts together. Cecil Madden had arranged everything. Cecil remembered Bing's arrival well. 'He really wanted to help with broadcasts to the troops. One thing I will always remember about him was that he had very bright hand-painted ties. They showed naughty girls on them. I said you can't wear them over here. He began to laugh, and then took them off. He was a real joy to work with and he remained a good friend until his death in 1977.'

After recording some shows with Glenn's various units, Bing, Glenn and Don Haynes drove into London. Bing was to appear with the British AEF Band that evening. After the broadcast at the Queensbury Club, Glenn, Bing and Don went to Kettners Restaurant next door. A crowd started to form. Bing himself recalled: 'We were informed that quite a crowd were forming

Fred and Adelle Astaire with Cecil Madden and Ken Tredwell at The American Eagle in Britain, *London, 31 August 1944 (Photo: Cecil Madden)*

outside the restaurant and the British Bobbies were having trouble trying to disperse them. So I went out onto the balcony and the crowd started yelling for me to sing. Glenn and I were worried, because there was a law in England at that time about big crowds and the bombing. I asked, would you like me to sing? If I did, would they disperse? They yelled they would. The majority wanted *Pennies From Heaven*. I then sang the song; at the end, they turned, cheered and were gone. We finished our meal, and that night a fog came down. We crawled along, feeling the kerb, back to our hotel.' Glenn, Don Haynes and Bing stayed overnight at the Mount Royal Hotel, near Marble Arch.

The next day, Thursday, 31 August, the orchestra came into London for their weekly American Band of the AEF broadcast. However, during the afternoon, they again appeared at Rainbow Corner for another of Cecil Madden's *American Eagle in Britain* broadcasts. This time, Fred Astaire was also on hand and did a dance number with the trio from the dance band. This included Ray McKinley on drums, Mel Powell on piano and Michael 'Peanuts' Hucko on clarinet. Later, at the Paris Cinema, the full orchestra broadcast their live show. Their very special guest star was Bing Crosby. Bing again tells the story, just before his death in 1977: 'Glenn walked in during the early evening rehearsal, and I was handing out bottles of Scotch to the orchestra. Somehow, he did not seem to like the idea, but I said this is a freebee for the guys. That seemed to calm him down.' Cecil Madden was also present during the broadcast. He remembered: 'Bing did not rehearse with the orchestra and at the time of the broadcast went straight into the four songs. It was a great broadcast.'

After the broadcast, Glenn asked Bing where he was heading for next. Bing said he was going over to France and the Western Front. Glenn offered Bing his relief pianist, Jack Russin. The next day, Bing went to France. Russin followed two days later, but never did catch up with Crosby.

On Friday, 1 September, Glenn and the orchestra flew by B-24s to the 445th bomb group base at Tibbenham (also known as Tivetshall), in Norfolk. The afternoon concert was in a very cold hangar, before 3,000 personnel. This was the base at which Colonel James Stewart was based. Jimmy would later star in the Hollywood bio-film about Glenn Miller. After the concert at Tibbenham, the orchestra were off again, this time in trucks to the 100th bomb group base at Thorpe Abbot's, about five miles east of Diss. After dinner at this base, they played an evening concert before 3,000 in the hangar. Once again, they had to curtail their departure, due to bad weather. They stayed overnight and returned in buses, a weapons carrier and a staff car, to London.

That evening the orchestra was the star attraction in the BBC series *Atlantic Spotlight*. This was a live broadcast, heard simultaneously in both Britain and the USA. The programme was short-waved across the Atlantic. Also taking part in the USA were Roy Fox, The Modernaires (Glenn's pre-war singing group) and Marion Hutton. Marion sang with the Crew Chiefs and the band in London, *Jukebox Saturday Night*. After the broadcast, Glenn and the orchestra did another show, which was not broadcast, at the Queensbury All Services Club.

For the next seven days, the orchestra stayed in Bedford, recording broadcasts in advance for the BBC. Their live Thursday night broadcast came from there. Their special British guest star on 7 September was Gloria Brent. Gloria sang *Time Alone Will Tell*. Gloria still holds fond memories of Glenn and the boys in the orchestra. 'I was touring around the British Isles when I got a telegram from my agent, telling me I was to perform with Glenn and his orchestra. I was really thrilled. I still have that telegram. Every time I hear *Moonlight Serenade* I still remember with pride that special moment when I sang with the Moonlight Serenader in Bedford.'

On Sunday, 10 September, Glenn and the orchestra were back on their tour of the bases. This time, they were at Horham, three miles east of Eye, in East Suffolk. Haynes noted in his diary that Horham was yet another air-conditioned hangar. The next day, the band played for 4,000 men of the 82nd Airborne Division in De Montfort Hall, near Leicester. Within the week this division would be in action in Holland, at Nijmegen, for Operation Market Garden. Johnny Desmond was given an airborne outfit by the division, Glenn extended the concert to an hour and a half after roars of applause from the audience.

The next day, 12 September, Glenn and the orchestra played at their coldest concert so far in the United Kingdom, at Hardwicke, close to the North Sea. Haynes noted once again, 'Another air-conditioned hangar.' It was so cold that several musicians, including Glenn, performed wearing gloves.

Thursday, 14 September: the orchestra and Major Miller were back in London for their weekly big show for the Allied Forces. Once again, the Swing Shift unit under Ray McKinley did *American Eagle in Britain*, recording during the afternoon. Also on hand to perform with the dance band was Geraldo's drummer, Maurice Burman. Maurice sat in for one number. Later that evening, the orchestra, with their British guest star, Paula Green, gave their first live broadcast from the packed Queensbury All Services Club. This was Paula's second broadcast with the orchestra. Paula remembers, 'To sing once with Glenn was such an honour, but to sing twice was the highest commendation of all.' Paula's song that evening was Glenn's big hit from his second film, made in 1942, *At Last*.

From now on, Glenn and the orchestra would be in London once or twice a week at the Queensbury Club for their regular weekly AEFP broadcasts. The V-1 'Doodle-bug' raids had declined fortunately but since 8 September the capital city had been under bombardment from a yet more deadly Nazi weapon — the V-2 long-range rocket (which could be fired from inside Germany). While in London, Glenn had recorded a special interview for the BBC for their series *Here's Wishing You Well Again*. It was broadcast the very next day, 15 September. The request for the interview had asked Glenn to perform a trombone solo. This Glenn declined. The interview went ahead with Vernon Harris.

On 15 September Glenn was unwell, and stayed in Bedford. The orchestra, however, directed by Ray McKinley, travelled by road transport to the Rougham base, near Bury St Edmunds, to perform with Dinah Shore at a 200 mission party at that base. Dinah, who had just returned from the Western Front, was not too happy to find Glenn was not there.

The very next day Glenn and the orchestra teamed up again with Dinah Shore to produce four recordings for special issue, around Christmas. The two 78rpm recordings were to raise funds for British and American service charities. However, they were never issued. A row followed. SHAEF had given permission for Glenn and the AEF Orchestra to record at HMV studios in St John's Wood, London. However, USO, whom Dinah Shore worked for during her tour of Europe, had written back a week later saying that they did not approve of the recordings. Dinah left for home the following day and, needless to say, the four titles are now quite rare. Copies are held by collectors but, to this day, HMV in London say they have no trace of the masters.

The day after the HMV recording session, the American Band of the AEF were given their first furlough since their arrival in the United Kingdom. Glenn was still feeling unwell, with a bad sinus problem. Many of the unit stayed in and around London. Others headed for Newmarket and the race course there.

The orchestra personnel reported back for duty on Thursday, 21 September for their live American Band of the AEF show at the Queensbury All Services Club. Their guests that evening were the US Navy Dance Band of the

Liberation Forces, led by Musician First Class Sam Donahue. Cecil Madden was on hand that night. 'It was the greatest broadcast of them all. I will never forget that final number played by the greatest American musicians we ever had over here: the title was Count Basie's *One O'Clock Jump*. It was one of the great sights and sounds of World War Two.'

On Sunday, 24 September, the orchestra and Major Miller resumed their tour of the bases. That afternoon, they travelled in their buses to North Witham, about ten miles south of Grantham, to play for 2,500 airborne troops in a hangar. After this concert the entire orchestra then went on to the State Cinema in Grantham for a public concert to say 'thank you' to the people of the town for their funds for the forces.

The next day, Monday, 25 September, the orchestra travelled in their buses to Oxford. Despite its being a cold day, Glenn and the orchestra performed on the lawn outside the 91st General Hospital. After the concert they travelled by their buses to the 7th Photographic Reconnaissance Group airfield at Mount Farm, about five miles south-east of Oxford. Three thousand attended the concert there. After the concert, the band piled into their buses and headed back to Bedford. However, it was not until after midnight that they got back to their billets. Due to the blackout, their drivers had got lost in the countryside.

For the next two days the members of the orchestra stayed in Bedford. Their next trip was into London for their weekly big broadcast on Thursday, 28 September. Their special British guest star was film star and singer Pat Kirkwood. Pat sang her own well-known title, *My Kind of Music*, which she had introduced in a London show during the 1940 blitz on London. The show was *Top of the World*, which lasted only a few weeks due to the heavy bombing of London.

The very next day Major Miller was asked to go to see Colonel Ed Kirby at SHAEF at Bushey Park. Kirby informed Miller he was to proceed to Paris. Haynes drove Miller to Bovingdon Airfield, and Glenn flew by the SHAEF shuttle over to Paris. Upon arrival Glenn was ordered to SHAEF at Versailles. Here, Glenn was to meet General Eisenhower's Chief of Staff, Lieutenant General Walter Bedell Smith. The meeting lasted three minutes. The general offered Glenn the leadership of the US Army Band, which was then stationed in Paris. Glenn refused the appointment.

While Glenn was in Paris the orchestra, led by Ray McKinley, performed for the 385th Bomb Group at Elmswell, Great Ashfield. Among the guests was General Doolittle. Fifteen minutes of the 200th mission party was relayed by the BBC back to the USA.

The next day, Monday, 2 October, the band went by road transport to the 398th Bomb Group airfield at Nuthampstead, about five miles south-west of Royston. This was yet another very cold day and the band performed in another hangar.

It was now well into autumn, and October 1944 was a very wet and cold month. The orchestra did one final concert on 3 October. Glenn was on hand, having returned on the Monday from Paris. The final concert in the United Kingdom was for the 20th fighter group at Kingscliffe, Northants, about twelve miles west of Peterborough. From now on, the band were to concentrate on their broadcasting schedule.

The following Thursday, Glenn and the orchestra travelled by road transport into London for their weekly broadcast live from the Queensbury All Services Club. That evening (of 5 October) their British guest star was not a girl, as was the usual custom, but the leader of the British Band of the AEF, RSM George Melachrino. Multi-instrumentalist George sang *Goodnight Good Neighbour*, from the film *Thank Your Lucky Stars*. Half-way through this live broadcast, a 'Buzz-Bomb' (V-1 rocket) flew over the Queensbury Club. The club was packed with 2,500 Service personnel. Miller quietened the orchestra until it passed over. About twelve minutes of this broadcast is preserved in the archives of the BBC.

The very next day, 6 October, Colonel Ed Kirby was transferred back to Washington, D.C. Kirby had done a wonderful job in setting up the AEFP back in June. Just before his death, he said, 'You know, I have never really got over Glenn's death. You know it was through me that he died. If I had not asked him to join me for that cup of coffee, he would never have come over to England and wound up dead.' Colonel Kirby's next job was in Washington and he finished the war out in the Pacific Theatre of Operations.

For the next two weeks the orchestra concentrated on their broadcast schedule. However, on Sunday 15 October, Glenn and the American Band of the AEF gave the second of their public performances in London. The special concert was at the 1944 Jazz Jamboree at the Stoll Theatre in Kingsway. The 1944 event, as always, was staged on behalf of the British Musicians' Social and Benevolent Fund. Glenn had been approached by Ted Heath and had said he would see what could be done. During the Sunday afternoon all the British bands had performed, including the RAF Squadronaires, but, while they were on stage, Ted Heath was beginning to get worried. As he recalls: 'Then, into Kingsway came a line of American trucks. Not only had Glenn brought the band, but everything including their bandstands from Bedford.'

The next Thursday, 19 October, Glenn and the orchestra were again in London for their weekly show. Their guest was Sally Douglas.

The final AEF show to include a British guest star was the broadcast of 26 October. Anne Shelton was the guest on that programme. Unlike the 27 July broadcast, which was recorded in Bedford, this one was a live broadcast from the Queensbury All Services Club before 2,500 service personnel. Anne's song that evening was the new song *Spring Will Be a Little Late This Year*. Anne remembers that Queensbury Club show very well: 'You know, he used to conduct the orchestra with either a pencil or cigarette during the rehearsal. I can still see him directing the orchestra, with his cap stuck on the back of his head. I will always remember standing there with my knees knocking just before air-time. You know, he gave me a wonderful gold bracelet as a birthday gift. He said it was for someone with a voice of gold. He said to me, ''Do you know you fit my sound?'' I just did not know what he meant. I guess I do now. It was very sad when we heard he was missing over Christmas.'

Cecil Madden was asked just before his death if he was at the Glenn Miller Queensbury Club broadcasts. He said, 'I was at every one Glenn did from there. Myself, Stephen Williams, and Teddy Gower were always there. You know, the Queensbury Club was owned by the Marquis of Queensbury, Sir Simon Marks. He turned it over for the war to the Forces and it became a Forces canteen and entertainment centre. The lighting came from the T.V. studios at Alexandra Palace and every day of the week there was always a show at the Queensbury. It was part of my empire, the AEFP Empire. It was a great time and I enjoyed meeting so many famous people and they all became such great friends.'

During mid-October, Glenn and the orchestra were asked to begin a series of broadcasts over ABSIE (The American Broadcasting Station In Europe). The recordings were to be beamed into Nazi Germany as propaganda broadcasts. The series was to be broadcast every Wednesday afternoon. The orchestra started to record the shows at HMV studios on Monday, 30 October 1944. Then, every Monday up until late November, Glenn would drive down from the Mount Royal Hotel at Marble Arch in London and meet the orchestra who had come down from Bedford. They would then team up with ABSIE's German girl announcer, Ilsa, and record the broadcasts. Johnny Desmond also appeared and sang his songs in German. Glenn also introduced some items in very poor German.

On Monday, 6 November 1944, the American Band of the AEF once again travelled by road into London for further HMV/ABSIE recording sessions in St John's Wood. They were met by Major Miller and they spent the afternoon in the studios. Later, at 7.15 p.m., the strings section went over to the Maida Vale Studios for their regular Monday evening *Strings With Wings* broadcast. They had special guest conductor Sir Adrian Boult conducting. They performed three titles under his direction: *Serenade for Strings* (Elgar), *Clouds Nocturne* (Debussy), and *Annie Laurie*.

On 13 November the orchestra and its sub-units started a complete new broadcasting schedule. With the winter nights and the tour of the bases over for the time being, Glenn, it seemed, had given up playing for troops in outside areas. The BBC had, with Cecil Madden's help, increased the number of broadcasts but had they convinced Glenn? He, it seems, had other ideas and, on the very day the new schedule started, he flew from Bovingdon on the SHAEF Shuttle to Paris. Glenn missed the two American Band of the AEF broadcasts on Tuesday and Friday, both from the Queensbury Club. Upon Glenn's arrival in Paris on 13 November, he went out to see General Barker and Major May at SHAEF, Versailles Palace. Glenn spent the next five days in Paris, and had many meetings with Barker and May. Finally, he convinced them to bring the large orchestra over to entertain American troops on furlough in Paris over the Christmas and New Year period. Glenn obtained permission for the orchestra to stay just six weeks in France and then return to Bedford, England. It took some lengthy telephone conversations between SHAEF and the BBC (who were running the AEFP) for them to come up with an answer and, in the end, they said Glenn and his orchestra and sub-units would have to pre-record at least six weeks' reserve broadcasts in advance.

Meanwhile, the full orchestra broadcasts from the Queensbury All Services Club had been compèred by Sergeant Keith Jameson of the US Army in Glenn's absence. The orchestra was conducted by Sergeant Jerry Gray.

Before Glenn had left on Monday, 13 November, the orchestra had recorded four titles at HMV with visiting USO star Irene Manning, for use by ABSIE.

Glenn was away in Paris from 13 November until 18 November. When he arrived back on 18 November, he told Haynes that he would be leaving for Paris on 25 November to obtain billets for the personnel. During that week Glenn approached Cecil Madden for discs from the BBC for the reserve recordings. They added up to nearly 129 in all. Cecil told Glenn that, due to wartime restrictions, the BBC could not supply so many discs. Glenn went next to Johnny Hayes, the head of the American Forces Network, in London. Hayes said he would see what could be done. The discs started to arrive at Bedford on 24 November. The orchestra started their enormous task of stock-piling recordings on 25 November, the day before Haynes left for Paris to secure their new billets.

For the next three and a half weeks, they spent their time in Bedford, recording all the weekly shows they could — everything from full band shows, *Swing Shifts*, *Uptown Hall*, *Strings With Wings*, *Piano Parades* and *Sgt. Johnny Desmond Shows*. They also had a couple of trips into London for ABSIE and full orchestra shows.

By 12 December all the reserve broadcasts had been recorded. Haynes flew back on 2 December with the news that he had obtained billets for the three officers and a hotel at 22 Rue Clignancourt, in the Montmartre district of Paris. The hotel was the Hôtel des Olympiades.

On the 12th, Glenn and the orchestra travelled by bus into London for their very last live broadcast from the Queensbury All Services Club. Another American star was in London with the USO during this time. This was the Irish-American, Morton Downey. He appeared as a special surprise guest on the last show with Glenn. Downey sang *I'll Get By*. The last title on the broadcast was the *Red Cavalry March* or *Meadowlands*. As Ray McKinley recalls, 'The show went on much longer than the broadcast. Our last title was *Tuxedo Junction*.'

After the show and broadcast at the Queensbury Club, the band went back to Bedford. Glenn, Haynes and Dudley stayed on in London at the Mount Royal Hotel. The weather was terrible. Thick fog and drizzle. Haynes was due to fly in advance of the orchestra on or about 14 December. During the evening of the 12th, Glenn asked Haynes to drive out to SHAEF at Bushey

Major Glenn Miller with two musicians at the Carnival of Bands at the Granada Cinema, Bedford, 26 November 1944 (Photo: Louis Lawrence)

Park the next day to have his orders transferred to himself (Major Glenn Miller), so he could fly out in advance. This Haynes did and reported back to Miller at the Mount Royal. Haynes then drove by staff car to Bedford. He noted in his diary: 'The weather was so bad that the conductors of the big red buses were walking out in front with a torch to show the driver the way.'

Haynes stayed in Bedford overnight. That evening, he went for a meal with an old friend of his and Glenn's, Lt. Colonel Norman Baessell, at the Officers' Club in Milton Ernest Hall, just outside Bedford. While they were eating, Haynes was called to the telephone. It was Major Miller in London. Glenn told Haynes that he had been in touch with Bovingdon and no planes were flying over to Paris. However, during their phone conversation, Baessell informed Haynes that he was flying over to Paris on the morning of the 15th in General Goodrich's plane. So, if Glenn wanted to, he could come along for the ride. Haynes relayed the message to Miller in London. It was now clear to Glenn that, even if the SHAEF Shuttle was flying the next day (the 14th), he would not be able to pull rank and obtain a flight over to Paris. Glenn accepted the colonel's offer. Haynes said he would drive into London in the afternoon and pick Miller and Dudley up from the Mount Royal Hotel.

The weather was the same on the 14th. Before Glenn left the hotel, he spoke to Cecil Madden. Cecil recalled just before his death: 'I pleaded with him not to go on the small aircraft on the 15th. He said he had an appointment in Paris and I was not to worry. I asked him to wait and go with the full orchestra on

One of the final photographs taken of Major Glenn Miller, with W/O Paul Dudley and 2nd Lt. Don Haynes, taken at the Queensbury All Services Club, London, on Tuesday, 12 December 1944

the large transport planes, but he said it was no use, he had arrangements in Paris. That was the last I ever saw of him.'

The last letter Glenn ever wrote was on 1 December to his younger brother, Herb. Before Herb's own death in September 1987, he showed me that letter. It was eerie to read. Part of it said, 'Other than a nose-dive into the Channel, we should be in Paris, etc.' Herb said he received the letter around about 15 December, at about the time Glenn died. Glenn also recorded a special 78rpm message for his wife, Helen, on 6 December at the HMV studios in St John's Wood, London. Helen received the recording on or about 22 December.

During the evening of Thursday, 14 December, Glenn, Don and Norman Baessell played poker with Major Bill Koch and Warrant Officer Neal Earlywine into the early hours of the morning of the 15th.

On the morning of 15 December, Don Haynes was wakened early to answer the telephone. The caller was Colonel Norman Baessell, who informed Haynes that the original pilot, Lt. George Ferguson, had been grounded by his Commanding Officer because of the bad weather conditions. In fact, George, who is still alive, informed Baessell that everything was grounded due to fog on the Continent. Ferguson, who was stationed just outside Brussels, told the Colonel that it was so bad on the Continent that any idea of flying should be postponed, at least for twenty-four hours. However, Baessell did not inform Haynes of this. He went on to inform Don that he had spoken with Flight Officer Johnny 'Nipper' Morgan at station 595, and he had informed him that the weather was clearing over the Continent. He went on to say that he would arrange clearance from Abbots Ripton (station 595), and pick up a plane to fly down to Twinwoods Farm, just after lunch, to pick them up! If Haynes had taken a look out of the window, he could have seen that conditions were still terrible and flying was out of the question.

Later that morning, Haynes informed Glenn that, providing Morgan could arrange for the plane and clearance, he should be ready to drive out to Milton Ernest. They awaited the phone call from Colonel Baessell to confirm their travel arrangements. Around 11 a.m., Baessell phoned and Haynes drove Glenn out to Milton Ernest Hall. The Colonel had told them they would be flying from Twinwoods Farm airfield at 1.45 p.m. The three officers were joined for lunch by Major Koch and Warrant Officer Earlywine. After the meal, Baesselle went to see his Commanding Officer, General Goodrich, at the Hall. Then Haynes drove Glenn and the Colonel out to Twinwoods Farm Airfield. The weather was still very bad.

Glenn, who was very worried about his flight, got out of the staff car and stood on the runway. It was 1.45 p.m., and there was still no sign of the aircraft. Then suddenly, they heard the sound of a single engine aircraft overhead. Morgan landed and then took on board the luggage and the passengers. Haynes said his farewell to Major Miller. Miller asked, 'Where are the parachutes?' Baessell jokingly said, 'What the f---, Miller, do you want to live forever?' Haynes closed the hatch, and the plane took off from the runway and into the fog. It was 1.55 p.m. and that was the last time Glenn Miller was seen alive. Haynes got back into the staff car and drove back to the American Red Cross Club in Bedford.

Over the last 45 years many people have tried in vain to find the wreck of the plane in the English Channel. Many details have come to light. The two most popular theories concerning the plane's disappearance are that the plane iced-up and then got into trouble over the Channel and crashed into the sea. All three men would have stayed alive only for about thirty minutes at that time of year. The other is just as horrendous. This is the theory that RAF bombers dropped bombs onto the aircraft when it strayed into a ditching zone. Either way, the three men would have died within thirty minutes. The first theory was that laid down by the US AAF and SHAEF during the Court of Inquiry at Bedford on 20 January 1945. Many other ideas have come to light, many of them bizarre and disturbing to the Major's family. Herb Miller, who sadly died on 30 September 1987, had as his last wish that his remains be with Glenn in the Channel, so that everyone else should believe that was his brother's resting-place. After all, the American Air Force believe 100% that the Channel was Glenn's last resting-place and perhaps so should everyone else. The last puzzle about this terrible affair is that so far no information on the flight clearance has ever come to light. The biggest question surrounds the UC-64-A Norseman, serial number 44-70285. What state was this plane in? After all, Abbots Ripton was a repair depot. Was the plane under repair when Morgan took it? Did he obtain clearance and where did he get his weather information from when Ferguson was not allowed to fly and Morgan was?

These and many other questions were asked during the January 1945 Court of Inquiry. Some of that inquiry has come to light, thanks to ex-President Ronald Reagan. Mr Reagan tried during his term of office to find out some of the answers. Being a Hollywood film star and a former member of the Army Air Forces, the ex-President, who is also a great fan of Glenn's music, did obtain some rare insights into Major Miller's life and death.

It goes without saying that Glenn's death signalled the end of the big-band era. Even today, his band brings the era of World War Two to life. Perhaps one day we will all find out just what happened on that cold foggy Friday of 15 December 1944, when the Moonlight Serenader took off and lost his life.

On Saturday, 16 December 1944, the German Panzer Armies attacked a weak section of the Western Front in the Ardennes. The famous 'Battle of the Bulge' was under way. Telephone lines from Paris to London were jammed. Haynes had no idea what was happening. The weather was still very bad and the orchestra was still held up in Bedford. They tried to get away on the 17th. Still bad weather. When they did get away on the Monday, 18 December, it was sunny. They travelled in three C-47 transport planes. Upon arrival at Orly, Haynes reported to the despatcher, hoping to find Glenn waiting there. There was no sign of him, nor was there any sign of the transport that Glenn was to have arranged. Glenn's flight should have landed at A-42, Villacoublay

Captain Glenn Miller at the RCA Studios, in New York City, 29 October 1943
(Photo: RCA Victor)

Airfield. So Orly knew nothing of a UC-64-A Norseman Aircraft. Anyway, after an hour or so, transport did turn up. Haynes had contacted General Barker and Major May at SHAEF. Haynes was told to report to SHAEF once the orchestra were in their billets.

Haynes got a staff car and drove out to SHAEF at Versailles. Major May met him upon his arrival. Then he went in to see Barker. They telephoned everywhere for a trace of Glenn, but nothing could be found. Over the next few days, SHAEF checked everywhere — at every Allied base in France, Belgium and over in England. No one had seen or heard of Major Miller since 15 December, at Twinwoods Farm Airfield. Haynes even asked the Allied press for their help in tracing Glenn. Nobody found anything at all. The whole flight path was checked. Nothing again. Blank after blank. News did come through that a light plane was tracked by Allied troops on the south coast on 15 December. It was tracked as flying out to sea, in the general direction of Normandy. Nothing could be traced on the French side.

A month later, on 20 January, Don Haynes was called back to Bedford to the Court of Inquiry. Their findings were that the UC-64-A Norseman, serial number 44-70285, had crashed into the English Channel on 15 December 1944, killing the two passengers and the pilot. Even to this day, the rumours continue. Looking at the facts I believe that Glenn either died in the way the Court of Inquiry suggested or perhaps he was killed in a terrible accident by discarded bombs. Either way, he is dead. He achieved what he set out to do. He brought a much needed 'Hunk o' Home' to millions of Allied servicemen and women.

The orchestra continued with its mighty task. Now firmly based in Paris, the great phenomenon that Major Glenn Miller had produced picked up the pieces and continued. Their first concert on 21 December 1944 found a new leader from within their own ranks — T/Sgt. Ray McKinley. A former peacetime bandleader and drummer, McKinley would lead the orchestra on its many concerts on the Continent. Another who would come to the fore for live and recorded broadcasts from Paris was S/Sgt. Jerry Gray, the chief arranger. Jerry had been an arranger and composer with Glenn's pre-war civilian band. Before joining Glenn, Jerry had worked with Artie Shaw. It fell to Jerry to conduct the orchestra on that much-remembered Christmas Day broadcast of 1944. Jerry once recalled that Christmas: 'It was dark and cold at morning rehearsal, but that Christmas in Paris, it was dark and cold most of the time. Don Haynes got the boys out and told them about Glenn. It all worked out, but I never want to have to do a job like that ever again.'

A great many of the orchestra's concerts were cancelled due to the curfew caused by the Battle of the Bulge. However, they did do a few during the daylight hours. Many were at freezing venues. On New Year's Eve, they did another live broadcast for the AEFP.

By late January, with the BBC lines from Paris to London improving, SHAEF said that the orchestra would be staying for the duration of the war in

Paris. So it was, then, that the eleven rear echelon who had stayed behind in Bedford, were brought over to Paris.

From January right through the very cold winter the orchestra continued with its broadcasts and concerts, often performing under very extreme conditions indeed. Their billets were not up to scratch either. They were very cold and quite often the men had to sleep in their overcoats. Food was not much better either. Still, spring was round the corner and their hardships were soon forgotten. The Allied war-machine was now crossing the Rhine into Nazi Germany. The war was fast drawing to a close. The orchestra's concert schedule was still very heavy. They performed again at airfields, camps, and hospitals, just as their boss had planned.

The orchestra members in Paris had some very 'adverse' problems to cope with during that long hard winter which ushered in 1945, as former singer Johnny Desmond remembered just before his death in 1985: 'I'll always remember that mess-hall in Paris where we had to go for our meals. Food was kept warm there 24 hours a day for G.I. truck drivers passing through Paris on their way to the front. The food was horrible and being kept warm around the clock didn't help.' Singer Artie Malvin, from the Crew Chiefs, also remembers Paris during that terrible winter of 1945: 'I'll always remember the night Harry Hartwick, one of our scriptwriters, was carried out of our Hôtel des Olympiades on a stretcher, with a virulent case of food poisoning. Other arrangements were quickly made for meals, although we had to travel halfway across Paris: the American rations were prepared by French chefs — a vast improvement, we thought. The winter was terrible and Parisiens swore it was the coldest ever. We had no heat and couldn't bathe. We slept in every item of clothing we could get into and still nearly froze. I recall learning, with appropriate dismay, that the one big shipment of coal that had been sent to our billet was quickly sold on the black market by our very own concièrge, the infamous Monsieur Gombere.'

Quite a few of the scheduled concerts in the Palais de Glace, a former ice rink, had to be cancelled because of the intense cold. The few that were performed by the orchestra at the beginning of January were warmly received, although the orchestra performed in overcoats and gloves. Violinist George Ockner even played his famous version of *The Flight of the Bumble Bee* wearing gloves. The brass players were even worse off. Their mouth-pieces were so cold that it hurt them even to perform. In the end, the Palais de Glace concerts were cancelled until the Spring, and warmer weather.

The BBC, meanwhile, continued broadcasting the 118 stock-piled reserve broadcasts that the orchestra and its sub-units had recorded in Bedford prior to their Paris trip. As Cecil Madden remembers: 'We had one problem with the American Band of the AEF full-orchestra broadcasts — they were all introduced by Major Glenn Miller and, after it was announced that he was missing, we had to re-dub other announcements onto them by Dick Dudley and Keith James, both of AFN.'

On Sunday, 18 February 1945, the orchestra performed at a special public concert at the Théâtre National de l'Opéra in aid of the French Prisoner of War Fund. It was a two-and-a-quarter-hour concert before 2,200 paying French civilians. Part of the concert was broadcast by French radio. It was an outstanding success. It was at this concert that many French girls lost their hearts to the young singer Johnny Desmond. He was nicknamed by them 'Le Crémier.' Late in the spring, *Time* magazine picked up on the nickname and changed it to the 'The Creamer.'

By late March, with both spring and victory in the air, the orchestra's schedule began to increase. The winter had been very cold indeed. Paris had received very grave rationing during the winter of 1945 and heavy snowfalls. The string orchestra did a special show in March with Andre Kostanlanetz and his wife, Lilly Pons. Both were in Paris with the USO.

All through this period and into April, the orchestra and its sub-units continued their weekly pre-recordings for the AEFP from the Olympia Theatre in Paris. In between, they also performed at the Marigan Theatre and at the various American Red Cross Clubs in the city. They also played at many field hospitals and airfields. Often they performed competing with the roar of 'Flying Fortresses' and fighters, taking off to bomb the Nazis. They also performed at the Palais de Glace. During the winter, they had, as pointed out, stopped performing at this venue because of the severe cold. The whole schedule was less hectic than it had been in England. Many of the members still lived in hope that Glenn would suddenly turn up. But it was not to be. Haynes and Dudley checked out every rumour and every slim chance that their boss was still alive. Every report, no matter how slim, would be checked out by Haynes through SHAEF. One report about a crashed light plane in Normandy looked very hopeful, but, as it turned out, it was not the Norseman 44-70285 which Glenn had been in.

It was during this period that Sergeant Ray McKinley was asked to become an officer. 'Mac' declined the offer because, as he later said, 'It would alienate me from the orchestra, like Glenn had been.'

Paris was just like one of those wild-west towns you see in the movies. It was a rest centre for American troops on 48-hour furloughs from the Western Front. They would come to Paris, still in their muddy uniforms, direct from the front. All they wanted was rest, wine, women and song. The songs were provided by Major Miller's American Band of the AEF. Paris was the rest centre for American troops while Brussels was the rest centre for British troops. The only British troops in Paris were RAF Signal Corps and SHAEF personnel. The Commodore Hotel in Paris was a centre for these British troops and on 28 March 1945, the orchestra performed for 600 at this venue.

By April, with the Allied armies pouring into Nazi Germany from both east and west, the orchestra were given leave from Paris, in the south of France. They would spend six days giving concerts at various rest centres around Nice and Cannes. The other seven would be a well-earned furlough.

The American Band of the AEF at a BBC recording in the Olympia Theatre, Paris, spring 1945

So, on 25 April 1945, the orchestra were flown by C-47 transport planes from Paris to Nice. For the next few days they entertained in the beautiful sunny climate for US troops on rest furlough from the fighting. What a backdrop it was too! The beautiful blue Mediterranean was somewhat different to what the orchestra had been used to in Paris. While the orchestra gave its first concert, it was snowing in Paris.

Well rested, the unit flew back to Paris on 6 May. Upon arrival, all they heard was news that the war in Europe was nearly over. Other news came through that Adolf Hitler was dead. Could it all be true? Then, the news came through the very next day that Nazi Germany had surrendered. On VE Day, 8 May 1945, the orchestra played at a very special Victory Concert for 3,200 at the Palais de Chaillot. Paris would celebrate for the next five days. Everything was closed. Like Paris, the rest of the Allied world went wild.

Eight days later, the entire orchestra were flown in three C-47 transport aircraft from Paris to the US 12th Army group headquarters in the heart of Germany. The transports landed at Fitzlaur Airfield, which was littered with smashed Luftwaffe planes, and the unit were taken in a fleet of Cadillacs to the Hotel Furstenhof in Bad Wildungen. The orchestra, which by this time was known as 'Major Glenn Miller's Band of the AEF', were scheduled, along with Hollywood film star Mickey Rooney, to perform for a very special guest of honour, Russian General, Marshal Ivan Koniev, Commander of the First

Ukrainian Army Group. The next day, 17 May, the orchestra performed the concert for the Russian guests. General Bradley, who had arranged everything, was very pleased indeed.

The orchestra's missing leader would have loved the place. Not only was Bad Wildungen a health spa, but also had very large golf courses and fishing, both of which Glenn loved.

Later, during the evening, the orchestra gave a second show, this time for troops stationed in the area. During the outside show, it started raining. Even that did not deter the US troops in the large audience from enjoying the music of Glenn Miller's Band.

The next morning, the band were taken back to the airfield and flew back to Paris. On the way back, they flew over the Belgium town of Bastogne, where the 101st Airborne Division had held out during the Battle of the Bulge in December 1944. They arrived back at Villacoublay airfield at 1 o'clock.

On Monday, 21 May, the orchestra resumed its concert and recording schedule for the BBC. Haynes went over to SHAEF and Major May told him that the AEFP was scheduled to close down on 28 July 1945. Haynes asked if there was any news as to when the orchestra would be returning home to the USA. He was informed that, because the orchestra had done such a great job entertaining the Russian generals, they would be asked to do one more tour before returning home. The tour was to start as soon as their BBC pre-recorded broadcasts had been completed. The tour was of the Allied bases in Germany. Haynes confirmed that within the next three weeks there should be enough pre-recorded broadcasts for the tour to begin by mid-June.

Between 22 May and 4 June 1945, all the broadcasts were completed. Then, on 13 June after several delays, the orchestra flew from Villacoublay to Regensburg, Germany. That evening, they performed their first concert for the 1137th Engineering group of the US Army at Regensburg. From now until the end of June, they performed another 23 concerts throughout southern Germany, to many thousands of US Army and Army Air Force personnel. Then, on 1 July, they played at perhaps their largest concert so far in the ETO, at the former Nazi Stadium in Nuremberg. It had been the scene of some of Hitler's pre-war rallies. Now, it was packed with 40,000 American G.I.s, hearing and seeing in person the famous Glenn Miller Band, directed by Ray McKinley. Also appearing was Paul Dudley's wife, singer Joy Hodges, who was on a USO tour of Europe. Joy, backed by the orchestra, sang her songs to 40,000 screaming G.I.s. It was a never-to-be-forgotten concert and marked the first anniversary of the orchestra's arrival in the ETO.

The tour continued with further concerts throughout Germany, eastern France and Venlo in Holland. Their last concert in Germany was at SHAEF at Frankfurt on 21 July 1945.

The SHAEF concert was outdoors before 10,000. The orchestra was awarded a citation from General Eisenhower for their tremendous work in the ETO since 28 June 1944. Part of this concert was recorded by the American Forces Network and still exists.

1st Lt. Don Haynes with Private Mickey Rooney, the Hollywood film star, at Bad Wildungen, Germany. 17 May 1945

Frank Ippolito in the Nuremberg Stadium prior to the concert on 1 July 1945
(Photo: the late Frank Ippolito)

The orchestra had a few more concerts to do in the ETO, all of which took place in France. One was at Villacoublay Airfield and the other two were at Le Havre. The second two began on 28 July at Camp Herbert Tareyton, near Le Havre, before 10,000 G.I.s awaiting ships to be sent home to the USA. Camp Herbert Tareyton was a vast tented camp just outside Le Havre, which acted as an embarkation area for US service personnel. Here the Glenn Miller Orchestra would wait 11 boring days for their transport ship. The very last concert the band performed in Europe was on the quayside in Le Havre. The dance band performed under Ray McKinley. However, no mention has ever been made of their performing on the actual quayside itself. The details here come from eight photographs taken of this concert just hours before Glenn's famous band sailed for home.

Glenn's dream had come true. His famous 'Hunk o' Home' had performed for millions of Allied Service personnel both on the radio and in concert. In all, the orchestra had played on 625 radio broadcasts and had made 525 personal appearances at many Allied airfields, camps, and hospitals throughout England and Europe during their 13 months overseas. Perhaps more than anyone else, the Moonlight Serenader and his music had brought pleasure and boosted morale when it was most needed during those dark days just before victory. It must be added that he became a legend, and so did his music.

The orchestra sailed home on 4 August 1945. While they were at sea, news came through that Japan had also surrendered. This spread great joy throughout the members of the orchestra. For, although they were sailing home for much-needed furloughs, they all knew they might be needed out in the Pacific Theatre of War. Now they all knew they would be staying in the USA.

200

The orchestra, conducted by T/Sgt. Ray McKinley, perform at one of the many concerts for American G.I.s in Germany, July 1945

They arrived home in New York City on Sunday, 12 August 1945. They were treated as heroes by everyone. Their mission was over and they looked forward to just over a month's much-needed rest.

The orchestra reported for duty during September and quite a few members had already left and returned to civilian jobs. Mel Powell had left and returned to his former job with Benny Goodman's band. Those that were still in uniform continued with their weekly *I Sustain the Wings* broadcasts over NBC. They did eight broadcasts under Jerry Gray. Ray McKinley left on 6 October and, slowly, the others began to be demobbed. Their last public concert was on 13 November at the National Press dinner in Washington D.C. before President Truman and Generals Eisenhower and Arnold. Their last *I Sustain the Wings* broadcast was on 17 November 1945.

By 15 December 1945, most of the orchestra were back in Civvy Street. On that day, Glenn was declared dead by the US Army Air Forces. The orchestra's wartime role was now taken over by other bands. So ended perhaps the greatest American service band of all time. In early 1946, Don Haynes started to put together a new Glenn Miller Orchestra directed by Tex Beneke. It would continue the music even further. Others started to form Glenn Miller bands, both in America and in England. And now, nearly 50 years after Glenn died, his music lives on in America with the Glenn Miller Orchestra directed by Larry O'Brian, in England with Syd Lawrence, and also with Glenn's younger brother's band, directed by John Miller. John, who now directs the Herb Miller Orchestra, recently said, 'The more bands we have that can play Glenn's music the better. That is, providing they play it well and the public enjoy every minute of it. That's just how Glenn would have wanted it.'

The No. 1 Balloon Centre Dance Orchestra
'The Skyrockets' 1940 – 1945

The Skyrockets were the better known name of the No. 1 Balloon Centre Dance Orchestra, one of the two famous Royal Air Force service bands formed after the outbreak of the Second World War. Their friendly rivals were the RAF Dance Orchestra, better known as the 'Squadronaires'. The 15-year history of the Skyrockets began in Blackpool in October 1940, where a group of professional musicians, mostly from the Jay Wilbour band (from the *High Gang* radio series), who had volunteered for the RAF, were on a training course. They decided to play together in their off-duty periods, under the leadership of saxophonist Buddy Featherstone, in *Contact* — an Air Force revue. They were then transferred to Number 1 Balloon Centre at Kidbrooke. There, in addition to servicing the silver barrage balloons, the twelve-piece dance orchestra formed under the direction of Corporal George Beaumont. When Beaumont was posted away in June 1941, Corporal Paul Fenoulhet took over the leadership. Paul, a highly respected musician and arranger, had toured with Jack Hilton and had also spent nine years at the Savoy Hotel, with Carroll Gibbons.

The initial personnel was: Corporal Paul Fenoulhet (ex-Carroll Gibbons) on trombone; leader and arranger, Chick Smith (ex-Lew Stone); Les Lambert (ex-Roy Fox) and Ted Allaby on trumpets; Basil Skinner, Bill Apps (ex-Lew Stone), Izzy Duman (ex-Teddy Joyce) and Cliff Timms on saxophones and clarinets; Jock Reid and Jock Purvis on bass; Pat Dodd (ex-Al Collins) on piano and Reg Sargeant on drums. Official duties meant deputies often had to be found either from the services or civilians. Among the drummers used by the Skyrockets during the war were Jack Parnell and George Fierstone (ex-Harry Roy).

The Skyrockets were booked first for a series of broadcasts to the Luftwaffe. These were broadcast by the BBC as propaganda on the European Service of the BBC. Then, from July 1941, the Skyrockets were on the air regularly in their own dance session, with vocalists Sergeant Leslie Douglas and Corporal Denny Dennis. They also used Beryl Davis as a guest singer on many of their broadcasts.

They broadcast every fortnight in the BBC radio series *Ack-Ack, Beer-Beer* over the next two years. They also broadcast on the *Music While You Work* series. Their first public appearance was in the 1941 Jazz Jamboree at the London Palladium on 7 September 1941, and their first Sunday concert was at Bristol on 5 October 1941. The Skyrockets played many times in Bristol and Pat Dodd recalls playing at Colston Hall there for a Mr Lockyer: 'We played two shows that evening — one at 6 p.m. and another at 8 p.m. on a Sunday evening. We had played at an officers' mess dance at a station near Birmingham on the Saturday and on the Sunday we had caught a train for Bristol, changing at Worcester on the way. All in all, the train journey took eight hours (what joy!) and we arrived at Bristol at 5 p.m. to discover that British Railways had removed the guard's van at Worcester and, apart from Izzy Duman's sax, which never left his side, we had no instruments and no music! On the way to Colston Hall, by taxis, I remembered a guitar player whose father owned a musical instrument shop in Bristol, and we sent our 'Gaffer' post-haste to the shop, and asked him to loan us some instruments. When we arrived at the hall, we had a wire from Leslie Douglas, who could not get away from his station. So now we had no vocalist. Jack Parnell was doing this weekend with us, and he volunteered to sing. We opened up with *In the Mood*, which we knew backwards. Paul Fenoulhet then explained our problem, and Jack Parnell played a drum solo, which lasted about ten minutes. Jack then joined me on the piano and we played four or five numbers. Paul then played a lengthy trombone solo. Incidentally, they were all borrowed instruments. Jack had a military drum kit, but he never complained. The hall was packed and the audience enjoyed every minute. During the interval, the music and instruments turned up. So all was well again. What joy!'

The Skyrockets recorded their first four titles for Rex records in March 1943. Their main output on records was, however, for EMI, followed by Parlophone and then HMV. Their first recording session for Parlophone was on 3 November 1943. This session produced two instrumental titles, *October Mood* and *Saturday Night Jump*, winners of the first and second awards at the 1943 *Jazz Jamboree*. Unfortunately, Corporal Denny Dennis never made any commercial recordings with the band, but Sergeant Leslie Douglas did and recorded Paul Fenoulhet's impressive arrangement of their famous signature tune, Matty Malneck's *Stairway to the Stars*.

From late 1943 to early 1944, the Skyrockets, along with the RAF Squadronaires, recorded broadcast discs for ENSA and ORBS. ENSA and ORBS also took recorded BBC broadcasts by both bands and then issued them overseas for various service networks including the American Forces Network. Both bands became involved in several BBC programmes of the time. One of the most famous was *Fanfare*, which included both bands, plus army pianist Ronnie Selby, from the Army Radio Orchestra, which later became the British Band of the AEF. The series was a truly inter-Allied affair, with Corporal Keith Jameson, from the US Army and AFN, as compère.

The recording sessions at EMI continued right into 1944. It was during this period that the Skyrockets teamed up with one of their future singers — Miss

Corporal Paul Fenoulhet outside the stage door entrance to the Stoll Theatre, 1943
(Photo: Ivor R. Richman)

Doreen Lundy, WAAF, who would sing again with the Skyrockets during 1946. The late Paul Fenoulhet remembered: 'We often had Beryl Davis as our guest on many of our concerts and broadcasts. Young Beryl was the daughter of Oscar Rabin's partner, Harry Davis. She later sang with Geraldo. Beryl recorded two songs with us, *No Love, No Nothing* and *My Heart Tells Me.*' Many of the band were also used by other bands of the time. Pat Dodd remembers: 'On one occasion I had a broadcast to do with one of the other big bands at that time (I can't remember which one), and when I arrived at the camp (Kidbrooke) on Saturday morning (I had a living-out pass), I discovered I was on guard duty that night. Panic! I rushed around and paid an airman ten shillings to do my guard duty. When I arrived back at camp on Sunday morning, I was told that this airman let a round off in the guard room, narrowly missing his foot. I was straight away put on a charge for not doing my guard duty. Fortunately for me, Dorothy Carless had asked me to accompany her at the New Cross Empire the following week and, when I offered the duty officer six tickets, all was forgiven with a telling off!'

The Skyrockets travelled all over the United Kingdom, playing for both the services and for civilians. Like all bands during the war, they had their hardships. Pat Dodd recalls: 'I also remember doing a week's engagement at six ice rinks in Scotland. We played with our greatcoats on — boy was it cold! On this occasion, we travelled to Scotland by train and returned by train, and most of us played poker there and back. We had another trombone player added for this engagement (I forget his name), and we were pulling into Kings

Cross station, from Scotland. He opened the carriage window and threw his wallet away. He said he could not tell his wife he had lost his money playing poker. Oh, happy memories!'

The Skyrockets used many musicians as well as their full line-up. The drummer was always a problem. They never had one, although they mainly used George Fierstone. Paul Fenoulhet remembers: 'We used to borrow civilians and stick them in uniform!' Most of the arrangements were either by Pat Dodd or Paul Fenoulhet. They included *American Patrol, Time On My Hands, No Love, No Nothing* and many others. Pat Dodd still holds fond memories of Paul: 'I had a great admiration for Paul, who was not only a gentleman, but could sit in a railway carriage with pen, pencil, rubber and a board on his lap, and score two or three new numbers for the band while we were playing poker — and what scores! Copperplate writing, and each instrument as it sounds.'

By the spring of 1944, the whole of southern England was one vast camp and, with everything set for the invasion of Europe, the Skyrockets were really playing their hearts out at Allied bases all over the place. A week after the D-Day landings on 13 June, a new Nazi blitz started on London. The first V-1 'Doodle-bugs' began hitting London. The Skyrockets were bombed out of their base at Kidbrooke in the first week of the blitz. They were transferred to Chessington to restore damaged balloons. Pat Dodd remembers this time very well: 'I was put in charge of a balloon crew. It was the height of the 'Doodle-bug' blitz and we were despatched by RAF lorry, complete with balloon and winch, and sent down through Kent to just outside Dover, and to await our orders. Sure enough, about 10 p.m., I got the signal to hoist the balloon. I told the winch man to release the balloon, but forgot to tell him to stop the winch! Whereupon our balloon disappeared in the clouds. As it was a terrible night, with many 'Doodle-bugs' brought down, we got away with it. Talk about skating on thin ice.'

The Skyrockets, along with many other famous services bands, were often featured on the newly-opened Allied Expeditionary Forces Programme. Among their AEFP shows was *AEFP Special* together with several other programmes. On 3 October 1944 the Skyrockets recorded a Paul Fenoulhet instrumental called *Heavy Gang*, which was a reminder that they had to lift the five hundredweight balloons onto lorries for transit.

Another recording session for EMI-Parlophone on 30 October 1944 produced another hit for the band's leader and composer — *It's Alright for You.*

Then on Sunday, 17 December 1944, the Skyrockets were featured on *Variety Bandbox.* During December 1944, they were transferred to fighter command at Bentley Priory, Stanmore, Middlesex. This would be their base until the end of the war in Europe.

The Skyrockets were demobilised in the autumn of 1945. The band decided to stay together as a co-operative civilian band. The twelve owner-members,

The No. 1 Balloon Centre Dance Band, better known as the Skyrockets, perform at the 1944 Jazz Jamboree (Photo: Ivor R. Richman)

with Paul Fenoulhet as musical director and Les Lambert as manager, employed the remaining musicians. They embarked on a tour of theatres and one-night stands. They were engaged by Val Parnell for the London Palladium revue *High Time*, which opened on 20 April 1946, and ran for ten months. The Skyrockets became so popular at the London Palladium that Val Parnell asked them to stay on as the resident band. The band stayed together with only minor changes right through until August 1955. Their stay at the London Palladium involved appearing in every Royal Command Performance at that theatre. Pat Dodd stayed on at the London Palladium for a further four years until 1959. Paul Fenoulhet died on 29 December 1979, and only three of the musicians are still alive and well. Of these, Pat Dodd, the pianist, is the most famous for his version of the wartime Skyrockets tune *In Pipetop's Footsteps*.

No. 1 BALLOON CENTRE DANCE ORCHESTRA 'THE SKYROCKETS' — DIRECTED BY CPL. PAUL FENOULHET 1941 – 1945

Sunday, 7 September 1941   JAZZ JAMBOREE
Broadcast live from the London Palladium, London
Over the BBC General Overseas Service
Featuring: The Skyrockets, the RAF Dance Orchestra, the RAOC Bluerockets, and many others
No details exist of the Skyrockets concert or the titles broadcast by the BBC.

Sunday, 5 October 1941   **CONCERT**
Live concert in Bristol
No further details exist on this live public concert.

Circa **March 1943**   **REX RECORDING STUDIOS, LONDON**
At this present time, details on the four titles recorded at the Rex Records
Studios by the Skyrockets are not available.

Wednesday, 3 November 1943   **HMV STUDIOS, LONDON**
(3.10) October Mood (Milne) EMI Saville SVL 161
(2.21) Saturday Night Jump (Rees) EMI Saville SVL 161

Wednesday, 9 February 1944   **HMV STUDIOS, LONDON**
(2.49) Stairway to the Stars (Parish-Malneck-Signorelli) -VR- Leslie Douglas
EMI Saville SVL 161
(2.55) No Love, No Nothing -VR- Beryl Davis EMI Saville SVL 161
(3.15) My Heart Tells Me -VR- Beryl Davis EMI Saville SVL 161

Tuesday, 3 October 1944   **HMV STUDIOS, LONDON**
(3.37) Heavy Gang (Fenoulhet) EMI Saville SVL 161

Monday, 23 October 1944   **DANCE ORCHESTRA OF THE**
13.30   **No. 1 BALLOON CENTRE**
(Pre-recorded, date unknown — BBC Disc No. SLO unknown)
Over AEFP
Featuring: The Skyrockets, conducted by Cpl. Paul Fenoulhet
Compère: Unknown
Details remain unknown.

Monday, 30 October 1944   **HMV STUDIOS, LONDON**
(3.09) It's Alright for You (Fenoulhet) EMI Saville SVL 161

Tuesday, 19 December 1944   **VARIETY BANDBOX**
13.01- 14.00
(Pre-recorded at the Queensbury All Services Club, on Sunday, 17 December
1944 — BBC Disc No. O.P. 116 – SLO 66020)
Over AEFP and the BBC General Overseas Service
Featuring: Uriel Porter, Morton Frazer, Patricia Morne, Eric Winstone,
Talbot O'Farrell, Elsie Carlisle, The ATS Pipers and the RAF Skyrockets
Orchestra, conducted by Cpl. Paul Fenoulhet
Compère: Patricia Medina
Producer: Stephen Williams
Editor: Cecil Madden
Opening Theme (I Love to Sing)/Stairway to the Stars – Theme
(Skyrockets)/Here We Go Again (Skyrockets)/O Blessed Day -VR- Uriel
Porter/Stephan Foster River Medley (featuring Uriel Porter)/Kiss Me -VR-
Morton Frazer/Frenesi -VR- Morton Frazer/Brazil -VR- Morton Frazer/My
Prayer -VR- Morton Frazer/Medley (featuring Morton Frazer): It's a Lovely
Day Tomorrow; 12th Street Rag; Yes Sir that's My Baby/Medley (featuring

Patricia Morne): Look for the Silver Lining; Blue Room; I'll Get By; My Heart Tells Me; Look for the Silver Lining/Medley (featuring Patricia Morne): My Heart Stood Still; Small Hotel; White Christmas/It Must be Jelly (Skyrockets)/O'Rafferty's Daughter -VR- Talbot O'Farrell/'Patter' (featuring Talbot O'Farrell)/If You Ever go to Ireland -VR- Talbot O'Farrell/ Somebody's Waiting for You -VR- Talbot O'Farrell/Marches featuring the ATS Pipers: March Atholl Highlanders; Strathspey, Market Place of Inverness; Devil Among the Tailors; Rhodesia Regiment/It Could Happen to You -VR- Elsie Carlisle/Medley (-VR- Elsie Carlisle): A Little Fond Affection; Cuddle Up a Little Closer; Never Been so Many Bonny Babies and Close.

Thursday, 19 April 1945   SERVICE DANCE BAND
12.02-12.30
(Pre-recorded at the Queensbury All Services Club, Soho, London, on Monday, 2 April 1945 — BBC Disc No. SLO 72058)
Over AEFP
Featuring: The RAF Skyrockets Dance Band, directed by Cpl. Paul Fenoulhet
Guest Star: Billy Campbell
Compère: Jill Balcon
Opening Theme (Stairway to the Stars)/Indiana/Come Out Wherever You Are -VR- Billy Campbell/The Sheik of Araby/I'll be Seeing You -VR- Denny Dennis/Two o'Clock Jump/The Man I Love/On the Sunny Side of the Street/ Jivin' at the Jamboree -VR- Billy Campbell/High Society/Theme and Close (Stairway to the Stars).

Saturday, 28 April 1945   RAF 'SKYROCKETS'
12.30-13.00   DANCE ORCHESTRA
(Pre-recorded at the BBC Studios, London, date unknown — BBC Disc No. unknown)
Over AEFP and the BBC General Overseas Service
Details remain unknown.

Sunday, 27 May 1945   SERVICES DANCE
19.35-20.00   BAND SESSION
(Pre-recorded at the BBC Studios, London, on Tuesday, 22 May 1945 — BBC Disc No. SLO 74696)
Over AEFP
Featuring: The RAF 'Skyrockets' Dance Orchestra, conducted by Cpl. Paul Fenoulhet with Cpl. Denny Dennis and WAAF Doreen Lundy
Compères: Jill Balcon and S/Sgt. Wilf Davidson
Opening Theme (Stairway to the Stars)/Anchors Aweigh/There Goes that Song Again -VR- Denny Dennis/Do You Ever Think Of Me/I Didn't Know About You -VR- Doreen Lundy/Swinging on a Star -VR- Denny Dennis/ Cossack Patrol/I'm Gonna Love that Guy -VR- Doreen Lundy/Two o'Clock Jump/Closing Theme (Stairway to the Stars).

The Royal Air Force Dance Orchestra
'The Squadronaires' March 1940 – October 1945

Early in 1940, the RAF asked a number of the leading British dance band musicians to form an RAF Dance Orchestra, the idea being that the service band would complement the military brass ensembles playing for dances, accompanying artists at concerts and entertaining generally as a morale-booster. The musicians selected were the cream of the pre-war dance bands. Among these were pianist and singer Jimmy Miller, Vera Lynn's new husband, clarinet player Harry Lewis, arranger and trombonist George Chisholm, pianist Ronnie Aldrich, drummer Jock Cummings, guitarist and singer Sid Colin, Eric Breeze, Tommy McQuater, Jimmy Durrant, Archie Craig, Andy McDevitt, Arthur Maden, Tom Bradbury and leader Leslie Holmes (real name Les Brannally).

The band was formed during March 1940 at RAF Uxbridge, Middlesex, during the period known as the 'Phoney War'. From the outbreak of the Second World War on Sunday, 3 September 1939, until the spring of 1940, the British dance bands had carried on very much in the manner of the pre-war period. Their whole concept, technique and performance, however, would change within a very short period of time. The American Swing bands would influence the whole era and the newly-formed RAF Dance Orchestra, better known under their popular name as 'The Squadronaires', would be one of the forerunners of the Swing dance music. The style was very much like the Bob Crosby bands, with added music tones of Sam Donahue and Glenn Miller added during late 1944. A whole section of the newly formed Squadronaires came from the Ambrose Orchestras, while others came from Lew Stone's and many other famous British dance bands. It was perhaps prophetic that many of the newly-formed band musicians were playing in a part-time group called the 'Heralds of Swing' just before their joining-up papers were served.

Their main base was RAF Uxbridge for the duration of the war and Jimmy Miller still remembers their hut at that camp: 'We were in Mons block — they were all named after First War battles.'

When the group of musicians reported to RAF Uxbridge in March 1940, many of the musicians had been working right up until the very evening they were to go into the RAF. Jimmy Miller recalls: 'We were all still in our evening dress when we arrived by tube train at Uxbridge. The best example was Jock — Jock Cummings — because we had to report at 11.59 p.m., just before midnight. Jock came straight from the Embassy, I think, and the next morning at 5.30 a.m., it was "wakey wakey, rise and shine." He was still lying there in his evening dress. Iron beds with a straw mattress, and this Sergeant walked in and Jock told him where to go and he gave him the job of cleaning out the latrines. Jock was still wearing his evening suit while he cleaned them out. It was quite funny to see him that morning. The night before, he had been playing drums in the West End.'

Over the next few weeks, the musicians were put into RAF training at Uxbridge — drills and all the military activities that would turn them into an RAF band. RAF Flying Officer Ticquet once wrote in the *Melody Maker*: 'At first, they had to overcome a few inevitable service difficulties. Sympathetic as the RAF has always been, the ambitious idea of a top-line service dance orchestra found a few opponents among the military band first school. Sometimes it took time — and unorthodox methods! — to secure scope which the band needed for full development. But things soon settled down and the work went smoothly on, with the blessing of Wing-Commander R. P. O'Donnell, M.V.O., director of Music to the RAF.'

Circumstances became very difficult in the formative days, when the band started to tour around the British Isles. They performed at airfields, camps, factories and in halls for dances. The main difficulties involved travel and the Blitz. The Squadronaires were on the road performing at the height of the 1940 Blitz. Once, while the band were playing at Bristol, a bomb literally blasted them out of the hall and they finished the night dragging victims from bombed houses. But the band played two shows at the Gaumont Cinema in Manchester during the early days, and the *Manchester Evening News* called them the greatest dance band this country had ever produced! The phrase was coined by Jerry Dawson, *Melody Maker*'s provincial editor.

On Friday, 3 May 1940, the RAF Squadronaires, as they were called at that time, were in the Decca recording studios in London. Under the leadership of Leslie Holmes, they recorded four titles. It was the start of a long recording contract with Decca. The four titles included two instrumental and two vocal tracks, one by their future leader Jimmy Miller, and one by guitar player Sid Colin. Leslie Holmes did not remain long as the band's leader, as Jimmy Miller recalls: 'When the band was formed, Wing-Commander O'Donnell was the commanding officer — the musical director. He was Squadron-leader O'Donnell then and, when the band got together, this fellow Leslie Holmes fronted the band. His uncle was Joe Brannally, ex-guitar player, who worked for Peter Maurice, the music publisher. Holmes was quite a tall, nice-looking chap, but he could not conduct a bus. Our first broadcast for the BBC was at the Maida Vale studios in Stadland Avenue and David Miller, the Canadian broadcaster chap, was there. Miller was like a sort of Pete Murray in those days. The band under Holmes was so bad, the tempos were all wrong and, in the end, David Miller asked him to join him in the control box with the engineers. David then asked me to front the band — it was not staged or anything; after all, we were in the BBC studios. Leslie Holmes did not know the arrangements or anything, and that is how I took over the band. All the boys in the band asked me to carry on fronting the band from then on. I don't know what happened to Holmes after that or where he went to!'

So Sergeant Jimmy Miller took over the leadership of the band just before the 'Battle of Britain' and the Blitz. Under Jimmy Miller, the RAF Dance Orchestra, 'The Squadronaires', became perhaps Britain's greatest dance band. Britain has produced no finer saxophone section and the brasswork was excellent in itself, providing the inspiration for the later brass-dominated Ted Heath Orchestra. George Chisholm was the most important soloist in the band and his highly individual arrangements were a major influence in shaping the band's personality. George also introduced the Chisholm/Breeze unison trombone duets, which became a style unique to the Squadronaires. The name itself 'Squadronaires' was shortened by many of its fans to just the 'Squads'. On Decca records, they were called The Royal Air Force Dance Orchestra, by permission of the Air Council, although, after the war and demobbing, they carried on with the name 'The Squadronaires'.

The first recording session with Jimmy Miller fronting the band took place at the Decca studios in London on Friday, 10 January 1941. Once again they produced four titles. Exactly one month later, they were back in the Decca studios for more recordings. On radio broadcasts, the band were introduced by their theme, *There's Something in the Air* which included vocals by their leader Jimmy Miller. This, however, would not be recorded by the Squadronaires until 13 November 1941. The arrangement was by George Chisholm and the song itself was by Adamson and McHugh. One of their first records really to catch the public's ear was an arrangement, again by George Chisholm, called *That's A-Plenty*, recorded on 10 June 1941. This used the famous Chisholm/Breeze unison. Ronnie Aldrich remembers: 'The arrangement was by George, whose nationality is betrayed by the Scottish bit he inserted in the middle of the number. There is an exciting trombone duet and a trumpet solo by Tommy McQuater. The recording was unusual in its time because it was one of the earliest to finish with a mechanical fade-out, a deliberate device which is used nowadays by arrangers who have difficulty in thinking of an end for their arrangements.'

On Sunday, 7 September 1941, the RAF Dance Orchestra, 'The Squadronaires', took part in the *Jazz Jamboree* at the famous London Palladium. Three titles were broadcast by the BBC General Forces programme. Jimmy Miller remembers the *Jazz Jamboree* shows very well: 'The Squadronaires were on first, then Geraldo second and then the Skyrockets third. We all appeared on the *Jazz Jamboree* shows, following the *Melody Maker* polls. We were involved in every one right up until 1946.'

During this period, the Squadronaires also broadcast in Cecil Madden's *American Eagle in Britain* series. Cecil Madden has said of these now legendary short-wave broadcasts to America: 'This series was all my own idea. It came about because of the American Eagle Squadrons in the RAF. These were American volunteers who came over here via Canada to join the RAF and fight the Nazis. I never missed a show, right through from 1940 until 1945. Right through all the bombing, and V-bombs. Even when I was in hospital, they brought a microphone for me to talk into. The shows were recorded every Thursday afternoon and broadcast on Saturday evenings. We broadcast from ''Dunker's Den'' in the American Red Cross Club. You have to remember America was still not at war at that time and these boys were fighting for us, over here. I had every famous band and artist available and used them whenever I could. They all came down to the American Red Cross Club in Piccadilly in London at some time. When America came into the war in December 1941, the whole scene changed. American stars began to arrive and we really had some grand old times with these broadcasts.'

By mid-December 1941, the Squadronaires' trumpet section was increased to three with the addition of Clinton French. Clinton was in the band for a BBC Home Service broadcast on Christmas Day, 1941.

The Squadronaires were performing everywhere from Scotland to Cornwall. They played at every major camp for soldiers, sailors and airmen. They broadcast at least once a week, and were often heard by millions of people, many of whom were involved in war production in factories and work in hospitals all over the country. Their fame quickly spread, as George Chisholm remembers: 'We may not have been the best band in the world, but we were the best drinking band in the world. As soon as the landlords heard, they would say, ''Quick, the Squadronaires are coming,'' and stock up.'

Wartime travelling often took its toll. The Squadronaires often used RAF trucks, but hold-ups caused by bombing often caused delays, although the fans would often wait and gave them a tremendous reception. Airfield concerts were often a problem during the winter months, due to the cold and unheated hangars, but the band always gave a tremendous performance wherever they played. Often, after playing at a dance or at a services concert, they would end up in some far-off camp in the back of beyond. George Chisholm remembers: 'One night we drove up to some camp, very late at night, and the airman on guard asked who we were. ''We're the band.'' ''The what?'' came his reply. Anyway, they billeted us in this Nissen hut. At 5.30 a.m. the next morning, in came the duty sergeant. ''Wakey, wakey — rise and shine.'' Jock Cummings told him where to go! There were no lights and he asked, ''Who said that? Name and number.'' Jock replied, ''Hitler,'' and he said, ''Yes, but what's your first name?'' '

During the first week of February 1942, the Squadronaires were playing at the Palace Theatre in Blackpool. Anne Shelton was guest vocalist with the band at this venue.

The spring of 1942 saw the RAF Squadronaires very busy at the Decca recording studios. During late February, arranger Woolf Phillips had joined the

Sergeant Jimmy Miller conducts the orchestra, as Dame Vera Lynn's husband, Harry Lewis, gets a down-beat for one of his famous clarinet solos. Taken at the Stoll Theatre, Kingsway, during one of the Jazz Jamboree *concerts, circa 1942-43 (Photo: Ivor R. Richman)*

line-up of musicians. Also added during this period for a short while was singer Billy Nicholls. Billy also worked with the band during their subsequent tour of the Continent from November to December 1944. The Decca recording session of 21 May 1942, produced another well-known recording for the Squadronaires — *South Rampart Street Parade*. This tune had already been recorded by Bob Crosby and his band in the USA. As George Chisholm remembers: 'The band was basically a collective organisation like the Bob Crosby Orchestra. Unlike that American band, they were subject to RAF discipline and pay. The spirit was tremendous: there was no working to rule, the rule was to work, whether blowing in an officers' mess, concert hall or dance hall, anywhere from Scotland to the German border.'

The summer of 1942 was the turning-point in the war for the Allies. The Squadronaires were as busy as ever, with BBC broadcasts, concerts, camp shows, hospitals and even concerts in munitions factories throughout the country. During this period, they worked a lot with Vera Lynn, the forces' sweetheart. Jimmy Miller remembers: 'After all, Vera's husband, Harry Lewis, was a member of the band and we often worked with Vera during the war, on many broadcasts and concerts. I still have a chat now and again with Vera and Harry on the telephone and we always talk about the war. Oh, sorry, I should say Dame Vera.'

The Squadronaires also worked with another famous female singer of that period, Miss Dorothy Carless. Jimmy also remembers doing duets with the blonde bombshell, Miss Evelyn Dall, during the war.

On Saturday, 26 September 1942, the day Glenn Miller disbanded his famous civilian band in America and went into the army, the RAF Squadronaires were broadcasting over the BBC Home Service. Eight days later, on Sunday, 4 October 1942, the RAF Squadronaires were again on the bill of the *Jazz Jamboree* but, unlike the 1941 *Jamboree*, which came from the London Palladium, the venue had changed to the Stoll Theatre in Kingsway, London. The only tune by the Squadronaires broadcast by the BBC from that event was the George Chisholm arrangement of *Anchors Aweigh*.

Once again, on Christmas Day, 1942, the RAF Squadronaires were featured in a special broadcast over the BBC Home Service.

During April 1943, the Squadronaires were involved in the technicolour film, *The Life and Death of Colonel Blimp*, directed by Michael Powell and Emeric Pressburger. The Squadronaires played *Commando Patrol*. The film was an Archers production and was released by the General Film Distributors on 26 July 1943.

In the month before the Squadronaires performed for the soundtrack of the film, they broadcast over the BBC, with compère Phillip Brown. This broadcast went out live on Sunday, 14 March 1943.

During the summer of 1943, the Squadronaires played at many factories producing 'Spitfires' and 'Hurricane' fighters. They were also engaged in a heavy broadcasting schedule and were involved with ENSA and ORBS in producing broadcast discs for overseas use by short-wave stations. Among the various broadcasts were those for the *Fanfare, Swing Time* and *Top of the List* series. There were many others for *Best Sellers* and other ENSA programmes. So their fame and musicianship spread all over the world. From the Far East to the Arctic convoys, the Squadronaires were heard.

By 1944, the Squadronaires were really at the top of the British dance band list. Early in March, they teamed up with Beryl Davis at the Decca studios to record two titles. The two were recorded on 17 March and both became very popular indeed. They were *A Journey to a Star* and *No Love, No Nothing*, both from the 1943 smash-hit musical film *The Gang's All Here*. The teaming of young Beryl Davis with the RAF Dance Orchestra, the Squadronaires, would continue later in the year on the newly-opened Allied Expeditionary Forces Programme, on the *Top Ten* series.

1944 was to be quite a year for the Squadronaires. Their touring schedule increased with the preparations for the invasion of Europe. Jimmy Miller remembers: 'We were everywhere, performing for Americans, British and Canadian soldiers, sailors and airmen. Everyone seemed in uniform and they all enjoyed everything we had to offer.'

Also during the early spring of 1944, the Squadronaires appeared in the Vera Lynn film, *One Exciting Night*, made by Columbia Pictures. Unlike in *The Life and Death of Colonel Blimp* the previous spring, the Squadronaires, directed by Jimmy Miller, were shown performing in the film.

On 6 June 1944, the greatest invasion of all time took place in Normandy.

'D-Day', the day everyone had waited for so long, had arrived. The following day, after several dry runs, the BBC and SHAEF opened the Allied Expeditionary Forces Programme. The Squadronaires were to form an important part of the radio programme. On Monday, 17 July, at 21.15 DBST, the Royal Air Force Dance Orchestra took to the air with a programme. The next Thursday, 20 July, Jimmy Miller would be the guest star on Captain Glenn Miller's American Band of the Supreme Allied Command broadcast, along with Vera Lynn.

Jimmy was introduced on the broadcast by Captain Franklin Englemann to Captain Glenn Miller. Glenn's introduction on the broadcast was: 'How d'you do, Sergeant Miller?' Jimmy: 'Very well indeed, Captain Miller. I've looked forward to this moment.' Captain Glenn Miller: 'No more than we have, Sarge. Sharin' the same mission with a band like yours is nice work, and we've got it.' Jimmy Miller: 'Well, Captain, I do a bit of singing, y'know, and I've been hoping to share the same song with a band like yours.' Captain Miller: 'All right, Jimmy, you name it and we'll play it.' Jimmy Miller: '*This is a Lovely Way to Spend an Evening.*'

After the broadcast that evening, Jimmy remembers that Vera Lynn drove them both back from Bedford to London: 'It was the blackout and Vera nearly drove us off the road. Now I look back on it, it was quite funny.'

The following Monday evening, the RAF Dance Orchestra were on the air over the AEFP with their own series, *Top Ten*. The first broadcast on Monday, 24 July 1944, was introduced by Sergeant Broderick Crawford, and was performed from the Paris Cinema, a BBC studio in Lower Regent Street, which is still in use today..

The *Top Ten* series included three bands, the Squadronaires, the Brass Hats, with Kenny Baker, and the Singing Strings under Reg Leopold. The vocals on the programme were supplied by Beryl Davies, Sergeant Jimmy Miller and Sid Colin, the latter two both from the Squadronaires. It was a very large orchestra as Jimmy Miller remembers: 'It was a very large band, because we augmented it by four trumpets and four trombones. That was people like Kenny Baker, Woolfe Phillips, and Laddie Busby, plus a few others. Of course, there were the 'Singing Strings' under Reg Leopold — my brother played violin in that string orchestra. I conducted all three orchestras in the final number on the show. Just about the best type of programme for featuring the best jazz players we had. During the war we had the best through the RAF. Then we had three or four very fine arrangers, and they used to do the big arrangement at the end of the show every week, augmented with the strings. Lots of people thought in the old days, that if you stood in front of a band all you did was jump about or sing a bit. I think it surprised a lot of people I could read and conduct a concert arrangement with strings at the finish.'

A week later, the *Top Ten* programme was introduced by Captain Franklin Englemann, and once again the programme was a great hit. *Top Ten* was a sort of British version of the AFRS *All Time Hit Parade*, and included the top

Beryl Davis sings and LAC Ronnie Aldrich plays during a Top Ten *programme, summer 1944*

tunes being broadcast by Britain, the United States of America and Canada at that time. It also included the top tune from *Your Hit Parade*, which was really the forerunner of today's chart hits programmes. *I'll be Seeing You* was often performed on the *Top Ten* programmes, along with *A Lovely Way to Spend an Evening* — both were Frank Sinatra songs.

Right through July and into August 1944, the Squadronaires were very busy with the *Top Ten* series. Then, in the last week of August, the Old Groaner himself came over. Yes, Bing Crosby made his first trip to England. On Wednesday, 30 August 1944, he was the special guest on the British Band of the AEF broadcast. In the audience was Jimmy Miller and his wife Mary. Jimmy remembers that broadcast very well: 'Mary and I were in the front row, along with Glenn Miller, Don Haynes, Broderick Crawford and many other famous stars. RSM George Melachrino was an old friend of mine from the Carroll Gibbons Orchestra back in the thirties. It was a great broadcast.'

This was at the height of the V-1 'Doodle-bug' blitz on London, and on the following day, Thursday, 31 August 1944, the Stage Door Canteen in Piccadilly opened. Among the people who opened the now legendary Canteen were the RAF Squadronaires, Bing Crosby, Fred and Adele Astaire, Jack Buchanan, Anthony Eden, and Dorothy Dickson. The opening was pre-recorded by the BBC AEFP and broadcast on Friday, 1 September 1944. Jimmy Miller recalls: 'Everybody wanted to be there at the opening because Bing Crosby was there. Denny Dennis begged me to get him a ticket, just to see his idol. He even went down on his knees, just to see Crosby. He was in the front row when Bing made his entrance. He [Bing] was as bald as bald could

216

The rhythm section of the Squadronaires, winter 1944

be. The Squadronaires performed two songs with him. We also backed Fred Astaire while he danced. It was a great night.'

Just over a week later, on Saturday, 9 September 1944, the Squadronaires, along with Sam Donahue's US Navy Dance Band played on the stage of the Queensbury All Services Club for 2,000 Allied service men and women. Beryl Davies was on hand with the RAF Squadronaires and sang some memorable songs with them. The Sam Donahue US Navy Band had as their singer Bill Bassford. Once again, it was another great night. AEFP recorded and broadcast the show.

During the summer and early autumn of 1944, the RAF Squadronaires had some narrow escapes with V-1 'Doodle-bugs' and V-2 rockets in and around London. The *Top Ten* series was still being broadcast every Monday evening over the AEFP and, from 25 September onwards, it was introduced by Roy Williams. Captain Franklin Englemann had been sent over to the Continent for AEFP broadcasts from the fighting troops. In between the AEFP broadcasts and personal appearances, the RAF Squadronaires were still making records for Decca. On 29 August they had recorded another title with Beryl Davis — *Milkman, Keep Those Bottles Quiet*, from the Tommy Dorsey film *Broadway Rhythm*. They also recorded an instrumental that day called *The Blues in C Sharp Minor*. It became one of their famous hits.

Sunday, 15 October 1944, was the day of the 1944 *Jazz Jamboree* and, among the bands that were featured in that show from the Stoll Theatre in Kingsway, London, were the RAF Squadronaires, directed by Jimmy Miller.

Also featured in the 1944 *Jazz Jamboree*, were the entire American Band of the AEF, under the direction of Major Glenn Miller. The only portion of the RAF Squadronaires part of this charity show that was broadcast by the BBC was their famous signature tune, *There's Something in the Air*. The Glenn Miller part was not even broadcast, Also on hand were the *Melody Maker* reporters and their photographer, Ivor Richmond, who took many photographs of the orchestras and bands taking part. The yearly *Jazz Jamboree* charity concerts were a major event during the war years and many famous musicians and bands were featured. On the council that year was the Geraldo trombone star, Ted Heath. Ted was in the process of forming a new band, which would soon take over the AEFP *Top Ten* series from the Squadronaires. His band, 'Ted Heath and His Music' would become the greatest 'big band' to be formed in the United Kingdom in the post-war years. It was Ted's idea to have the great Glenn Miller AEF Orchestra on that year's *Jazz Jamboree*. With the RAF Squadronaires was singer Beryl Davis, from the *Top Ten* series. Also included in the RAF Dance Orchestra's line-up of musicians was their new tenor saxophone and clarinet player, Jimmy Durrant. Jimmy had taken over Harry Lewis's position in the band during August 1944. Harry had been demobbed and by October 1944 was with his wife, Vera Lynn, on a tour for the forgotten army in Burma. Harry never did return as a musician to any band, and has spent the last 45 years working as Dame Vera Lynn's manager — a job he has done extremely well!

The following day, 16 October 1944, the RAF Squadronaires were back on their famous *Top Ten* series. This was a *Top Ten* with a difference, because it featured four bands, instead of the normal three. The fourth was the Sam Donahue US Navy Band of the Liberation Forces. Also with the Donahue Band was their singer, Bill Bassford, while the RAF Squadronaires had Beryl Davis and their own Sid Colin together with their lead singer, Sergeant Jimmy Miller. The show was broadcast live from the BBC studios at Aeolin Hall. The compère was Douglas Marshall and the final title, which featured the RAF Squadronaires and the Sam Donahue US Navy Band, was an arrangement by guardsman George Evans of *All Alone*. BBC producer Pat Dixon, who produced all the *Top Ten* series, had teamed up the two famous service bands for this broadcast in the same fashion as Cecil Madden had done with the famous Glenn Miller AEF Orchestra and Sam Donahue a month earlier.

Also on the show were the famous 'Singing Strings' under Reg Leopold and the 'Brass Hats'. As with all the *Top Ten* series, it lasted half an hour from 21.15 to 21.45, Double British Summer Time. Like all the broadcasts in the series, it was not so much a hit parade show, but tended to highlight famous composers such as Irving Berlin, and many others on both sides of the Atlantic. The Americans had their *All Time Hit Parade* at that time which featured Tommy Dorsey and his Orchestra but, unlike that series (which was also broadcast by the AFRS and the AEFP), the *Top Ten* Series featured three regular bands with a grand finish in which all three played together — or, as on this special one, two!

Not to be outdone, the following Saturday Cecil Madden teamed up three Allied service bands representing America, Britain and Canada. They were the RAF Squadronaires, the Sam Donahue US Navy Band and the Canada Dance Band, directed by Captain Robert Farnon (the Canada Dance Band were a sub-unit of the Canadian Band of the AEF). The three performed at the Queensbury All Services Club, in Soho, London, which opened in 1942, in the large former Casino Theatre, now better known as the Prince Edward Theatre. It was sponsored by a group of wealthy sporting and entertainment celebrities, presided over by the Marquis of Queensbury, Sir Simon Marks (who was better known as the owner of Marks and Spencer). The manager for the club was John Harding. As well as supplying films, bands and stage shows the club also provided meals, a wash and brush-up and dancing downstairs. Both Cecil Madden and Stephen Williams recognised its potential as a regular broadcasting venue for the BBC, especially as it could supply a large and enthusiastic service audience. By 1944 some of the best light entertainment broadcasts were coming from the club. The three-orchestra show on Saturday, 21 October 1944, was pre-recorded by the BBC for their *AEFP Special* series and broadcast by the AEFP on Sunday, 22 October 1944. With the Squadronaires was singer Beryl Davis, while the Sam Donahue outfit had Bill Bassford as their singer. The Canada Dance Band had their own Paul Carpenter. Jimmy Miller remembers that evening very well: 'You could have had orchestras of that high standard only during a war. It would never happen again in a life-time! The only time it could ever happen again as if there was another war. God forbid!'

On Monday, 13 November, the RAF Squadronaires were featured for the last time in 1944 on the *Top Ten* series. For the next six weeks the band were scheduled to tour the continent. During their six weeks away, the George Evans Orchestra took over their broadcasting schedule. Their next broadcast for *Top Ten* was on Monday, 1 January 1945. Their tour of the liberated Continent took them from Belgium through into France and up into Holland. They also performed at many advanced bases very close to the German border. Jimmy Miller remembers the start of that famous tour, which, as he recalls, nearly never came about: 'While we were waiting to go abroad, we were down at Purfleet, awaiting embarkation, on an LST, to go across to follow the troops through Belgium and Holland. We waited at Purfleet two days, and we were getting fed-up because we had no British money — we had converted all our money into Belgian francs. We could not go down to the pub or anything, because we had no British money and the rockets were coming down. These were the V-2 rockets, not the 'Doodle-bugs', and they made an awful mess of the camp. And then finally we got into an LST. They had made us miss the one the day before, which had made us all feel worse. I had argued with the commanding officer about taking the one the previous day. Anyway, we finally arrived in Ostend and in the mouth of the harbour was the LST that I'd argued over, with only two masts sticking out the water. There were about three to four hundred airmen lost. The bodies washed ashore days afterwards and we learned to be a bit more patient after that!'

From Ostend, the band travelled and performed mostly for British troops and airmen in Belgium, Holland and northern France. The tour of the Continent lasted nearly six weeks, and they performed at many troop concerts, some very near the front line. They also performed at many advanced fighter bases and had to compete with fighters taking off to attack Nazi positions. At the beginning of December, they spent several days in Paris, performing for SHAEF personnel. Jimmy Miller recalls their stay in Paris: 'We just arrived from Brussels, and it was our first night in Paris, and we were stationed in a place in Montmartre. The RAF squadron leader, who was also the entertainments officer, gave me a batch of 20 tickets to see Jasha Heifitz, the famous violinist, performing in a recital. As it turned out, only Ronnie Aldrich and myself went along to the recital. All the others in the band went out on the town to see the girls at the ''Folies Bergère''. My main reason was to try to understand the violin parts and, after all, my brother was a violinist in the Singing Strings, under Reg Leopold, on the *Top Ten* series. Another funny thing happened at that time. We were scheduled to do quite a lot of shows for the fighting troops and RAF chaps. On one of the billings, they made an awful error. They listed the concert as the RAF Dance Orchestra by permission of the Air Marshall Commanding Sergeant, Jimmy Miller. Lady Cunningham thought it was very funny and said to me, ''I must show my husband.'' I've kept that billing to this day. It put me in charge of the RAF over the continent.'

On 12 December 1944, the Squadronaires, with singer Billy Nicholls, performed at an RAF airfield just outside Brussels. A portion of that concert was recorded by Radio Diffusion Nationale Belge and used by the AEFP in their series *AEFP on the Spot*. The compère was Captain Franklin Englemann. The AEFP broadcast this programme on Friday, 22 December 1944.

On that Friday, however, the RAF Squadronaires were returning home, having cut short their tour of the Continent, as Jimmy Miller remembers: 'We got as far as the German border, and von Rundstedt started his attack through the Ardennes. Our commanding officer up where we were said to me, ''If I were you, I'd get back to the old country as quickly as you can with the band, because we could be cut off by the Germans.'' He went on to say, ''They're coming through the Ardennes. If I were you, I'd get back to Ostend, if you can.'' We packed our truck and I said to Jock, ''Pack your drums.'' He said, ''Leave the bloody drums! I can always get another kit at Boosey and Hawks.'' '

'When we got back to Ostend and were queuing for an LST, a coach arrived from Paris, I think, and it was Joe Loss and the boys — they were all ENSA. They were all young, long-haired characters. I don't think they were outstanding, but Joe had to use what musicians he could get in those days. The Warrant Officer on the quay said to me, ''You've got a band here, get your boys to carry Mr Joe Loss and his band's instruments onto the LST.'

Joe was so embarrassed when he saw George Chisholm, Tommy McQuater and myself carrying his boys' instruments.

'When we got back to England, we heard an announcement that Major Glenn Miller was missing. We were scheduled to go back to the Continent to meet Glenn and his band for a concert at the Garrison Theatre in Paris. We never went back over again.'

The RAF Squadronaires' first 1945 broadcast with the *Top Ten* series was on Monday, 1 January. It was a live broadcast over the AEFP, which was repeated during March 1945 over the BBC General Forces Programme. The broadcast was from the Paris Cinema in Lower Regent Street. It is interesting to note that the Paris Cinema is still in use by the BBC to this day.

Two weeks later, on Monday, 15 January 1945, the *Top Ten* series featured the newly-formed 'Ted Heath and His Music'. The RAF Squadronaires were touring the UK and their spot was filled by the new orchestra in its first-ever broadcast. The band featured drummer Jack Parnell on drums and vocals. They also had their own vocalist on hand in future shows. Ted and his boys were a great hit with the radio audience and the show's producer, Pat Dixon. The following week, on Monday, 22 January 1945, the RAF Squadronaires were back again in their regular spot in the series. They would remain there until Monday, 30 April 1945. 'Ted Heath and His Music' took over the RAF Squadronaires spot in the series from Monday, 7 May 1945 — the day before 'VE Day'. Although Ted and his boys took over the series, the 'Singing Strings' and the 'Brass Hats' remained with the series and so too did singer Beryl Davis. As Jimmy Miller recalls: 'Beryl Davis sang with us a lot. After the war, Beryl went to America with Mel Powell, the pianist with Glenn Miller. Beryl later married Peter Potter, the famous disc jockey in the USA. Dorothy Carless also went to the USA and became a producer on the west coast.'

Towards the end of the RAF Squadronaires' stay with the series, Jimmy Miller was replaced as the singer by Bill Bassford of the US Navy, who had been with the Sam Donahue US Navy Band until early April 1945. When Sam and his band returned home to the United States in early April, Bill was for some reason left behind in England. During mid-April 1945, he appeared on many AEFP shows. He broadcast on several of the *Top Ten* shows during April with the RAF Squadronaires. Although Jimmy Miller did not sing on the programmes, he was there directing the Squadronaires.

From 'VE Day' until mid-July 1945, the RAF Squadronaires were back out on a tour of the United Kingdom. After all, the war in Europe was over, but not the war against Japan. The RAF Squadronaires' tour included further services camps and munitions factories. They also performed quite a bit at the Queensbury All Services Club.

On Wednesday, 18 July 1945, the Squadronaires were back in London and recorded four titles at the Decca studios. Among the four was a Mel Powell composition, *Mission to Moscow*. They had already recorded a Mel Powell composition back in February, *Lead With Your Left*. Such was the inter-Allied feeling among the bands on the Allied Expeditionary Forces Programme that Glenn Miller's pianist and arranger, Sergeant Mel Powell would supply arrangements and compositions to the Squadronaires. As Cecil Madden recalls: 'All the bands and orchestras were so very friendly. There was a great Allied spirit in everything they did. It was a wonderful time working with all the bands and artists — something I will remember as long as I live.'

Sergeant Jimmy Miller and the RAF Squadronaires were on hand for one of the last AEFP shows to be broadcast, on Saturday, 28 July 1945, at 21.05 DBST, from the Queensbury All Services Club. The show, called *Farewell AEFP*, was produced by Cecil Madden. Among the bands featured were the Canadian Band of the AEF, directed by Captain Bob Farnon, with Paul Carpenter, and Joanne Dallas. The RAF Squadronaires performed *Marie*. RSM George Melachrino, the Ronnie Selby Trio, Dorothy Carless, Corporal Jack Powers, and many others took part in the show. The AEFP closed down that very evening. The next day, the BBC Light Programme was born. This remained on the air until 1967, when BBC Radio 2 was launched.

This was not the end for the RAF Squadronaires: they stayed in the RAF until early 1946. On 17 October 1945, they were back in the Decca studios in London and again recorded four titles. Dorothy Carless recorded two titles with the Squads, on that session and they also recorded two instrumentals. Among their broadcasts over the war years, they had played as guests on *Variety Bandbox* and Cecil Madden's *American Eagle in Britain* series. They had been featured many times in one-off broadcasts and, of course, there had been their *Top Ten* series. During 1946, they were demobbed from the RAF, but they had become so popular with their British fans that they exchanged their RAF blues for black and white tuxedos . . . and the band played on!

From 1946 until 1959, they carried on where they had left off with the RAF. They became one of Britain's top bands. They produced many records and even formed a small quartet singing group called 'The Quads'.

Sadly, only five members of the band are still alive: Jimmy Miller, George Chisholm, Ronnie Aldrich, Harry Lewis and Tommy McQuater. They were so good in their day that today we have two bands bearing their name — the official RAF dance band 'The Squadronaires' and the 'New Squadronaires', directed by Harry Bence.

The personnel of the Squads remained constant even after they had left the Royal Air Force. They provided Britain with the Big Band Sound well into the 1950s, along with Ted Heath and His Music. And, of course, they are very much remembered for their contribution to the war effort back in those dark days between 1940 and 1945, when they gave everyone their music in concerts and over the BBC.

THE RAF DANCE ORCHESTRA —
'THE SQUADRONAIRES'
MARCH 1940 – OCTOBER 1945

Friday, 3 May 1940   DECCA STUDIOS, LONDON

DR 4610 –   (   ) The Man Who Comes Around Decca F7480
                       -VR- Sid Colin -arr- RA
DR 4611 –   (   ) With the Wind and Rain   Decca F7480
                       in Your Hair -VR-
                       Jimmy Miller -arr- RA
DR 4612 –   (   ) By the Waters of Minnetonka Decca F7572
                       (J.M. Cavanass –
                       T. Lieurance) -arr- GC
DR 4613 –   (   ) The Song is Ended   Decca F7572
                       -arr- JD

Friday, 10 January 1941   DECCA STUDIOS, LONDON

DR 5234 – 1   (   ) All of Me   Decca F7782
DR 5235 – 1   (   ) Indiana   Decca F7782
DR 5236 – 1   (   ) Beat Me Daddy, Eight to   Decca F7720
                       a Bar -VR- Sid Colin
                       (Raye-Prince-Sheehy)
DR 5237 – 1   (   ) The Nearness of You -VR-   Decca F7720
                       Jimmy Miller
                       (Ned Washington –
                       Hoagy Carmichael)

Wednesday, 19 February 1941   DECCA STUDIOS, LONDON

DR 5361 –   (   ) Constantly   Decca F7743
DR 5362 –   (   ) Rock-a-bye Baby   Decca F7743
DR 5364 –   (   ) One Look at You   Decca F7744
DR 5364 –   (   ) Li'l Boy Love   Decca F7744

Monday, 19 May 1941   DECCA STUDIOS, LONDON

DR 5703 – 1   (   ) It's Foolish, but it's   Decca F7861
                       Fun -VR- Jimmy Miller
DR 5704 – 1   (2.47) Boogie Woogie Bugle Boy   Decca F7862
                       -VR- Sid Colin (Raye-Prince) Decca RLF 19
                       (From the 1941 film, *Buck
                       Privates*)
DR 5705 – 1   (   ) There I Go -VR- Jimmy   Decca F7862
                       Miller (Hy Zaret – Irving
                       Meiser)
DR 5706 – 1   (   ) Love at Last -VR- Jimmy   Decca F7861
                       Miller

Tuesday, 20 May 1941   DECCA STUDIOS, LONDON
DR 5765 – 1 ( ) South American Way -VR- Decca F7880
          Sid Colin (Al Dubin-Jimmy
          McHugh) (from the musical
          production *Streets of Paris*)
DR 5766 – 1 ( ) Amapola -VR- Jimmy Miller Decca F7880
          (Lacalle-Gamse)

Tuesday, 10 June 1941   DECCA STUDIOS, LONDON
DR 5842 – ( ) Dolores -VR-   Decca F7893
          Jimmy Miller
DR 5843 – ( ) That Day it Rained -VR- Decca F7893
          Jimmy Miller
DR 5844 – 1 ( ) That's A-Plenty (Pollack) Decca F8127,
          -arr- GC   Ace of Clubs
          Chisholm/Breeze (unison) ACL 1121,
          McQuater   Decca ECM 2112
DR 5845 – 1 ( ) Way Down Yonder in New Decca F8127
          Orleans (Layton-Creamer)

Tuesday, 29 July 1941   DECCA STUDIOS, LONDON
DR 6038 – ( ) Down Forget-me-not Lane Decca F7926
DR 6039 – ( ) Beneath the Lights of Home
– Unissued
DR 6040 – ( ) I'll Think of You   Decca F7927
DR 6041 – ( ) I Wish I Could Fish
– Unissued

Saturday, 2 August 1941   DECCA STUDIOS, LONDON
DR 6039 – 2 ( ) Beneath the Lights of Home Decca F7926
DR 6041 – 2 ( ) I Wish I Could Fish Decca F7927
DR 6087 – 1 ( ) Darktown Strutters Ball
– Unissued
DR 6087 – 2 ( ) Darktown Strutters Ball
– Unissued
DR 6088 – 1 (2.51) Drummin' Man (Krupa) Decca F7968
Sunday, 7 September 1941   JAZZ JAMBOREE
Broadcast live by BBC General Forces Programme from the London Palladium
South Rampart Street Parade/Dolores -VR- JM/Drummin' Man.
Note: This was the only part of this special concert that was broadcast which
featured the RAF Dance Orchestra.
Tuesday, 9 September 1941   DECCA STUDIOS, LONDON
DR 6220 – 1 ( ) Sand in My Shoes -VR- Decca F7967
          Jimmy Miller
DR 6221 – 1 ( ) I'll Never Let a Day Pass by Decca F7967
          -VR- Jimmy Miller

DR 6222 – 1   (   ) My Sister and I -VR-
– Unissued   Jimmy Miller
DR 6223 – 1   (   ) Maria Elena -VR-   Decca F7984
                    Jimmy Miller

Saturday, 13 September 1941   DECCA STUDIOS, LONDON
DR 6087 – 3   (   ) Darktown Strutters Ball   Decca F7968
DR 6222   (   ) My Sister and I -VR-
– Unissued   Jimmy Miller

Monday, 29 September 1941   DANCE ORCHESTRA OF
11.15   HM ROYAL AIR FORCE
BBC General Forces Programme
Compère: Unknown
Intro: Theme (There's Something in the Air)/South Rampart Street Parade/
My Sister and I -VR- JM/My Heart Stood Still/Maria Elena -VR- JM/Swinging
the Blues/I Hear a Rhapsody -VR- JM/Drummin' Man/I Wish I Could Fish
-VR- SC/Slow Freight/Delores -VR- JM/These Foolish Things (Ronnie
Aldrich, Piano Solo)/I'll Think of You -VR- JM/Copenhagen and Close.

Thursday, 2 October 1941   DECCA STUDIOS, LONDON
D 6222 – 2   (   ) My Sister and I -VR-   Decca F7984
                    Jimmy Miller
DR 6316 –   (   ) Where You Are   Decca F7994
DR 6317 –   (   ) You Started Something   Decca F7994
DR 6318 –   (   ) Woodland Symphony   Decca F7995

Tuesday, 7 October 1941   DECCA STUDIOS, LONDON
DR 6319 –   (   ) Estrellita (Little Star)   Decca F7995

Thursday, 13 November 1941   DECCA STUDIOS, LONDON
DR 6429 – 1   (   ) Blue Champagne -VR-   Decca F8020
                    Jimmy Miller (Watts-Ryerson)
DR 6430 – 1   (   ) Lament to Love -VR-   Decca F8020
                    Jimmy Miller
DR 6431 – 1   (3.14) There's Something in the Air Decca F8062
                    -VR- Jimmy Miller   Decca ECM 2112
                    (Adamson-McHugh)   Decca RLF 19
DR 6432 –   (   ) I'm Coming, Virginia   Decca F8062

Tuesday, 9 December 1941   DECCA STUDIOS, LONDON
DR 6531 –   (   ) My Paradise   Decca F8048
DR 6532 –   (   ) My Mother Would Love You   Decca F8048
DR 6533 –   (   ) Some Sunny Day   Decca F8049
DR 6534 –   (   ) A Sinner Kissed an Angel   Decca F8049

Thursday, 25 December 1941
18.30
BBC General Forces Programme
Compère: David Miller

THE NAVY, THE ARMY
AND THE AIR FORCE

Featuring: The RAF Dance Orchestra, the RAOC Blue Rockets, the RN Nautical Septet

Trumpet Fanfare (all bands)/Honeysuckle Rose (Naval Septet)/When My Ship Comes In (Blue Rockets)/South Rampart Street Parade (RAF Squadronaires)/ The Song is Ended (Naval Septet)/Why Don't We do this More Often? (Blue Rockets)/We Three (RAF Squadronaires)/Yours (Naval Septet)/Greatest Mistake of My Life (Blue Rockets)/Fed Up and Far From Home (Blue Rockets)/Chattanooga Choo Choo (RAF Squadronaires)/Out of Nowhere (Blue Rockets)/I'm Coming, Virginia (RAF Squadronaires)/ Medley (featuring all three bands): 'Tribute to the British Commonwealth of Nations' – (England) Here's Health unto His Majesty; (Ireland) Mountains of Mourne; (Wales) Land of My Fathers; (Scotland) Annie Laurie; (Australia) We Are the Boys from Down Under; (New Zealand) Waiata Poi; (South Africa) The Trek Song; (India) Song of India; (England) Hearts of Oak; British Grenadiers and Close.

Tuesday, 20 January 1942 DECCA STUDIOS, LONDON

DR 6226 – 1	(	) Russian Serenade -VR-		
– Unissued		Jimmy Miller		
DR 6626 – 2	(	) Russian Serenade -VR-	Decca F8068	
		Jimmy Miller		
DR 6627 – 2	(	) Jealousie -VR-	Decca F8068	
		Jimmy Miller		
DR 6628 –	(	) The Man with the Lollipop	Decca F8069	
		Song -VR- Jimmy Miller		
DR 6629 –	(	) Tropical Magic -VR-	Decca F806	
		Jimmy Miller		

Monday, 9 February 1942

The RAF Squadronaires performed for one week at the Palace Theatre in Blackpool. Anne Shelton was the special guest during the week, and there were possible broadcasts from this venue over the BBC Home Service and General Forces networks. However, no trace can be found in the BBC archives.

Wednesday, 11 February 1942 DECCA STUDIOS

DR 6679 – 2	(	) Chattanooga Choo Choo	Decca F8095
		-VR- Sid Colin	
		(Gordon-Warren) (from the	
		1941, 20th Century Fox film	
		Sun Valley Serenade)	
DR 6680 – 2	(	) The Nango -VR- Jimmy Miller Decca F8111	

DR 6681 – 2   (   ) Bounce Me Brother with   Decca F8095
                         a Solid Four -VR- Sid Colin
                         (Raye-Prince) (from the 1941
                         film *Buck Privates*)

DR 6682 – 2   (   ) Ringle Dingle -arr- GC   Decca F8142
                         (Cummings-Chisholm)   Decca ECM 2112

Note: As the RAF Squadronaires were performing at the Palace Theatre in Blackpool during this week, this Decca recording session may have been recorded at the Decca Studios in Manchester. Alternatively the recording session may have taken place the week before.

Friday, 13 March 1942   DECCA STUDIOS, LONDON

DR 6732 – 2   (   ) The Whistler's Mother-in-Law Decca F8111
                         -VR- Sid Colin

DR 6733 – 2   (   ) I've Found a New Baby   Decca F8180
                         (Palmer-Williams)

DR 6734   (   ) Blue Room (Rogers-Hart)
– Unissued

DR 6735   (   ) Black Eyes
– Unissued

Thursday, 14 May 1942   DECCA STUDIOS, LONDON

DR 6830 – 2   (   ) Who'll Buy a Rose from   Decca F8139
                         Margareta?

DR 6831 – 2   (3.06) Blues in the Night -VR-   Decca F8139
                         Sid Colin (Arlen-Mercer)   Decca RFL 19
                         (from the 1941 film *Blues in
                         the Night*)

DR 6832 –   (   ) Tangerine -VR- Jimmy Miller Decca F8141
                         (Schertzinger-Mercer)   BBC REC 140M
                         (from the 1942 film
                         The Fleet's In)

DR 6833 –   (   ) I Remember You -VR-   Decca F8141
                         Jimmy Miller (Schertzinger-
                         Mercer) (from the 1942 film
                         The Fleet's In)

Thursday, 21 May 1942   DECCA STUDIOS, LONDON

DR 6836 – 2   (   ) South Rampart Street Parade Decca F8142
                         (Haggart-Bauduc-Crosby)   Ace of Clubs
                                                       ACL 1121
                                                       Decca ECM
                                                       2112

DR 6837 – 2   (   ) Oh! You Beautiful Doll   Decca F8180

Thursday, 2 July 1942　　　　　　　　　DECCA STUDIOS, LONDON

DR 6874 − 1	(3.21)	Pennsylvania Polka (Lee-Manners)	Decca F8166 / Decca RLF 19
DR 6875 − 1	( )	Me and My Melinda -VR- Jimmy Miller	Decca F8166
DR 6876 − 1	( )	Jersey Bounce (Plater-Bradshaw-Johnson-Wright)	Decca F8167
DR 6877 − 1	( )	String of Pearls (Jerry Gray)	Decca F8167

Friday, 11 September 1942　　　　　　DECCA STUDIOS, LONDON

DR 6958 −	( )	Conchita Marquita, Lopez -VR- Jimmy Miller (Magidson-Styne) (from the Paramount film *Priorities on Parade*)	Decca F8194
DR 6595 −	( )	Be Careful it's My Heart -VR- Jimmy Miller (Irving Berlin) (from the 1942 Paramount film *Holiday Inn*)	Decca F8194
DR 6960 − 2	( )	Jealousie -VR- Jimmy Miller -arr- RA	Decca F8195
DR 6961 − 2	( )	Daybreak -VR- Jimmy Miller (Adamson-Grofe) (from the MGM film *Thousands Cheer*)	Decca F8195

Saturday, 26 September 1942　　　　DANCE ORCHESTRA OF
General Forces Programme　　　　　HM ROYAL AIR FORCE
Compèred and produced by: David Miller
Opening Theme (There's Something in the Air)/Anchors Aweigh -arr- GC/ Blue Lou/Pennsylvania Polka -Arr- WP/Massachusetts/Jealousie -VR- JM/Be Careful It's My Heart -VR- JM/I Remember You -VR- JM/I've Found a New Baby and Close.

Sunday, 4 October 1942　　　　　　　　JAZZ JAMBOREE
Live from the Stoll Theatre, Kingsway, London
BBC General Forces Programme
　　　　　　　　　　( ) Anchors Aweigh -arr- GC
Note: This was the only title from the RAF Squadronaires portion that was broadcast.

Friday, 25 December 1942   DANCE ORCHESTRA OF
18.30   HM ROYAL AIR FORCE
Compèred and produced by: David Miller
Opening Theme (There's Something in the Air)/Anchors Aweigh/Daybreak
-VR- JM/Dark Eyes/Breathless -VR- SC/Clarinet à la King/To a Wild Rose/
Quiet Please -arr- Jimmy Durrant/White Christmas -VR- JM and Choir/South
Rampart Street Parade/Closing Theme (There's Something in the Air).

Thursday, 7 January 1943   DECCA STUDIOS, LONDON

DR 7153 – 2	(	)	Anchors Aweigh (Miles-Lovell-Charles-Zimmerman)	Decca F8262 Ace of Clubs ACL 1121 Decca ECM 211
DR 7154 – 2	(	)	I've Got a Gal in Kalamazoo -VR- Sid Colin (Gordon-Warren) (from the 20th Century Fox film *Orchestra Wives*)	Decca F8261
DR 7155 – 2	(	)	Manhattan Serenade -VR- Jimmy Miller (Louis Alter) (from the MGM film *Broadway Rhythm*)	Decca F8261
DR 7156 – 2	(	)	Blue Lou -arr- GC	Decca F8262

Friday, 15 January 1943   DECCA STUDIOS, LONDON

DR 7179 – Unissued	(	)	To a Wild Rose	
DR 7180 –	(	)	Cherokee (Ray Noble)	Decca F8288
DR 7181 – 2	(	)	You're My Baby	Decca F8288
DR 7182 – 2	(	)	Jazz Me Blues	Decca F8453

Saturday, 6 March 1943   DANCE ORCHESTRA OF
BBC Radio Orchestra   HM ROYAL AIR FORCE
Further details remain unknown.

Sunday, 14 March 1943   DANCE BAND OF THE
BBC Radio Broadcast   ROYAL AIR FORCE
Compère: Phillip Brown
Opening Theme (There's Something in the Air)/South Rampart Street Parade/
Blue Lou/Ol' Man River/Anchors Aweigh/Dearly Beloved -VR- JM/Daybreak
-VR- JM/There Are Such Things and Close.

Circa **April 1943**   THE LIFE AND DEATH OF COLONEL BLIMP
Technicolour film, directed by Michael Powell and Emeric Pressburger, in
which the RAF Dance Band, the Squadronaires played *Commando Patrol* on
the soundtrack. An Archers production, the film was released by General Film
Distributors on 26 July 1943.

Wednesday, 19 May 1943   DECCA STUDIOS, LONDON

DR 7336 – 2   (   ) I've Heard that Song Before   Decca F8315
                     -VR- Jimmy Miller
                     (Styne-Cahn)
                     (from the 1942 Republic film
                     Youth on Parade)

DR 7337 – 2   (   ) All Our Tomorrows -VR-   Decca F8315
                     Jimmy Miller

DR 7338 –   (   ) Keep an Eye on Your Heart   Decca F8319
                     -VR- Sid Colin
                     (Manners-Leeds-Shirl)

DR 7339 –   (   ) Lover's Lullaby -VR-   Decca F8319
                     Jimmy Miller

Friday, 28 May 1943   DANCE BAND OF THE
23.11   ROYAL AIR FORCE
BBC Home Service
Compère: Unknown
Opening Theme (There's Something in the Air)/Swingin' the Blues/Lover's
Lullaby -VR- Jimmy Miller/Hit the Road to Dreamland -VR- Sid Colin/
Clarinet à la King/I See You Everywhere -VR- Jimmy Miller/Cow Cow Boogie
-VR- Sid Colin/You're My Baby/That Old Black Magic -VR- Jimmy Miller/
Estrellita/The Mill Went Round and Around/Keep an Eye on Your Heart
-VR- Sid Colin/Slow Freight/Jealousie -VR- Jimmy Miller/There are Such
Things -VR- Jimmy Miller/Massachussetts -VR- Sid Colin and Close.

Sunday, 13 June 1943   DANCE BAND OF
16.20-17.00   THE ROYAL AIR FORCE
BBC General Forces Programme and Home Service
Compère: Phillip Brown
Opening Theme (There's Something in the Air)/Sun Valley Jump/I See You
Everywhere -VR- JM/Ol' Man River -VR- JM/Cow Cow Boogie -VR- SC/
Quiet Please/Lover's Lullaby -VR- JM/Dark Eyes/Keep an Eye on Your Heart
-VR- SC/The Man I Love/I've Heard that Song Before -VR- JM/
Stardust/Swinging the Blues/There's Something in the Air -VR- JM and
Close.

Saturday, 24 July 1943   DANCE BAND OF
23.25   THE ROYAL AIR FORCE
BBC Home Service
Guest Star: Dorothy Carless
Compère: Phillip Brown
Opening Theme (There's Something in the Air)/Fan It/You'd be so Nice to
Come Home to -VR- JM/Keep an Eye on Your Heart -VR- SC/Stardust/I've
Heard that Song Before -VR- JM/Poor Butterfly -VR- Dorothy Carless/In
Pinetops Footsteps/Where's My Love -VR- JM/American Patrol/Stormy
Weather -VR- Dorothy Carless/Ol' Man River -VR- JM/There's Something in
the Air and Close.

Tuesday, 27 July 1943   DECCA STUDIOS, LONDON
DR 7438 – 3   (   ) Harlem Sandman -VR-   Decca F8348
                       Sid Colin (Adamson-Styne)
                       (from the 1943 Republic film
                       Hit Parade of 1943)

DR 7439 – 2   (   ) Cow Cow Boogie -VR-   Decca F8364
                       Sid Colin   Decca ECM
                       (Don Raye-Gene De Paul)   2112
                       (from the 1943 film
                       Reveille with Beverly)

DR 7440 – 2   (   ) Commando Patrol   Decca F8364
                       (Gray-Ridley-Bousher)   Decca ECM
                       (from the 1943 film *The Life* 2112
                       and Death of Colonel Blimp)

Tuesday, 10 August 1943   DECCA STUDIOS, LONDON
DR 7459   (   ) Stardust
– Unissued

DR 4760 – 2   (   ) Do Those Old Eyes Deceive   Decca F8348
                       Me -VR- Jimmy Miller
                       (Adamson-Styne)
                       (from the 1943 Republic film
                       Hit Parade of 1943)

DR 4761 – 1   (   ) American Patrol   Decca F8453
                       (F. W. Meacham)
                       (from the 1942 20th Century
                       Fox film *Orchestra Wives*)

Thursday, 19 August 1943   DANCE BAND OF
23.17-24.00   THE ROYAL AIR FORCE
BBC Home Service
Compère: Phillip Brown
Producer: Rex Burrows
Opening Theme (There's Something in the Air)/South Rampart Street Parade/
All or Nothing at All -VR- JM/OK for Baby/In the Blue of Evening -VR-
Dorothy Carless/Sans Culottes/Cow Cow Boogie -VR- SC/American Patrol/All
This and Heaven Too -VR- Dorothy Carless/Leap Frog/You Rhyme with
Everything that's Beautiful -VR- JM/Dawn on the Desert/Don't Get Around
Much Anymore -VR- Dorothy Carless/Fan It/You're My Baby/There's
Something in the Air and Close.

Tuesday, 5 October 1943   DECCA STUDIOS, LONDON
DR 7723 – 1   (   ) Walk Jenny Walk   Decca F8442

DR 7724 – 2 ( ) How Sweet You Are -VR-   Decca F8386
Jimmy Miller
(Schwartz - Loesser)
(from the 1943 Warner Bros
film *Thank Your Lucky Stars*)

DR 7725 – ( ) I Know that You Know
– Unissued (Vincent Youmans)
(from the 1943 film
The Powers Girl)

DR 7726 – 1 ( ) Goodnight Good   Decca F8386
Neighbour -VR- Jimmy Miller

Tuesday, 18 January 1944   RAF DANCE ORCHESTRA
13.30
(Recorded for future use by the BBC — BBC Disc No. OP 876 – SOX
27001)
Guest Star: Beryl Davis
Compère: Frank Phillips
Intro: Theme (There's Something in the Air)/I Know that You Know/Lazy
River/Massachusetts/Swanee River/Wrap Your Troubles in Dreams/Good-
night Good Neighbour -VR- JM/Everybody Step/The Army Air Corps Song/
RAF March Past/There's Something in the Air and Close.

Wednesday, 23 February 1944   DECCA STUDIOS, LONDON
DR 8207 – ( ) Liza (Gus Kahn-George and
– Unissued Ira Gershwin)

DR 8208 – 2 (3.20) Shoo Shoo Baby -VR-   Decca F8424
Sid Colin (Phil Moore)   Decca RLF 19
(from the 1943 Universal film
Chip Off the Old Block)

DR 8209 – 2 ( ) Is My Baby Blue Tonight   Decca F842
-VR- Jimmy Miller

Tuesday, 14 March 1944   RAF DANCE ORCHESTRA
17.00
(Pre-recorded Tuesday, 18 January 1944 — BBC Disc No. OP 876 – SOX
27001)
Guest Star: Beryl Davis
Compère: Frank Phillips
Recorded repeat of a programme first broadcast by the BBC General Forces
Programme on Tuesday, 18 January 1944.

Friday, 17 March 1944   DECCA STUDIOS, LONDON
DR 8280 – 2 ( ) A Journey to a Star -VR-   Decca F8419
Beryl Davis (Robin-Warren)
(from the 1943 20th Century
Fox film *The Gang's All Here*)

DR 8281 – 1   (3.25) No Love, No Nothin' -VR-   Decca F8419
                       Beryl Davis (Robin-Warren)   Decca RLF 19
                       (from the 1943 20th Century
                       Fox film *The Gang's All Here*)
DR 8282   (   ) Truckin'
– Unissued

Friday, 14 April 1944   DANCE BAND OF
12.15   THE ROYAL AIR FORCE
BBC General Forces Programme
Guest Star: Beryl Davis
Compère: Unknown
Intro: Theme (There's Something in the Air)/Commando Patrol/Think About
the Wabash -VR- Beryl Davis/Shoo Shoo Baby -VR- SC/Truckin'/Is My Baby
Blue Tonight -VR- JM/Everybody's Step -VR- Beryl Davis/Runnin' Wild/A
Journey to a Star -VR- Beryl Davis/Liza/Carolina Moon/You're the Rainbow
-VR- Beryl Davis/Blue Lou/I'm Getting Tired so I can Sleep -VR- JM/
Loveable and Sweet/American Patrol/There's Something in the Air and Close.

Friday, 28 April 1944   DANCE BAND OF
13.15   THE ROYAL AIR FORCE
BBC Home Service
(Recorded for future use by the BBC — BBC Disc No. SBS 415 – DB 29)
Guest Star: Beryl Davis
Compère: Unknown
Opening Theme (There's Something in the Air)/Jealousie -VR- Beryl
Davis/Star Eyes -VR- Beryl Davis/I Know that You Know/My Heart Tells Me
-VR- JM/ The Blues/You're the Rainbow -VR- Beryl Davis/Don't Ask Me
Why/Shoo Shoo Baby -VR- SC/Thinkin' About the Wabash -VR- Beryl
Davis/Cherokee/ Is My Baby Blue Tonight -VR- JM/Loveable and Sweet/All
My Life -VR- Beryl Davis/Put on Your Old Grey Bonnet/Stardust and Close.

Friday, 26 May 1944   DANCE BAND OF
12.15   THE ROYAL AIR FORCE
BBC General Forces Programme
(Pre-recorded by the BBC on Friday, 28 April 1944 — BBC Disc No. SBS
415 – DB 29)
Guest Star: Beryl Davis
Recording of a programme first broadcast by the BBC Home Service on Friday,
28 April 1944.

Monday, 12 June 1944   DECCA STUDIOS, LONDON
DR 8508   (   ) Reverse the Charges
– Unissued
DR 8509 – 2   (   ) Canteen Bounce   Decca F8442
DR 8510   (   ) When Buddha Smiles
– Unissued

DR 8511 –　　　(　) Hobo's Prayer
Unissued

Sunday, 25 June 1944　　　　　TOMMY HANDLEY'S HALF-HOUR
14.00-14.30

(Recorded repeat of a programme first broadcast by the BBC General Overseas
Service on Tuesday, 2 May 1944 — BBC Disc No. unknown)

Over AEFP

Featuring: The RAF Dance Orchestra, conducted by Sgt. Jimmy Miller,
Beryl Davis, Maudie Edwards, Carl Carlisle and Clarence Wright

Compère and host: Tommy Handley

Details remain unknown

Sunday, 2 July 1944　　　　　TOMMY HANDLEY'S HALF-HOUR
14.00-14.30

(Recorded repeat of a programme first broadcast by the BBC General Overseas
Service on Tuesday, 9 May 1944 — BBC Disc No. unknown)

Over AEFP

Featuring: The RAF Dance Orchestra, conducted by Sgt. Jimmy Miller,
Beryl Davis, Maudie Edwards, Carl Carlisle and Clarence Wright

Compère and host: Tommy Handley

Details remain unknown.

Monday, 3 July 1944　　　　　MUSIC IN THE RAF
21.35-22.38

BBC Home Service

(Pre-recorded earlier the same day — BBC Disc No. unknown)

Featuring: The RAF Symphony Orchestra and Central Band, conducted by
Wing Commander R. P. O'Donnell, MVC, the Griller String Quartet, the
RAF Dance Orchestra (the Squadronaires), directed by Sgt. Jimmy Miller

Solo pianist: LAC Dennis Matthews

Compère: Frank Phillips

Produced by: Fred Hartley

RAF March Past (Military Band and Orchestra)/Overture: Prince Igor (RAF
Symphony Orchestra)/Song of Loyalty (Military Band)/Movement from Haydn
Quartet Op. 32, No. 2 in 'E' Flat (Griller Quartet)/There's Something in the
Air -VR- Jimmy Miller (RAF Dance Orchestra)/Swanee River (RAF Dance
Orchestra)/Don't Ask Me Why (RAF Dance Orchestra)/South Rampart Street
Parade (RAF Dance Orchestra)/Toccata and Fugue in 'D' minor (RAF
Military Band)/Nocturne (Griller Quartet)/Piano Concerto in 'B' flat minor –
1st Movement (RAF Symphony Orchestra with LAC Dennis Matthews).

Sunday, 9 July 1944　　　　　TOMMY HANDLEY'S HALF-HOUR
14.00-14.30

(Pre-recorded and a repeat broadcast of the programme first broadcast by the
BBC General Overseas Service on Tuesday, 16 May 1944 — BBC Disc No.
unknown)

Over AEFP

Featuring: The RAF Dance Orchestra, conducted by Sgt. Jimmy Miller, Beryl Davis, Maudie Edwards, Carl Carlisle and Clarence Wright
Compère and host: Tommy Handley
Details remain unknown

Sunday, 16 July 1944   TOMMY HANDLEY'S HALF-HOUR
14.00-14.30
(Repeat programme first broadcast by the BBC General Overseas Service on Tuesday, 23 May 1944 — BBC Disc No. unknown)
Over AEFP
Featuring: The RAF Dance Orchestra, conducted by Sgt. Jimmy Miller, Beryl Davis, Maudie Edwards, Carl Carlisle and Clarence Wright
Compère and host: Tommy Handley
Details remain unknown

Monday, 17 July 1944   ROYAL AIR FORCE
21.15   DANCE ORCHESTRA
BBC General Forces Programme and AEFP
Guest Star: Beryl Davis
Compère: Unknown
Opening Theme (There's Something in the Air)/Anchors Aweigh/Long Ago and Far Away -VR- Beryl Davis/Canteen Bounce/My Heart isn't in it -VR- JM/Hobo's Prayer/Amor Amor -VR- Beryl Davis/It's Love, Love, Love -VR- SC/Somebody Loves Me/Do Nothin' Till You Hear from Me -VR- Beryl Davis/Oh! You Beautiful Doll/Time Alone will Tell -VR- JM/Reverse the Charges/I'll Get By -VR- Beryl Davis/That's A-Plenty/Theme (There's Something in the Air) and Close.

Monday, 24 July 1944   TOP TEN
21.15-21.45
Broadcast live from the Paris Cinema, Lower Regent Street, London
Over AEFP
Featuring: The RAF Dance Orchestra (the Squadronaires), directed by Sgt. Jimmy Miller, the Brass Monkeys (later known as the Brass Hats), led by Kenny Baker, the Singing Strings, led by Reg Leopold, Beryl Davis
Compère: Sgt. Broderick Crawford, US AAF
Producer: Pat Dixon
The programme is a weekly review of the big song hits in Britain, the United States and Canada
Opening Theme (A Pretty Girl is Like a Melody)/I'll Get By -VR- Beryl Davis (RAF Squadronaires)/My Ideal -VR- Jimmy Miller (The Singing Strings)/I'll See You in My Dreams (The Brass Monkeys)/I Couldn't Sleep a Wink Last Night -VR- Beryl Davis (RAF Squadronaires)/It's Love, Love, Love -VR- Sid Colin (RAF Squadronaires)/Anita (The Brass Monkeys)/Embraceable You -VR- Beryl Davis (The Singing Strings)/The Royal Garden Blues (Swing

Saxophone Sextet, better known as 'The Swing Shift'*)/Long Ago and Far Away -VR- Beryl Davis (RAF Squadronaires)/Stardust (entire ensemble − all three orchestras, conducted by Jimmy Miller)/Closing Theme (A Pretty Girl is Like a Melody).

* Note: This saxophone sextet was made up mainly of members of the RAF Dance Orchestra, plus visiting guest musicians. The name was changed after this first programme, mainly because Captain Glenn Miller's American Band of the AEF were using this title for one of their programmes also broadcast by the AEFP.

Thursday, 27 July 1944   DECCA STUDIOS, LONDON

DR 8595 − 2	(3.04)	Rhapsody for Reeds	Decca F8472
		(Buck Ram)	Decca RLF 19
DR 8596 − 2	(2.54)	Concerto for Drums	Decca F8472
		(Buck Ram-Marty Gold)	Decca RLF 19
		(featuring Jock Cummings, Drums)	

Monday, 31 July 1944   TOP TEN
21.15-21.45
Broadcast live from the Paris Cinema, Lower Regent Street, London
Over AEFP
Compère: Capt. Franklin Englemann
Opening Theme: (A Pretty Girl is Like a Melody)/Don't Sweetheart Me (RAF Squadronaires)/Look for the Silver Lining (The Singing Strings)/I'm Bidin' My Time (The Brass Hats)/Swinging on a Star -VR- unknown (RAF Squadronaires)/A Lovely Way to Spend an Evening -VR- Jimmy Miller (RAF Squadronaires)/They Didn't Believe Me -VR- Beryl Davis (The Singing Strings)/Copenhagen (The Brass Hats)/Do Nothin' Till You Hear From Me -VR- Beryl Davis (RAF Squadronaires)/I'll Walk Alone -VR- Jimmy Miller (RAF Squadronaires)/Begin the Beguine (complete ensemble − all three bands, conducted by Jimmy Miller)/Closing Theme (A Pretty Girl is Like a Melody).

Circa late July 1944   ENSA 'TOP OF THE LIST'
Recorded at the Criterion Theatre, Piccadilly Circus, London
Guest Star: Dorothy Carless
Compère: Flying Officer Bill McClerk
Producer: Cpl. Charles Chilton

(0.32)	You're the Tops (Cole Porter)
(2.33)	I Ain't Got Nobody
(1.50)	How Many Hearts Have You Broken -VR- Jimmy Miller
(2.26)	I Can't Get Started -VR- Dorothy Carless (Gershwin-Duke)
(2.25)	All This and Heaven Too -VR- Dorothy Carless
(3.53)	Rhapsody for Reeds (Buck Ram)
(0.40)	You're the Tops

ENSA 'TOP OF THE LIST'

Recorded at the Criterion Theatre, Piccadilly Circus, London
Compère: F/O Bill McClerk

(0.32)	You're the Tops (Cole Porter)
(4.01)	Boston Bounce
(2.28)	Come Out Wherever You Are -VR- Sid Colin (Styne-Cahn) (from the 1944 RKO film *Step Lively*)
(2.40)	It Must Be Jelly -VR- Sid Colin (Williams-MacGregor-Skylar)
(1.59)	I'll be Seeing You -VR- Jimmy Miller (Fain-Kahal)
(2.18)	I Ain't Got Nobody (Spencer Williams)
(3.35)	I Heard You Cried Last Night -VR- Jimmy Miller (Kruger-Grouya)
(1.45)	I've Found a New Baby (Palmer-Williams)

Sunday, 6 August 1944 RAF DANCE ORCHESTRA
14.00-14.30
Broadcast live from the Paris Cinema, Lower Regent Street, London
Over AEFP
Featuring: The RAF Dance Orchestra, conducted by Sgt. Jimmy Miller, with Beryl Davis
Compère: Unknown
Details remain unknown.

Monday, 7 August 1944 TOP TEN
21.15
Broadcast live from the Paris Cinema, Lower Regent Street, London
Compère: Capt. Franklin Englemann
All My Life -VR- Beryl Davis (RAF Squadronaires)/The Man I Love (Singing Strings)/Holiday for Strings (The Brass Hats)/I'll be Around (RAF Squadronaires)/Poinciana -VR- Beryl Davis (Singing Strings)/Don't Believe Everything You Dream -VR- Beryl Davis and Jimmy Miller (RAF Squadronaires)/Mandy (The Brass Hats)/Lazy River (RAF Squadronaires)/ Stormy Weather (entire ensemble)

Monday, 14 August 1944 TOP TEN
21.15
Broadcast live from the Paris Cinema, Lower Regent Street, London
Compère: Capt. Franklin Englemann
If I Had My Way/Darktown Strutters Ball/Tea for Two (Singing Strings)/ G.I. Jive -VR- Sid Colin (RAF Squadronaires)/Star Eyes (RAF Squadronaires)/ Remember/Going My Way/Milkman Keep Those Bottles Quiet -VR- Beryl Davis (RAF Squadronaires)/Deep Purple (entire ensemble).

Monday, 21 August 1944 TOP TEN
21.15
Broadcast live from the Paris Cinema, Lower Regent Street, London
Compère: Capt. Franklin Englemann

What Do You Do in the Infantry -VR- Jimmy Miller (RAF Squadronaires)/It Had to be You (The Brass Hats)/I'll be Seeing You -VR- Beryl Davis (Singing Strings)/I Know that You Know (RAF Squadronaires)/Wrap Your Troubles in Dreams -VR- Beryl Davis (RAF Squadronaires)/Everybody Loves My Baby (RAF Squadronaires)/Suddenly it's Spring -VR- Jimmy Miller (RAF Squadronaires)/ Bugle Call Rag (The Brass Hats)/How Blue the Night (Singing Strings)/After You've Gone (complete ensemble).

Sunday, 27 August 1944   THE ROYAL AIR FORCE
14.00 - 14.30   DANCE ORCHESTRA
Broadcast live from the Paris Cinema, Lower Regent Street, London
Over the General Overseas Service and AEFP
Compère: Unknown
Details remain unknown.

Circa **late August to early September 1944**   SWING TIME
ENSA recordings recorded at the Criterion Theatre, London, for future use by ENSA and ORBS
Compère: Cpl. Sally Rogers
Opening Theme (There's Something in the Air)/Somebody Loves Me/The Minor Drags/Rosetta (RAF Swing Sextet*)/Georgia Blues (composition by and featuring George Chisholm, Trombone)/Concerto for Drums (featuring Jock Cummings, Drums)/unknown title/Jazz Me Blues/Clarinet à la King (featuring Andy McDevitt, Clarinet)/Dr Heckle and Mr Jive (RAF Swing Sextet*)/G.I. Jive -Vocal- Sid Colin/Darktown Strutter's Ball/Closing Theme (There's Something in the Air).
* The RAF Swing Sextet was made up of the rhythm section with George Chisholm on trombone, Andy McDevitt on clarinet and one of the trumpet players from the full RAF Dance Orchestra.
Note: The RAF Dance Orchestra, 'The Squadronaires', were also featured on many other ENSA broadcasts during this period. They were also featured in the series *Fanfare for Rhythm Fans* which was broadcast by the BBC and later produced by ORBS.

Monday, 28 August 1944   TOP TEN
21.15
Broadcast live from the Paris Cinema, Lower Regent Street, London
Over the AEFP
Compère: Capt. Franklin Englemann
You'll Never Know -VR- Beryl Davis (complete ensemble)/Somebody Loves Me -VR- Jimmy Miller (Singing Strings)/Louise -VR- Jimmy Miller (Singing Strings)/Tess's Torch Song -VR- Beryl Davis (RAF Squadronaires)/I Got Rhythm (The Brass Hats)/Besame Mucho -VR- Beryl Davis (Singing Strings)/ Canteen Bounce (RAF Squadronaires)/Goodnight Wherever You Are -VR- Beryl Davis (RAF Squadronaires)/I Can't Give You Anything but Love (The Brass Hats)/St Louis Blues -VR- Sid Colin (complete ensemble).

Tuesday, 29 August 1944　　　　　　　DECCA STUDIOS, LONDON

DR 8644 – 2　(　) Blues in 'C' Sharp Minor　　Decca F8485

DR 8645 – 2　(　) Milkman Keep Those Bottles　Decca F8477
　　　　　　　　　Quiet -VR- Beryl Davis
　　　　　　　　　(Don Raye-Gene De Paul)
　　　　　　　　　(from the 1944 MGM film
　　　　　　　　　Broadway Rhythm)

DR 8646　　　(　) Dear Old Southland
– Unissued

DR 8647 – 2　(　) G.I. Jive -VR- Sid Colin　　Decca F8477
　　　　　　　　　(Johnny Mercer)

Friday, 1 September 1944　　　　　　STAGE DOOR CANTEEN
18.15-18.59

Broadcast recorded from the opening of the 'Stage Door Canteen' in Piccadilly, London

(Pre-recorded 31 August 1944 — BBC Disc No. DOX 38476)

Over the BBC — AEFP

Featuring: The RAF Dance Orchestra, Fred Astaire, Bing Crosby, Jack Buchanan, Beatrice Lillie, Carole Lynne, Joan Hammond

Compères: Dorothy Dickson, Fred Astaire, Gerry Wilmot

Special introduction by Dorothy Dickson/San Fernando Valley -VR- Bing Crosby (RAF Squadronaires)/If I Had My Way -VR- Bing Crosby (RAF Squadronaires)/Rhythm -VR- Beatrice Lillie/Three Little Fishes -VR- Beatrice Lillie/Medley of musical comedy from *The Student Prince* -VR- Carole Lynne/ 'Showboat' -VR- Carole Lynne/Ad lib patter and dance by Fred Astaire with the RAF Squadronaires – impromptu 'Boogie Woogie'/One Fine Day (featuring Joan Hammond)/Jack Buchanan with an American soldier and an English WAAF/Stage Door Canteen -VR- Jack Buchanan, with three male factory workers.

Monday, 4 September 1944　　　　　　　　TOP TEN
21.15

Broadcast live from the Paris Cinema, Lower Regent Street, London

Over the BBC — AEFP

Compère: Capt. Franklin Englemann

Produced by: Pat Dixon

You're My Little Pin-Up Girl -VR- Sid Colin (complete ensemble)/Brazil -VR- Beryl Davis (Singing Strings)/Goodbye Blues (The Brass Hats)/Time Alone Will Tell -VR- Jimmy Miller (RAF Squadronaires)/Exactly Like You (RAF Squadronaires)/You Must Never Say Goodbye -VR- Beryl Davis (Singing Strings)/Is You Is or Is You Ain't My Baby? -VR- Sid Colin (RAF Squadronaires)/Solitude (The Brass Hats)/Now I Know -VR- Beryl Davis (Singing Strings)/The Way You Look Tonight (complete ensemble)

Saturday, 9 September 1944   HANDS ACROSS THE SEA
12.15-13.00
Broadcast recorded at the Queensbury All Services Club, Soho, London —
BBC Disc No. TLO 61626
Over AEFP, Wednesday, 13 September 1944
Featuring: The RAF Dance Orchestra, conducted by Sgt. Jimmy Miller, with
Beryl Davis and the US Navy Dance Band of the Liberation Forces, directed by
MFC Sam Donahue
Compères: A/C2 Ronald Waldman RAF and Sgt. Dick Dudley (US Army)
Opening theme (There's Something in the Air — RAF Squadronaires)/
Convoy (US Navy Dance Band)/When Buddha Smiles (RAF Squadronaires)/
Wrap Your Troubles in Dreams -VR- Beryl Davis (RAF Squadronaires)/How
am I to Know (US Navy Dance Band)/Amor Amor -VR- Bill Bassford/Walk
Jenny Walk (RAF Squadronaires)/Milkman Keep Those Bottles Quiet -VR-
Beryl Davis (RAF Squadronaires)/Goodnight Wherever You Are (US Navy
Dance Band)/It's Love, Love, Love -VR- Rocky Coluccio (US Navy Dance
Band)/Blues in 'C' Sharp Minor (RAF Squadronaires)/Hobo's Prayer (RAF
Squadronaires)/My Melancholy Baby (US Navy Dance Band)/I Got Rhythm
(US Navy Dance Band)/Closing Themes: There's Something in the Air —
RAF Squadronaires; Convoy — US Navy Dance Band.

Monday, 11 September 1944   TOP TEN
21.15
Broadcast live from the Paris Cinema, Lower Regent Street, London
Over AEFP
Compère: Capt. Franklin Englemann
You're the Dream, I'm the Dreamer (RAF Squadronaires)/My Prayer -VR-
Beryl Davis (Singing Strings)/I'm Just Wild About Harry (The Brass Hats)/
Sweet Lorraine -VR- Beryl Davis (RAF Squadronaires)/Stomping at the Savoy
(RAF Squadronaires)/I Didn't Know what Time it was (Singing Strings)/
Emmaline (The Brass Hats)/San Fernando Valley (RAF Squadronaires)/I Get a
Kick Out of You -VR- Jimmy Miller (Singing Strings)/Smoke Gets in Your
Eyes (complete ensemble).

Monday, 18 September 1944   TOP TEN
21.15
Broadcast live from the Paris Cinema, Lower Regent Street, London
Over AEFP
Compère: Cpl. Douglas Marshall
Sweet and Lovely -VR- Beryl Davis (complete ensemble)/Eager Beaver (RAF
Squadronaires)/The Music Stopped -VR- Beryl Davis (Singing Strings)/
Copenhagen (The Brass Hats)/When They Ask About You -VR- Jimmy
Miller (RAF Squadronaires)/Way Down Yonder in New Orleans (RAF
Squadronaires)/The Day After Tomorrow -VR- Beryl Davis (The Singing
Strings)/California Here I Come (The Brass Hats)/You're the Rainbow -VR-
Beryl Davis (RAF Squadronaires)/More Than You Know (complete
ensemble).

Monday, 25 September 1944   TOP TEN
21.15
Broadcast recorded from the Paris Cinema, Lower Regent Street, London
Over AEFP
(Pre-recorded Thursday, 21 September 1944 — BBC Disc No. TLO 61490)
Compère: Jack Bentley
An Hour Never Passes -VR- Beryl Davis (complete ensemble)/The Best Things in Life are Free (The Brass Hats)/They Didn't Believe Me -VR- Beryl Davis (Singing Strings)/Is You Is or Is You Ain't My Baby? -VR- Sid Colin (RAF Squadronaires)/Hallelujah! (The Brass Hats)/Don't Ask Me Why -VR- Beryl Davis (Singing Strings)/A Lovely Way to Spend an Evening -VR- Jimmy Miller (RAF Squadronaires)/Rose of Washington Square (The Brass Hats)/ Blue Moon -VR- Beryl Davis (The Brass Hats)/Blue Skies (complete ensemble).

Monday, 2 October 1944   TOP TEN
21.15 - 21.45
Broadcast live from the Paris Cinema, Lower Regent Street, London
Over AEFP
Compère: Cpl. Douglas Marshall
My Sunny Tennessee (complete ensemble)/I Can't Believe that You're in Love with Me -VR- Beryl Davis (RAF Squadronaires)/The World is Waiting for the Sunrise (The Brass Hats)/Something to Remember You by -VR- Beryl Davis (The Singing Strings)/I'm Coming, Virginia (small group, including Dennis Brain on French horn)/Crazy Me -VR- Beryl Davis (RAF Squadronaires)/Liza -arr- George Chisholm (The Brass Hats)/At Last -VR-Beryl Davis (The Singing Strings)/Waiting for the Evening Mail -VR- Sid Colin (RAF Squadronaires)/Perfidia — Tonight -arr- Paul Fenhoulet (complete ensemble, directed by Jimmy Miller).

Monday, 9 October 1944   TOP TEN
21.05 - 21.35
Broadcast live from the Paris Cinema, Lower Regent Street, London
Compère: Cpl. Douglas Marshall
Swinging on a Star -VR- Beryl Davis (RAF Squadronaires)/My Buddy (The Brass Hats)/Tico Tico -VR- Beryl Davis (The Singing Strings)/I'm In Love with Someone -VR- Jimmy Miller (RAF Squadronaires)/I'll Walk Alone (Swing Wing — Dixieland Band)/Long Ago and Far Away -VR- Beryl Davis (RAF Squadronaires)/Holiday for Strings (The Brass Hats)/Something to Remember You by -VR- Beryl Davis (The Singing Strings)/Waitin' for the Evening Mail -VR- Sid Colin (RAF Squadronaires)/Make Believe (combined bands, conducted by Sgt. Jimmy Miller).

Sunday, 15 October 1944   JAZZ JAMBOREE
Broadcast live from the Stoll Theatre, Kingsway, London
Over BBC General Forces Programme
There's Something in the Air (Theme) — (RAF Squadronaires).

Note: This was the only portion of the RAF Dance Orchestra's part of the concert that was broadcast by the BBC.

Monday, 16 October 1944   TOP TEN
21.05-21.35
Broadcast live from studio No. 1, Aeolian Hall, London
Over AEFP
Special Guests: MFC Sam Donahue and the US Navy Dance Band of the
Liberation Forces, with singer Bill Bassford
Compère: Cpl. Douglas Marshall
Unknown title (US Navy Band)/Spring Will Be a Little Late This Year -VR-
Beryl Davis (The Singing Strings)/Yearning (RAF Squadronaires)/My Prayer
-VR- Bill Bassford (US Navy Band)/Chinatown My Chinatown (The Brass
Hats)/I'm Gonna Sit Right Down and Write Myself a Letter -VR- Beryl Davis
(RAF Squadronaires)/When it's Sleepy Time Down South (combined bands)/
Vous Qui Passez Sans Me Voir -VR- Beryl Davis (The Singing Strings)/
unknown title (US Navy Band)/All Alone -arr- George Evans (combined RAF
Squadronaires and US Navy Band).

Tuesday, 17 October 1944   HOOP LA
19.15-20.00
(Pre-recorded Sunday, 15 October 1944 — BBC Disc No. OP 824 – SOX
39893)
Over AEFP and the BBC General Overseas Service
Featuring: Robb Wilton, Max Wall, Freddie Forbes, Polly Ward, Doris
Nichols, Kenneth Blain, John Rorke, Dorothy Carless and the RAF Dance
Orchestra, augmented by Reg Leopold, with five strings from the 'Singing
Strings'
Opening Theme (Hoop La)/Tico Tico -VR- Polly Ward/Loveable and Sweet/
Yes Sir that's My Baby/I'll be Seeing You -VR- Dorothy Carless /Begin the
Beguine/Let Me Love You Tonight/Till the Stars Begin to Shine/We Three/
Comedy Spot (featuring Mr Lovejoy, Enoch and Ramsbottom)/The Baby in the
Flat Up Above/South Rampart Street Parade and Close.

Saturday, 21 October 1944   AEF SPECIAL
17.15-18.00
Recorded from the Queensbury All Services Club, Soho, London, for broadcast
on Sunday, 22 October 1944 — BBC Disc No. SLO 62783
Featuring: The Canada Show Dance Band (a unit of the Canadian Band of the
AEF), directed by Capt. Robert Farnon; The RAF Dance Orchestra, directed
by Sgt. Jimmy Miller; The US Navy Dance Band, directed by MFC Sam
Donahue
Compère: Lt. Charmian Samson, CWAC
Introduction/Isle of Capri (Canada Dance Band)/I Heard You Cried Last Night
-VR- Beryl Davis (RAF Squadronaires)/What can I Say Dear After I Say I'm
Sorry (US Navy Dance Band)/Basin Street Blues/Somebody Loves Me/The
First Few Days -VR- Paul Carpenter (Canada Dance Band)/Stompin' at the
Savoy (US Navy Dance Band)/Do Nothin' till You Hear from Me -VR- Beryl
Davis (RAF Squadronaires)/Is You Is or Is You Ain't My Baby -VR- Don

Jacoby (US Navy Dance Band)/Swinging on a Star -VR- Paul Carpenter (Canada Dance Band)/The Touch of Your Lips (RAF Squadronaires)/'C' Jam Blues (US Navy Dance Band) and Close.

Monday, 23 October 1944   TOP TEN
21.05-21.35
Broadcast live from studio No. 2, Aeolin Hall, London
Over AEFP
Compère: Cpl. Douglas Marshall
I Just Can't Take it Baby (combined bands)/Rose of Washington Square (The Brass Hats)/Sambi Sambi -VR- Beryl Davis (The Singing Strings)/Truckin' (RAF Squadronaires)/Stars Fell on Alabama -VR- Beryl Davis (RAF Squadronaires)/There's Honey on the Moon Tonight (The Brass Hats)/Poinciana -VR- Beryl Davis (The Singing Strings)/Junk Man (RAF Squadronaires)/It was a Lover and His Lass -VR- Beryl Davis (RAF Squadronaires)/St Louis Blues (combined bands, conducted by Jimmy Miller).

Tuesday, 24 October 1944   HOOP LA
19.15
(Pre-recorded at the Paris Cinema, Lower Regent Street, London, on Sunday, 22 October 1944 — BBC Disc No. OP 848 – SOX 40072)
Over AEFP and the BBC General Overseas Service
Featuring: Robb Wilton, Max Wall, Freddie Forbes, Polly Ward, Doris Nichols, Kenneth Blain, Sidney Keith, Benny Lee, the Debonnaires and the augmented RAF Dance Orchestra, conducted by Sgt. Jimmy Miller with Reg Leopold and five members of the Singing Strings
Guest Stars: Bruce Trent, Kenway and Young
Opening Theme (Hoop La)/The Snake Charmer -VR- Polly Ward/Anchors Aweigh (RAF Squadronaires)/Yes Sir that's My Baby (RAF Squadronaires)/G.I. Jive -VR- Debonnaires (RAF Squadronaires)/Echo of a Serenade -VR- Bruce Trent (RAF Squadronaires)/Without a Song -VR- Bruce Trent (RAF Squadronaires)/Very Tasty, Very Sweet (featuring Kenway and Young)/ Hoop La/South Rampart Street Parade and Close (RAF Squadronaires).

Wednesday, 25 October 1944   DECCA STUDIOS, LONDON
DR 8788 – 2   (   ) Business Unusual   Decca F8485
DR 8789   (   ) I Ain't Got Nobody
– Unissued
DR 8790   (   ) Loveable and Sweet
– Unissued
DR 8791   (   ) Carolina Moon
– Unissued

Monday, 30 October 1944   TOP TEN
21.05-21.35
Broadcast live from the Paris Cinema, Lower Regent Street, London
Over AEFP

Compère: Cpl. Douglas Marshall

I'll Get By -VR- Beryl Davis (RAF Squadronaires)/I'm Just Wild About Harry (The Brass Hats)/I Didn't Know what Time it was (The Singing Strings)/ Chicago (RAF Squadronaires)/I'll Be Around -VR- Jimmy Miller (RAF Squadronaires)/Remember (The Brass Hats)/Embraceable You -VR- Beryl Davis (The Singing Strings)/Minor Drag (RAF Squadronaires)/When They Ask About You -VR- Jimmy Miller (RAF Squadronaires)/Stardust (combined orchestras, conducted by Jimmy Miller).

Tuesday, 31 October 1944   HOOP LA
19.15

(Pre-recorded at the Paris Cinema, Lower Regent Street, London, on Sunday, 29 October 1944 — BBC Disc No. OP 894 – SOX 40433)

Over AEFP and the BBC General Overseas Service

Featuring: Robb Wilton, Max Wall, Freddie Forbes, Polly Ward, Doris Nichols, Kenneth Blain, Sidney Keith, Benny Lee, the Debonnaires and the augmented RAF Dance Orchestra, conducted by Sgt. Jimmy Miller with Reg Leopold and five members of the Singing Strings

Special Guest Stars: Ronald Chesney, Tessie O'Shea, Hatton and Manners

Opening Theme (Hoop La)/I Go For You -VR- Polly Ward (RAF Dance Orchestra)/The Touch of Your Lips (RAF Squadronaires)/Yes Sir that's My Baby (RAF Squadronaires)/Hallelujah! (featuring Ronald Chesney, Harmonica)/Two Ton Tessie/It all Belongs to Me (featuring Tesssie O'Shea)/ Don't Sweetheart Me (featuring Tessie O'Shea)/Me and My Gal (Hatton and Manners Spot/The Same Little Words -VR- Hatton and Manners/South Rampart Street Parade (RAF Squadronaires) and Close.

Monday, 6 November 1944   TOP TEN
21.05-21.35

Broadcast live from the Paris Cinema, Lower Regent Street, London

Over AEFP

Compère: Roy Williams

It Could Happen to You -VR- Jimmy Miller (RAF Squadronaires)/It Had to be You (The Brass Hats)/Once in a While -VR- Beryl Davis (The Singing Strings)/You're the Cream in My Coffee (Saxophone Sextet)/Time Waits for No One -VR- Beryl Davis (RAF Squadronaires)/Aggrivatin' Papa (RAF Squadronaires)/Now I Know -VR- Beryl Davis (The Singing Strings)/Shine on Harvest Moon (The Brass Hats)/Waitin' for the Evening Mail -VR- Sid Colin (RAF Squadronaires)/Dardanella (combined bands).

Tuesday, 7 November 1944   HOOP LA
19.15

(Pre-recorded at the Paris Cinema, Lower Regent Street, London, on Sunday, 5 November 1944 — BBC Disc No. OP 927 – SOX 40592)

Over AEFP and the BBC General Overseas Service

Featuring: Robb Wilton, Max Wall, Freddie Forbes, Polly Ward, Doris

Nichols, Kenneth Blain, Sidney Keith, Benny Lee, the Debonnaires and the augmented RAF Dance Orchestra, conducted by Sgt. Jimmy Miller with Reg Leopold and members of the Singing Strings
Guest Stars: Stephane Grappelli, Jose Fearon, Charles Gillespie, Jewel and Warriss
Opening theme (Hoop La)/Dance with a Dolly -VR- Polly Ward/Oh! You Beautiful Doll/Yes Sir that's My Baby/It Had to be You (featuring Stephane Grappelli, Violin)/The Girl Friend (featuring Stephane Grappelli, Violin)/ Medley (featuring Jose Fearon and Charles Gillespie): You Are My Heart's Delight; Count of Luxembourg; Love Here Is My Heart; When You Come Home; Where the Blue Begins/With Plenty of Money and You (Jewel and Warriss theme)/Sketch/South Rampart Street Parade and Close.

Monday, 13 November 1944   **TOP TEN**
21.05-21.35
Broadcast live from the Paris Cinema, Lower Regent Street, London
Over AEFP
Compère: Roy Williams
The First Few Days -VR- Beryl Davis (RAF Squadronaires)/Bugle Call Rag (The Brass Hats)/My Ideal -VR- Beryl Davis (The Singing Strings)/Swanee River (RAF Squadronaires)/The Jumping Jive -VR- Sid Colin (RAF Squadronaires)/Cherry (RAF Squadronaires)/Brazil -VR- Beryl Davis (The Singing Strings)/Poor Butterfly (The Brass Hats)/Everybody Step (RAF Squadronaires)/Tonight – 'Perfidia' (combined bands).
This was the last *Top Ten* programme featuring the RAF Dance Orchestra, The Squadronaires. For the next six programmes, their place would be taken by the George Evans-led Dance Band. The RAF Dance Orchestra were on a tour of the Western Front, on the continent of Europe. Their first *Top Ten* show following this would be on Monday, 1 January 1945.

Tuesday, 14 November 1944   **HOOP LA**
19.15-20.00
(Pre-recorded at the Paris Cinema, Lower Regent Street, London, on Sunday, 12 November 1944 — BBC Disc No. OP 951 – SOX 40879)
Over AEFP and the BBC General Overseas Service
Featuring: Robb Wilton, Max Wall, Freddie Forbes, Polly Ward, Doris Nichols, Kenneth Blain, Benny Lee and the augmented RAF Dance Orchestra, conducted by Sgt. Jimmy Miller with Reg Leopold and five members of the Singing Strings
Produced by: Pat Dixon
Guest Stars: Rita Marlowe, Cicely Courtnidge, Nat Mills and Bobbie
Opening Theme (Hoop La)/I've Got a Feeling You're Fooling -VR- Polly Ward/I Know that You Know (RAF Squadronaires)/Yes Sir, that's My Baby (RAF Squadronaires)/Echo of a Serenade -VR- Rita Marlowe/Something About a Soldier/Patter – 'Pre-Fabricated Homes' (featuring Cicely Courtnidge)/ Song Home -VR- Cicely Courtnidge/Monologue – 'This World is Very

Homesick' (featuring Cicely Courtnidge)/Let Us Climb an Apple Tree -VR-Nat Mills and Bobbie/South Rampart Street Parade (RAF Squadronaires) and Close.

On 15 November the RAF Dance Orchestra were in camp awaiting transport ships to take them to the Continent. Their continental tour of the Western Front between 17 November 1944 and 20 December 1944 was cut short due to the German Panzer attack through the Ardennes. Their first tour included concerts throughout France and Belgium. They performed at airfields, hospitals and army camps, some very close to the front lines near the German-French Border.

Tuesday, 12 December 1944   AEFP ON THE SPOT
18.10-18.30
(Recorded for future use by the AEFP, from an RAF airfield, near Brussels, Belgium)
Over AEFP, Friday, 22 December 1944
(Recording made by Radiodiffusion Nationale Belge, on mobile equipment)
Featuring: the RAF Dance Orchestra, directed by Sgt. Jimmy Miller
Compère: Capt. Franklin Englemann
South Rampart Street Parade/San Fernando Valley -VR- Billy Nichols/Jingle Bells/Concerto for Drums/In the Mood/Closing theme (There's Something in the Air).

Monday, 1 January 1945   TOP TEN
21.05-21.35
Broadcast live from the Paris Cinema, Lower Regent Street, London
Over AEFP
Compère: Roy Williams
As Long as There's Music -VR- Jimmy Miller (RAF Squadronaires)/ Coquette (The Brass Hats)/Some Other Time -VR- Beryl Davis (The Singing Strings)/Five Flat Flurry (RAF Squadronaires)/How Many Hearts have You Broken -VR- Jimmy Miller (RAF Squadronaires)/Stardust (RAF Squadronaires)/It Was a Lover and His Lass -VR- Beryl Davis (The Singing Strings)/Moonlight on the Ganges (The Brass Hats)/I'm in the Mood for Love -VR- Beryl Davis (The Singing Strings)/New Orleans* (combined bands, conducted by Jimmy Miller).

*This is not the famous *Way Down Yonder in New Orleans*, but another composition by Phil Cardew.

Monday, 8 January 1945   TOP TEN
21.15
Broadcast live from the Paris Cinema, Lower Regent Street, London
Over AEFP
Compère: Roy Williams
Knock Me a Kiss -VR- Beryl Davis (complete ensemble)/You're Blasé (The Brass Hats)/Let Me Love You Tonight -VR- Beryl Davis (The Singing

Strings)/Zing Went the Strings of My Heart (RAF Squadronaires)/So Dumb, But So Beautiful -VR- Jimmy Miller (RAF Squadronaires)/I'll Walk Alone (Swing Wing − Dixieland Band)/After Twelve o'Clock (RAF Squadronaires)/ Whispering (The Brass Hats)/Echo of a Serenade -VR- Beryl Davis (The Singing Strings)/These Foolish Things (combined bands).

Monday, 15 January 1945   TOP TEN
21.05-21.35
Broadcast live from the Paris Cinema, Lower Regent Street, London
Over AEFP
Compère: Roy Williams
Featuring: Ted Heath and His Music* (replacing the RAF Squadronaires), The Singing Strings, The Brass Hats
Breezing Along with the Breeze -VR- Beryl Davis (Ted Heath and his Music)/ Rockin' Chair (The Brass Hats)/What a Difference a Day Made -VR- Beryl Davis (The Singing Strings)/East of the Sun (Ted Heath and His Music)/Dance with a Dolly -VR- Beryl Davis (Ted Heath and His Music)/My Guy's Come Back (Ted Heath and His Music)/Come Easy, Go Easy Love -VR- Beryl Davis (Ted Heath and His Music)/Somebody's Wrong (The Brass Hats)/By the Light of the Silvery Moon -VR- Beryl Davis (The Singing Strings)/Tonight − 'Perfidia' (combined bands, conducted by Ted Heath)
*The RAF Squadronaires were replaced for this one broadcast by the newly-formed Ted Heath and His Music. This new band would later take over the series and become Britain's finest post-war big band. This was their debut broadcast.

Monday, 22 January 1945   DECCA STUDIOS, LONDON
DR 9067 − 2   (   ) Boston Bounce   Decca F851
DR 9068 − 2   (   ) Jumpin' Jiminy   Decca F851

Monday, 22 January 1945   TOP TEN
21.05-21.35
Broadcast live from the Paris Cinema, Lower Regent Street, London
Over AEFP
Compère: Roy Williams
Don't be that Way -VR- Beryl Davis (RAF Squadronaires)/Poor Butterfly (The Brass Hats)/Together -VR- Beryl Davis (The Singing Strings)/Yearning (RAF Squadronaires)/The Jumping Jive -VR- Sid Colin (RAF Squadronaires)/ Judy (RAF Squadronaires)/My Favourite Dream -VR- Beryl Davis (RAF Squadronaires)/Moon Country (The Brass Hats)/When a Woman Loves a Man -VR- Beryl Davis (The Singing Strings)/Deep Purple (combined bands, conducted by Jimmy Miller).

Monday, 29 January 1945   TOP TEN
21.05-21.35
Broadcast live from the Paris Cinema, Lower Regent Street, London
Over AEFP

Compère: Roy Williams
There Goes that Song Again -VR- Jimmy Miller (RAF Squadronaires)/South Rampart Street Parade (RAF Squadronaires)/The Boy Next Door -VR- Beryl Davis (The Singing Strings)/Bugle Call Rag (The Brass Hats)/Come with Me My Honey -VR- Beryl Davis (RAF Squadronaires)/Easter Sunday (Saxophone Sextet)/It was so Beautiful -VR- Beryl Davis (The Singing Strings)/Can't We Talk it Over (The Brass Hats)/unknown title (combined bands).

Monday, 5 February 1945   TOP TEN
21.05-21.35
Broadcast live from the Paris Cinema, Lower Regent Street, London
Over AEFP
Compère: Roy Williams
Details remain unknown.

Monday, 12 February 1945   TOP TEN
21.05-21.35
Broadcast live from the Paris Cinema, Lower Regent Street, London
Over AEFP
Compère: Roy Williams
Accentuate the Positive -VR- Beryl Davis (RAF Squadronaires)/Yesterdays (The Brass Hats)/A Kiss in the Night -VR- Jimmy Miller (The Singing Strings)/Harlem Nocturne (RAF Squadronaires)/You're the Cream in My Coffee (Saxophone Sextet)/Do it Again -VR- Beryl Davis (RAF Squadronaires)/Suddenly it's Spring -VR- Jimmy Miller (RAF Squadronaires)/ Peg o' My Heart (The Brass Hats)/And then You Kissed Me -VR- Beryl Davis (The Singing Strings)/That Old Black Magic (combined orchestras, conducted by Jimmy Miller).

Saturday, 17 February 1945   DECCA STUDIOS, LONDON
DR 9138   (   ) Piccolo Pete
– Unissued
DR 9139 –   (   ) Lead with Your Left   Decca F975
                        (Mel Powell) -Piano-
                        Ronnie Aldrich
DR 9140   (   ) Mop Mop
– Unissued
DR 9141   (   ) Harlem Nocturne
– Unissued

Monday, 19 February 1944   TOP TEN
21.05-21.35
Broadcast live from the Paris Cinema, Lower Regent Street, London
Over AEFP
Compère: Roy Williams
You Fascinating You (RAF Squadronaires)/Dapper Dan (The Brass Hats)/I Love You Too Much (The Singing Strings)/You Go to My Head (The Brass

Hats)/Since You Went Away (RAF Squadronaires)/Do, Do, Do (Saxophone Sextet)/Who Said Dreams Don't Come True (RAF Squadronaires)/There's Honey on the Moon (The Brass Hats)/Vous Qui Passez Sans Me Voir -VR-Beryl Davis (The Singing Strings)/In the Still of the Night (complete ensemble).

Monday, 26 Febrary 1945 TOP TEN
21.05-21.35
Broadcast live from the Paris Cinema, Lower Regent Street, London
Over AEFP
Compère: Roy Williams
Details remain unknown.

Monday, 5 March 1945 TOP TEN
21.05-21.35
Broadcast live from the Paris Cinema, Lower Regent Street, London
Over AEFP
Compère: Roy Williams
Straighten Up and Fly Right -VR- Beryl Davis (RAF Squadronaires)/If I Didn't Care (The Brass Hats)/You're so Sweet to Me -VR- Jimmy Miller (The Singing Strings)/High Society (RAF Squadronaires)/Knock Me a Kiss -VR-Beryl Davis (RAF Squadronaires)/I've Got the World on a String (Saxes)/More and More -VR- Jimmy Miller (RAF Squadronaires)/Moonlight on the Ganges (The Brass Hats)/Waiting in the Rain -VR- Beryl Davis (The Singing Strings)/Frenesi (complete ensemble).

Monday, 12 March 1945 TOP TEN
21.05-21.35
Broadcast live from the Paris Cinema, Lower Regent Street, London
Over AEFP
Later broadcast by the BBC General Forces Programme
Compère: Roy Williams
Details remain unknown.

Monday, 19 March 1945 TOP TEN
21.05-21.35
Broadcast live from the Paris Cinema, Lower Regent Street, London
Over AEFP
Compère: Roy Williams
How Many Hearts have You Broken -VR- Jimmy Miller (RAF Squadronaires)/ Can't We Talk it Over (The Brass Hats)/I'll Remember April -VR- Beryl Davis (The Singing Strings)/Mission to Moscow (RAF Squadronaires)/The Trolley Song -VR- Beryl Davis (RAF Squadronaires)/ Lullaby of the Leaves (The Brass Hats)/It's a Blue World -VR- Jimmy Miller (RAF Squadronaires)/Lying in the Hay (The Brass Hats)/Once in a While -VR- Beryl Davis (The Singing Strings)/New Orleans (combined bands, conducted by Jimmy Miller).

Monday, 26 March 1945   TOP TEN
21.05-21.35
Broadcast live from the Paris Cinema, Lower Regent Street, London
Over AEFP
Compère: Roy Williams
Details remain unknown.

Monday, 2 April 1945   TOP TEN
21.15-21.45
Broadcast live from the Paris Cinema, Lower Regent Street, London
Over AEFP
Compère: Roy Williams
Special Guest Star: Bill Bassford, USN
Accentuate the Positive -VR- Beryl Davis (RAF Squadronaires)/My Silent
Love -VR- Bill Bassford, USN (The Singing Strings)/Texas Polka (RAF
Squadronaires)/What's New? (RAF Squadronaires)/Phil the Fluter's Ball (The
Brass Hats)/Sleigh Ride in July -VR- Beryl Davis (RAF Squadronaires)/Isle of
Capri (The Brass Hats)/Ghost of a Chance -VR- Bill Bassford (The Singing
Strings)/Who? (combined orchestras, conducted by Jimmy Miller).

Monday, 9 April 1945   TOP TEN
21.15-21.45
Broadcast live from the Paris Cinema, Lower Regent Street, London
Over AEFP
Compère: Roy Williams
Special Guest Musician: Ted Heath
Wouldn't it be Nice -VR- Beryl Davis (RAF Squadronaires)/Memories of You
(The Brass Hats, featuring Ted Heath, Trombone)/I'm in the Middle of
Nowhere (The Singing Strings)/Rosetta (RAF Squadronaires)/ I'm Gonna Love
that Guy -VR- Beryl Davis (RAF Squadronaires)/ To a Wild Rose (Saxophone
Sextet)/I Promise You -VR- Jimmy Miller (RAF Squadronaires)/There's a
Blue Ridge Round My Heart (The Brass Hats, featuring Ted Heath on
Trombone)/I Love You Much Too Much -VR- Beryl Davis (The Singing
Strings)/That Old Black Magic (combined bands, conducted by Sgt. Jimmy
Miller).

Monday, 16 April 1945   TOP TEN
21.05-21.35
Broadcast live from the Paris Cinema, Lower Regent Street, London
Over AEFP
Compère: Roy Williams
Come Easy, Go Easy -VR- Beryl Davis (RAF Squadronaires)/Peg o' My Heart
(The Brass Hats)/It's the Talk of the Town -VR- Bill Bassford, USN (The
Singing Strings)/Marie (RAF Squadronaires)/I Didn't Know -VR- Beryl Davis
(RAF Squadronaires)/You Turned the Tables on Me (Saxophone Sextet)/
I Cover the Waterfront -VR- Beryl Davis (RAF Squadronaires)/Lonesome and

Sorry (The Brass Hats)/There's a Small Hotel -VR- Beryl Davis (The Singing Strings)/These Foolish Things (complete ensemble, conducted by Jimmy Miller).

Monday, 23 April 1945   TOP TEN
21.05-21.30
Broadcast live from the Paris Cinema, Lower Regent Street, London
Over AEFP
Compère: Roy Williams
RAF Dance Orchestra, The Squadronaires, were replaced on this broadcast by the newly-formed Ted Heath and His Music orchestra.

Monday, 30 April 1945   TOP TEN
21.05-21.35
Broadcast live from the Paris Cinema, Lower Regent Street, London
Over AEFP
Compère: Roy Williams
Don't Fence Me In (RAF Squadronaires)/Jada (The Brass Hats)/One Morning in May -VR- Beryl Davis (The Singing Strings)/Mission to Moscow (RAF Squadronaires)/Just a Little Fond Affection -VR- Jimmy Miller (RAF Squadronaires)/I've Got the World on a String (Saxophone Sextet)/Knock Me a Kiss -VR- Beryl Davis (RAF Squadronaires)/Somebody's Wrong (The Brass Hats)/Let Me Love You Tonight -VR- Beryl Davis (The Singing Strings)/After You've Gone (combined bands, conducted by Jimmy Miller).
From Monday, 7 May 1945, the RAF Dance Orchestra were replaced on the *Top Ten* radio series by Ted Heath and His Music. The series would continue on the AEFP until 23 July 1945. Ted and his new orchestra would be featured in all the remaining 12 programmes. The Squadronaires were on a second Continental tour of Western Europe. This tour started just after VE Day, 8 May 1945. It lasted almost six weeks.

Saturday, 16 June 1945   AEFP ON THE SPOT
21.15-21.43
(Recorded from the Dufayel Barracks, Paris, by the 'AEFP On the Spot Team' — BBC Disc A.E.F. 391)
Broadcast by AEFP, Sunday, 8 July 1945
Featuring: The RAF Dance Orchestra, directed by Sgt. Jimmy Miller
Compère: Capt. Franklin Englemann
Intro: Theme (There's Something in the Air)/High Society/A Little on the Lonely Side -VR- Jimmy Miller/The Touch of Your Lips/Mission to Moscow/ Accentuate the Positive -VR- Sid Colin/Marie/You Fascinating You -VR-Jimmy Miller/Dont Fence Me In -VR- Sid Colin/South Rampart Street Parade/ Closing Theme (There's Something in the Air).

Wednesday, 18 July 1945 DECCA STUDIOS, LONDON

DR 9567 –	(	) Please Don't Say No -VR-	Decca F8548
		Jimmy Miller	
DR 9568 –	(	) I Should Care -VR-	Decca F8548
		Jimmy Miller	
DR 9569 – 2	(	) 'C' Jam Blues	Decca F8568
			Decca ECM 2112
DR 9570 – 2	(	) Mission to Moscow	Decca F8568
		(Mel Powell)	Decca ECM 2112

Saturday, 28 July 1945 FAREWELL AEFP
21.05-22.00

Broadcast live from the Queensbury All Services Club, Soho, London
Over AEFP (Repeated by the BBC Light Programme, Sunday, 29 July 1945)

Featuring: Capt. Robert Farnon and the Canadian Band of the AEF, RSM George Melachrino, The Ronnie Selby Trio, The RAF Dance Orchestra – 'The Squadronaires' – directed by Sgt. Jimmy Miller

Introduction/Marie (RAF Squadronaires)/Candy -VR- Paul Carpenter (Canada Show – AEF)/Don't Fence Me In -VR- Dorothy Carless (Canadian AEF Band – Canada Show)/On Another Track (featuring Pat Frost with the RAF Squadronaires)/Patter by Cam Ritchie and PFC Flapjack/My Heart Sings -VR- Beryl Davis (Canadian AEF Band)/Red White and Blue (Canadian AEF Band)/ What a Difference a Day Made -VR- Jack Powers (Canadian AEF Band)/A Brown Bird Singing -VR- Joanne Dallas (Canadian AEF Band)/'Patter' by Ronald Waldman and Dick Dudley/Rise and Shine (Ronald Waldman)/SHAEF theme (Canadian Band)/The More I See You -VR- George Melachrino (Canadian Band)/What is this Thing Called Love (Ronnie Selby Trio)/ Whisperings in the Vienna Woods -VR- Richard Tauber (accomp. by Percy Kahn piano)/Talk by General Eisenhower from SHAEF/ Auld Lang Syne (RAF Squadronaires and The Canadian Band of the AEF) and Close.

Wednesday, 17 October 1945 DECCA STUDIOS, LONDON

DR 9728 – 2	(	) Out of Nowhere -VR-	Decca F8575
		Dorothy Carless	
DR 9729 – 1	(	) My Heart Sings -VR-	Decca F8575
		Dorothy Carless	
DR 9730 – 2	(	) Gotta be This or That	Decca F8621*
		-VR- Sid Colin	
DR 9731 – 2	(	) Down in Chi-Chi-Hotcha	Decca F8621*
		Watchee -VR- Sid Colin	

* These two titles listed on record label as 'The Squadronaires', directed by Jimmy Miller.

The Royal Army Ordnance Corps Dance Orchestra 'The Blue Rockets' 1941 – 1945

The RAOC Dance Orchestra, better known as 'The Blue Rockets', were formed in early 1941 under the leadership of Eric Robinson. The band specialised in swing arrangements of light classics, and backing entertainers at ordnance factories and warehouses all over the United Kingdom. Later, the band often did BBC radio broadcasts, often being featured on BBC *Music While You Work* broadcasts and other series on both the Home and General Forces programmes.

Around September 1941, Eric Robinson was transferred to the Army Radio Unit, which became the British Band of the AEF during July 1944, although he did return occasionally to make guest appearances with the Blue Rockets from time to time. The leadership of the Blue Rockets was taken over by Eric Tann. Eric had worked pre-war for Roy Fox, Henry Hall and Lew Stone, and was well respected by all the musicians under his command. Under Tann, the band began to play more varied music and, in early 1942, a recording contract was signed with HMV.

The first recording session took place on 23 February 1942, in the Regimental Theatre of the RAOC (a slight echo is audible on the first two 78rpm records). Eric Robinson was in the violin section as a guest musician.

During February 1942, there was a press campaign, begun by irritable civilian bandleaders, against musicians in the services — even though they only got normal army pay, plus an allowance of 9 shillings and 6 pence per week towards wear and tear of instruments, as against the substantial earnings available in war-torn London for a freelance musician. The service bands were considered unfair opposition and the result was the disbandment of the Blue Rockets. However, fair play eventually ruled and, late in March 1942, the Blue Rockets were back in business.

During April and May 1942, the Blue Rockets made a number of BBC broadcasts, including some for the daily *Music While You Work* series. Arrangers Burton Gillis and Claude Grant were added to the line-up during this period.

The next recording sessions for HMV took place at the HMV studios in Abbey Road, St John's Wood, London, on 24 and 25 June 1942. A further recording session took place at the HMV studios on 5 August 1942.

During late August or early September 1942, Julie Dawn and Glenn Martin became the featured vocalists with the band. Glenn Martin made six sides with the Blue Rockets during a two-day recording session at HMV studios on 14 and 15 October 1942. Julie Dawn also recorded with the band at HMV studios on 26 November 1942.

It was rumoured in the press that the Blue Rockets were to be featured in a film for the Ministry of Information, entitled *Swinging into the Attack*. For the film, arranger Miff Ferrie was to reorchestrate several Spike Hughes compositions. Many years later, it was thought that reels of this film were lost in an air-raid, but this has never been confirmed, and there could be a copy of the film in existence.

The Blue Rockets next and last recording session was at the HMV studios on 1 March 1943. Four titles were recorded, including two with Glenn Martin on vocals.

Very little is known about the band for the rest of the war, and the recording contract was never renewed. Eric Tann was invalided out of the Army on 2 April 1943 and Benny Daniels took over as director of the band. Benny remained the leader of the Blue Rockets until the band were demobbed in 1945.

After the war, a peacetime band called the Blue Rockets Dance Band, led by Eric Robinson, was formed, with many of the wartime personnel. In early 1947 the leadership of this band passed to Benny Daniels who toured Britain with them, featuring Bertie King on alto and vocalist Judy Johnson.

The band lasted until 1952.

THE ROYAL ARMY ORDNANCE CORPS DANCE ORCHESTRA 'THE BLUE ROCKETS' 1941 − 1945

Monday, 23 February 1942   REGIMENTAL THEATRE
OF THE RAOC

OER 595 − 1   (   ) Katy Did Katy Didn't -VR-   HMV BD 5745
Ernest Polfer

OER 596 − 1   (   ) Couple in the Castle   HMV BD 5745
-VR- Eric Whitley

OER 597 − 1   (   ) Peace on Earth -VR-   HMV BD 5743
Eric Whitley

OER 598 − 1   (   ) Ma, I Miss Your Apple Pies   HMV BD 5743
-VR- Eric Tann and Lee Street

Wednesday, 24 June 1942   HMV STUDIOS, LONDON

OEA 9818 − 1   (   ) Anchors Aweigh -VR- Band   HMV BD 5767
-arr- Claud Grant

OEA 9819 − 1   (   ) National Emblem -arr-   HMV BD 5767
Burton Gillis

Thursday, 25 June 1942   HMV STUDIOS, LONDON

OEA 9827 − 1   (   ) Miss You -VR- Ernest Polfer   HMV BD 5751

OEA 9828 − 1   (   ) A Zoot Suit -VR- Alan Kane   HMV BD 5751

Wednesday, 5 August 1942   HMV STUDIOS, LONDON

OEA 9787 − 1   (   ) Great Little Army   HMV BD 5775

OEA 9788 − 1   (   ) Desert Patrol   HMV BD 5775

OEA 9789 − 1   (   ) Unknown title

OEA 9790 − 1   (   ) Unknown title

OEA 9791 − 1   (   ) Tell Me Teacher -VR-   HMV BD 5769
Ernest Polfer

OEA 9792 − 1   (   ) The Girl Who Broke the   HMV BD 5769
RSM's Heart -VR- Eric Tann
and Lee Street

Wednesday, 14 October 1942   HMV STUDIOS, LONDON

OEA 9580 − 1   (   ) Over There -VR- Glenn   HMV BD 5783
Martin (George M. Cohen)
(from the 1942 Warner Bros
film *Yankee Doodle Dandy*)

OEA 9581 − 1   (   ) Side by Side -VR-   HMV BD 5783
Glenn Martin

Thursday, 15 October 1942   HMV STUDIOS, LONDON

OEA 9582 − 1   (   ) Easter Parade -VR-   HMV BD 5790
Glenn Martin
(Irving Berlin)
(from the 1942 Paramount
film *Holiday Inn*)

OEA 9583 – 1 (   ) Love is a Song -VR- HMV BD 5785
         Glenn Martin
OEA 9584 – 1 (   ) The Last Bus Home -VR- HMV BD 5785
         Glenn Martin and Band
OEA 9585 – 1 (   ) My Melancholy Baby -VR- HMV BD 5790
         Glenn Martin

Thursday, 26 November 1942   HMV STUDIOS, LONDON
OEA 9901 – 1 (   ) Red Moon Over Havana HMV BD 5780
         -VR- Julie Dawn
OEA 9902 – 1 (   ) Idaho -arr- Burton Gillis HMV BD 5780
Monday, 1 March 1943   HMV STUDIOS, LONDON
OEA 9922 – 1 (   ) Sons of the Brave -arr- HMV BD 5797
         Burton Gillis
OEA 9923 – 1 (   ) On the Sunny Side of the HMV BD 5803
         Street -VR- Glenn Martin
OEA 9924 – 1 (   ) Time on My Hands -VR- HMV BD 5803
         Glenn Martin
OEA 9925 – 1 (   ) Girls in Grey -arr- HMV BD 5797
         Charles Williams

The Royal Marines Commando Training Unit Dance Band 'The Marineers'

The 'Marineers', a fourteen-piece dance band of the Royal Marine Commando Training Unit, led by ex-Edmundo Ros trumpet star, 'Buzz' Trueman, was a lesser-known band of the war years. However, they were often mentioned in the *Melody Maker* during 1944 – 45. At the very end of the war in Europe, they toured the Continent entertaining the fighting forces. They also appeared on several occasions at the London Stage Door Canteen. On 6 April 1945, they broadcast for the BBC in the Mediterranean edition of *Merry-Go-Round*. The drummer with this band was Norman Wisdom, who later became one of Britain's top comedians and film stars.

Melody Maker said of this unit: 'We know the band, with its stylish tendencies and fine arrangements, will be wildly missed by service personnel in the United Kingdom.' This write-up was in the 21 April 1945 edition.

Buzz Trueman and his band were often used for dances and concerts in the United Kingdom. As far as we know, they did not record for any of the major record companies and no known examples of their work exist. The other personnel in this band remain unknown. However, we believe this band was demobbed sometime during 1946.

Saturday, 9 June 1945   HALF-WAY HOME
12.00
(Pre-recorded at a Returned Prisoner of War Transit Camp, in Brussels on VE Day, Tuesday, 8 May 1945 — AEF Disc No. 376)
Over AEFP
Featuring: The Royal Marine Training Unit Band — The Marineers, directed by L/Cpl. Buzz Trueman, with vocals by Joe Royal
Compère: Capt. John Burgess
AEFP Announcer: S/Sgt. Wilf Davidson
Details remain unknown.

The Royal Navy Swing Octet 'The Blue Mariners' 1942 – 1945

The Royal Navy Dance Orchestra, better known as 'The Blue Mariners', were formed in 1942 by pianist George Crow for entertaining at Royal Navy installations throughout the United Kingom, and making broadcasts for the BBC and forces networks. This small band was built around the talents of multi-reedman, Freddy Gardner, and the personnel remained intact throughout the war, until late 1945.

Freddy Gardner, like all British musicians who were in the services during the war, made records during leaves. Freddy recorded several titles for Decca under the title of 'Freddy Gardner and his Mess Mates', but this was a civilian outfit, led when he was on leave from the Navy, and must not be confused with the 'Blue Mariners'.

In late 1943, the Royal Navy Blue Mariners signed a recording contract with Decca and, interestingly, each 78rpm record had the words 'By permission of Commodore de Pass RN', inscribed on the label. The records cut were unusual in that they featured two titles per side, linked by George Crow on piano.

Only three recording sessions are known to have taken place by this eight-piece band. The first recording session was on 30 November 1943 at the Decca Studios in London. The second and third also took place in London on 14 and 15 March 1944. The three sessions are listed overleaf.

The Blue Mariners' personnel included George Crow directing and playing piano, Harry Latham and Hugh Radcliffe on trumpets, Fred Clitheroe on trombone, Freddy Gardner on clarinet, baritone, soprano and alto saxophone, Reginald Pink on tenor saxophone, plus Al Jennings on clarinet, guitar and bass, with, lastly, Al Craig on drums. It was quite a neat little line-up, and the recordings with Gardner are very outstanding indeed.

They also did quite a few broadcasts over the BBC General Forces and AEFP networks, as well as recording for ENSA and other forces' transcription services from 1944 to 1945.

During the spring of 1945, the Royal Navy Blue Mariners Swing Octet toured the continent of Europe, playing for Allied troops. They were recorded by the AEFP *On the Spot* team at an ENSA garrison theatre on Sunday, 20 May 1945. P/O George Crow directed the octet and Harry Latham appeared with the group. They started the broadcast with their own theme (by George Crow), called *Up Spirits*. Sub-Lt. Eric Barker compèred the show, which was part of the *Merry-Go-Round* series. Further information on this now forgotten tour remains unknown.

This small octet was disbanded during late 1945. No other details exist and it is now sadly forgotten among the other larger dance bands and orchestras of the time.

All the musicians went back to civilian jobs. Sadly, Freddie Gardner died in 1949, although, happily, his saxophone solos on recordings are still played nearly 50 years later.

THE ROYAL NAVY SWING OCTET
'THE BLUE MARINERS' 1942 – 1945

30 November 1943   DECCA STUDIOS, LONDON
DR 7912 – 2   Three Little Words/   DeMW 187
                   You're Driving Me Crazy
    7913 – 2   Touch of Your Lips/One More
                   Chance
    7914 – 2   Undecided/Deed I Do   DeMW 188
    7915 – 2   April in Paris/June in January

14 March 1944   DECCA STUDIOS, LONDON
DR 8264 – 2   Who?/I Wish I Were Twins   DeMW 250
    8265 – 2   Thanks for the Memory/
                   By the Fireside
    8266 – 2   Sleepy Time Gal/   DeMW 265
                   Life is Just a Bowl of Cherries
    8267 – 2   Crazy People/Gypsy in My Soul

15 March 1944   DECCA STUDIOS, LONDON
DR 8268 – 2   I've Got the World on a String/   DeMW 306
                   Couldn't Say Goodbye
    8269 – 2   Dancing With Tears in My Eyes/
                   You Can't Stop Me Dreaming
    8270 – 2   I'll Never Say Never Again/   DeMW 331
                   It's . . . D'Lovely
    8271 – 2   Amapola/Stop You're Breaking My
                   Heart

Monday, 11 June 1945   AEF EXTRA
18.15
(Pre-recorded on Wednesday, 4 April 1945 — BBC Disc No. SLO 72071)
Over AEFP
Compère: Jill Balcon

Featuring: The Blue Mariners Dance Band, directed by P/O George Crow, with Wren Audrey Pullen

Opening Theme (Up Spirits -comp- George Crow)/Hallelujah/Latin American Medley: Frenesi; Amor Amor -VR- Freddie Latham; Brazil/ Heavenly Music -VR- Audrey Pullin/Struttin' Like a Peacock/Closing Theme (Up Spirits).

Sunday, 24 June 1945   AEFP ON THE SPOT
21.15-21.43

(Pre-recorded at an ENSA garrison theatre, somewhere on the Continent, on Sunday, 20 May 1945 — BBC Disc No. AEF 383)

Over AEFP

Featuring: The Blue Mariners Dance Band, directed by P/O George Crow, with leading seaman Ivor Pye, P/O Hector Hall, P/O Freddie Gardner RN, leading seaman Freddie Latham

Compère: Sub-Lt. Eric Barker

Opening Theme (Up Spirits)/Come Out Wherever You Are -VR- Freddie Latham/Memories Live Longer than Dreams (featuring Ivor Pye)/Music Makers/Bless this House -VR- Hector Hall/Embraceable You (featuring Freddie Gardner, Saxophone)/Comedy Routine — Eric Barker/Put on Your Old Grey Bonnet/Theme (Up Spirits) and Close.

Sunday, 22 July 1945   SERVICE DANCE
18.10-18.40   BAND SESSION

(Pre-recorded at the BBC Studios, London, on Friday, 20 July 1945 — BBC Disc No. SLO 76795)

Over AEFP

Featuring: The Blue Mariners Dance Band, directed by P/O George Crowe

Guest Stars: Marilyn Williams (accomp. by Lt. Harry Jacobson, Wren Audrey Pullin)

Compère: Roy Williams

Opening Theme (Up Spirits)/I'm Beginning to See the Light -VR- Freddie Latham/The Night has Known My Tears -VR- Audrey Pullin/Embraceable You (featuring Freddie Gardner, saxophone)/Covered Wagon/Say that We're Sweethearts -VR- Marilyn Williams (accomp. by Harry Jacobson, Piano)/ Confessin' -VR- Marilyn Williams (accomp. by Harry Jacobson, Piano)/ Pablo the Dreamer (featuring Billy Farrell, Accordion)/Forever -VR- Audrey Pullin/Put on Your Old Grey Bonnet -VR- Ensemble/Closing Theme (Up Spirits).

The 718th Army Air Forces Band

When Captain Glenn Miller was building his large orchestra at Yale University in the early spring of 1943, many dance band musicians were transferred from Atlantic City to the new headquarters. Many of the overflow went out to other Army Air Force bands and orchestras throughout the United States. Glenn did hold on to the cream, even though many were never used. The overflow, however, built up a small seventeen-piece dance band. Among this unit's ranks were Nat Peck, Louis Stein and vocalist Bob Carroll. A few others had been with Glenn and were transferred and used by him during illness, etc. During the summer, Glenn's band had been designated the 418th Army Air Forces Training Command Band. On 7 December 1943, Miller's radio orchestra was separated from the 418th, and became the 2nd AAFTC Radio Orchestra. On 27 December, the remaining members of the 418th were designated the 718th Army Air Force Band.

The 718th consisted of a nucleus of 15 musicians (four from the old 418th, and 11 transferred from other units at Yale University); by additional transfers from other AAF bases, the band soon obtained its full shape, with a total strength of 25 men, including George T. Simon, Marty Blitz and many more. The unit was first commanded by Lieutenant Harry Dawson, with Warrant Officer Thomas Nichols as bandleader. On 15 February 1944, Warrant Officer Robert Boucher, who had been part of the Glee Club, under Captain Glenn Miller, on the early CBS *I Sustain the Wings* broadcasts, returned to Yale and became both commander of the unit and bandleader.

Boucher took the band a step further and introduced small units from within the 25 members of the 718th. These included a classical trio, a quintet, an octet (the 'El Morocco Octet') and a Spike Jones-type novelty group, led by Ambrose 'Perry' Burgett. Pianist Louis Stein organised an eight-piece swing unit (known as the 'G.I. Jivesters'). Later, sufficiently experienced men were available for a large dance band which became known as '17 Skymen of the 718th AAF Band'. The 17 were under the direction of trombonist/composer Aron 'Kahn' Keene. Six members of the G.I. Jivesters group also played in the dance band and all played in the 25-piece military marching band.

The 718th remained in the old Durfee Hall after Glenn Miller's orchestra relocated. Rehearsal halls were a problem, but the band was assigned a rowing room in the basement of the Payne Whitney Gymnasium. This proved unsatisfactory, and they ended up using their own 10 by 15-foot dayroom.

The 718th AAF Band marches in review through the streets of New Haven, Connecticut, in the spring of 1944

Even though they had problems, they did turn into a great band. While Glenn Miller and the 2nd AAFTC Orchestra were taking part in the Fourth War Loan drive during January 1944, the 718th AAF Dance Band took over the *Wings For Tomorrow* series on CBS. Although the *Wings For Tomorrow* broadcasts were only on the local CBS network, the 718th did do a very good job. The 718th Marching Band were often featured on parades throughout New Haven in the spring of 1944. They took part in WAC, Red Cross and war bond rallies throughout Connecticut during the spring and summer of 1944.

In mid-May 1944, Corporal George T. Simon brought a portable recording unit to Durfee Hall and recorded the 718th AAF Band. These recordings were submitted to Captain Vincent at V-Disc headquarters and a V-Disc session was arranged for the band. Before it took place in June, Captain Glenn Miller and his band left for England, taking with them four important members of the 718th: Nat Peck (trombone), Mannie Thaler (baritone saxophone), Jack Russin (piano), and Joe Shulman (bass). Trombonist Jim Harwood and baritone saxist Charles 'Chuck' Gentry came from the Miller band to replace the four who had gone overseas. In late July, George T. Simon was transferred from the 718th to the V-Disc project in New York City. The 718th AAF Band went to New York City on 26 July 1944 for their one and only V-Disc recording session. From it came only one issued V-Disc title, *Summer Holiday*. Others were recorded but never issued. The one title would cause great problems for collectors, because it sounds very like the Glenn Miller-led orchestra. To make matters worse, the 718th often used Miller arrangements, such as the *St Louis Blues March* and, with a similar sound, this has led many people to the erroneous assumption that this band was Miller's orchestra.

After 1 November 1944, the 3510th Base Unit (the name assigned to the 718th after May 1944) gradually deactivated.

Retreat ceremonies and parades ended at Yale University on 19 November 1944. The band moved from Durfee Hall to the Graduate Hall at Yale. They were involved in the Sixth War Loan drive from November until 31 December 1944. On the last day of 1944, they were transferred intact to the Headquarters detachment, at the 1st Service Command of the Army Services Forces at Boston.

As far as is known, the unit was disbanded in mid-1945.

Artie Shaw and the US Navy Rangers Band 1942 – 1944

The tale of how one of the world's most talented and popular bandleaders, who wound up fronting an all-star band on lonely sun-drenched atolls in the Pacific, is quite a story. It involves a young clarinet genius who, during the period of the Depression, had toured as a sideman in the orchestras of Austin Wylie and Irving Aaronson. Artie wound up in New York City as a studio and radio musician. Then, in 1936, he put together a band, which included violins, a viola and cello, but this unique orchestra was not a success. So Artie dumped the strings and formed a conventional dance band in 1937. By 1938, Artie and his new orchestra really started to take off. They recorded their first sides for RCA Victor Bluebird, and among them was a Cole Porter song called *Begin the Beguine*. It was a million-seller hit and is still selling today.

The ominous war clouds hovered over Europe and Asia as Artie and his band enjoyed enormous popularity both in the USA and overseas. The band included many of the all-time greats. Among them was Tony Pastor, a sensitive tenor saxophonist, trumpeters John Best and Bernie Priven, drummer Buddy Rich, and a petite brunette from Atlantic City named Helen Forrest who handled all the vocals. It was a sleek aggregation that Shaw led through 1938 until the autumn of 1939. By this time, Europe was at war, and the big bands were all the rage in the USA. Artie Shaw was one of the top bandleaders in the USA, but he succumbed to the pressures of being the top man in music, and abandoned his orchestra abruptly, fleeing to Mexico. Tony Pastor and Georgie Auld tried vainly to keep the band together, but without Shaw's ever-brilliant clarinet, the group had no focus or glamour.

Then, in 1940, Artie returned to music. This time, he put together an even larger orchestra, which included a string section. Once again it was a great success with the public. More hits poured forth, among them *Frenesi*, *Stardust*, and many others. This new band included the trumpet of Billy Butterfield and another star line-up.

That same year, Artie and his new orchestra completed the film *Second Chorus* with Fred Astaire and Paulette Goddard. Another first happened when the talented Shaw put together a band within a band with his small jazz group, called the 'Gramercy Five', which introduced the harpsichord into jazz. The small group's titles were hits from their first release.

While Artie was out in Hollywood, he had married the film star Lana Turner. Their marriage did not last long. Later, Artie married Jerome Kern's daughter, Betty.

In 1941, America was on the eve of war, but Artie did not seem to notice much of what was going on. The draft — or call-up — of America's young men had started in January and, although they were still at peace, United States ships had been attacked by Nazi U-boats in the Atlantic. Japan seemed to be on the road to war. The top bands performed every night on the radio and at night spots through the States. Artie was still leading the large orchestra with strings. Then, on Sunday, 7 December 1941, Japan attacked the US fleet in Pearl Harbour. Because of the time difference, it was evening when the news came through to the eastern coast. Artie and his orchestra were playing at a dance in Providence, Rhode Island. Most of the audience was made up of navy personnel from the large navy base nearby. During the interval, Artie went for a smoke backstage. One of the theatre bands had a radio on and Artie heard a newsflash telling everyone about the Japanese attack. Artie later said, 'I was asked to tell the audience what had happened. After the interval, I went on stage and informed everyone . . . I was also asked to tell everyone who was in the Armed Forces that they should report back to their bases. Three-quarters of the audience walked out. It then dawned on me what was going on, and what I was doing just did not seem to matter any more. The next day, I went down to join the navy.'

Early in April 1942, Artie went into the US Navy, completed boot training, was stationed on Staten Island in New York Harbour and served for a couple of months on a minesweeper. During that period, Artie was an apprentice seaman. Then he was transferred to Newport, Rhode Island.

After his transfer to Newport, he was put in charge of a pretty terrible band. Artie later said: 'If I was going to lead a band, it ought to be a worthwhile one.' Then, in complete desperation, Artie went to Washington D.C. He succeeded in reaching some influential ears and requested permission to form a good band and to take it out into the battle zones. Permission was granted and he jumped in rank right up to Chief Petty Officer.

He was told to report for duty to the US Navy base at Treasure Island, near San Francisco, California. It was at this west-coast base that the newly promoted Shaw began to select the members of his new swing band. It became a terrific band and included the brilliant trumpet section of Conrad Gozzo, Frank Beach, Johnny Best and Max Kaminsky. Sam Donahue stood out in the saxes; Davey Tough played drums; ex-bandleader Claude Thornhill played piano and wrote some arrangements along with Dick Jones and Dave Rose (later changed to Rhodes). The new title for this band was 'Naval Reserve Band 501', better known as 'The Rangers'. The band was completed in November 1942.

On Christmas Day 1942, CPO Artie Shaw and his US Navy Rangers Band landed at Pearl Harbour, after a trip over to the Hawaiian Islands by navy transport from San Francisco. For the next six weeks, Artie and the band performed at nearly every base in the islands. They played for nearly 40,000 army, navy and marine personnel.

The band played mainly from the Artie Shaw book, although a few new arrangements did appear. The troops and sailors loved the old titles. Many of their concerts were outdoors on hastily constructed bandstands. Wherever they performed, they would be greeted by excited cheers from their audiences.

On 30 January 1943, Artie and his Rangers band performed *Begin the Beguine* on a short-wave hook-up with the AFRS in Hollywood, in a programme called *America Salutes the President*. It was heard coast-to-coast as a salute on Roosevelt's birthday. Needless to say, it is the only known title that exists by this wonderful service band.

Within that same week, Claude Thornhill was transferred to Admiral Halsey's staff to form another navy band and Artie and his boys were on their way again by ship heading for the South Pacific. Although they were on their way to the fighting front, they performed many concerts on the decks of ships. None was more impressive than the special concert for the ship's crew of the largest aircraft carrier in the world at that time — the USS Saratoga. Artie later recalled: 'The bandstands were put on the flight deck, on the aircraft lift, which brought aircraft from the flight deck down to the aircraft deck. They slowly lowered the lift with the band down and, as we played it, it seemed just like the Paramount in New York City. When we got down there, there were 3,000 men in dress whites who started to applaud. The band finished with the *Star Spangled Banner* — such a corny tune, but it took on a new meaning in front of all those sailors.'

Another group of shows followed in New Caledonia. It was a back-breaking tour. They performed in jungles, airplane hangars, field hospitals, and even in the outdoor areas, camouflaged for protection from Japanese attacks.

In an interview, Artie later told *Metronome*, 'Was I scared? You bet I was. Conditions were grim. Nearby boats were being torpedoed. You just quake and wonder if it's you or the next guy who got hit. You take your battle station and you do your job. We hitch-hiked everywhere, sometimes on a large ship, then a small one, and sometimes by plane. We travelled any way we could.' Artie and the band survived seventeen bombing attacks by Japanese aircraft trying to hit the warships and transports taking them from island to island.

Slowly, the strain began to tell on the highly-strung bandleader. At some bases, the Marines, Seabees, and flyers would lap up everything the band played. At others, they would say terrible things. Max Kaminsky recalls one story: 'Artie came back after one meeting in, of all places, the officers' latrine. A young officer was standing next to Shaw. He said, "You're Artie Shaw?" Shaw said yes. The officer said, "Can I shake the hand of the hand that held Lana Turner's tit." Artie was really cut up by this.' It was terrible that Shaw had gone to war for such insults. After all, Artie was doing a hell of a job entertaining the fighting troops under such extreme conditions. The band not

CPO Artie Shaw and his US Navy Rangers Band perform during their tour of the Pacific during 1943

only travelled such great distances, but performed under all sorts of handicaps. Artie picks up the story again: 'Even our instruments were under attack — by the weather. I found it not unusual to be playing a solo and a pad would drop out of my clarinet. In addition, reeds were impossible to come by; guitar and bass strings were continually snapping, and most of the time there wasn't a PA system, the guys had to blow their brains out to be heard.'

After a while, Artie got so bad that he wandered off and was picked up by a navy doctor. He wound up with a nervous breakdown in a field hospital. Slowly he recovered after rest.

By mid-June 1943, Artie had recovered and was back leading the 'Rangers' band. This time, they were heading for another war zone. While being transported, they played one concert on board a Royal Navy battleship. Their destination was Guadalcanal. Although this island had seen some bitter fighting, it was now firmly in Allied hands, albeit that the Japanese were still bombarding the place with bombing raids. Shaw and his band saw many dogfights between Japanese Zeros and US Army Air Force P-38 fighters. The Rangers band was the first entertainment group in these islands. They performed everywhere, including one concert on Henderson field, which was the forward airbase at that time. Artie recalled: 'We played many of the old arrangements. It's amazing how the kids out there are familiar with the band. And they got so excited when we showed up on some godforsaken island unexpectedly. Some would throw gifts at the band. Others cry. Most would just sit there and just listen, devouring everything we kicked off.'

Artie also reported hearing Radio Tokyo playing his records and announcing that the band were appearing at the St Francis Hotel in San Francisco. 'The idea was to make the Yanks feel homesick,' he pointed out.

Altogether, Artie and the band stayed on Guadalcanal and the other islands in that chain for nearly six weeks. Then, in mid-August, they were transported to New Zealand.

Artie and the Rangers band performed at many shows throughout New Zealand. However, the most important performances were the ones throughout the war zones, in the front line. Artie recently recalled in an interview: 'We resisted playing at officers' dances. Then, a Mrs Dillingham, the wife of a magnate down there, asked them to play at one. She said, "I understand that back home in the USA, you could be asking and earning $20,000 for such an appearance." I said we were there to do what we could. Then Commander Hicky said to us, "Sooner or later, all the big shots come down and work for me." I said, "I thought we were all working for the same boss".'

The tour began to tell on other members of the band and, by September 1943, the unit was withdrawn back to Pearl Harbour. On 11 November 1943, Artie and his Rangers band arrived back in San Francisco. The tour had been a complete success, but the strain on the entire unit was terrible. The band had done very well and performed to the highest standard but, according to some members, there was a great deal of friction, and several of them had some very unkind words to say about their leader — which was not surprising. Throughout his career, not many had been able to penetrate his façade very deeply. At least in civilian days, Artie had found it easy to withdraw from his musicians. In the navy, such seclusion was virtually impossible.

Upon their return from overseas, many of Artie's friends reported that he seemed unusually nervous. Davey Tough had received his medical discharge, and Max Kaminsky was in very bad shape too. All three men were in no fit state to continue in the service of their country. The rest of the unit were given six weeks' furlough and rest.

When the members of the band reported back for duty in early 1944, their leader, Shaw, drummer Tough and trumpet man Kaminsky were no longer in the service. Artie had another breakdown and the other two were completely unfit for further service. The band Shaw had formed continued under their new leader, Sam Donahue, and would see further service overseas in the European Theatre of Operations, during 1944 and 1945.

After nearly a year, Artie Shaw formed another civilian band and continued with his career in recording and broadcasting.

The 64th Army Band 1942-1945

The 64th Army Band were based at Fort Ord, and the leader of this little-known band was Captain Marion Walters. Among the trumpet section was a young trumpet player, and brother of one of America's bandleaders, John Herbert Miller (better known as Herb). Herb spoke very little of his army service from mid-1944 until late-1945. Like Tex Beneke, Herb stayed in the United States with the band, although they did appear on quite a few War Bond rallies around Fort Ord. Unlike his elder brother, who died in Europe, Herb saw little overseas action.

However, because the band played swing and many of the members came from swing bands, the outfit must be included in this book. Herb Miller, along with his son John, would later form and run the Herb Miller Orchestra over in the United Kingdom during the 1980s. Herb Miller died on 30 September 1987. He had played trumpet for the Charlie Spivak Band, and many others. He had also been a road manager for his brother Glenn during 1940.

The US Army Band 1942 – 1945

This band had become famous as the 100-piece military band that was offered to Major Glenn Miller during early October 1944 by General Walter 'Beetle' Bedell Smith. Major Miller turned down the leadership point-blank, telling the general 'they didn't play his kind of music'!

This band had been formed in 1942 as part of the Military District of Washington Band, stationed at Fort Meyer, Virginia. In June 1943, under the direction of Captain Thomas Darcy, the band was shipped overseas to the North African Theatre of War. For the next two years, they performed in seventeen countries. In 1944, they were in newly-liberated Paris. They also broadcast over the Allied Expeditionary Forces Programme of the BBC during late 1944 and early 1945. Often, they performed in their army overcoats because of the very cold conditions during the winter of 1945. Their tour of Europe took them right into Berlin at the end of the war.

While the band was away in Europe, another group of 40 musicians led by Master Sergeant (later Warrant Officer) Clarence Hurrell remained in Washington D.C. to play for parades, ceremonies and other functions. This forty-piece band recorded V-Discs for the *Music For Marching Men* series. No other details exist on this band or the larger band that toured Europe.

Claude Thornhill and His US Navy Band
October 1942 – September 1945

Bandleader Claude Thornhill disbanded his orchestra in the early autumn of 1942 and entered the US Navy on 26 October 1942. Claude enlisted in the navy as an apprentice Seaman. He joined Artie Shaw's Naval Reserve Band 501 ('The Rangers'). When Artie and the Rangers left Pearl Harbour in early February 1943 for a tour of the South Pacific Theatre of War, Thornhill remained behind to form his own US Navy Orchestra. Claude attained the rank of Chief Petty Officer. Claude returned to the United States in June 1944 and organised a small band for a tour of the Pacific Theatre of War. Like his former boss in the US Navy, Artie Shaw, Claude and his small naval unit toured right across the war zone. The tour lasted right through the war and included the liberated Phillipines and many small atolls. Performing under such conditions, Thornhill became ill during the tour and was discharged in September 1945.

In April 1946, Claude Thornhill formed a new civilian orchestra, which made its debut on 29 May at the Boston Post Lodge in Larchmont, New York. A number of Claude's pre-navy musicians joined the new orchestra. His musical activity diminished in the 1950s and, after disbanding in 1959, he retired to New Jersey. Thornhill died in Caldwell, New Jersey, on 1 July 1965.

Lt. Rudy Vallee and the US Coast Guard Band

Rudy Vallee entered the US Coast Guard in late 1942 as a Chief Petty Officer and was stationed at the 11th Naval District's Coast Guard Training Centre at Alameda, California. As Lieutenant Vallee, he led a band of about 20 musicians (mostly former Hollywood studio musicians). The band recorded Treasury Star Parade transcriptions, for war bond sales promotion, at the studios of RCA Victor Records, Twentieth Century Fox and Warner Brothers.

In 1943, Vallee was joined by former bandleader Jimmie Grier as assistant bandleader and arranger. At this time, the band was enlarged to about 30 musicians for shows and War Bond tours. The full personnel of the band is largely unknown; however, it did include Max Herman and Dave Wade (trumpets), J. Myron 'Mickey' Folus and Henry 'Hank' Howe (saxes), Elliot Daniels or Peter Lance (piano), Clint Wardrup (drums), Bob Caudana (accordion) and Bobby Maxwell (harp).

Lieutenant Rudy Vallee retired from the Coast Guard in July 1944 and, on 2 September 1944, began the NBC Thursday night Drene Show (Proctor and Gamble). The US Coast Guard Band was now led by Lieutenant Jimmie Grier. The Coast Guard Band did not participate in any of the Drene Show broadcasts, but the chorus participated in a special tribute to the US Navy programme on 28 October 1944. In 1945, the band, now enlarged to 47 men, toured the Pacific Theatre of War. Grier was discharged from the navy in October 1945 and formed a band mostly of former US Coast Guard band members for a Hollywood Bowl concert.

Jimmie Grier died in mid-1959. Rudy Vallee gave up radio work in 1947, but has continued to appear in films, clubs and shows.

Major Meridith Willson and the Armed Forces Radio Service Orchestra 1942 – 1945

Meridith Willson led orchestras on a number of radio programmes in the early 1940s on the west coast of the USA. In mid 1942, he volunteered his service to AFRS, and was commissioned in late 1942, with the rank of Major. He was put in charge of AFRS musical activities until mid 1945. Willson was responsible for instituting the AFRS Basic Music Library Transcription series in mid 1943. Later, in early 1944, he organised the AFRS Orchestra and its various sub-units.

The Armed Forces Radio Orchestra under Willson's leadership was heard on many AFRS-produced programmes. These included *Mail Call, Swing Time* (with Dinah Shore), *G.I. Journal, Command Performance* and special Christmas programmes. Among the famous members of this large concert-style orchestra was Les Paul, the famed guitar player. Smaller groups were formed from within the orchestra to perform on many different types of programmes. From light music right through to jazz Willson's AFRS Orchestra were to be heard. They played for many stars, including Frank Sinatra, Bing Crosby, Dinah Shore, Morton Downey, Bob Hope, and even for comedy shows.

The orchestra performed and were based in Hollywood, but they were heard in every corner of the war-torn world, from the cold of the Arctic to the heat of the jungle — anywhere an AFN or AFRS station was broadcasting. Millions heard them.

After the war, Meridith Willson went back to conducting orchestras on many American radio shows. He even had his own programme in the late 1940s. Later, he became famous again with his show and film *The Music Man*.

Winged Victory Show

Moss Hart's Army Air Forces' stage show *Winged Victory* made its New York City debut in late 1943. The 47-soldier pit band was directed by Technical Sergeant David Rose, who also scored the incidental music. Technical Sergeant Rose's assistant was Master Sergeant Joe Bushkin, former pianist with the Tommy Dorsey Orchestra. Other members of this pit orchestra also came from the top big bands and included, on bass, Benny Goodman's brother, Harry Goodman. From the Glenn Miller Orchestra came trumpet player Steve Lipkins, and many other top swing musicians. The clarinet player was Steve Aaronson. The show played for nearly two years to packed audiences. In November 1944, the orchestra was taken over by Master Sergeant Joe Bushkin, when Rose became ill. A V-Disc was produced from the show in December 1943, and included vocals by Sergeant Zeke Manners and Miss Rosalie Allen. The title was *Nobody's Love is Like Mine*. PFC Johnny Desmond was scheduled to go to this show, but was transferred to the 418th AAF Orchestra at Yale University, led by Captain Glenn Miller, in October 1943.

After the war, Joe Bushkin would go on to greater fame as Frank Sinatra's personal pianist. Most of the others would go back into the swing world and continue what they had been doing pre-war.

Sound Recordings

RECORDINGS PRESERVED IN THE SOUND ARCHIVES OF THE BRITISH BROADCASTING CORPORATION

1. British Band of the AEF (announcements by Ronald Waldman): Theme: SHAEF Signature Tune; Put on Your Old Grey Bonnet; Spring Will Be a Little Late This Year (sung by Cpl. Jack Powers); His Rocking-Horse Ran Away (sung by Paula Green). (This is the first 12 minutes of a live broadcast from the Queensbury All Services Club on Wednesday, 27 December 1944 at 8.30 for the Allied Expeditionary Forces Programme.)

2. Sam Donahue and His US Navy Dance Band of the Liberation Forces (announcements by Margaret Hubble): Theme: 'Convoy'; St Louis Blues; Spring Will Be a Little Late This Year (sung by Bill Bassford); Dinah; East of the Sun (partial). (This is the first 15 minutes of a programme recorded on Friday, 15 December 1944, at 13.30, from the Paris Cinema, London, and first broadcast on Saturday, 16 December 1944 at 18.30 for the Allied Expeditionary Forces Programme.)

3. Canada Show (announcements by Cpl. Wilf Davidson and Pvt. Dick Misener): Theme: 'March Along, Joe Soldier' (sung by The Canada Show Chorus); Oh! Dear what Can the Matter be (sung by The Canada Show Chorus); The Isle of Capri (featuring The Canada Dance Band); Poinciana (sung by Pvt. Paul Carpenter); My Prayer (featuring Ronald Chesney, Harmonica). (This is the first 15 minutes of a live broadcast from the Queensbury All Services Club on Monday, 25 September 1944 at 20.30 for the Allied Expeditionary Forces Programme.)

4. American Band of the AEF (announcements by Major Glenn Miller): Theme: 'Moonlight Serenade'; Great Day; Goodnight Good Neighbour (sung by RSM George Melachrino); String of Pearls (This is the first 12 minutes of a live broadcast from the Queensbury All Services Club on Thursday, 5 October 1944 at 20.30 for the Allied Expeditionary Forces Programme.)

5. The American Dance Band – 'Swing Shift' (announcement by T/Sgt. Ray McKinley): Theme: 'Song and Dance' (sung by T/Sgt. Ray McKinley); Tail End Charlie; Embraceable You (sung by Sgt. Johnny Desmond); Bubble Bath. (This is the first 12 minutes of a programme recorded on 20 April 1945, from the Olympia Theatre in Paris, and first broadcast on Saturday, 19 May 1945, in the Allied Expeditionary Forces Programme.)

6. The Swing Sextet – 'The Uptown Hall' (announcements by Cpl. Paul Dubov): Theme: 'My Guy's Come Back'; Hallelujah!; Louise; If Dreams Come True (played by a quartet consisting of Mel Powell (Piano), Peanuts Hucko (Clarinet), Trigger Alpert (Bass), and Frank Ippolito (Drums); I'm Through With Love (sung by Sgt. Johnny Desmond); Night In Tunisia (arranged by Addison Collins, Jnr). (This is a programme recorded from Bedford on 3 December 1944, and first broadcast on Thursday, 11 January 1945, at 21.15 in the Allied Expeditionary Forces Programme.)

7. Strings With Wings (announcements by Cpl. Paul Dubov): Theme: 'I Sustain the Wings'; The Song is You; Pavanne (Ravel); Indian Summer (sung by Sgt. Johnny Desmond); I Love You Truly. (This is a programme recorded from the Olympia Theatre in Paris on 31 May 1945, and first broadcast on Friday, 20 July 1945, at 21.45, in the Allied Expeditionary Forces Programme.)

8. American Eagle in Britain (announcements by Cecil Madden): Theme: It's a Long Way to Tipperary (sung by Artie Malvin accomp. by S/Sgt. Mel Powell); 'Roving Microphone' (partial). (This is the first five minutes of a recording made at the American Red Cross Club – 'Rainbow Corner', in Piccadilly, London, on Thursday, 28 September 1944, and first broadcast by the BBC American Service (Red) on 1 October 1944 at 00.30. It was relayed by short-wave to the USA and broadcast on Saturday, 30 September 1944* over MBS at 20.30 EWT.)

* The two different dates are due to the time difference between England and the USA.

9. 'Farewell AEFP' (announcements are made by various guest announcers): Theme: 'Fanfare' (announcer Gerry Wilmot); Announcement by Sgt. Keith Jameson; Marie (RAF Squadronaires, introduced by Gerry Wilmot); Candy (sung by Pvt. Paul Carpenter — Canadian AEF Band, introduced by Douglas Marshall); Don't Fence Me In (sung by Dorothy Carless – Canadian AEF Band, introduced by Jill Balcon); On Another Track (featuring Pat Frost accomp. by RAF Squadronaires, introduced by Gerry Wilmot); 'Comedy Spot' with Cam Ritchie; All of a Sudden My Heart Sings (sung by Beryl Davis – Canadian AEF Band, introduced by Margaret Hubble); Red, White and Blue (Canadian AEF Band); What A Difference A Day Made (sung by Cpl. Jack Powers – Canadian AEF Band, introduced by Keith Jameson and George Monahan); A Brown Bird Singing (sung by Joanne Dallas – Canadian AEF Band, introduced by Wilf Davidson); Rise 'n' Shine Blues (played by Ronald Waldman and Dick Dudley, introduced by Charmian Samson); SHAEF Signature Tune (Canadian AEF Band); The More I See You (sung by RSM George Melachrino – Canadian AEF Band, introduced by Ronnie Waldman); What is this Thing Called Love (trio consisting of Ronnie Selby (Piano), Freddie Phillips (Guitar), and Bob Roberts (Bass), introduced by Ronald Waldman); Whisperings of the Vienna Woods (sung by Richard Tauber accomp. by Percy Kahn (Piano), introduced by Ronald Waldman);

277

'Speech' by General Dwight D. Eisenhower (from SHAEF at Frankfurt); Auld Lang Syne (sung by combined bands, guests and audience); Closing announcements by Gerry Wilmot. (This entire live programme was first broadcast on Saturday, 28 July 1945, at 21.05 on the Allied Expeditionary Forces Programme.)

10. 'Oranges and Lemons' (announcements by Ronald Waldman). This special programme tells the story of the Allied Expeditionary Forces Programme and the old nursery song. Also included are several small theme songs from the many service bands that performed on this network between 1944 and 1945. These include: the American Band of the AEF, the British Band of the AEF, the Canadian Band of the AEF, and the RAF Squadronaires in the *Top Ten* series. (This 15-minute recording was first broadcast on Saturday, 28 July 1945, at 22.45 on the Allied Expeditionary Forces Programme.)

Note: These ten recordings are strictly for use within the corporation, but researchers may be able to listen to them (by appointment only) at the National Sound Archives, 29 Exhibition Road, London SW7.

ARMED FORCES RADIO SERVICE
RECORDINGS HELD IN WASHINGTON D.C.

1. Down Beat No. 162 – Featuring Sam Donahue and his US Navy Dance Band (announcements by Sam Donahue and AFRS announcer): Theme: Gypsy Love Song; My Melancholy Baby; LST Party; Theme. (This 15-minute AFRS transcription was recorded in New York City, some time during the spring and early summer of 1945.)

2. Down Beat No. 163 – Featuring Sam Donahue and his US Navy Dance Band (announcements by Sam Donahue and AFRS announcer): Theme: Just You, Just Me; Dinah; I Can't Give You Anything but Love (sung by Rocky Coluccio); Homeward Bound; Theme. (This 15-minute AFRS transcription was recorded in New York City during the late spring or early summer of 1945.)

3. Yank Bandstand No. 89 – Featuring Sam Donahue and his US Navy Dance Band (announcements by AFRS announcer): Theme; It was Only a Paper Moon; Somebody Loves Me; Out of this World; Convoy; I Found a New Baby and Close. (This 15-minute AFRS transcription was recorded in New York City, some time in the summer of 1945.)

4. Yank Bandstand No. 223 – Featuring Sam Donahue and his US Navy Dance Band (announcements by AFRS announcer): Theme: 'C' Jam Blues; Out of this World; Take Me in Your Arms; 'C' Jam Blues and Close. (This 15-minute AFRS transcription was recorded in New York City some time during the summer of 1945.)

5. Yank Bandstand No. 23 – Featuring Jimmy Heffner and his SeaBees

Dance Orchestra (announcements by AFRS announcer): Theme: Always; I Dream of You; Two Guitars; Do You Ever Think of Me; Close. (This 15-minute AFRS transcription was recorded at the AFRS Studios in Los Angeles during late 1944.)

6. Yank Bandstand No. 24 – Featuring Jimmy Heffner and his SeaBees Dance Orchestra (announcements by AFRS announcer): Theme: Together; I Promise You; Pan American; Out of Nowhere; Close. (This 15-minute AFRS transcription was recorded at the AFRS Studios in Los Angeles some time in late 1944.)

7. Yank Bandstand No. 28 – Featuring Major Glenn Miller's American Band of the AEF (announcements by W/O Paul Dudley): Theme: Moonlight Serenade; Sun Valley Jump; Long Ago and Far Away (sung by Sgt. Johnny Desmond); On Wisconsin; Theme (Moonlight Serenade). (This 12-minute insert of an American Band of the AEF programme, which was originally recorded by the BBC from the Olympia Theatre in Paris, was recorded on Monday, 28 January 1945, and was re-dubbed by the AFRS from early February to March 1945.)

8. Yank Bandstand No. 30 – Featuring Major Glenn Miller's American Band of the AEF (announcements by W/O Paul Dudley): Theme: Moonlight Serenade; It Must Be Jelly; Chant by Orchestra; I Only Have Eyes for You (sung by Johnny Desmond and the Crew Chiefs); Medley: Silver Threads Among the Gold; Rainbow Corner (sung by Sgt. Johnny Desmond and the Crew Chiefs); My Guy's Come Back; Theme (Moonlight Serenade). (This 15-minute programme was original material recorded by the American Band of the AEF for BBC use on Monday, 5 February 1945, from the Olympia Theatre, Paris, and re-dubbed by AFRS some time during late February or early March 1945).

9. America Salutes the President (various announcers); Introduction; At the President's Birthday Ball (Sammy Kaye and his Orchestra); The Call of Freedom (Speech); Basil O'Connor (Speech); Mrs Roosevelt; Happy Birthday to the President; Let's Bring New Glory to Old Glory (sung by Tommy Ryan and Choir – Sammy Kaye and his Orchestra); Night and Day (sung by Frank Sinatra – with the Axel Stordahl Orchestra); Beautiful Dreamer (US Naval Training Station Band); I Dream of Jeanie (US Naval Training Station Band); Yellow Rose of Texas (sung by Sgt. Gene Autrey – Army Air Force Western Band); Army Air Corps Song (sung by Gene Autrey and ensemble – Luke Field AAF Country Band); The Caisson Song (The WAC's Band, directed by June Norman – from Fort Des Moine); WAC Hymn (WAC's Choir); Fibber McGee and Molly; Nightmare (Theme) (CPO Artie Shaw and his US Navy Rangers Band from the US Navy Base at Pearl Harbour); Begin the Beguine (CPO Artie Shaw and his US Navy Rangers Band from the US Navy base at Pearl Harbour, Hawaii – announcements by CPO Artie Shaw); Home on the Range (sung by Bing Crosby – Charlie Dance and his Band – announcements by Bing Crosby – from Hollywood, California); Anchors

Aweigh (sung by Dick Powell – announcements by Bing Crosby and Dick Powell – from Hollywood, California); National Anthem (sung by ensemble – announcements by Bing Crosby) and Close. (This one-hour special programme was broadcast live coast to coast by NBC, CBS and Mutial Networks, on Saturday, 30 January 1943.)

Note: This is the only known broadcast and recorded item by CPO Artie Shaw and his US Navy Rangers Band.

10. Yank Bandstand No. 19 – Featuring Sgt. Joe Stabile and the Air Transport Command Band (announcements by AFRS announcer): Theme: V Mail Special; Embraceable You; Alexander's Ragtime Band; I Didn't Know About You; What's New and Close. (This 15-minute transcription was recorded at the AFRS Studios in Hollywood, California, some time during late 1944.)*

11. Yank Bandstand No. 20 – Featuring Joe Stabile and the Air Transport Command Band (announcements by AFRS announcer): Blue Skies; Ghost of a Chance; He's My Guy; Somebody Loves Me; Close. (This 15-minute transcription was recorded at the AFRS Studios in Hollywood, California, some time during late 1944).*

* Although this band is not listed in the text, it is included in these details. We have notes on the following bands that were featured in the Yank Bandstand series, all of which were service bands, but many details are now missing: Lt. Bob Crosby and his Fleet Marine Force Orchestra, Cpl. Paul Tanner and his Solid Seven; Jimmy Grier and his Coast Guard Band, and Sgt. Milt De Lugge and his Swing Wing.

ENSA DISCS HELD BY PRIVATE COLLECTORS

1. ENSA-ORBS Disc No. unknown — Top of the List No. unknown — featuring the Royal Air Force Dance Orchestra (The Squadronaires) (announcements by F/O Bill McClerk): Theme (You're the Tops); I Ain't Got Nobody; How Many Hearts Have You Broken (sung by Jimmy Miller); I Can't Get Started (sung by Dorothy Carless); All This and Heaven Too (sung by Dorothy Carless); Rhapsody for Reeds; Close (You're the Tops).
2. ENSA-ORBS Disc No. unknown — Top of the List No. unknown — featuring the Royal Air Force Dance Orchestra (The Squadronaires) (announcements by F/O Bill McClerk): Theme (You're the Tops); Boston Bounce; Come Out Wherever You Are (sung by Sid Colin); It Must be Jelly (sung by Sid Colin); I'll Be Seeing You (sung by Jimmy Miller); I Ain't Got Nobody; I Heard You Cried Last Night (sung by Jimmy Miller); I've Found a New Baby.
3. ENSA-ORBS Disc No. unknown — Swing Time No. unknown — featuring the Royal Air Force Dance Orchestra (The Squadronaires) (announcements by Cpl. Sally Rogers): Theme (There's Something in the Air); Somebody Loves Me; The Minor Drags; Rosetta; George's Blues; Concerto for Drums; Unknown title; Jazz Me Blues; Clarinet à la King; Dr Heckle and Mr Jive. G.I. Jive (sung by Sid Colin); Darktown Strutter's Ball; Close (There's Something in the Air).
4. ENSA-ORBS Disc No. unknown — Top of the List No. unknown — featuring the Royal Army Ordnance Corps Dance Orchestra (The Blue Rockets) (announcements by Hugh Shillet): Theme (You're the Tops); Paper Doll; It Can't be Wrong (sung by Anne Lenner); Califronia Here I Come; A Garden in the Rain (sung by Anne Lenner): Ice Cold Katty (sung by Ann Lenner): Two Sleepy People (sung by Anne Lenner and RSM George Melachrino); Theme (You're the Tops).
5. ENSA-ORBS Disc No. unknown — Services Music Box No. unknown — featuring the Royal Marines Commando Training Unit Dance Band (The Marineers) (announcements by Unknown Announcer): Theme; I Want to be Happy; Roses of Piccardy (featuring Marcus Hughes, Violin); If You Ever go to Ireland (sung by Burt Kelly); Brazil; My Prayer (sung by Joe Royal); The Lark Leaps In; Theme.
6. ENSA-ORBS Disc No. unknown — Services Music Box No. unknown —

featuring the Royal Marines Commando Training Unit Dance Band (The Marineers) (announcements by Unknown Announcer): Theme (The Melody Lingers On); A Sultan Goes to Harlem; Frankie and Johnny (sung by Burt Kelly): Samba Medley; Where or When; In a Little Spanish Town; Little Grey Home in the West.

Note: This Band was directed by L/Cpl. Buzz Trueman.

7.   ENSA-ORBS Disc No. unknown — Services Music Box No. unknown — featuring the Royal Navy Swing Octet (The Blue Mariners) (announcements by Unknown Announcer): Theme (Up Spirits); Mr Ghost Takes the Air; Honey Suckle Rose (featuring guest L/Cpl. Freddie Phillips, RAOC); Stardust (featuring guest L/Cpl. Freddie Phillips, RAOC); All of My Life (featuring guest Jack Coles, RAOC Trumpet); How About a Cheer for the Navy (sung by Freddie Latham); Theme (Up Spirits).

8.   ENSA-ORBS Disc No. unknown — Services Music Box No. unknown — featuring the Royal Navy Swing Octet (The Blue Mariners) (announcements by Unknown Announcer): Theme (Up Spirits); You're the Rainbow (sung by Freddie Latham); Could it be You; St Louis Blues (featuring guest L/Cpl. Freddie Phillips, RAOC); I Got Rhythm (featuring L/Cpl. Freddie Phillips, RAOC); Time On My Hands (featuring Freddie Gardner, Saxophone); Sitting on a Cloud (sung by Freddie Latham); Theme (Up Spirits).

9.   ENSA-ORBS Disc No. unknown — Services Music Box No. unknown — featuring the Royal Navy Swing Octet (The Blue Mariners) (announcements by Unknown Announcer): Theme (Up Spirits); Music Makers; The Basic Language of Love (sung by Freddie Latham); Straighten Up and Fly Right; Theme (Up Spirits).

Index

286